Omnibus Press

Published 1980 by Omnibus Press,
78 Newman Street, London W1P3LA, England.

Exclusive Distributors:
Book Sales Limited,
78 Newman Street,
London W1P 3LA, England (and their Agents),
Quick Fox,
33 West 60th Street,
New York,
NY 10023,
USA.
Music Sales Gmbh,
Kolner Strasse 199,
Koln 90, D-5000,
West Germany.

© 1980 Colin Cross

Cover and book design by Pearce Marchbank.
Layout by John Frewin.

ISBN 0.86001.638.2
UK Order No. OP 40534

Printed in England by
J.B. Offset Printers (Marks Tey) Limited.
Reprinted 1981, 1982(2)

ENCYCLOPEDIA OF BRITISH BEAT GROUPS & SOLO ARTISTS OF THE SIXTIES

COMPILED BY COLIN CROSS WITH PAUL KENDALL & MICK FARREN

ABDABS—ANIMALS

ARCHITECTURAL ABDABS

THE ABDABS Roger Waters (bass), Rick Wright (keyboards) and Nick Mason (drums) were at Regent Street Polytechnic studying architecture when they formed Sigma 6. With the addition of Juliette Gale (who later became Mrs. Wright) as vocalist, guitarist Bob Close and singer/guitarist Roger 'Syd' Barrett, an art student from Camberwell, they called themselves The T-Set, then The Screaming Abdabs and finally just The Abdabs.

The group was mainly R&B orientated, despite Close's preference for traditional jazz, and when the guitarist left after clashing with Syd Barrett, the name changed to The Pink Floyd Sound (after a blues record Barrett owned by Pink Anderson and Floyd Council), and shortly afterwards to Pink Floyd (q.v.).

THE ACCENT One of the many groups signed by Decca in the mid-sixties who made no impact at all. Their singles included 'Red Sky At Night from 1967.

THE ACTION Reggie King (vocals), Alan King (rhythm guitar), Nick Evans (bass) and Roger Powell (drums) started off in Kentish Town during 1963 as The Boyfriends, backing Sandra Brown (q.v.). They later became The Boys, and with the addition of Peter Watson on lead guitar changed their name to The Action.

Their pop/soul sound was very popular in the clubs of London, but despite a number of singles on Parlophone (including versions of 'Land Of A Thousand Dances' and 'Shadows And Reflections) between 1965-67, record success eluded them.

Watson left the group in 1966 to be replaced by Ian Whiteman. Whiteman was in turn supplanted by Martin Stone the following year, after which the group became Azoth and later Mighty Baby (q.v.).

Reggie King went on to make a solo album for United Artists, and Alan King played with Ace, who had an American Number One in 1975 with 'How Long'.

THE ADDICTS A beat group from Widnes in Lancashire who recorded for Decca in the early sixties. Their singles included 'That's My Girl'.

AFTER TEA Featuring guitarist Ray Fenwick and Hans van Eijck, they recorded an album of the same name for Decca's Ace of Clubs label in the late sixties. Fenwick went on to join the Spencer Davis Group (q.v.), and subsequently began a solo career.

SKIP ALAN TRIO A London-based group who played the clubs for a short while in 1965 before Skip Alan became drummer with The Pretty Things (q.v.).

THE ALLISONS This lookalike duo represented Britain in the Eurovision Song Contest of 1961. They were runners-up with 'Are You Sure', and their recording of the song on Fontana gave them a Number One hit. They followed this up with an album, also entitled 'Are You Sure', and promptly disappeared before anyone could make up their minds.

AMBROSE SLADE Noddy Holder (guitar/vocals), Jim Lea (bass), Dave Hill (guitar) and Don Powell (drums) were four lads from the Wolverhampton area, formerly known as The 'N Betweens, (q.v.) playing cover versions until they met Chas Chandler, Jimi Hendrix's manager.

They recorded a single, 'Genesis', and an album, 'Ballzy', for Fontana and were promoted as the first skinhead group, with a predictable reaction from promoters, before shortening their name to Slade and enjoying a considerable run of success in the early seventies.

AMEN CORNER Andy Fairweather-Low (vocals), Neil Jones (lead guitar), Blue Weaver (organ), Allan Jones (baritone sax), Mike Smith (tenor sax), Clive Taylor (bass) and Dennis Byron (drums) came from Cardiff in 1966. They charted the following year with the slow, bluesy 'Gin House', and enjoyed a string of more obviously commercial hits during the next two years, including a Number One with '(If Paradise Was) Half As Nice'.

Four singles for Deram were accompanied by the 'Round Amen Corner' album, before the group switched to the Immediate label for three more singles and two albums, 'National West Coast Live' and 'Farewell To The Real Magnificent Seven'.

With the demise of Immediate in 1969 the group split in two. The brass section formed Judas Jump (q.v.), while the remainder became Fairweather, who made the Top Ten in 1970 with 'Natural Sinner'.

Blue Weaver became a ubiquitous sessionman and band member later in the seventies, playing with The Strawbs and Mott The Hoople (q.v.) among others, and Fairweather-Low has had a sporadically successful solo career with A&M.

AMM Cornelius Cardew, Lou Gare, Eddie Prevost, Keith Rowe and Lawrence Sheaff played strange free form music using cellos, saxes, transistor radios and assorted bits and pieces, recording albums for Elektra and DNA. They appeared at Sunday afternoon "spontaneous underground" sessions at the Marquee during 1967, and later developed into The Scratch Orchestra.

TIM ANDREWS In 1966 this gentleman nearly joined The Monkees, America's answer to the Beatles-led British Invasion. His chance of immortality was thwarted, however, when the TV company assembling the group decided that one English boy (Davy Jones from Manchester) was enough.

Being only 5'5" tall, Andrews became affectionately known as Tiny Tim (not to be confused with the American of the same name), and back in the UK his career assumed equally modest proportions. His singles for Parlophone, including 'Sad Simon Lives Again', 'Smile If You Want To', and 'How Many More Hearts Must Be Broken' with Paul Korda, all failed to make the charts.

ANDROMEDA John Cann (guitar), Mick Hawksworth (bass) and Ian McLane (drums) were a heavy rock band operating in 1968-9. They recorded an album called 'Andromeda' for RCA, and their singles included 'Go Your Way'. John Cann later played with Atomic Rooster (q.v.) and then Bullet, who became Hard Stuff.

ANDWELLA'S DREAM Dave Lewis (guitar, piano, organ, vocals), Nigel Smith (bass, vocals) and Gordon Barton (drums) made up this interesting late sixties group. They recorded the 'Love And Poetry' album and two singles, 'Sunday' and 'Mr.Sunshine', for CBS in 1969, and 'Every Little Minute' for Reflection in 1970. Lewis re-emerged several years later as a solo artist on the Polydor label.

THE ANIMALS Alan Price (keyboards), Chas Chandler (bass), Hilton Valentine (guitar) and John Steel (drums) began playing together round the Newcastle area as The Alan Price Combo in 1959. In 1962 they were joined by vocalist Eric Burdon, playing regularly at the aptly named Downbeat Club and the more salubrious Club A Go-Go.

The wildness of the group's R&B based act resulted in the Geordie punters dubbing them "animals", and it was as The Animals that they descended on London in early 1964, at the encouragement of producer Mickie Most (q.v.).

The group's primary source of inspiration was the music of black Americans like Jimmy Reed, Chuck Berry and Bo Diddley, but they were also impressed by the comparatively unknown folk singer Bob Dylan. These two influences came together on their first single for the Columbia label, 'Baby Let Me Take You Home. Taken from 'Baby Don't You Tear My Clothes', an old blues song, it was not dissimilar from Dylan's own version of the song, 'Baby Let Me Follow You Down', and it nearly made the Top Twenty in April 1964.

It was their follow-up single which gave them their international breakthrough, however, and again it was a traditional tune recorded previously by Bob Dylan. 'House Of The Rising Sun' was nearly never released, and Columbia were worried about its length (some five and a half minutes), but it reached the Number One position on both sides of the Atlantic.

Seven further hit singles followed over the next two years for Columbia and then Decca, and three albums. 'The Animals', 'Animal Tracks' and 'Animalisms', made up largely of first rate R&B covers.

In 1965 Alan Price (q.v.) left the group, his fear of flying being exacerbated by their American success, and was replaced by Dave Rowberry from The Mike Cotton Sound (q.v.). John Steel also left in February 1966, making way for Barry Jenkins from The Nashville Teens (q.v.), and in July of the same year the group broke up altogether.

Chas Chandler went into management, guiding the careers of Jimi Hendrix (q.v.) and Ambrose Slade (q.v.). Burdon, meanwhile, moved to California, lured by the twin sirens of LSD and the burgeoning West Coast music scene.

While in San Francisco he formed The New Animals, whose personnel during their year long existence included John Weider (guitar), who was later in Family (q.v.), Mick Briggs from Steampacket (q.v.), Zoot Money (q.v.),

5

ANTEEKS – BRIAN AUGER TRINITY

bassist Danny McCullough and Barry Jenkins.

With this group, Burdon moved away from The Animals original raw R&B sound to the gentler tones of flower power and psychedelia. Nevertheless, he made three hit singles with them, including the quintessential 'San Franciscan Nights', and an album, 'Love Is'.

After breaking up this group in early 1968, Burdon had further modest singles success in the States with 'Monterey' and 'Sky Pilot' and dabbled briefly in films. In 1970 he changed stance yet again with the formation of War, from the nucleus of a black band called Nite Shift and Lee Oskar, a Danish harmonica player. They recorded an album together and had a big American hit with 'Spill The Wine', and after Burdon's departure in 1971, War went on to become one of the world's top-selling bands.

Burdon recorded several further albums during the seventies without notable artistic or commercial success, and in 1976 the five original Animals reformed to make an album for Chas Chandler's Barn label.

THE ANTEEKS A mid-sixties group who recorded a single, 'I Don't Want You', for Phillips in 1966.

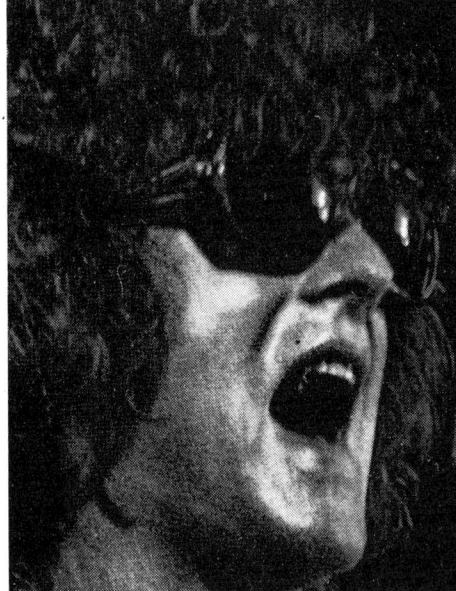

THE APEX RHYTHM AND BLUES ALL STARS This group came out of Northampton in the mid sixties, and their main claim to fame was the membership of Ian Hunter, who went on to find fortune with Mott The Hoople (q.v.). They also recorded an EP for John Lever Records, which featured 'Tall Girl', 'Reeling And Rocking', 'Down The Road Apiece' and 'Sugar Shack'.

APPLE An outfit from the late sixties who had two singles, 'Let's Take A Trip Down The Rhine' and 'Dr.Rock', released on the Page One label, as well as recording a cover of the Scaffold (q.v.) hit 'Thank U Very Much' for the American market.

THE APPLEJACKS Originally called The Crestas and The Jaguars, Al Jackson (vocals), Martin Baggott (lead guitar), Phil Cash (rhythm guitar), Don Gould (organ), Megan Davies (bass) and Gerry Freeman (drums) emerged from Solihull in 1964 with a Decca recording contract.

Their first single, 'Tell Me When', was a Top Ten hit, and the follow-up, 'Like Dreamers Do', reached No.20, allowing them the luxury of an LP release.

They were basically a very lightweight pop group, however, with a female bassist as their only noteworthy feature. After 'Three Little Words' made the Top Thirty in late 1964, all their remaining singles bombed...a situation made worse by a lack of live appeal, which sometimes almost saw them outnumbering their audiences.

ARGENT Formed by keyboard player Rod Argent after his departure from The Zombies (q.v.). Two of the original members were Argent's cousin Jim Rodford (bass) from the Mike Cotton Sound (q.v.), and ex-Roulettes (q.v.) Russ Ballard (guitar) and Robert Henrit (drums).

Their first album, 'Argent', for the CBS label in 1969, was in the melodic Zombies tradition, but later recordings developed a heavier feel, yielding hit singles in 'Hold Your Head Up' and 'God Gave Rock And Roll To You'.

Ballard's exit in 1974 started a string of personnel changes, and the group eventually split up in 1976. Rodford went on to play in Phoenix with other latterday Argent members; Henrit opened a successful drum shop in London's West End; and Argent himself returned in early 1979 with a solo album, 'Moving Home', on MCA.

P.P.ARNOLD A tiny black American girl with an enormous voice, Pat Arnold came to England in 1967 after a spell with Ike and Tina Turner's Ikettes. Signed by Andrew Oldham's (q.v.) Immediate label she had a debut Top Twenty hit with Cat Stevens (q.v.) 'The First Cut Is The Deepest'. This was followed by minor successes with 'The Time Has Come' and 'If You Think You're Groovy', and another Top Thirty entry in mid-1968 with an emotional rendition of 'Angel Of The Morning'.

She toured with The Nice (q.v.) as her backing group, and after they had gone off on their own, with T.N.T. (q.v.). She featured on The Small Faces' (q.v.) 'Tin Soldier' in 1967, and when the group reformed a decade later she went on the road as one of their backing vocalists. In the same year her version of 'The First Cut Is The Deepest' was reissued to coincide with Rod Stewart's hit.

ARRIVAL They arrived from Liverpool in the late sixties, and visited the Top Twenty in 1970 with 'Friends' and 'I Will Survive' on Decca. Their three singers, Dyan Birch, Frank Collins and Paddy McHugh, all reappeared a few years later in Kokomo.

ART One of the first groups signed by Island in 1967, they made one album, 'Supernatural Fairytales', which was re-released in 1976. Soon after this album they evolved into Spooky Tooth (q.v.).

THE ARTWOODS Arthur Wood (vocals), Jon Lord (organ), Derek Griffiths (guitar), Malcolm Pool (bass) and Keef Hartley (drums) were a blues and R&B outfit formed in 1964 by Wood, the elder brother of Ron Wood, of Faces (q.v.) and Rolling Stones (q.v.) fame.

The group were always popular on the London club scene, but had little success with their series of singles released by Decca and Parlophone between '64 and '67, or with their one album, 'Art Gallery'. In 1973 the Spark label issued a budget album of Artwoods' material, entitled just 'The Artwoods'.

Hartley left in May 1967 to join John Mayall (q.v.), before forming The Keef Hartley Band, and the group metamorphosed into St.Valentine's Day Massacre (q.v.). Jon Lord found international notoriety in the seventies with Deep Purple (q.v.).

ASHKAN Steve Bailey (vocals), Ron Reading (bass), Terry Sims (drums) and Bob Weston (guitar) recorded one album, 'In From The Cold', for Decca's 'progressive' Nova label in 1969. They specialised in self-penned, somewhat overlong ditties of a bluesy nature, and the public declined to warm to them.

ATOMIC ROOSTER Organist Vincent Crane and drummer Carl Palmer formed Rooster after the break-up of The Crazy World of Arthur Brown (q.v.) in 1969. Palmer left shortly afterwards to inaugurate E.L.P., and during its four year lifespan the group suffered numerous changes in personnel, including drummers Rick Parnell and John Hammond, guitarists Johnny Mandala and John Cann from Andromeda (q.v.), and vocalist Chris Farlowe (q.v.).

The group's moment of glory came in 1971, when 'Tomorrow Night' and 'Devil's Answer' were both hits. They failed to maintain their momentum, however, and their five albums for B&C and Dawn represent an inexorable slide into obscurity.

THE ATTACK Notable chiefly for their controversy with Jeff Beck (q.v.) over their respective versions of 'Hi Ho Silver Lining', The Attack launched several further singles on Decca without results. Guitarist with the group was David O'List, who left to join The Nice (q.v.).

THE ATTRACTIONS Released cover versions of The Stones' 'Stupid Girl' and The Kinks' 'Party Line' on Columbia in 1966.

BRIAN AUGER TRINITY Auger was originally a jazz pianist, but in 1964 he moved over to organ and the flourishing R&B scene. The first Trinity was Rick Laird (bass) and Phil Kinorra (drums), but they were soon augmented by guitarist John McLaughlin and saxophonist Glen Hughes. This line-up disbanded after a few months, but McLaughlin and Laird teamed up again nearly a decade later in The Mahavishnu Orchestra.

With Rick Brown on bass and Mickey Waller on drums, Auger recorded two singles, 'Fool Killer' and 'Sixty Five Green Onions', for Columbia in 1965, before Trinity became the backing group for Steampacket (q.v.).

Also in Steampacket was singer Julie

Driscoll (q.v.), and after the group's demise they formed yet another Trinity, comprising Clive Thacker (drums), Dave Ambrose (bass) and Gary Boyle (guitar), who led the jazz rock band Isotope during the seventies.

Signed to Giorgio Gomelsky's Marmalade label, they had a hit throughout Europe in 1968 with Bob Dylan's 'This Wheel's On Fire'. They looked set to become huge, but after two albums, 'Open' and 'Streetnoise', Julie Driscoll departed, leaving the Trinity to struggle on without a record contract until July 1970, when Auger called it a day.

Auger returned to active service fronting Oblivion Express, who made several albums which achieved more recognition in the States than his home country.

PETER B'S – BEACHCOMBERS

THE PETER B'S Peter Bardens (keyboards), Peter Green (guitar), Dave Ambrose (bass) and Mick Fleetwood (drums) were an instrumental group, originally known as Peter B's Looners. They toured round the clubs in early 1966, and made a single for Columbia, an instrumental version of 'If You Wanna Be Happy' which was Green's recording debut. Later in the year they became the backing group for Shotgun Express (q.v.).

BABYLON A rock band from 1968, who featured girl vocalist Carol Grimes. Grimes joined Delivery (q.v.) in early 1969, and was with Uncle Dog during the seventies before going solo.

THE BACHELORS An Irish vocal trio with short hair, suits and bow ties, John Stokes, Con Cluskey and Dec Cluskey were popular with mothers everywhere. Between 1963 and 1967 they had thirteen Top Thirty hits on Decca, including a Number One with 'Diane'. The Bachelors are still regular workers in cabaret and television.

BADFINGER Peter Ham (guitar, piano, vocals), Tom Evans (bass), Mike Gibbins (drums) and Ron Griffiths (guitar, vocals) began their career as The Iveys (q.v.) in South Wales.

In 1968 they were signed to Apple, after submitting demo tapes to Paul McCartney, but at the end of the year Griffiths left to be replaced by Liverpudlian Joey Molland, and the group name changed to Badfinger.

Their first single was McCartney's 'Come And Get It', the only non-original on their debut album, 'Magic Christian Music', which was the soundtrack for the film starring Ringo. The single scored on both sides of the Atlantic, and the group looked set for great things.

Unfortunately, despite five more albums for Apple and Warner Bros. during the next five years, and sporadic single success, especially in the States, they never really broke big.

In April 1975 Pete Ham, who had written Nilsson's chart-topping 'Without You', left the group, disillusioned by their constant frustrations with management, and a few days later he committed suicide.

The group split up at this point, but Evans and Gibbins reappeared in 1976 with The Dodgers, recording for Island and Polydor.

BAKERLOO Dave "Clem" Clempson (guitar), Keith Baker (drums) and Terry Poole (bass) were a Birmingham blues group, who started in the mid-sixties as The Bakerloo Blues Line. They abbreviated their name, and recorded an album with the same title for Harvest in 1969. After breaking up, Poole played with Graham Bond (q.v.), Baker was briefly a member of Uriah Heep (q.v.), and Clempson replaced Peter Frampton in Humble Pie (q.v.) before joining Colosseum (q.v.).

LONG JOHN BALDRY A ubiquitous figure on the London R&B scene, Baldry owes his nickname to his 6'7" height. He began singing in folk clubs and coffee bars during the late fifties, often with Alexis Korner, and in 1961 became frontman for Korner's Blues Incorporated (q.v.).

After appearing on Korner's 'R&B at The Marquee' album in early 1962 he spent time touring on the Continent, returning in 1963 to join Cyril Davies' All Stars (q.v.). When Davies died in 1964, Baldry took over leadership of the group, changing their name to The Hoochie Coochie Men (q.v.).

After the demise of this group in autumn '65, Baldry helped form the Steampacket road show (q.v.), which again only lasted for about a year. During the lifespan of both these ventures, Baldry made a number of solo singles for United Artists and two albums, 'Long John's Blues' and 'Looking At Long John'.

While performing with Bluesology (q.v.) after the breakup of Steampacket, however, Baldry moved to the Pye label and changed his recording style from R&B to big ballads.

This tactic brought results in the form of four Top Thirty entries in fifteen months, including a Number One, 'Let The Heartaches Begin', from November 1967. It also brought about the alienation of his grassroots following, however, and Baldry has searched in vain for a new audience ever since.

Seventies albums like 'It Ain't Easy' on Warner Brothers, produced by ex-sidemen Rod Stewart (q.v.) and Elton John, and 'Everything Stops For Tea' and 'Good To Be Alive', have done little to further this search.

A BAND OF ANGELS Mike d'Abo (vocals, piano), Christian (John) Gaydon (guitar, vocals), John Baker (guitar), Dave Wilkinson (bass) and James Rugge-Price (drums) had all been to Harrow public school, as emphasised by their straw boaters trademark.

From 1964 onwards, they released a series of quite acceptable pop singles for United Artists and Piccadilly, but couldn't graduate to the big time.

They split up in 1966 when d'Abo took over from Paul Jones in Manfred Mann (q.v.). Gaydon later became the 'G' in EG Management, along with David Enthoven, who had been the Band Of Angels's manager. Their stable was to include King Crimson (q.v.), T.Rex (q.v.) and Roxy Music.

BAND OF JOY Known primarily as the group which once included Robert Plant and John Bonham of Led Zeppelin (q.v.), this Midlands rock and blues combo soldiered on to become a rather mundane heavy band by 1977, at which point they were signed (largely on the strength of their more illustrious connections) by Polydor, for whom they recorded an equally mundane album.

THE BANSHEES A Newcastle group of the early sixties, their vocalist was Bryan Ferry, who left his Geordie roots for Roxy Music and a tuxedo-clad solo career. Their singles for Columbia included Ray Charles' 'I Got A Woman' in 1964.

THE BARRON KNIGHTS Duke D'mond (vocals), Paul Longford (guitar), Butch Baker (guitar), Barron Anthony (bass) and Dave Ballinger (drums) hailed from Leighton Buzzard, and were a popular act on package shows in the early sixties.

They had several hits in the mid-sixties with comic medleys of other groups' hits, such as 'Call Up The Groups' and 'Pop Go The Workers', but all their efforts to stray from this formula were substantially less successful.

They subsequently moved onto the cabaret circuit, where their blend of humour and genuine vocal talent made them a perennial attraction.

In late 1977, the group signed to CBS, after a decade of independent releases, and made the Top Ten with 'Live In Trouble'. The following year, their original line-up still intact after more than fifteen years together, they enjoyed their biggest success of all, as 'A Taste Of Aggro' and the accompanying album, 'Night Gallery', both went gold.

THE BASKERVILLES Brian Tatum (organ, vocals), Peter Berryman (vocals), Will Slater (guitar), Red (bass) and Lester Dinney (drums) were the proteges of Phil May, vocalist with the Pretty Things (q.v.). Playing R&B with harmony vocals, they had evolved from Sudbury group Brian and The Comets. Having failed to hound the British public into appreciating them, The Baskervilles went to the dogs in 1966.

THE BEACHCOMBERS A rocking instrumental group who recorded a single called 'Mad Goose' for Columbia in 1963. Perhaps appropriately, in view of that title, their drummer was Keith Moon, who shortly afterwards joined The Who (q.v.).

BEATLES

THE BEATLES Although their actual record sales have been eclipsed in recent years, thanks to the tremendous expansion of the music industry, there can be no disputing that The Beatles were the most universally popular group in the history of pop music, and their influence on its developement was immense.

John Lennon and Paul McCartney had first joined forces during 1956 in The Quarrymen, a schoolboy skiffle group. In 1958 they added George Harrison, a friend of McCartney's, and in 1959, with Stuart Sutcliffe on bass and various drummers, they became The Silver Beatles.

The following year they found a permanent drummer in Pete Best, shortened their name to The Beatles, and began playing regularly in the clubs and ballrooms round Liverpool, and making frequent visits to Germany. It was during one such trip to Hamburg that they recorded some sessions for Polydor with Tony Sheridan. These tapes were later released to cash in on The Beatles success, and 'My Bonnie' and 'Ain't She Sweet' were minor hits. When they returned to Liverpool after this visit, in June 1961, Stuart Sutcliffe stayed behind, and died shortly afterwards of a brain tumour.

During these formative years The Beatles were managed by Liverpool clubowner Alan Williams, who wrote 'The Man Who Gave The Beatles Away', a scurrilous exposé of their alleged experiences together, in 1976.

In late 1961, however, they were spotted at The Cavern club by Brian Epstein (q.v.), a local record shop owner, and he took over their management.

After being turned down by numerous record companies, who insisted that groups were a thing of the past, Epstein got a contract with EMI during 1962. The unfortunate Pete Best was ousted before any recordings were made, and his place was taken by Ringo Starr (Richard Starkey) from another Liverpool group, Rory Storm and The Hurricanes (q.v.). Rumours abound, however, that Ringo himself didn't play on many of the early Beatles sessions.

Although producer George Martin was anxious for them to record 'How Do You Do It' (which later gave Gerry and The Pacemakers (q.v.) a Number One), The Beatles insisted on using their own material, and their first single, 'Love Me Do', reached No.17 in late 1962.

This turned out to be the lowest chart placing achieved by an official Beatles release, and their string of 31 hit singles in the UK included no less than seventeen Number Ones.

During 1963 the media seized on The Beatles' "loveable moptop' image, complete with matching suits and Beatle boots, which was in fact a far cry from the dirty rock'n'roll they had played in the clubs of Liverpool and Hamburg. "Beatlemania" gripped the nation, and crossed the Atlantic in early 1964, giving British pop its first foothold in America.

Beatles singles, EPs and LPs occupied the charts of the world in unprecedented quantities, and their virtually non-stop touring programme was accompanied by fan hysteria of an intensity never witnessed before.

At the same time, Lennon and McCartney had established themselves as songwriters of a unique calibre, and their material provided hits for numerous artists, apart from The Beatles.

Their popularity was further enhanced by 'A Hard Day's Night' in 1964 and 'Help' in 1965, two films very different in character, but both light years away from the pap normally associated with pop stars in the cinema.

After another hugely successful American tour in July 1966, The Beatles announced their retirement from touring, but it made no appreciable difference to their popularity. In fact, the extra time that they could now devote to recording and the influence of the general creative upsurge in the pop world at that time seemed to spur them on to new heights, and their next album, 'Revolver', was arguably the finest they ever made.

As the age of psychedelia dawned, The Beatles continued to set the pace for the rest of the world to follow. They made a much-publicised trip to India to see the Maharishi Mahesh Yogi, investigated the possibilities of 'mind expanding' drugs, and experimented with more adventurous lyrics and fast-developing studio technology.

This broadening of horizons was manifested in the monumental 'Strawberry Fields Forever/ Penny Lane' single (which ironically became the first Beatles single in four years not to reach Number One in the UK), and the 'Sgt Pepper' album. This latter release was hailed as a watershed in the growing sophistication of pop music, although the passing years have tended to highlight its flaws.

Soon after 'Sgt.Pepper' had been unleashed on the world, Brian Epstein met his untimely death, and in retrospect this event can probably be seen as marking the beginning of the end for The Beatles.

Their next project, a television film called 'Magical Mystery Tour', was a very offbeat affair, and was greeted with a mixture of derision and bewilderment. The accompanying single, 'Hello Goodbye', was another huge seller, however.

1968 saw the foundation of the ill-fated Apple empire, which started as a boutique in Baker Street, but grew into a major publishing and record company, handling all the Beatles activities. Their first album for the new label was the double White Album, a sporadically excellent though often over-indulgent effort, which nonetheless did little to diminish their reputation.

In the same year, the 'Yellow Submarine' cartoon was premiered, but from then on things fell into increasing disarray. Apple, despite some success with their other acts, lacked a strong guiding hand and degenerated into a complete shambles, overrun by hangers-on and incompetents.

The four Beatles were also growing apart. John Lennon had met Japanese artist Yoko Ono, while Paul had a very homely set-up with American Linda Eastman and her child from a previous marriage. The ideological split between the two inevitably affected the whole group, and the internal tension was graphically illustrated by the 'Let It Be' film.

BEAT MERCHANTS—BEE GEES

Through 1969, John became increasingly involved with his own projects with Yoko and The Plastic Ono Band, as well as 'political' activities like the Amsterdam bed-in and the return of the MBE which he, along with the rest of The Beatles, had been awarded in 1965.

The Beatles came together in the studio for the last time to record 'Abbey Road', although 'Let It Be' was actually the final release. It was a high point for them to go out on, perhaps surprisingly in view of the atmosphere surrounding it, but after its release the end came swiftly and bitterly.

By 1970, Apple and the Beatles affairs were in chaos. McCartney wanted to bring in Linda's family to sort out the mess, while the other Beatles favoured an American lawyer called Allen Klein. Later events suggest that they should probably have taken McCartney's advice, but they didn't, and on December 31st McCartney started legal action to dissolve The Beatles officially and appoint a receiver.

All The Beatles embarked on successful solo careers without ever scaling the heights they had achieved together. There have been sporadic rumours of a reunion almost ever since their break-up, but such an occurrence is highly unlikely, especially since McCartney's group Wings, which he formed with Linda and Denny Laine from The Moody Blues (q.v.), has become one of rock's greatest attractions.

THE BEAT MERCHANTS These gentlemen played a harsh-sounding R&B from the early to mid-sixties. They recorded for Columbia, and got as far as appearing on ITV's 'Thank Your Lucky Stars' to promote their single 'Pretty Face'.

The composition of this single is credited to G.Daneski, R.Worman, C.Boyle, V.Sendall and G.Farndell, who presumably were The Beat Merchants.

The group's vocalist had long thick, black curly hair and bore a slight resemblance to King Charles II, and their other singles included 'So Fine'.

THE BEATSTALKERS Ronnie Smith (guitar, vocals), Davis Lennox (vocals), 'Tudge' Williamson (drums), Alan Mair (bass) and Eddie Campbell (organ) hailed from Glasgow, and were sometimes billed as 'The Scottish Beatles'.

In 1965 they signed to Decca and moved to London. They recorded with Denny Cordell and made three good singles, but without chart success.

Mair and Williamson were replaced by Jeff Allen and Joe Gaffney in early 1967, at which point the group moved to CBS. They made five singles for their new company, including three David Bowie songs 'Silver Treetop School For Boys', 'Everything Is You' and 'When I'm Five'. Still unable to track down that elusive hit The Beatstalkers went their separate ways in 1969. Eddie Campbell joined another Scottish group, Tear Gas, but sadly for him was not part of the group when it was taken over by Alex Harvey (q.v.) in 1972.

JEFF BECK One of the major "guitar heroes" of the sixties, Beck first established a reputation during 1964, while still a student at Wimbledon Art College, playing in jam sessions at the Eel Pie Island in Twickenham.

His first proper group was The Yardbirds whom he joined in March 1965, replacing Eric Clapton, and during his two year stay with them, he became acknowledged as one of the country's foremost guitarists.

In early 1967 Beck left The Yardbirds and spent a few months working with producer Mickie Most (q.v.). The quirky pop which resulted was something of a surprise after Beck's previous work, but 'Hi Ho Silver Lining', 'Tally Man' and 'Love Is Blue' were successive Top Thirty entries during the next year.

It was during this period that the first Jeff Beck Group was put together, with vocalist Rod Stewart (q.v.), Ron Wood (guitar), ex-Shadow (q.v.) Jet Harris (bass), and drummer Viv Prince from The Pretty Things (q.v.). Harris and Prince never even made it to the first rehearsal, however, so Wood moved over to bass guitar, and after a quick succession of drummers, including Aynsley Dunbar (q.v.), the position was occupied by Micky Waller.

This line-up was frequently augmented by Nicky Hopkins (q.v.) on keyboards, and they made the tremendous 'Truth' album for Columbia in 1968. Waller was replaced by Tony Newman, however, before 'Beckola' in 1969. The whole group also participated, together with Donovan (q.v.), in the 'Goo Goo Barabajagal' hit single.

The pairing of Beck and Stewart was one of the most formidable combinations rock music has ever seen, and the group's live appearances earned them a huge following, particularly in the States, where they spent most of their time.

Unfortunately, Beck's notoriously erratic temperament put the group's future in constant jeopardy. In 1969 Wood was sacked, only to be reinstated when his replacement, Junior Woods from Tomorrow (q.v.), didn't fit, and shortly afterwards he left to join The Faces (q.v.). Rod Stewart went with him, and that was the end of that.

Beck was then going to form a new band with Tim Bogart and Carmine Appice, whose work with Vanilla Fudge he had long admired, but a serious car accident put him on the sidelines for nearly two years.

When he returned to action in 1971, the new Jeff Beck Group comprised Bobby Tench (vocals) Max Middleton (piano), Clive Chaman (bass) and Cozy Powell (drums). They made two albums for CBS, 'Rough And Ready' and 'Jeff Beck Group', before they went the same way as their predecessors.

At the end of 1972 came the long-awaited Beck, Bogart and Appice. Their performances and one studio album lived up to the high expectations, but after recording a live album in Japan, they too split up.

Since then, Beck has moved in more of a jazz-rock direction, recording several albums with various musicians, without ever really capturing the fire or the public interest of his golden years in the late sixties.

THE BEDROCKS This group of British-based West Indians sneaked into the Top Twenty in January 1969, with a version of 'Ob La Di, Ob La Da' on Columbia. Sadly for them it was eclipsed by Marmalade's (q.v.) version, which went to Number One.

THE BEE GEES Although many people believe them to be Australian, The Bee Gees are actually British. Barry Gibb was born in Douglas, Isle of Man, while his twin brothers, Robin and Maurice, were born in Manchester two years later. It was in Manchester that they began their singing career, in 1956, as The Blue Cats. Most of their appearances were between films at Saturday morning cinema shows.

In 1958 the Gibb family emigrated to Australia, and by 1963, while still in their early teens, The Bee Gees had become one of the country's top groups.

Returning to Britain three years later with drummer Colin Peterson, a former child actor, and bassist Vince Melouney, their first single, 'Spicks and Specks', flopped. The follow-up, 'New York Mining Disaster 1941', reached the Top Twenty in June 1967, however, and over the next two years they had a whole string of hits with their melodic, self-penned numbers, including Number Ones in 'Massachusetts' and 'I Gotta Get A Message To You'.

In 1969 the brothers split up, after differences of such bitterness that they said they would never work together again. Barry concentrated on songwriting, Maurice went into acting and married Lulu (q.v.), while Robin had a big solo hit with 'Saved By The Bell'.

Despite earlier threats, the brothers were

JEFF BECK

BELFAST GYPSIES—BLIND FAITH

reconciled in late 1970, and The Bee Gees were revived with just the three of them. During the early seventies they continued to have spasmodic singles success, especially in the States, but public taste had swung away from their lush ballads, and it looked as if they would slip gracefully away from prominence to live very comfortably on the proceeds of their much-covered song catalogue.

In 1973 they switched labels from Polydor to RSO, and two years later, with 'Jive Talkin', hit upon the blend of sophisticated harmony vocals and superbly produced and arranged disco-style music which, with the 'Saturday Night Fever' soundtrack in 1978, was to make them the world's biggest-selling group.

Throughout their career The Bee Gees have been prolific recorders of albums, although until recently these have never received the same attention as their singles, and they have also been regular producers and writers of hits for other artists, including their younger brother Andy.

BELFAST GYPSIES Formed by Ken McLeod, Jackie and Patrick McAuley, and M.Scott after the demise of Them (q.v.), the Belfast Gypsies continued the early group's tradition, and made a single, 'Gloria's Dream', which was written and produced by Kim Fowley, for Island in 1966. Later the same year they recorded another Fowley song, 'People, Let's Freak Out' under the name of The Freaks of Nature.

CLIFF BENNETT AND THE REBEL ROUSERS Bennett came from Slough, and after singing with various groups in the late fifties, he put together The Rebel Rousers in late 1961. Despite the name, they had a very clean cut image, with nice haircuts and smart tartan suits, and they were popular in British ballrooms and continental clubs.

They recorded for Parlophone, and had Top Ten hits with 'One Way Love' in 1964 and 'Got To Get You Into My Life' in 1966, (the latter produced by Paul McCartney, the man who wrote it), as well as minor success with 'I'll Take You Home'. They also made two albums, 'Cliff Bennett & The Rebel Rousers' and 'Drivin' You Wild'.

The seven man line-up was changing constantly over the years, but it included veteran keyboard player Roy Young, who later formed his own band, and recorded several albums in the seventies, and bassist Frank Allen, who joined The Searchers (q.v.) in 1964.

The Rebel Rousers were finally put down during 1969, at which point Bennett grew his hair and went "progressive" with Toe Fat Their debut album for Regal Zonophone was distinguished only by one of the most unpleasant sleeves in history, and Bennett lay low for a few years to get over it. He re-emerged in 1975 to form Shanghai, with guitarist Mick Green from The Pirates (q.v.), but they were equally short-lived.

DAVE BERRY AND THE CRUISERS Berry (real name Grundy) and his backing boys were an R&B group from Sheffield. They were regulars at the city's Esquire Club and Club 60 during 1962, when they were sometimes joined by Joe Cocker (q.v.), before signing with Decca in 1963.

Their first single, Chuck Berry's 'Memphis Tennessee', made the Top Twenty, despite having to compete with the original version. Another R&B cover, Arthur Crudup's 'My Baby Left Me', reached the charts as well in the following January, but then Berry switched to a slower ballad style, and began doing most of his studio and television work without his backing band.

Berry had a great stage presence, resembling a gay vampire as he slithered about, peeping round trees and rocks, sliding his microphone down his back, and hiding his face behind the collar of his leather jacket. His TV appearances were always something special, and in July 1964 he had his first Top Ten hit with 'The Crying Game'.

Not surprisingly, The Cruisers were less than happy at being pushed into the background, and in October of the same year they all walked out. Berry, however, merely replaced them with Frank White (lead guitar), Alan Taylor (rhythm guitar), Peter Cliff (bass) and John Riley (drums), who were originally The Frank White Combo from Dave's home town, and carried on as before.

Bobby Goldsboro's 'Little Things', and 'Mama', which had been an American hit for B.J.Thomas, gave him further Top Ten entries in 1965 and 1966 respectively, but then Berry, like so many of his Beat Era contemporaries, had his career badly ruffled by the winds of change that blew through the pop scene in 1967

He disappeared onto the Northern club circuit, leaving behind him two albums, 'Dave Berry' and 'One Dozen Berries', as well as his singles, and a new contract with CBS in 1971 did nothing to revive his fortunes.

BIG BERTHA Formed by bassist Ace Kefford (q.v.), who was previously with The Move (q.v.), they made a single, 'The World Is An Apple', for Atlantic in 1969.

THE PETE BEST FOUR Best was the unfortunate drummer ousted by The Beatles (q.v.) shortly before they shook the world. Ironically, his new combo were promptly snapped up by Decca, one of the companies who had turned down his previous group, but past associations were not enough to bring Best success in his own right.

THE BIG THREE Brian Griffiths (guitar, vocals) John Gustafson (bass, vocals) and John Hutchinson (drums) were an integral part of the Merseybeat scene. Originally called Cass and The Casanovas (q.v.), they claimed to have been the first beat group in Liverpool, and were certainly one of the country's first three-piece groups.

Very popular among Merseyside audiences, and highly respected by fellow musicians, they were soon signed, by Decca, when the eyes of the record company scouts started scouring Liverpool for anything that moved with a guitar. Their first two singles, 'Some Other Guy' and 'By The Way', both entered the lower regions of the charts, and they also recorded a great EP, 'The Big Three Live At The Cavern', which is their most treasured legacy.

In November 1963, however, Griffiths and Gustafson left to form The Seniors, and although Hutchinson tried to carry on with two ex-members of Faron's Flamingos (q.v.), The Big Three were irrevocably diminished in stature.

Gustafson later joined The Merseybeats (q.v.), and in the seventies has worked with Roxy Music and Quatermass, among others. He and Griffiths got together with drummer Nigel Olsson to make a very worthwhile Big Three revival album, entitled 'Resurrection', for Phonogram in 1972.

THE BIRDS Alistair McKenzie (vocals), Ronnie Wood (guitar), Tony Monroe (guitar), Kim Gardner (bass) and Pete McDaniels (drums) hailed from Middlesex, and came together in 1961 while at art college, as The Thunderbirds.

Shortening their name to The Birds, their R&B and Motown-influenced music was popular in the clubs and ballrooms, and they made three singles for Decca during 1964 and 1965.

They made an appearance in 'The Deadly Bees', a horror movie, but apart from that their main public exposure came from the legal battle with the American Byrds over rights to the name.

In 1966 the group split when Gardner and then Wood joined Creation (q.v.), but one more single, 'Say Those Magic Words', was released on Reaction, originally as The Bird's Birds.

Gardner later got his name in lights with Ashton, Gardner and Dyke, while Wood achieved notoriety with The Jeff Beck Group (q.v.), The Faces (q.v.) and The Rolling Stones (q.v.).

CILLA BLACK The definitive Liverpool lass, she started in show business as a cloakroom attendant at The Cavern (q.v.), and occasionally singing with the groups. In 1963 she changed her name from Priscilla White, and was signed by Brian Epstein (q.v.). From then on, her rapid rise to stardom was little more than a formality.

With her marmalade coloured hair, clogs and short (but not too short!) dresses, she was a favourite with kids and parents alike, and after 'Love Of The Loved' had sold moderately well, she had two successive number ones in 1964 with 'Anyone Who Had A Heart' and 'You're My World'.

The hits kept on coming throughout the latter half of the sixties, and when Epstein died in 1967 she was managed by Bobby Willis, whom she later married.

In the seventies she has upgraded her image with a nosejob and a new wardrobe, without losing her essential girl-next-door charm, and has become a popular TV performer, while still making sporadic forays into the charts.

BLACK CAT BONES A semi-professional blues band from London, their line-up during 1967 and 1968 included guitarist Paul Kossoff and drummer Simon Kirke, who later formed Free (q.v.).

THE BLACKWELLS One of numerous Merseyside groups to secure a recording contract in the wake of The Beatles (q.v.), in their case with Parlophone, and to appear in 'Ferry Cross The Mersey', they were also one of numerous Merseyside groups to make a rapid return to obscurity.

BLIND FAITH The original 'supergroup' - a vile trend that blighted the rock landscape for some time in the early seventies - Blind Faith's illustrious membership was Eric Clapton (guitar) and Ginger Baker (drums) from Cream (q.v.), Stevie Winwood (keyboards, vocals) from Traffic (q.v.), and Ric Grech (bass) from Family (q.v.).

They rehearsed for several months in early 1969, before making their debut in the June before 100,000 people in Hyde Park. They made one reasonable album, which sold in predictably

BLODWYN PIG – BONZO DOG DOO DAH BAND

large quantities, and one tour of America before splitting up.

Winwood returned to Traffic duty, Clapton retreated to a low-key role with Delanie and Bonnie, and Baker formed the over-ambitious Airforce.

BLODWYN PIG Mick Abrahams (guitar), Jack Lancaster (flute, violin, saxes), Andy Pyle (bass) and Ron Berg (drums) joined forces in 1969 after the guitarist had left Jethro Tull (q.v.).

Their two Island albums, 'Ahead Rings Out' and 'Getting To This', both good rock albums tinged by Lancaster's jazz background, sold well before Abrahams moved on to form his own band.

Peter Banks from Yes (q.v.) came in to replace him, but the band split up shortly afterwards. An attempted reformation with ex-Tull drummer Clive Bunker in 1974 proved abortive after just a few gigs.

BLOSSOM As might be deduced from the name, Blossom flourished in London during the flower power boom. They played a mixture of soul and Tamla Motown material, but withered up before they could record.

Drummer with the group was Mick Blaikley, brother of The Tremeloes (q.v.) Alan, and he played in the early seventies with Christie, whose 'Yellow River' reached Number One.

BLOSSOM TOES Their 1967 album 'We Are Ever So Clean' introduced Blossom Toes as 'Little Brian known as Wellington, Jim known as Bartholomew, Kevin known as Plod and Big Brian known as Scarlet. They were, in fact, Brian Godding (guitar and vocals), Jim Cregan (guitar and vocals), Brian Belshaw (bass) and Kevin Westlake (drums).

They were certainly one of the better bands to surface in 1967, and they recorded several singles for Giorgio Gomelsky's Marmalade label, including a cover of Bob Dylan's 'I'll Be Your Baby Tonight', and two albums...the second one being 'If Only For A Moment'.

The band's merits weren't reflected by their lack of notable success, and they broke up when their record label folded. Godding, Belshaw and Westlake stayed together as B.B. Blunder, recording an album called 'Workers Playtime' for United Artists in 1971, while Cregan joined Family (q.v.) and later became a member of Rod Stewart's (q.v.) backing band.

Godding also played with Centipede, the free form jazz orchestra formed by Keith Tippett, the husband of his sister-in-law Julie Driscoll (q.v.), and was a member of Solid Gold Cadillac, who made a couple of albums on RCA in 1973.

THE BLUE BEATS They recorded several EPs for the Ember label during 1962-3, before becoming The Cossacks and later The Naturals (q.v.).

BLUE MINK Roger Cooke, Madeline Bell, Herbie Flowers, Alan Parkes and Roger Coulam were all in-demand session singers and musicians when they formed Blue Mink in 1969. Cooke was also a very successful songwriter, while Bell had starred in the 'Black Nativity' stage show and made a number of solo recordings.

They reached No.3 with 'Melting Pot', and had several more hits in the early seventies on the Philips, Regal Zonophone, and EMI labels, although the group was never a full-time project for any of its members.

THE BLUE RONDOS Their single, 'Little Baby' was nearly a hit on the Pye label in 1964, and their guitarist was Mick Stubbs, who went on to join The Syndicats (q.v.).

BLUES BY FIVE An early to mid-sixties R&B group, whose singles for Decca included a version of John Lee Hooker's 'Boom Boom'.

BLUESOLOGY Reg Dwight (keyboards), Stuart Brown (guitar), Rex Bishop (bass) and Mick Inkpen (drums) came from Middlesex, and started out in 1964 playing blues and R&B covers in the London clubs.

They got a lot of work backing visiting American stars, and did several stints on the continent, before becoming the backing group for Long John Baldry (q.v.). Baldry's switch to big ballads and the cabaret circuit eventually killed the group off in the summer of 1969, and Dwight went on to enjoy some modest success after changing his name to Elton John.

Bluesology recorded just one single together, 'Just A Little Bit' for Polydor in 1967, with vocalist Stu Brown, who joined Cochise in the seventies.

BODAST This short-lived outfit was formed by guitarist Steve Howe between his departure from Tomorrow (q.v.) and his joining Yes (q.v.). They made an album, produced by Howe's ex-Tomorrow colleague Keith West (q.v.), but it was never released.

The other members were Dave Curtis, Curtis and Clive Maldoon, who made albums as Maldoon and Curtis Maldoon during the seventies. Bassist Bruce Thomas, who later joined Quiver and Elvis Costello, was also with them for a short while.

BOILERHOUSE A blues band formed in the Brixton area during 1966-7, their guitarist was Danny Kirwan, who became a member of Fleetwood Mac (q.v.) in 1968.

THE GRAHAM BOND ORGANISATION Bond started his career as an alto sax player with the Don Rendell Quintet, but switched to the organ and R&B in 1962, when he joined Alexis Korner's Blues Incorporated (q.v.).

The following year he left the group, along with drummer Ginger Baker and bassist Jack Bruce, and together they were the Graham Bond Trio, which became a Quartet with the addition of guitarist John McLaughlin soon afterwards.

They began as a jazz outfit, but when McLaughlin left at the end of 1963 to be replaced by sax player Dick Heckstall-Smith, Bond reverted to R&B once again, and changed the name to The Graham Bond Organisation. They were a mighty combination, as the line-up suggests, and were very big in the London clubs, but never had any success with records.

'Long Tall Shorty' on Decca was followed by 'Tammy' on Columbia, and two albums, 'The Sound Of '65', featuring a tremendous interpretation of 'Wade In The Water', and 'A Bond Between Us'. None made any commercial impact, and in 1965 Baker and Bruce departed to form Cream (q.v.). John Hiseman briefly took over on drums, but went with Heckstall-Smith to join John Mayall (q.v.) and then Colosseum (q.v.), when Bond disbanded the Organisation later in the year.

Bond himself went to the States, where he made two solo albums, 'Love Is The Law' and 'The Mighty Graham Bond', before returning to London to start Initiation.

In 1971 Bond was reunited with Ginger Baker in the ill-fated Airforce, where he met his wife, coloured singer Diane Stewart. He formed Holy Magic with her, following his interest in white magic, and they made an album of the same name for the Vertigo label. He also had a brief alliance with poet and singer Pete Brown, and together they made the 'Two Heads Are Better Than One' album on Decca's Chapter One label.

A commercial breakthrough still evaded him, however, and he also had problems with his finances and drugs. During 1973 his marriage collapsed, as did an attempt to form a group called Magus with Carolanne Pegg from Mr.Fox, and in May 1974 he met a tragic death, falling under a train at Finsbury Park Station.

Like John Mayall, Bond was one of the great catalysts of British R&B, and his failure to achieve wider recognition is one of rock music's great mysteries.

THE BONZO DOG DOO DAH BAND Vivien Stanshall (vocals), Neil Innes (guitar, piano), Rodney Slater (horns), Legs Larry Smith (drums), Roger Ruskin Spear (assorted silly things), Vernon Dudley Bohay Newell (bass) and Sam Spoons (percussion) were a bizarre cross between a Twenties jazz band and an asylum revue show.

They were first formed in 1965, when the various members were still at college, and during 1966 they made two singles, 'My Brother Makes The Noises For The Talkies' and 'Alley Oop' for Parlophone. Widespread recognition, however, had to wait until the next year, when they appeared in 'Magical Mystery Tour', The Beatles (q.v.) TV film.

They switched to the Liberty label for their first album, 'Gorilla', and in 1968 they had their only single success when 'I'm The Urban Spaceman', produced by Paul McCartney, got to No.5.

They made three more albums, 'The Doughnut

BO STREET RUNNERS—DAVID BOWIE

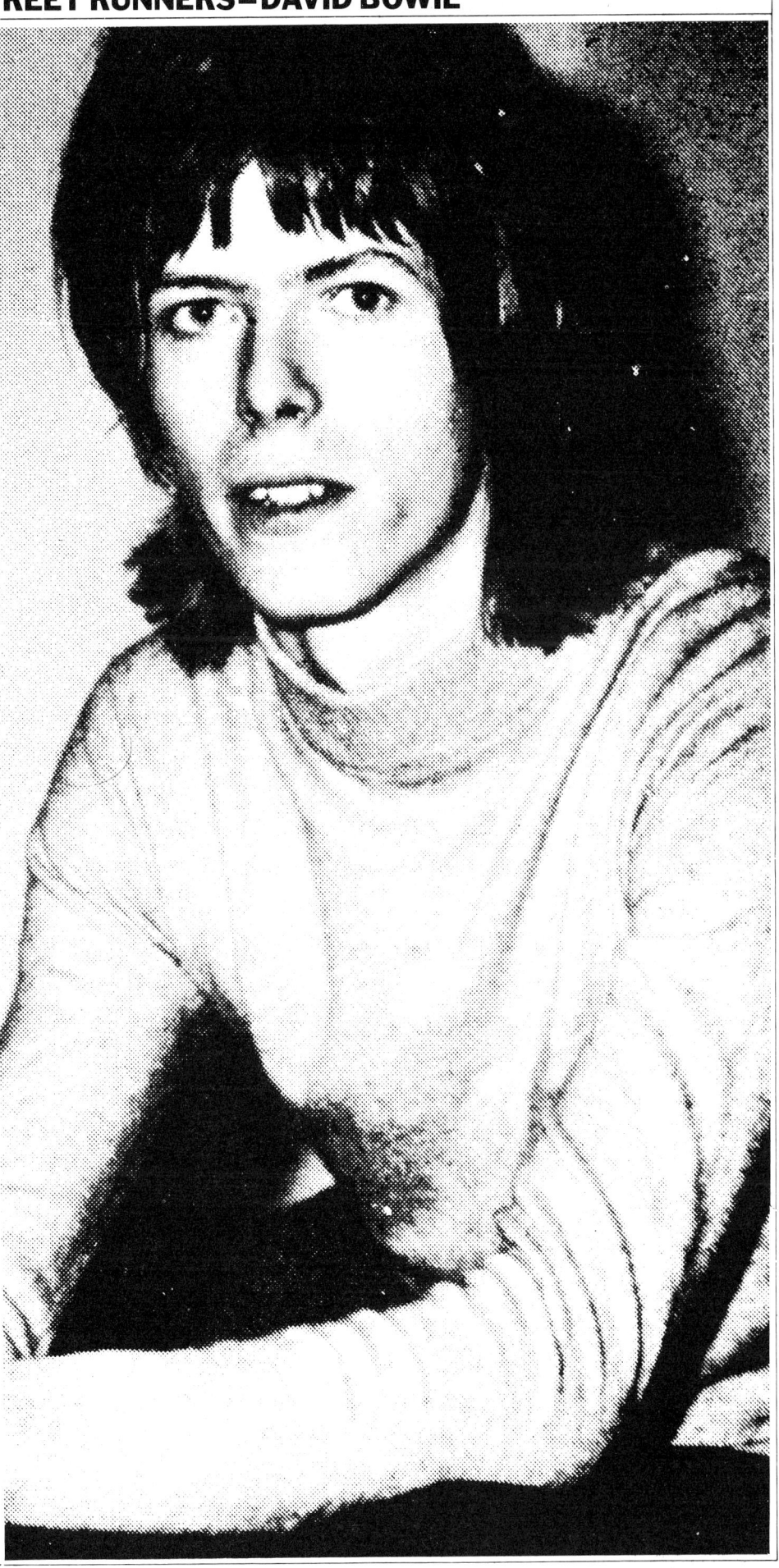

In Granny's Greenhouse', 'Tadpoles' and 'Keynsham, all featuring their unbeatable blend of lyrical and musical satire, before they went their separate ways in 1969.

Since then, Roger Ruskin Spear has been a popular live performer up and down the country with his Giant Kinetic Wardrobe of homemade robots, and Stanshall has made a couple of solo albums, 'Men Open Umbrellas Ahead' and 'Sir Henry Of Rawlinson End', as well as doing some eccentric broadcasting. But the most active has been Neil Innes, who became involved with the Grimms and Scaffold (q.v.) gang, working with Eric Idle from Monty Python as 'The Rutles', an affectionate lampoon of The Beatles, recording solo albums and singles, producing for other artists, and even getting his own TV show, 'The Innes Book Of Records' in early 1979.

THE BO STREET RUNNERS After winning the 'Ready Steady Go' R&B Contest in 1964, this group from Harrow in Middlesex went on to record three singles: 'Bo Street Runner' for Decca in 1964, and 'Tell Me What You're Gonna Do' and 'Drive My Car' for Columbia, in 1965 and 1966 respectively.

Throughout their existence, the group was led by keyboard player Tim Hinkley, and at various times included drummer Mick Fleetwood and vocalist Mike Patto (q.v.). In 1966 with Hinkley and Patto still as the frontmen, they metamorphosed into The Chicago Blues Line (q.v.).

THE BOSTON CRABS A mid-sixties group whose singles for Columbia included 'Down In Mexico', and covers of 'You Didn't Have To Be So Nice' and 'Gin House' in 1966. 'Gin House' cropped up again on EMI's 'My Generation' compilation in 1976.

THE BOSTON DEXTERS One of the few groups to emerge nationally from Edinburgh, The Dexters appeared on stage dressed as Chicago gangsters. They made two singles, 'I've Got Something To Tell You' and 'Try Hard' for Columbia in 1965, and then became The Buzz (q.v.).

DAVID BOWIE Born David Robert Jones at Brixton in 1947, he was in several groups, as singer and saxophonist, while still at school, before leading an R&B group called Davie Jones and The King Bees (q.v.) in 1963.

The following February he lost the chance to appear on the TV show 'Gadzooks! It's All Happening', because he refused to cut his 15" long hair (which really was outrageous for those days), and shortly afterwards had his first single release,'Liza Jane' on Decca, under the name of Tome Jones and The Jonahs. Over the next eighteen months, as well as making records with The King Bees and The Manish Boys (q.v.), he also did a single for Parlophone, called 'Digging My Potatoes', which came out by Davy Jones and The Mood.

In late 1965, he formed a new group, Davie Jones and The Lower Third (q.v.), and the next year changed his name to David Bowie, with the advent of a more famous Davy Jones (he of The Monkees).

He also changed the group name, to The Buzz (q.v.), but shortly afterwards went solo, recording two singles, 'Do Anything You Say' and 'I Dig Everything', for Pye.

By the end of 1966 he had secured a residency at The Marquee (q.v.), and moved to the Deram label, who put out three singles over the next year - 'Rubber Band/The London Boys', 'The Laughing Gnome' and 'Love You Till Tuesday' - and an album simply entitled 'David Bowie'. The album was re-released as 'The World Of David Bowie' in the seventies, and 'The Laughing Gnome' made the Top Ten when it was re-released in 1973 at the peak of Bowie's popularity.

Bowie also made a film, 'The Image', and then 'retired' from the music scene to spend most of 1968 studying mime under Lindsay Kemp.

When he returned in 1969 his music had changed radically from the almost child-like ditties on his Deram album, and he had his

ALAN BOWN SET — ELKIE BROOKS

first big hit with 'Space Oddity' in the October. There was also an album for the Mercury label, again just called 'David Bowie', which was re-released as 'Space Oddity' by RCA in 1973, but then Bowie retreated from the limelight yet again, spending several months forming and working in the Beckenham Arts Lab.

While he was doing this, he was persuaded to make another album for Mercury. 'The Man Who Sold The World' turned out to be an impressive, sombre work, but was largely ignored until three years after its original release, when it was seen to be the blueprint for the bleak visions of later albums.

Two of the sidemen on 'The Man Who Sold The World' were guitarist Mick Ronson and drummer Woody Woodmansey, and with the addition of bassist Trevor Bolder they started doing some low-key gigs around the country during 1971. Switching labels to RCA, they made 'Hunky Dory', which was critically acclaimed and gave Peter Noone a hit single with 'Oh You Pretty Thing', but in 1972 came the change of direction which was to make Bowie the biggest thing to hit British pop since The Beatles (q.v.).

Gone were the long blond hair, feminine taste in clothing, and self-effacing stage presence. The new Bowie sported short, spiky, bright orange hair, elaborate Japanese-style make-up, an equally startling wardrobe, and a stage act which drew heavily on his mime training. Adopting the pseudonym Ziggy Stardust, dubbing his band The Spiders From Mars, and grabbing publicity with the assertion that (although married with a son) he was bisexual, Bowie was a sensation on a scene that had been badly starved of sensations in recent years.

The album, 'The Rise And Fall Of Ziggy Stardust And The Spiders From Mars', gave all the hullabaloo a more-than-solid musical base, and 'Starman' was the first in a long chain of hit singles.

In July 1973, however, at the peak of his British success shortly after the 'Aladdin Sane' album, Bowie fulfilled the fate predicted for Ziggy, in the song 'Ziggy Stardust', by announcing his retirement from live work and disbanding The Spiders. Ronson made a couple of solo albums, and worked with Ian Hunter and Bob Dylan, among others, while Woodmansey and Bolder tried unsuccessfully to keep the Spiders name as a commercial proposition.

Bowie moved to the States, where rumours of health and management problems seemed to be substantiated by the relative disappointment of 'Diamond Dogs'. He thwarted the doommongers, however, with the triumphant 'Young Americans' and 'Station To Station', both of which demonstrated hitherto-unexpected R&B and soul influences.

In 1976 he moved yet again, to Berlin, where he has based himself ever since, mining a rich new creative vein inspired by European electronic music. He also made a return to the film world, though less successfully, starring in 'The Man Who Fell To Earth' in 1976, and 'Just A Gigolo' in 1979.

Nearly always at least one step ahead of public expectations, both in his image and his musical output, Bowie has undoubtedly been one of the seminal influences in seventies pop and rock.

THE ALAN BOWN SET A long-standing group formed in the mid-sixties, whose soul and blues influenced music earned them a strong following in the clubs. This was never turned into record success, although 'Toytown' on MGM came close, but they made several albums for Deram and Island, including 'Alan Bown', 'Stretching Out' and 'Outward Bown'.

Bown himself was a trumpeter, and vocalists with his band included Jess Roden and Robert Palmer, both of whom went on to solo careers in the seventies. Line-up changes were frequent, and among the sidemen at various times were John Helliwell (sax), Dave Lawson (keyboards) and Terry Stannard (drums), who later played with Supertramp, Greenslade and Kokomo respectively.

When the group finally disbanded in 1974, Bown went to work for the A&R department at CBS Records.

BOZ PEOPLE Featuring Boz Burrell on lead vocals, they originated in Kings Lynn, Norfolk, as The Tea Time Four (q.v.). They changed their name after moving to London in 1965, where they added a new keyboards player called Ian MacLagen, who struck lucky with The Small Faces (q.v.) and The Faces (q.v.).

On the group's demise, Burrell was taken under the wing of a businessman, who spent a great deal of money grooming and launching him as a solo artist. A couple of singles bombed, however, and Burrell returned to Norwich, where he teamed up with local soul band Feel For Soul (q.v.).

In the early seventies, back in London, he took up the bass guitar, and toured briefly with Alexis Korner (q.v.) before joining King Crimson (q.v.) and Bad Company.

BUDDY BRITTON AND THE REGENTS A Merseybeat group who recorded 'If You Gotta Make A Fool Of Somebody' coupled with 'Money' for the Oriole label in 1963. Unfortunately for them, Freddie and The Dreamers (q.v.) and Bern Elliott and The Fenmen (q.v.) respectively had the hits. They then recorded several singles for Piccadilly, but none of them were big sellers either.

ELKIE BROOKS One of the three girl singers to emerge from the Merseybeat scene (the others being Cilla Black (q.v.) and Beryl Marsden (q.v.) She was given a short, flicked-up hairstyle, pretty dresses, and a couple of singles which flopped, before ending up in London, singing with a dance band.

Completely changing her image, Elkie re-emerged in the early seventies fronting jazz-rock big band Dada, and then Vinegar Joe, whose funky rock gave her superb blues, soul and jazz voice plenty of scope. With her long, flowing hair, slit satin skirts and aggressive stage manner, she was the archetypal rock'n' roll lady.

When Vinegar Joe split up in 1973, she underwent yet another metamorphosis, with a more sophisticated image and material, high

ROBERT PALMER / THE ALAN BOWN SET

BROOK BROTHERS—BEAU BRUMMELL ESQ.

ELKIE BROOKS

quality production, and a new contract with A&M, which finally established her as one of Britain's top female vocalists.

THE BROOK BROTHERS Hailing from Southampton, they were Britain's answer to The Everly Brothers in the early sixties. They had several successful singles between 1960 and 1963, notably 'Warpaint' and 'Ain't Gonna Wash For A Week', which both made the Top Ten in 1961.

THE EDGAR BROUGHTON BAND Edgar Broughton (guitar, vocals), Steve Broughton (drums), Arthur Grant (bass), Victor Unitt (guitar, vocals) came from Warwick, and were one of the leading "underground" bands of the late sixties and early seventies.

When they moved down to London in 1968, Unitt stayed behind, but rejoined briefly in the seventies. Having been signed by Harvest and the Blackhill agency, the band soon established themselves both in this country and on the continent, where their brand of quasi-revolutionary heavy rock went down particularly well.

Their first album, 'Wasa Wasa', did quite well, but the second, 'Sing Brother Sing' got into the album charts in 1970, and around the same time they also had a couple of minor single successes, with their perennial stage favourite 'Out Demons Out' and 'Apache Dropout'.

Always very much a "people's band", the Broughtons were regular givers of free concerts, but such philanthropy did them little good, as they slowly disappeared into a mire of financial, managerial and record company problems in the mid-seventies.

ARTHUR BROWN Undoubtedly one of the most unforgettable figures to emerge during the sixties, the Yorkshire-born Brown was a student of philosophy at Reading University before forming The Crazy World of Arthur Brown.

The original band included Vincent Crane (keyboards) and Drachen Theaker (drums), but Theaker soon left, popping up again several years later with the American band Love, and was replaced by the teenaged Carl Palmer. They were regulars at London UFO (q.v.) club in the halcyon summer of 1967, and after 'Devil's Grip' had failed to catch on, they had a Number One hit with 'Fire' in August 1968.

With his fluorescent robes, painted face and flaming helmet, Brown had a quite amazing visual impact. He failed to capitalise on his breakthrough, however, and after the 'Crazy World of Arthur Brown' album on Track the band split up, like so many before and since, in the wake of an American tour. Crane and Palmer then formed Atomic Rooster (q.v.).

In 1970 Brown returned with Kingdom Come, who perpetuated his flair for theatrics and recorded three albums for Polydor, without reliving his past moment of glory. He has also made a solo album, 'Dance', on the Gull label, and appeared in the film of 'Tommy'.

PETE BROWN A poet whose various multi-media projects have included liaisons with Vincent Crane, John McLaughlin and Graham Bond (q.v.), Brown's main claim to fame is probably as the man who wrote most of the lyrics for Cream (q.v.).

In 1968 he put together Battered Ornaments, a rock band whose line-up included guitarist Chris Spedding, and they recorded an album for Harvest called 'Mantlepiece'. The following year they were superseded by Piblokto, with whom Brown made 'Thousands On A Raft' and 'The Art School Dance Goes On Forever'.

SANDRA BROWN AND HER BOYFRIENDS Formed in London during 1963, they recorded 'By Hook Or By Crook' for Columbia in the following year. The Boyfriends then stood Sandra up, and went on to be The Boys and then The Action (q.v.).

BEAU BRUMMELL ESQ. A real character from the mid-sixties, Mr. Brummell dressed in the style of the original Beau, carried a gold-topped

BRUNO—CHANTS

walking cane and claimed to clean his spats with champagne!

He made a single called 'I Know, Know, Know' which challenged the studio technology of the day by requiring the highlights of some fifty takes to be pieced together for the finished product!

When Mr. Brummell embarked on a nationwide tour, he was bright enough to employ a backing band whose volume disguised his vocal shortcomings. On retiring from the music business he confessed all to a well-known Sunday paper.

BRUNO A young man who had a brace of gentle, easy listening singles, 'The English Girl' and 'Wander Boy', on Parlophone in 1966. Both sank into instant obscurity, to be shortly followed by their perpetrator.

BUMBLEY HUM Originally a fairly successful New Zealand band called The Purple Hearts, Dave Dover-Masters (vocals), Tony Bird (organ), Harry Cherrell (bass) and John Callaghan (drums) came to England in 1967, basing themselves (for some bizarre reason) in Norwich.

They started out playing country rock, but gradually developed a more classical approach, somewhat akin to The Nice (q.v.). Neither style cut much ice, however, and after gigging round the country for three years they returned to their native land.

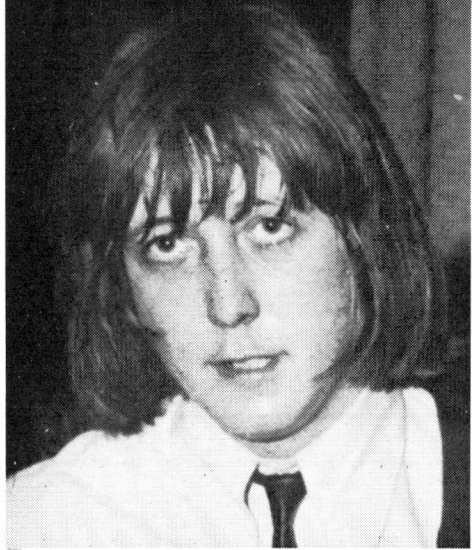

THE BUNCH OF FIVES Formed by drummer Viv Prince after his exit from The Pretty Things (q.v.) in 1966, the group made one single, 'Go Home Baby/At The Station', for Parlophone before counting themselves out.

THE BUZZ There seem to have been two different groups by this name in early 1966. The first was a new-look Boston Dexters (q.v.), and they had two singles on Columbia, 'Buzz Bomb' and 'You're Holding Me Down', the latter produced by Joe Meek.

The other Buzz were David Bowie's (q.v.) backing band, who had their name changed from David Jones and The Lower Third (q.v.). They were Dennis "T-Cup" Taylor (lead guitar), Graham Rivens (bass) and Phil Lancaster (drums).

THE BYSTANDERS Formed in Merthyr Tydfil during 1963, Gerry Braden (vocals), Mike Steel (guitar), Mark St. John (keyboards), Robin J. Selby (bass) and Jeff Paris (drums) specialised in harmony vocals *a la* Beach Boys and Four Seasons.

Braden was replaced by one Vic Oakley, and after doing a single called 'That's The End' for the local Pylot label, they had several singles on Piccadilly between 1966 and 1968, including a version of '98.6'.

In 1968, Oakley became a resident Top Rank vocalist, while the others (whose real names were Micky Jones, Clive John, Ray Williams and Jeff Jones) became Man (q.v.).

CARAVAN Pye Hastings (guitar, vocals), David Sinclair (keyboards), Richard Sinclair (bass, vocals) and Richard Coughlan (drums) were formed in Canterbury in January 1968, all four having previously been members of Wilde Flowers (q.v.).

Their first album, *Caravan* on MGM, came later the same year, along with a single called 'A Place Of My Own'. They then moved to Deram, making 'If I Could Do It All Over Again I'd Do It All Over You' and 'In The Land Of The Grey And Pink', which remain their most perennially popular albums.

In 1971 David Sinclair left to join Robert Wyatt's Matching Mole, and was replaced by Steve Miller, who had been in Delivery (q.v.). A year later cousin Richard also departed, to form Hatfield and The North.

The group has continued through numerous line-up changes, with Hastings and Coughlan as the nucleus, and recorded regularly for Deram and then BTM. They have always enjoyed a solid following both in Britain and the Continent without finding the widespread success that was originally forecast for them.

THE CARAVELLES Two girls with baby doll voices, whose reworking of Tennessee Ernie Ford's 'You Don't Have To Be A Baby To Cry' for Deram got to No.6 in 1963. Still a minor pop classic, this single was to be their only taste of fame and fortune.

CARL AND THE CHEETAHS An early sixties group from Birmingham, who got signed by EMI in 1963. Carl was Carl Wayne, who later fronted The Move (q.v.).

CARNABY As might be deduced from their name, Carnaby were a mid-sixties London mod group who dressed themselves in the latest gear. Despite their efforts to be fashionable none of their Piccadilly singles, including 'Jump And Dance', were up anyone's street.

JOHNNY CARR AND THE CADILLACS Johnny Carr (vocals), Ray Truscott (guitar), Mervyn Alexander (bass) and Dave Purslow (drums) started in 1958 as a Bristol rock'n'roll group. They had several vocalists, all of whom adopted the name Johnny Carr, and after changing to an R&B style in the sixties they joined the British caravan to Hamburg.

In 1965, while Johnny Carr was Con O'Sulli-

van, they had their only record success when 'Do You Love That Girl', on Fontana, crept into the lower reaches of the charts. They were still going in the late sixties, by which time they had been reduced to getting dates by impersonating The Zombies (q.v.).

CARTER LEWIS AND THE SOUTHERNERS Formed in the early sixties by vocalists John Carter and Ken Lewis, they made numerous appearances on BBC radio shows, and even had a minor hit in 1963 with 'Your Momma's Out Of Town'.

Carter and Lewis were also successful songwriters and session singers, and in 1964 they were two thirds of The Ivy League (q.v.). Among the various instrumentalists to pass through The Southerners were Jimmy Page and Viv Prince (q.v.).

CASS AND THE CASANOVAS Claiming to be the first group in Liverpool, they visited Hamburg along with almost every other group in Liverpool. In 1962 they became The Big Three (q.v.).

THE CASUALS After reaching the Top Three with 'Jesamine' on Decca in 1968 they scraped into the Thirty with the follow-up, 'Toy', and their fifteen minutes of fame were over.

THE CAVERN Actually just one of several cellar clubs which all played their part in making Liverpool such a thriving musical city in the early sixties, The Cavern is nevertheless the most celebrated club in pop.

All the Merseybeat groups played there, although it is best remembered as The Birthplace of The Beatles (q.v.), and The Big Three (q.v.) even recorded an EP there in 1963.

With the passing of the Mersey boom, The Cavern's golden years were over, although it stayed in existence until 1973. Now demolished, the only reminder of its location in Mathew Street is a rather kitsch plaque on the opposite side of the street, a madonna bearing the legend "Four lads who shook the world".

CHAD AND JEREMY Chad Stuart and Jeremy Clyde were two ex-public schoolboys and drama students who recorded a series of singles and albums, mainly self-penned, for Ember between 1963 and 1965. They had a minor hit with 'Yesterday's Gone' in this country, but were much bigger in the States, where three of their singles made the Top Twenty.

When their success petered out they both returned to acting careers, and in 1978 Clyde played the title role in the 'Sexton Blake' TV series.

THE CHANTS Yet another early sixties Liverpool group, The Chants were distinguished from their contemporaries by dint of the fact that

MICHAEL CHAPMAN – DAVE CLARK FIVE

they were the first coloured vocal group in the country.

They also outlasted most of their Merseybeat fellows, and during their career recorded for Pye, Fontana and Decca. This was despite the fact that none of their singles, which included 'Sweet Was The Wine', 'Come Back And Get This Loving Baby' and 'Lover's Story', had any impact.

Their lead singer was Eddie Amoo, who in the seventies had long-overdue success with The Real Thing.

MICHAEL CHAPMAN Originally a teacher in Hull, Chapman took up full-time folk-singing in 1967. The following year saw him gaining a contract with Harvest and making his first album, 'Rainmaker'. On this, as on later albums like the first rate 'Fully Qualified Survivor', Chapman used old acquaintances from Hull, including Mick Ronson, later guitarist with David Bowie (q.v.) and Rick Kemp. Chapman and Kemp actually toured as a duo in 1972, after which the bassist joined Steeleye Span (q.v.).

During the seventies, Chapman has emerged regularly from his self-imposed isolation in Cornwall to tour and record, but without ever achieving the recognition that his work deserves.

THE CHEROKEES John Kirby (vocals), Terry Stokes (guitar), Dave Dower (guitar), Mike Sweeney (bass) and Jim Green (drums) surprised everybody when their version of 'Seven Daffodils' made the Top Thirty in late 1964 at the expense of the better-known Mojos.

Despite being produced by hit-maker *extraordinaire* Mickie Most (q.v.), none of their other Columbia singles, including 'Wondrous Face' and 'Land Of 1000 Dances', could emulate even this modest success.

CHERRY SMASH A Decca recording group, their singles included 'Sing Songs Of Love' from late 1966, and 'Goodtime Sunshine' and 'Fade Away Maureen' from 1968.

THE CHEYNES Peter Bardens (keyboards), Roger Peacock (vocals), Phil Sawyer (guitar), Peter Hollis (bass) and Mick Fleetwood (drums) were formed at Chelsea Art School in 1964.

On stage they sported frilly yellow shirts and suede pullovers, which were slightly at odds with the raw R&B sound demonstrated on their three Columbia singles - 'Respectable', a cover of the Isley Brothers song which also appeared on the 'On The Scene' album, 'Goin' To The River' and Down And Out'.

When the group split in mid-1965, Bardens and Fleetwood formed The Peter B's (q.v.), while Sawyer later played bass for the second Spencer Davis Group (q.v.).

THE CHICAGO LINE BLUES BAND A short-lived outfit which developed out of The Bo Street Runners (q.v.) in 1966. The group featured keyboard player Tim Hinkley and vocalist Mike Patto, and among the other musicians were Louis Cennamo (bass), Viv Prince (q.v.) and trumpeter Mike Fellana.

During the seventies, Hinkley and Cennamo have both been in-demand session players, while Patto has fronted Patto and Boxer. They still occasionally gig together, along with numerous friends, as Dick and the Firemen or Hinkley's Heroes.

CHICKEN SHACK One of the main beneficiaries of the late sixties British "blues boom", Chicken Shack formed in Birmingham during 1965 as Stan Webb (guitar, vocals), Paul Hancox (bass) and John Glasgow (drums). By 1968, however, when the band moved to London after signing with Mike Vernon's Blue Horizon label, the line-up was Webb, Christine Perfect (piano, vocals), Andy Sylvester (bass) and Dave Bidwell (drums).

Their first album, '40 Blue Fingers Freshly Packed And Ready To Serve', sold well, and 'OK Ken' did even better in 1969. In the same

year, Chicken Shack also hit the singles chart with 'I'd Rather Go Blind', a cover of the Etta James R&B classic, and 'Tears In The Wind'.

In 1969 Christine Perfect left to join her husband John McVie in Fleetwood Mac (q.v.), and was replaced by Paul Raymond. This loss of their most distinctive voice, combined with a general decline in the popularity of the Blues, led to leaner years for Chicken Shack. They kept up their tireless gigging schedule, however, and were especially popular at festivals, when Webb's forays into the crowd on the end of a 200 ft. guitar lead were a memorable feature of the act.

They also kept making albums, for Blue Horizon and then Deram, but finally called it a day in 1973. Webb then joined Savoy Brown (q.v.), who also included Bidwell and Raymond, but shortly afterwards left again to form Broken Glass.

CHORDS FIVE Mick Rowley (vocals), Mal Luker (guitar), John "Zeke" Lund (bass) and Geoff Gill (drums) were also known as The Smoke (q.v.). As Chords Five they recorded 'I Am Only Dreaming' for Island in 1967, and 'Same Old Fat Man' for Polydor and 'Some People' for Jayboy in 1968.

THE CHOSEN FEW A mid-sixties combo from Newcastle led by Alan Hull, who later made himself famous with Lindisfarne (q.v.). Other members included Graham Bell and Micky Gallagher, who went on to form Skip Bifferty (q.v.). They recorded for Pye, but might as well not have bothered, for all the recognition it brought them.

NEIL CHRISTIAN AND THE CRUSADERS Remembered almost exclusively for the fact that their guitarist was a very youthful Jimmy Page, in his pre-Yardbirds (q.v.) and Led Zeppelin (q.v.) days. The Crusaders actually existed both before and after Page's stay with the group, and recorded several singles, including 'Oops' and 'Two At A Time' on Strike in 1966.

THE CITATIONS A rocking instrumental group from the early sixties, somewhat similar to The Tornadoes (q.v.), recorded a single entitled 'Moon Race' for Columbia in 1963. Far more interesting than this blatant mimickry of The Tornadoes' "space age" success was the flip-side, a full-blooded version of Little Richard's 'Slippin' And Slidin'', complete with vocals and saxes.

THE DAVE CLARK FIVE Originally a North London skiffle group formed in 1960, Dave Clark (drums), Mike Smith (keyboards, vocals), Lenny Davidson (guitar, vocals), Rick Huxley (bass) and Denny Payton (sax) first came to public attention in 1963, when they were dubbed "The Tottenham Sound" in the wake of Merseybeat.

After signing to Columbia their first two singles, 'Mulberry Bush' and 'Do You Love Me', were moderately successful, but then 'Glad All Over' went to No.1 in January 1964, starting a run of chart entries that was to last until 1970.

They had no further Number Ones in this country, but they were to become one of the biggest British bands in the States, and 'Over And Over' reached the top there in early 1966.

Their records had a distinctive stomping beat, and in fact their second hit, 'Bits And Pieces', inspired such dancing fervour that managers of ballrooms with sprung floors were prompted to ban the record.

In 1965 the group made a film, 'Catch Us If You Can', inspired no doubt by the success of The Beatles' (q.v.) celluloid ventures. Like almost everything else the group did, its commercial potential substantially outweighed its artistic merits.

Despite the name of the group, their guid-

The Dave Clark Five

CLASSMATES—CREAM

ing light was Mike Smith, who wrote most of their material. Clark himself did little but flash a clean-cut smile, and drum in a manner not unlike a clockwork soldier.

As well as their numerous singles The Dave Clark Five also made several albums, of which 'Session With The Five' and 'Catch Us If You Can' were the most successful.

When the group split up in the early seventies, Smith re-emerged in a duo with Mike d'Abo from Manfred Mann (q.v.). Clark, meanwhile, proved that although he was no Buddy Rich he certainly had more business suss than most of his contemporaries, by being able to resell the rights to all the group's material for a reputedly fabulous sum. The 'Twenty Thumping Great Hits' album culled therefrom gave The Dave Clark Five a large piece of posthumous chart action in 1977-8.

THE CLASSMATES A gospel beat group who made several singles for Decca, among them a version of 'Go Tell It On The Mountain' in 1963, without ever having their prayers answered.

THE CLAYTON SQUARES A Liverpool group who had the misfortune to arrive on the scene when the Merseybeat furore had died down, and interest in the 'Pool was waning. Their Decca singles included 'Come And Get It', but not many people did.

Members of the group were guitarists Mike Hart and Andy Roberts, both later in The Liverpool Scene (q.v.), and Albie Donnelly, now infamous as the bald-headed saxophonist with Supercharge.

THE CLIMAX CHICAGO BLUES BAND Pete Haycock (guitar, vocals), Colin Cooper (saxophone, vocals), Richard Jones (keyboards), Derek Holt (bass) and John Cuffley (drums) came together in Stafford during 1969 at the tail-end of the Blues boom.

Quickly signed up by Parlophone they made two albums, 'Climax Chicago Blues Band' and 'Play On', before transferring to EMI's "progressive" Harvest label.

During the seventies they have recorded several further albums for Polydor and BTM, during which time Jones (who originally played bass) left to go to college and then rejoined. Although perennially popular on the British concert circuit, they have always enjoyed a far greater response abroad.

CLOUDS Billy Ritchie (keyboards, vocals), Ian Ellis (bass) and Harry Hughes (drums) were a Scottish trio who made three albums, 'Clouds', 'Scrapbook' and 'Watercolour Days', for Island.

THE COASTERS An early sixties Liverpool group, completely unconnected with the Americans of the same name, The Coasters had a guitarist called William Howard Ashton who was persuaded to sing instead. Finding this more to his liking, he then changed his name to the more charismatic Billy J. Kramer (q.v.) and was soon signed by Brian Epstein (q.v.).

The rest of the group were left to back another Liverpool singer, Chick Graham, with whom they made a number of singles for Decca, including 'I Know'.

JOE COCKER A Sheffield gas-fitter who became one of rock's most lauded figures after his extraordinary performance in the 'Woodstock' film, Cocker began his musical career as a drummer and harmonica player with The Cavaliers, while still in his mid-teens.

On discovering his vocal talents he moved out to front the band, who changed their name to Vance Arnold and The Avengers, and later to Joe Cocker's Big Blues, under which name they spent some time touring USAF bases in France.

During this period, Cocker had a single released on Decca, a version of The Beatles' (q.v.) 'I'll Cry Instead' which fared disastrously in 1964. Returning to Sheffield after this chastening experience, Cocker put together his first Greaseband (q.v.) and worked Northern clubs and pubs on a semi-pro basis.

His time finally came in 1968, when he started recording again with producer Denny Cordell. The first single 'Marjorine' crept into the lower reaches of the charts, but with the superlative support of The Greaseband Cocker was making a considerable impact on live appearances, and at the end of the year 'With A Little Help From My Friends' shot to Number One.

Cocker had a very strong blues voice with a unique, orgasmic delivery, and this combined with a thoroughly demented (some said distasteful) presentation soon earned him star status, especially in America.

His first album, 'With A Little Help From My Friends' was recorded with an all-star line-up which included Jimmy Page and Stevie Winwood. The second, 'Joe Cocker' was made in Los Angeles the following year with supervision from Leon Russell, and when Cocker parted company from The Greaseband just prior to an American tour, it was Russell who put together the legendary Mad Dogs And Englishmen entourage to take their place.

The whole caravan was captured on a double album and a full-length feature film, but the exercise did more to launch the careers of Russell and some of the other sidemen than to further Cocker's. Apparently torn apart by the pressures of his sudden rise to fame and fortune, and by attendant financial and managerial disputes, Cocker went into a quite alarming decline, which was hastened by a reputedly monolithic ingestion of drugs and alcohol.

Several attempts have been made to revive his career, via albums for Cube, A&M and Asylum, but Cocker never seems to have been able to hold things together long enough to recapture his impact of the late sixties. A tremendous talent sadly lacking guidance and protection, Cocker's story is one of rock's great tragedies.

COLOSSEUM Jon Hiseman (drums), Dave Greenslade (keyboards), Dick Heckstall-Smith (saxophone), James Litherland (guitar) and Tony Reeves (bass) were an ambitious jazz-rock band formed out of John Mayall's (q.v.) 'Bare Wires' group in 1968.

Hiseman and Heckstall-Smith had both been with Graham Bond (q.v.) previously, and his influence was strongly felt on 'Those Who Are About To Die Salute You' and 'Valentyne Suite', both from 1969. Litherland and Reeves left after these albums to be replaced by Dave Clempson from Bakerloo (q.v.) and Mark Clarke. Vocalist Chris Farlowe (q.v.) also joined in time for 'Daughter Of Time'.

After a live album the band broke up, with Greenslade reuniting with Tony Reeves in Greenslade, Clempson joining Humble Pie (q.v.), Heckstall-Smith forming his own band, and Hiseman and Clarke starting Tempest. In 1975 Hiseman tried again with Colosseum II, but without recapturing the respect or interest engendered by the original band.

THE CONRADS An early sixties R&B band who featured David Jones on saxophone and vocals. Jones later became David Bowie (q.v.).

CONSORTIUM They recorded several singles for Pye in 1968-9, including 'All The Love In The World', 'When The Day Breaks' and 'I Don't Want Her Anymore', as well as 'Tell Me My Friend' for the Trend label.

COPS 'N' ROBBERS "Smudger" Smith (vocals), Terry Fox (organ), Steve Smith (bass) and Henry Harrison (drums) were an R&B group from Watford, who were popular on the mid-sixties club circuit and recorded for Pye and Decca.

Mostly covers, like 'St James Infirmary', none of their singles made the charts, although their version of Dylan's 'It's All Over Now Baby Blue' sold steadily for a while.

"Smudger" was eventually superseded by Duffy, and then Dane Stephens from The Fairies (q.v.). When the band split up in 1966, Henry Harrison formed The New Vaudeville Band (q.v.).

THE MIKE COTTON SOUND Originally The Mike Cotton Jazz Band during the late fifties, Cotton turned to soul and blues with the passing of the trad boom, and his group became regular performers on package tours, playing their own short set before backing other acts on the bill.

As well as playing with artists like Stevie Wonder, The Four Tops and Gene Pitney, they recorded in their own right for Columbia and had a small hit with 'Swing That Hammer' in 1963. Other singles included versions of 'Midnite Flyer' and 'Round And Round', and they also recorded an EP of music from the film 'The Wild And The Willing' and an album, comprising such diverse standards as 'Love Potion Number Nine' and 'Night Train'.

In 1966 the group were joined by black American singer Lucas and moved to Polydor and later to Pye, making further singles including 'Harlem Shuffle' and 'Soul Serenade'.

The group personnel changed constantly over the years, and among the members were keyboard player Dave Rowberry, who later joined The Animals (q.v.), and bassist Jim Rodford, who was to be with Argent (q.v.).

In 1969 The Sound provided the backing on Mary Hopkin's 'Postcard' album, and in the early seventies, having trimmed down to just the brass section, they concentrated on session work, and toured and recorded with The Kinks (q.v.) for a while.

THE COUGARS An early sixties group from Bristol, they had a modest hit on Parlophone in February 1963 with an instrumental called 'Saturday Night At The Duckpond'. This was actually a popped-up version of the theme from 'Swan Lake'. After following it with 'Red Square', the group vanished.

THE COUNTRY GENTLEMEN A Manchester beat group, their Decca singles included 'Baby Jean'.

THE CRAWDADDY A club at The Station Hotel in Richmond, Surrey, run by an eccentric Russian film director called Giorgio Gomelsky, The Crawdaddy started off as a jazz club, but moved to R&B in 1962 after the London success of Alexis Korner's Blues Incorporated (q.v.).

The Rolling Stones (q.v.) first came to public notice playing Sunday afternoon sessions there, and when they moved on to greater things, their residency was taken over by The Yardbirds (q.v.).

CREAM Jack Bruce (bass) and Ginger Baker (drums) from The Graham Bond Organisation (q.v.) linked up with guitarist Eric Clapton from John Mayall's (q.v.) Bluesbreakers in 1966. Since each member was widely acknowledged to be the premier British exponent of his particular instrument, Cream seemed to be an appropriate name for the band.

Followers of Bond and Mayall expected them to pursue a straightforward blues direction, but in fact they displayed strong jazz and pop influences, as well as a distinctive line in lyrics, courtesy of Pete Brown (q.v.).

Their first single, 'Wrapping Paper' on Reaction, was unashamedly poppy, and only made

the lower reaches of the charts. Their debut album, 'Fresh Cream', featured several classic blues covers, and was a substantial success.

Top Twenty singles in the shape of 'I Feel Free' and 'Strange Brew' followed during 1967, and at the end of the year came the second album, 'Disraeli Gears', yet again a balance of blues and jazzy pop, and probably Cream's definitive album.

During 1968 Cream took off in a big way in the States and started spending most of their time there. They changed labels to Polydor, found a new producer in Felix Pappilardi and, perhaps because their success was giving them less time for writing, began to rely increasingly on the virtuoso improvisational style which had always been evident in their live performances.

The turning-point album was 'Wheels Of Fire', a half-studio and half-live double set recorded in America, much of which can only be described as indulgent and uninteresting.

The strain of overwork and three strong egos finally took its toll, and the band played their farewell concert at the Royal Albert Hall on November 26th, 1968.

Their final purpose-built album, the appropriately named 'Goodbye', demonstrated the same flaws as 'Wheels Of Fire', but was, perhaps unsurprisingly, their most successful in commercial terms. Two further live volumes were released posthumously, along with various compilations and bootlegs, but their merits must have been more obvious to the record company accountants than anybody else.

All three members had built up very loyal followings - as proven by their consistent prominence in popularity polls, even during their leanest years in the seventies - so it was inevitable that their activities after the demise of the band would attract considerable interest.

Clapton and Baker went on to the short-lived Blind Faith (q.v.), while Bruce recorded a very well-received solo album, 'Songs For A Tailor', which pursued his jazzier influences. Bruce made several further solo efforts during the seventies, interspersed with stints in Tony Williams Lifetime, a jazz-rock combo which included guitarist John McLaughlin, and West, Bruce and Laing, a thoroughly uninspired sub-Cream outfit with two members of the American band Mountain.

Baker made ill-fated forays with Airforce and The Baker Gurvitz Army, before concentrating his interests on polo and his studio in Nigeria. Clapton meanwhile adopted a low-key profile with the American duo Delaney and Bonnie before putting together Derek and The Dominoes. They made one tremendous studio album, 'Layla And Other Love Songs', and a less amazing live album, but then Clapton spent some two years in self-imposed isolation, suffering from psychological and drugs problems.

In January 1973 he did a one-off comeback concert at the Rainbow, organised by Pete Townshend of The Who (q.v.). As an event it was overblown, to say the least, but it got Clapton back into playing, and in the following year he formed the band which, with an occasional change, has stayed with him ever since.

This alliance has led Clapton to a new, countryfied style, much more laid back than of yore, and with much less of Clapton's legendary guitar work than most people would like to see. It has, however, given rise to at least one excellent album '461 Ocean Boulevard' and lifted Clapton to multi-platinum level in the States.

Although often erratic as a group, Cream's place in rock history is assured, and their influence in the late sixties and early seventies was widespread...if not always beneficial.

CREATION Eddie Phillips (lead guitar), Kenny Pickett (vocals), John Dalton (bass) and Jack Jones (drums) were originally called The Mark Four (q.v.), but changed their name during early 1966. Dalton was soon replaced by Kim Gardner from The Birds (q.v.), and when Phillips left in 1968 they brought in Ronnie Wood from the same group.

Although popular at a grassroots level and very big on the continent, Creation never really cracked the charts in Britain, and minor hits with their first two singles, 'Makin' Time' and 'Painter Man' on the independent Planet label, were the closest they came. In 1967 they moved to Polydor, where their sales went down, rather than up.

Apart from featuring a vivid climax to their stage show, when Pickett sprayed drawings onto sheets and then set fire to them, they were a fine, inventive group with an excellent guitarist in Phillips, who was actually the first person to use a violin bow with his guitar... a feat later popularised by Jimmy Page with Led Zeppelin (q.v.).

Creation's manager was Tony Stratton-Smith, and in 1974 his Charisma label released a very worthwhile compilation album containing several of their singles and some unreleased material, including a version of 'Hey Joe'.

When he left the group, Phillips spent a short while with T.N.T. (q.v.), but then became a bus driver for London Transport, before re-emerging as a solo artist with a single called 'Limbo Jimbo' on Charisma in 1976.

The rest of the band split up in 1968, with Gardner forming Ashton, Gardner and Dyke, and Ronnie Wood getting rich with The Faces (q.v.) and The Rolling Stones (q.v.). Former bassist Dalton was later a member of The Kinks (q.v.).

THE CRESTERS An early sixties beat group from Bramley, Yorkshire, their singles included 'I Just Don't Understand' on HMV.

THE CRYIN' SHAMES Another of Decca's innumerable signings in the mid-sixties, their singles included 'What's New Pussycat' in 1966, and 'Please Stay' which made the Top Thirty in the same year.

CUPIDS INSPIRATION Led by vocalist Terry Rice-Milton, they had a huge hit for NEMS with 'Yesterday Has Gone' in the summer of '68. This was followed by 'My World', which was a minor hit, and an album blending ballads and up-tempo pop. Rice-Milton then left to pursue a solo career, and neither he nor the group had anything further to inspire them.

LEE CURTIS AND THE ALL STARS Yet another Merseyside group who got signed up in the heady days of 1963. They had a single on Decca called 'The Stomp', but failed to live up to their name.

DAVE CURTISS AND THE TREMORS A group from Clacton in Essex, who made a version of 'Summertime Blues' for Philips in 1963.

THE CYMBALINE A mid to late sixties pop group, their singles included 'Peanut And Chewy Mac' and 'Top Girl' on the Mercury label, and 'Turn Around' and 'Comin' Home Baby' on Philips

DAKOTAS—DEEP FEELING

THE DAKOTAS Mike Maxfield (lead guitar), Robin McDonald (rhythm guitar), Ray Jones (bass) and Tony Mansfield (drums) were playing the Manchester clubs in 1963 when Brian Epstein (q.v.) offered them the job of backing his latest *protege*, Billy J. Kramer (q.v.).

They played on Kramer's hits, and had three singles and an EP of their own instrumentals on Parlophone, of which 'The Cruel Sea' reached the Top Twenty. In August 1964, when Jones left, McDonald moved onto bass and Mick Green came in on rhythm.

DANTALIONS CHARIOT Zoot Money (keyboards), Andy Somers (guitar), Pat Donaldson (bass) and Colin Allen (drums) came about when The Zoot Money Big Roll Band (q.v.) broke up, and their leader went psychedelic.

They made several flamboyant appearances at the Middle Earth club and made one memorable single, 'The Madman Running Through The Fields' on Columbia, before Money went to join Eric Burdon and The Animals (q.v.).

Allen joined John Mayall (q.v.) and then Stone The Crows (q.v.); Donaldson was in Fotheringay and did a lot of session work during the seventies; while Somers was with ex-Soft Machine (q.v.) bassist Kevin Ayers before belying his years with New Wave group The Police in 1978.

DAVE DAVANI AND THE D MEN An early sixties beat group who recorded for Columbia. Davani later formed The Dave Davani Four and moved to Parlophone.

DAVID AND JONATHAN Roger Cook and Roger Greenaway were songwriters and session singers who made a series of singles as David and Jonathan. 'Michelle' and 'Lovers Of The World Unite' on Columbia were both hits in 1966. They have also written numerous hits for other artists, and in 1969 Cook formed Blue Mink (q.v.).

THE CYRIL DAVIES RHYTHM AND BLUES ALL STARS Cyril Davies started playing blues harmonica in the mid-fifties, while working in Chris Barber's Jazz Band alongside Alexis Korner. Eventually the pair left to form Alexis Korner's Blues Incorporated (q.v.), and their work together is captured on 'R&B From The Marquee' on Decca's Ace of Clubs label.

Davies was a main vocalist with the group as well as playing harmonica, and in late 1962 he left to form the All Stars. They signed with Pye, and made two singles - 'Country Line Special' and 'Preachin' The Blues - and an EP - before Davies died of leukaemia in January 1964.

Numerous musicians played with the group during its existence including pianist Nicky Hopkins (q.v.), saxophonist Dick Heckstall-Smith, and vocalist Long John Baldry (q.v.) who took over leadership of the group after Davies' death, renaming them The Hoochie Coochie Men (q.v.).

In the seventies an album was released by Folklore Records, comprising material recorded in 1957 and 1961 with Alexis Korner's Breakdown Group and The Roundhouse Jug Four.

THE SPENCER DAVIS GROUP Spencer Davis (rhythm guitar), Steve Winwood (keyboards, guitar, vocals), Muff Winwood (bass) and Pete York (drums) had all been with Birmingham jazz bands before joining forces and turning to R&B in 1963.

Signing to Fontana they flopped with 'Dimples', and their next three singles - 'I Can't Stand It', 'Every Little Bit Hurts' and 'Strong Love' - were minor hits, before 'Keep On Running' broke through to Number One in early 1966.

Once established they had a second chart topper with 'Somebody Help Me' followed by a string of further successes. Their three albums - 'Their First LP', 'Second Album' and 'Autumn '66' were all strong sellers.

Despite the name of the group, however, it was the teenaged Steve Winwood who was the driving force of the band, writing much of their material as well as providing their distinctive instrumental sound. When he left in early 1967 to form Traffic, the group not surprisingly lost much of their appeal. He was replaced by Eddie Hardin on organ and ex-Cheynes (q.v.) and Fleurs-de-Lys (q.v.) guitarist Phil Sawyer on lead, but despite entries in the lower regions of the charts with 'Time Seller' and 'Mr. Second Class' (the latter after a switch to United Artists), the group's days of glory were over.

Sawyer was supplanted by Ray Fenwick from After Tea (q.v.) in December 1967, and in the following year Hardin and York left to work as a duo. Muff Winwood went into production and A&R work, and after soldiering on with the group for a little longer Davis had unsuccessful tries at various ventures during the seventies, before moving to California and going into the same line.

DEAD SEA FRUIT A London group who recorded a ditty called 'Kensington High Street' for the Camp label in 1967, they withered up soon afterwards.

PAUL DEAN AND THE SOUL SAVAGES A beat group operating in the London area during the early sixties, they later became Paul Dean and His Thoughts, recording for Decca.

KIKI DEE Born Pauline Matthews in Bradford, she sang with local dance bands before meeting producer Mitch Murray, moving south, changing her name, and making her debut single 'Early Night' in 1964.

She recorded a string of further unsuccessful singles for Philips, as well as an album called 'I'm Kiki Dee' in 1966. In 1970 she became the first white singer to be signed by Tamla Motown, but it wasn't until she moved to Elton John's Rocket label in 1973 that she had her first real taste of stardom.

'Amoureuse', 'I Got The Music In Me' and 'How Glad I Am' all made the charts during the next three years, and in 1976 her duo with John, 'Don't Go Breaking My Heart', got to Number One.

Since then her career has stagnated yet again, and despite being blessed with a strong voice, she has never really achieved the status that has regularly been predicted for her.

DAVE DEE, DOZY, BEAKY, MICK AND TICH David "Dave Dee" Harman (vocals), Ian "Tich" Amey (lead guitar), John "Beaky" Dymond (rhythm guitar), Trevor "Dozy" Davies (bass) and Mick Wilson (drums) began their collective career in Salisbury as Dave Dee and The Bostons.

They changed their name and their fortunes when they met songwriting team Ken Howard and Alan Blaikley in 1964. The duo were to be the group's managers, as well as the source of their material, and after 'No Time' had flopped and 'You Make It Move' sneaked into the Top Thirty in 1965, they finally cracked it in early '66, when 'Hold Tight' got to No.4.

They had a run of further chart entries on Fontana, including a Number One with 'The Legend Of Xanadu', which continued right up until 1969. Their first album, named after the group, also sold well, although the follow-up, 'If Music Be The Food Of Love...Prepare For Indigestion', was less successful.

An unabashed pop outfit, with a colourful and often humorous stage presence, they were unable to make their British success cross the Atlantic, like several of their contemporaries.

After Dave Dee had left to go solo in 1969 the group had a Top Thirty hit on their own with 'Mr.President', but then faded from sight. Dee himself had a minor hit, 'My Woman's Man', and then became A&R man for WEA Records. In 1974 the group got back together for a one-off single on that same label.

DEEP FEELING A mid-sixties Birmingham group whose members included Dave Mason (guitar, voc-

21

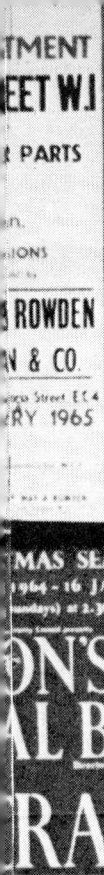

DEEP PURPLE – DOWNLINERS SECT

als) and Jim Capaldi (drums), who later joined Traffic (q.v.). The group carried on after their departure, and even managed a small hit with a version of 'Do You Love Me' on the Penny Farthing label in 1970.

DEEP PURPLE Jon Lord (keyboards), Ritchie Blackmore (guitar), Rod Evans (vocals), Nick Simper (bass) and Ian Paice (drums) were called Roundabout, before changing their name in early 1968.

Originally a pop-orientated group, they were more successful at first in America, where they had a big hit with 'Hush'. Their first three albums, 'Shades Of Deep Purple' on Parlophone, and 'The Book Of Taliesyn' and 'Deep Purple' on Harvest, also fared better in the States than in their own country.

In 1970, however, Evans and Simper were replaced by Ian Gillan and Roger Glover from Episode Six (q.v.), and the group moved in the direction of heavy rock.

The first album with the new line-up was actually 'Concerto For Group And Orchestra', a rather dubious attempt to amalgamate rock and classics, but 'Deep Purple In Rock' pioneered the style that made them into a huge international attraction.

Unfortunately, after forming their own Purple label in 1972, the group started running into problems. First Gillan left, to re-emerge later in the seventies with his own eponymous band; then Glover, to go into production and solo work; and finally Blackmore, who formed Rainbow.

This succession of changes had a detrimental effect both on the quality of the band's work and on their popularity, and in 1976 they called it a day. Lord, who had been with The Artwoods (q.v.) in the sixties, made a couple of solo albums, but ended up with Whitesnake, the group led by David Coverdale, Gillan's replacement in Deep Purple.

THE DEL RENAS A Liverpool quartet who were featured on Oriole's 'This Is Merseybeat' album in 1963, performing 'Sigh, Cry, Almost Die'.

DELIVERY Steve Miller (piano, vocals), Jack Monk (bass), Phil Miller (guitar), Lol Coxhill (saxes) and Pip Pyle (drums) forged their alliance in Canterbury during 1968. Originally a very blues-based band, they gradually widened their scope to embrace jazzier influences, and could often be found playing at the Aylesbury Arts Workshop.

In early 1969 they were joined by vocalist Carol Grimes, and Monk was replaced by Roy Babbington. This line-up survived until they disbanded in 1971.

Carol Grimes was then in Uncle Dog and had a spell as a solo artist before fronting The London Boogie Band. Coxhill was with Kevin Ayers and The Whole World, and has made a couple of albums with Steve Miller for the Caroline label. Both the Millers and Pip Pyle have been in Caravan (q.v.) at various times, and in the mid-seventies Babbington joined Soft Machine (q.v.). Jack Monk was a member of the very short-lived Stars in 1972 with Twink (q.v.) from The Pink Fairies and Syd Barrett of Pink Floyd (q.v.) fame.

THE DENNISONS Yet another Liverpool beat group who came to the attention of Decca while playing the Merseyside clubs and ballrooms. They climbed the lower rungs of the charts with 'Be My Girl' in 1963 and a cover of 'Walking The Dog' in 1964.

DENNY AND THE DIPLOMATS A Birmingham band who were one of the most popular in the Midlands during the early sixties, their line-up included guitarists Denny Laine and Roy Wood, and drummer Bev Bevan. The group split when Laine formed The Moody Blues (q.v.), and Wood and Bevan went on to make their mark with The Move (q.v.).

THE DEVIANTS Formed by vocalist Mick Farren in 1967 and originally known as The Social Deviants, they went through numerous personnel changes in their two year history, and earned themselves the reputation as one of the country's most untogether bands. If the group and their equipment actually managed to turn up in the same place at the same time, it was anybody's guess which would collapse first.

They did somehow manage to record three albums, 'Ptooff', 'Disposable' and 'Deviants Three' - probably best summed up by the second title - and by 1969 the line-up had more or less stabilised as Farren, Paul Rudolph (bass), Duncan "Sandy" Sanderson (bass) and Russell Hunter (drums)...a thoroughly disreputable collection of subhuman beings.

Farren had a loud raucous voice, and a stage act which involved staggering about supported by a mixture of alcohol and naughty narcotics; Sanderson had a disconcerting tendency to drop his guitar and fall retching to the floor in a methedrine haze; Rudolph was a large, leather clad Canadian; and Hunter added a little colour to the group's appearances with his nifty make-up and wardrobe of very fetching dresses.

To the unutterable relief of the entire civilised world, The Deviants broke up in September 1969 during an American tour. Farren returned to England and recorded a solo album, 'Mona', and also formed the first version of The Pink Fairies with Twink (q.v.) from Tomorrow (q.v.) and Steve Took from Tyrannosaurus Rex (q.v.). This line-up, perhaps unsurprisingly, never got as far as performing, and Twink soon formed the second Fairies with the other three ex-Deviants.

Farren went on to become a well-respected writer; Rudolph joined Hawkwind (q.v.) on bass after a spell with Uncle Dog; and Sanderson and Hunter kept making abortive attempts to resuscitate The Pink Fairies. An early member of The Deviants, Dennis Hughes, committed suicide in 1976 by jumping off Caernarvon Castle.

In 1977 Farren put together a new Deviants line-up to make an EP for Stiff Records, and the following year he recorded an album on Logo.

CHARLES DICKENS Not the novelist reincarnated, but fashion photographer David Anthony. His first single for Pye, 'That's The Way Love Goes' was a minor hit in 1965. After a tour of British ballrooms and another single, a cover of the Jagger/Richard composition 'So Much In Love' for Immediate in 1966, he fell on hard times and returned to his photography.

THE DIMPLES A London based R&B group who recorded for Decca in the mid-sixties.

DONOVAN Donovan Leitch came from Glasgow, and got his big break when he was discovered while bumming around southern England, and given a residency on ITV's Ready Steady Go (q.v.) in early 1965.

He sang his own gentle, melodic folky songs, and was a distinctive figure with his blue denim cap. Although criticised as a poor man's Bob Dylan, he was an instant success and had hits in 1965 with 'Catch The Wind', 'Colours' and 'Turquoise'. His first two albums, 'What's Bin Did And What's Bin Hid' and 'Fairytale', also got into the charts.

He then acquired a more up-tempo, drug-influenced style, but had several more hits, the biggest being 'Sunshine Superman'. In 1968, he changed stance yet again, denouncing drugs and recording a quintessential flower-power double album, 'A Gift From A Flower To A Garden'. The idea behind this album, his fourth was to have one record of children's songs and the other one for their young parents, and the album yielded another hit in 'Jennifer Juniper'.

In the following year he teamed up with Jeff Beck (q.v.) for 'Goo Goo Barabbajagal', and then returned to his Celtic heritage with the group Open Road, making an album for the Dawn label. This project met with little general interest, and in 1970 he retired to Ireland, concentrating his efforts on film scores.

He made another album for Dawn, the double 'H.M.S.Donovan', and then switched for the Mickie Most (q.v.) produced 'Cosmic Wheels' which marked something of a revival in his fortunes. Throughout the seventies he has maintained a low profile, spending much of his time in America with his wife Linda, an ex-girlfriend of Brian Jones, and their children.

He has continued to make albums, but whereas he was able to keep ahead of changing fashions in the sixties, changing lifestyle as well as musical direction with some regularity, he has been somewhat left behind in the seventies.

THE DOUGHNUT RING A pop group with a slight psychedelic tinge whose singles for Deram included 'Dance Around Julie'.

CARL DOUGLAS AND THE BIG STAMPEDE A popular club act in a blues and soul vein. The group were around for a long time during the sixties, but failed to stampede the public into buying their records. Douglas went solo in the seventies and had several hits, including a Number One with 'Kung Fu Fighting'.

THE DOWNLINERS SECT Don Crane (vocals, autoharp), Terry Gibson (guitar), Keith Grant (bass) and Johnny Sutton (drums) started out in London during 1963, and were joined the following year by harmonica player Ray Stone.

Their first record was actually an independent EP, 'A Nite At Great Newport Street', a live recording of R&B classics like 'Green Onions' and 'Shame, Shame, Shame'. Soon afterwards they were signed by Columbia, and over the next three years made numerous singles, including versions of 'Little Egypt' and 'I've Got Mine', another EP ('The Sect Sing Sick Songs'), and three albums - 'The Sect', 'The Country Sect' and 'The Rock Sect's In'.

None of these releases made any impact in Britain - although 'Little Eva' was a chart topper in Sweden - and the group's chances were probably harmed by the fact that although they played mainly raunchy R&B on stage, their records covered a bewildering variety of styles.

DR MARIGOLD'S PRESCRIPTION—EARTH

In 1965 Ray Stone left to be replaced by guitarist and banjoist Pip Harvey, who departed himself prior to the group's final album. In 1967 the group moved to Pye for 'I Can't Get Away From You', which was issued as Don Crane's New Downliners Sect, but then broke up after a final, desperate attempt to go psychedelic.

In 1977 Charly Records re-released 'Little Egypt' and all three albums, and the group reformed. Once again they failed to take the world by storm.

DR. MARIGOLD'S PRESCRIPTION As might be guessed from the name, this lot flowered in 1968. A middle-of-the-road outfit with a girl singer, they made an album named after them and a few singles, including 'Muddy Water', 'Breaking The Heart Of A Good Man' and 'Singalong' for Bell, and 'Pride Comes Before A Fall' and 'March Hare' for Santa Ponsa.

DREAM POLICE A Glasgow group of the late sixties, their singles for Decca included 'I'll Be Home' and 'I've Got No Choice'. Among their personnel were Onnie McIntyre and Hamish Stuart of the Average White Band, and Hugh McKenna and Dave Batchelor, who became keyboard player and producer respectively for Alex Harvey (q.v.).

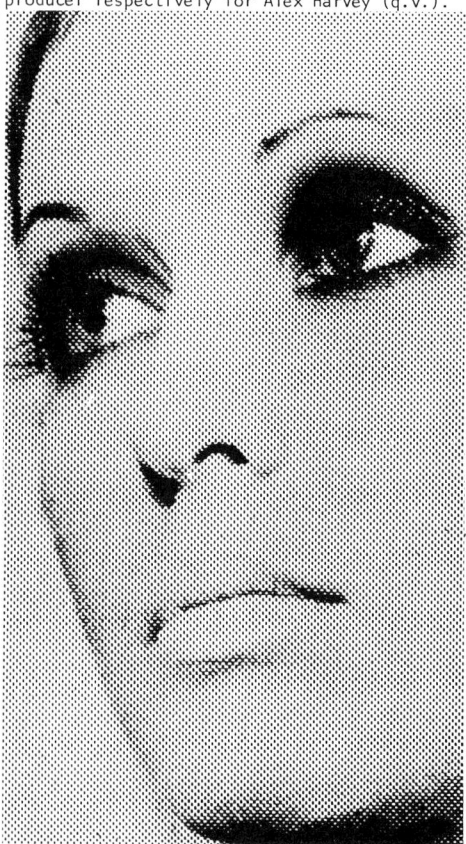

JULIE DRISCOLL After entering the wonderful world of showbusiness as fan club secretary for The Yardbirds (q.v.), Julie joined the Steam Packet (q.v.) road show as a vocalist in 1964.

When this venture was terminated she made some solo singles for Parlophone - 'Don't Do It No More' in 1965, 'Don't Want To Have To Do It' in 1966, and 'I Know You Love Me' in 1967 - before teaming up with Steampacket backing group, The Brian Auger Trinity (q.v.), and having a smash hit in 1968 with 'This Wheel's On Fire'.

At this point Julie - or Jools as she was more popularly known - was a very hot property, and her Afro hairstyle and bra-less look were very much de rigeur. Julie wasn't interested, however, and after leaving the Auger alliance later in 1968 during an American tour and starring in a TV play, 'Season Of The Witch' she stepped away from the public eye.

After marrying jazz pianist and composer Keith Tippett she made a few appearances with his Centipede "orchestra" in the early seventies, and in 1976 made an album, 'Sunset Glow', for Giorgio Gomelsky's Utopia label under her married name.

THE DRUIDS A mid-sixties R&B group from Chingford who followed the Hamburg trail, as well as playing the British clubs. Their singles included a version of 'Long Tall Texan' for Parlophone in 1964.

THE DUBLINERS A bunch of fearsome-looking bearded Irishmen, they created a stir with 'Seven Drunken Nights' on the Major Minor label in 1967. The song got to No.7 despite the fact that only five nights were actually on the record...the last two presumably being too outrageous for the sensitive ears of the British public!

Luke Kelly, Barny McKenna, Ronnie Drew, Ciaron Burke and John Sheahan made the Top Twenty again with 'Black Velvet Band', and at the end of 1967 'Maids When You're Young Never Wed An Old Man' was a minor hit.

The Dubliners have had no further chart success, but they have made numerous albums of Irish folk and rebel songs - 'A Drop Of The Hard Stuff' and 'More Of The Hard Stuff' did especially well at the time of their hit singles - and they are a perennial attraction on the folk circuit.

THE JOHN DUMMER BLUES BAND A lively, entertaining blues band, founded in the late sixties by drummer Dummer. They recorded four albums for Phonogram - 'This Is', 'Volume Two', 'Blue' and 'Oobleedooblee Jubilee'.

Besides Dummer the group featured violinist Nick Pickett and for a short while guitarist Tony McPhee, who left in 1969 to reform The Groundhogs (q.v.). When the group broke up in 1973 Dummer worked for record companies before picking up his sticks again with Darts.

THE AYNSLEY DUNBAR RETALIATION Dunbar was a Liverpool-born drummer who played with John Mayall (q.v.) and Jeff Beck (q.v.) before forming his own blues-based band in 1967. They recorded several albums on the Liberty label, including 'The Aynsley Dunbar Retaliation' and 'Remains To Be Heard'.

When Dunbar split up the band at the start of the seventies he moved to America, where he joined Frank Zappa's Mothers Of Invention. He subsequently did stints with several people, including David Bowie (q.v.) and launched a successful career as a session man, and in 1974 joined San Franciscan band Journey. When they elbowed him early 1979, Dunbar kept up his remarkable record of landing on his feet by filling the vacant drum stool in Jefferson Starship.

SIMON DUPREE AND THE BIG SOUND Ray, Derek and Phil Shulman were three brothers from Portsmouth who played in various local R&B groups, such as The Howlin' Wolves and The Roadrunners (q.v.). In 1966 they acquired a new manager, who changed their name to Simon Dupree and The Big Sound, and got them a contract with Parlophone.

The first single, 'I See The Light', did well enough for them to turn professional, and after 'Reservations' had again sold encouragingly, they hit the Top Ten at the start of 1968 with the ethereal 'Kites'.

The follow-up, 'For Whom The Bell Tolls', was a small hit, but the group were already having problems. 'Kites' had given them a public image more than somewhat removed from their rougher R&B-inclined aspirations. The success of the record pushed them towards the cabaret circuit and promotion as a ballad band, against the group's wishes.

By 1969 they had had enough and called it a day. The Shulman brothers formed Gentle Giant, an adventurous "progressive" combo who have achieved some success in foreign parts. The other members of The Big Sound - Eric Hine, Tony Ransley and Pete O'Flaherty - have not been heard of since.

THE EAGLES A Bristol group who provided the music for the film 'Some Girls' in 1962. In the following year they recorded a single for Pye called 'Come On Baby', which was actually a rock version of the traditional 'Cornish Floral Dance'. The group toured and even had their own weekly show on Radio Luxembourg, but despite this exposure were unable to sell records.

EARTH Formed in Birmingham during the late sixties, the group comprised Tony Iommi (lead guitar) and Bill Ward (drums) from a band called Mythology, and Ozzy Osbourne (vocals) and Geezer Butler (bass) from Rare Breed.

Playing mainly blues, the group acquired a tremendous reputation in the Midlands and the North, before changing their name to Black Sabbath at the turn of the decade and becoming one of the world's premier heavy rock bands.

There was another group called Earth doing the rounds at about the same time. They, presumably, didn't have the sense to change their name.

EAST OF EDEN – BRIAN EPSTEIN

EAST OF EDEN Dave Arbus (violin, flute), Ron Gaines (saxes), Geoff Nicholson (guitar), Andy Sneddon (bass) and Geoff Britton (drums) were a west country band of the "progressive" ilk.

They signed to Deram in 1969, making the 'Mercator Projected' and 'Snafu' albums. In 1971 they had a Top Ten hit with the catchy instrumental 'Jig-A-Jig', but as this was hardly typical of their normal style, it remained a one-off novelty hit.

The group then changed to Harvest for two more albums - 'East Of Eden' and 'New Leaf' - before breaking up. Britton had a brief spell later in the seventies with Paul McCartney's Wings.

THE EASYBEATS Stevie Wight (vocals), Harry Vanda (lead guitar), George Young (rhythm guitar), Dick Diamonde (bass) and Snowy Fleet (drums) came to England in 1966 as Australia's number one group...although Vanda and Diamonde were actually Dutch and the others British.

Their first United Artists single, 'Come And See Her' didn't happen, but 'Friday On My Mind' reached No.6. Despite several more good self-penned singles, they didn't score again until 'Hello How Are You' made the Top Twenty in early 1968. Shortly afterwards they broke up, leaving behind them two albums - 'Good Friday' and 'Vigil' - in addition to their singles.

Back down under, Vanda and Young concentrated on songwriting and production with some success, and in the seventies they were the brains behind AC/DC, a heavy rock band with Young's brothers Angus and Malcolm as guitarists.

THE ECCENTRICS A notable R&B-styled group who had a single on Pye in 1965. The A side was the Goffin/King composition 'What You Got', and the flip was entitled 'Fe Fi Fo Fum'.

ECLECTION Kerrilee Male (vocals), Mike Rosen (guitar), Trevor Lucas (guitar), Georg Hultgren (bass) and Gerry Conway (drums) were formed in August 1967, and were one of the first folk-rock groups. They were popular and well-respected, especially among fellow musicians, but despite an album for Elektra and numerous appearances live and on the radio, they never took off on a wide scale.

Male was replaced by Dorris Henderson in October 1968, and keyboard player Poli Palmer came in shortly before the group broke up at the end of 1969.

Lucas and Conway formed Fotheringay with Sandy Denny from Fairport Convention (q.v.), who later became Lucas' wife; Hultgren led Sailor under the name of Georg Kajanus; Palmer joined Family (q.v.); and Henderson tried to launch a solo career.

EIRE APPARENT An Irish rock group, naturally, who toured the States in 1967 with The Jimi Hendrix Experience (q.v.). They had one album produced by Soft Machine (q.v.) drummer Robert Wyatt, and another, called 'Sun Rise' produced by Hendrix himself.

Guitarist with the group was Henry McCullough, who later joined The Greaseband (q.v.) and Wings. Other members included guitarist Pete Tolson, who was later with the new-look Pretty Things (q.v.), and vocalist Ernie Graham, who had spells with Help Yourself and Clancy in the seventies, as well as making a solo single for Stiff in 1978.

THE ELIZABETHANS A late sixties group who sported frilly shirts and played mainly covers of other people's hits, they nevertheless made three singles for Decca and several broadcasts on Radio One.

At the start of the seventies they became Kindness and signed to RCA, then in 1973 the drummer left and the three remaining members - Alan Silson, Chris Norman and Terry Uttley - teamed up with Pete Spencer as Smokie.

BERN ELLIOTT AND THE FENMEN Bern Elliott (vocals), Alan Judge (lead guitar), Wally Allen (rhythm guitar), Eric Willmer (bass) and John Povey (drums) came from Erith, Kent, in 1961, and got most of their training in the Hamburg clubs.

Back in England, they signed to Decca in 1963 and had a Top Twenty hit with a version of 'Money'. Another classic cover, 'New Orleans' made the Top Thirty in the following year, but after another single, 'Good Times', and an EP Elliott and The Fenmen parted company.

Elliott formed a new backing group called The Klan and made several further singles, including 'Guess Who' and 'Voodoo Woman' in 1965. The Fenmen carried on without him, recording a version of The Four Seasons 'Rag Doll'. In 1968 Allen and Povey both joined The Pretty Things (q.v.).

THE END Despite having the advantage of being managed by Bill Wyman from The Rolling Stones (q.v.), The End never really got started. Wyman also produced their records, among them 'I Can't Get Any Joy' for Philips in 1965, and 'Loving Scared Loving' and the 'Introspection' album for Decca in 1968. The group later developed into Tucky Buzzard, and had a couple of albums on the Purple label during the seventies.

ENGLISH ROSE Formed by the original Love Affair (q.v.) organist Lynton Guest, they featured in the film 'Groupie Girl' and made a few singles for Polydor, 'Jackie' among them.

EPISODE SIX A late sixties sextet, they featured a fine female organist and vocalist, as well as male vocalist Ian Gillan and bassist Roger Glover, who left to join Deep Purple (q.v.) in 1970, and keyboard player Dave Lawson who later played with Greenslade.

Among their singles were versions of The Beatles (q.v.) 'Here There And Everywhere' and Tim Rose's 'Morning Dew' on Pye, and 'Mozart Versus The Rest' and 'Lucky Sunday' on Chapter One.

BRIAN EPSTEIN Originally heir to the NEMS record shops in Liverpool, Epstein became one of the driving forces behind the Merseybeat boom, launching The Beatles (q.v.), Cilla Black (q.v.), Gerry and The Pacemakers (q.v.), Billy J. Kramer and The Dakotas (q.v.), The Fourmost (q.v.), The Big Three (q.v.) and numerous others on their way to stardom.

He built NEMS into a management and publishing empire, and was in the process of expanding into other areas (such as the development of the Savile Row Theatre) as his management duties became less time-consuming, when he died from an accidental drug overdose on April 27th 1967.

BRIAN EPSTEIN

EQUALS—FAIRPORT CONVENTION

THE EQUALS A South London group, notable mainly for the fact that they comprised three West Indian and two English boys, The Equals had an exuberant, bubblegum style.

'I Get So Excited' on the President label was a minor hit in early 1968, but 'Baby Come Back' got to Number One later the same year. Over the next three years they had several further chart entries, the biggest being 'Viva Bobby Joe' in 1969 and 'Blackskin Blue-Eyed Boys' in 1971, and also made seven albums, of which 'The Unequalled Equals' made the album charts in 1967.

West Indian Eddie Grant was the group's lead vocalist and songwriter, as well as their visual focal-point with his bleached Afro hair style, and when the group broke up he went solo.

THE ESCORTS Terry Sylvester (guitar, vocals), John Kinrade (lead guitar), Mike Gregory (bass) and Johnny Sticks (drums) were voted Liverpool's 9th most popular group in 'Merseybeat's 1963 poll, and certainly they were one of the best groups to come out of the whole Liverpool furore.

Signed by Fontana, their singles included an ace version of 'Dizzy Miss Lizzy' and 'The One To Cry', which was a minor hit in the summer of 1964.

They suffered several personnel changes, but were still going in late 1966 when Paul McCartney produced 'From Head To Toe' for Columbia. Among their other members were drummer Pete Clarke and guitarist Paddy Chambers, from Paddy, Klaus and Gibson (q.v.). Sylvester and Gregory both left to join The Swinging Blue Jeans (q.v.), and Sylvester ended up replacing Graham Nash in The Hollies (q.v.) in 1968.

THE EVERONS A mid-sixties R&B group from East London, they changed their name to The China Plates at the suggestion of actress Susan Hampshire, but split up when they couldn't get a record deal. Their drummer and vocalist was one David Cook, now better known as David Essex.

THE EXCELLES Another of the constant stream of groups going round the clubs and ballrooms of Merseyside in the early sixties, The Excelles achieved the almost unique distinction of neither getting a record contract, nor appearing in 'Ferry Cross The Mersey'. Their three vocalists, Dyan Birch, Frank Collins and Paddy McHugh, were compensated in some way, however, when they formed Arrival (q.v.) later in the decade.

THE EXECUTIVES A mid-sixties instrumental outfit, whose singles for Columbia included 'Lock Your Door' in 1964.

THE EYES A mid-sixties group who recorded for the Mercury label. Among their singles were 'When The Night Falls' in 1965, and 'The Immediate Pleasure' and 'Man With Money' in 1966.

EYES OF BLUE A soul-based band from Neath who won the 'Melody Maker' group contest in 1966, they kept going until 1970 (having changed to a more West Coast influenced style) without making much impact.

Among their personnel were drummer John 'Pugwash' Weathers, who was later in Piblokto with Pete Brown (q.v.) and then Gentle Giant; Phil Ryan on keyboards, who was also with Piblokto before joining Man (q.v.); and vocalist Ritchie Francis who opted for an unspectacular solo career.

THE FACES Ronnie Lane (bass), Ian MacLagen (keyboards) and Kenny Jones (drums) teamed up with Ronnie Wood (guitar) and vocalist Rod Stewart (q.v.) from The Jeff Beck Group (q.v.), after The Small Faces (q.v.) had ceased functioning when Steve Marriott left to form Humble Pie (q.v.).

In view of the members previous illustrious associations, it was hardly surprising that they were quickly established as a major international act. Between 1969 and 1973 they made four studio albums - 'First Step', 'Long Player', 'A Nod's As Good As A Wink' and 'Ooh La La' - and a chaotic live set, 'Coast To Coast: Overtures And Beginners'. They also hit the singles charts with 'Stay With Me', 'Cindy Incidentally', 'Pool Hall Richard' and 'You Can Make Me Dance, Sing Or Anything', although the latter was released at the end of 1974, when the band were no longer really a going concern.

They were undoubtedly at their best as a shambolic, good-time live band, however, and none of their records really captured their true spirit.

In 1973 Ronnie Lane left to fulfil his own very attractive, low-key musical ambitions and was replaced (after much hassling with the Musicians Union) by Japanese bassist Tetsu Yamauchi, who had previously been with Free (q.v.).

The main stumbling block for the band however was the fact that Stewart was building his own solo career parallel to that of the band. This presented both contractual problems, since Stewart was with Mercury and the group with Warner Brothers, and internal problems, since Stewart's records were considerably more successful than the group's.

By 1974 the group had to all purposes ceased functioning, although there was no official disbandment. Stewart became one of the world's biggest-selling artists; Wood made a brace of solo albums before joining The Rolling Stones (q.v.); MacLagen and Jones joined up with Marriott again for an abortive Small Faces reunion, after which Kenny Jones filled Keith Moon's place in The Who (q.v.); and The Faces became just a sweaty, inebriated, lovable memory.

THE FAIRIES Dane Stephens, John Acutt, Johnny "Twink" Alder, Mick Weaver and John Gandy made up this first class R&B group. Originally hailing from Colchester in 1963 as Dane Stephens and The Deep Beats, they changed their name after signing with Decca the following year.

They recorded a version of Dylan's 'Don't Think Twice It's Alright' coupled with the self-penned 'Anytime At All', but then Stephens (whose real name was Dougie Orde) was forced to leave for personal reasons.

He was replaced as lead vocalist by Nick Wymer from Nix Nomads (q.v.), and in 1965 they released 'Get Yourself Home' on the HMV label. Stephens then returned until the group split up.

Drummer Twink (q.v.) went on to have a chequered career with Tomorrow (q.v.), The Pretty Things (q.v.) and The Pink Fairies (q.v.); Weaver has played with numerous bands during the seventies; and Stephens became vocalist with Cops 'N' Robbers (q.v.).

FAIRPORT CONVENTION The catalyst around which the British folk-rock scene revolved in the late sixties and early seventies. Based in London, and originally called Tim Turner's Narration, they became Fairport Convention (named after the house where they lived) in November 1967 with a line-up of Judy Dyble (vocals), Simon Nicol (guitar, vocals), Richard Thompson (guitar, vocals), Ian Matthews (guitar, vocals), Ashley Hutchings (bass) and Martin Lamble (drums).

They played regularly in the London clubs, in a style more akin to West Coast folk-rock, and in 1968 they signed to Polydor, recording their first album, 'Fairport Convention'. Dyble then left, later forming Trader Horne with Jackie McAuley from Them (q.v.), and was replaced by Sandy Denny, who had been with The Strawbs (q.v.). The group moved to the nascent Island label for their second album, 'What We Did On Our Holidays', after which Matthews also departed, forming Matthews Southern Comfort - who had a Number One with 'Woodstock' - and Plainsong with Andy Roberts from The Liverpool Scene (q.v.), before going solo and spending most of his time in the States.

Shortly before the release of their third album, 'Unhalfbricking', tragedy struck when Martin Lamble was killed in a motorway accident. The album yielded their only single success, however, in 'Si Tu Dois Partir', and also marked the beginning of their turn to English traditional sources, with the epic 'Sailor's Life'.

Dave Mattacks replaced Lamble and violinist Dave Swarbrick, who had guested on 'Unhalfbricking', joined full-time, and in 1970 they released 'Liege And Lief'. This album was completely dedicated to the direction opened up

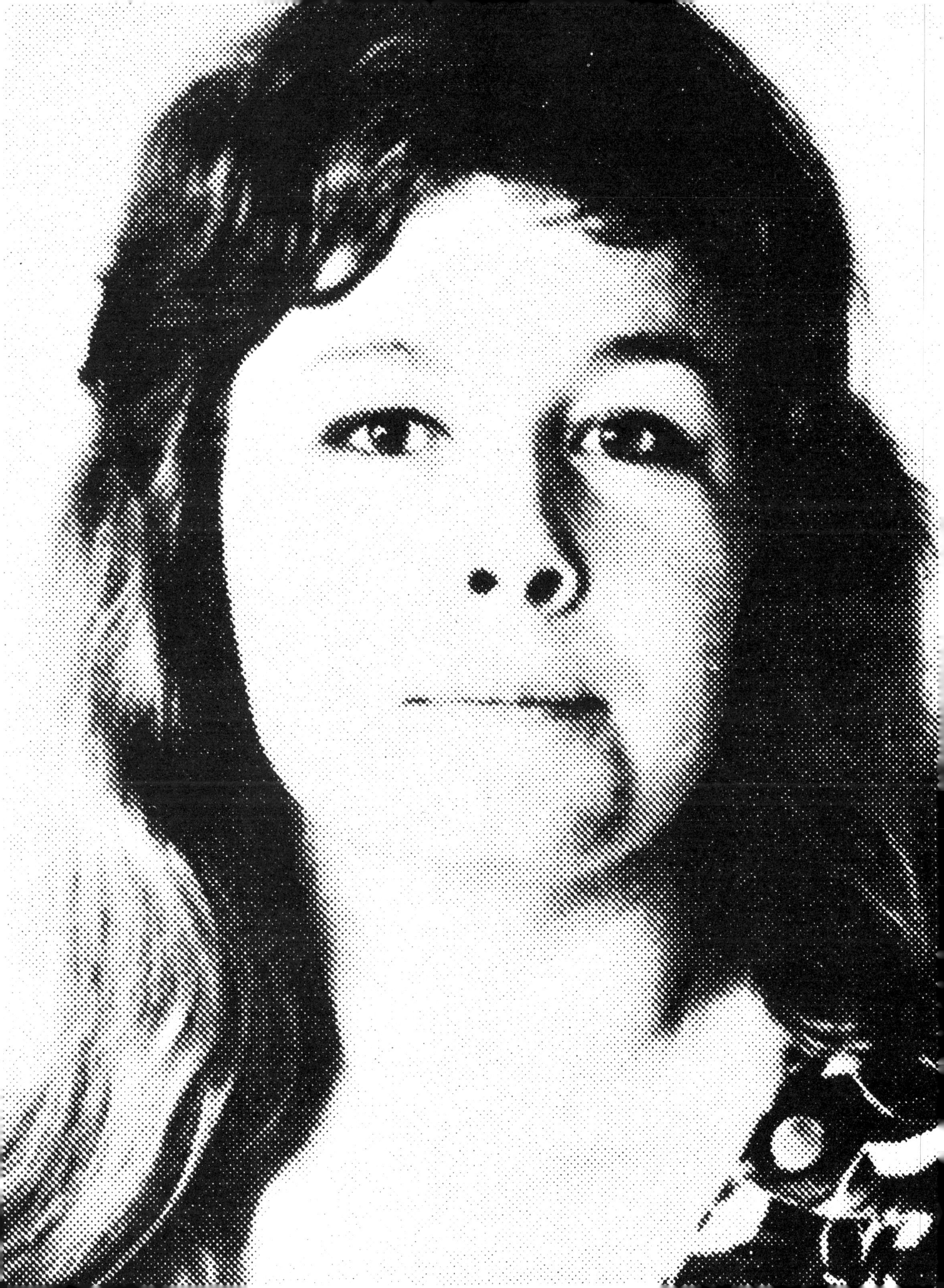

MARIANNE FAITHFULL

by 'A Sailor's Life', and is their most successful, both commercially and artistically.

After this zenith, however, Fairport became plagued by constant personnel changes, and ended up being held together by Swarbrick. They have kept on making albums throughout the seventies with some highlights - notably the 'John Babbacombe Lee' 'documentary' - but have sadly missed the songwriting ability which Denny and Thompson gave them.

Denny and Hutchings both left after 'Liege And Lief' to form Fotheringay and steeleye Span (q.v.)respectively.Denny also made several solo albums and rejoined Fairport briefly in 1975 to make 'Rising For The Moon', but met an untimely death in early 1978 after falling downstairs at a friend's home.

Mattacks has been kept busy playing sessions and appearing in various backing bands, including Andy Fairweather-Low's; and Thompson, who left in 1971, has made a series of formidable albums, firstly as a solo artist and then with his wife Linda, formerly folk singer Linda Peters. Thompson has teamed up regularly with Simon Nicol, after the latter had been the final original member to leave Fairport Convention in 1972.

MARIANNE FAITHFULL The life of 17-year-old Reading convent schoolgirl Marianne Faithfull changed irrevocably when she went to a London party in 1964 with her boyfriend John Dunbar, a Cambridge fine arts student, and Peter Asher of Peter and Gordon (q.v.). Among the revellers were The Rolling Stones (q.v.) and their manager, Andrew Loog Oldham (q.v.). Oldham decided she had a commercial face, and promptly signed her up.

His instincts were substantiated when her first single for Decca, the Jagger/Richard composition 'As Tears Go By', got into the Top Ten during the summer. The follow-up, Dylan's 'Blowing In The Wind', didn't do anything, but in 1965 she had further Top Ten hits with 'Come And Stay With Me', 'This Little Bird' and 'Summer Nights'.

She did indeed have a very photogenic face, as well as a delicate, wistful voice, and in addition to her singles her first two albums, 'Marianne Faithfull' and 'Come My Way', also made the charts...a particularly admirable feat, as they were both released on the same day, for some bizarre reason.

By 1966 Marianne was drifting away from Dunbar, whom she had married and had a child by, and also away from music. She did make one more album, 'North Country Maid', and had a minor hit in 1967 with 'Is This What I Get For Loving You Baby'. Her artistic aspirations since then have been largely concentrated on films and the stage, however, and most of her publicity has come from less happy activities.

She appeared in two films, 'I'll Never Forget Whatsisname' with Oliver Reed in 1967, and 'Girl On A Motorcycle' in 1968, and in the theatre she has played in Chekhov's 'The Three Sisters' alongside Glenda Jackson, and was Ophelia to Nicol Williamson's Hamlet in the Roundhouse production.

Her most famous role, though, was as Mick Jagger's girlfriend, and she achieved national notoriety for her portrayal of a naked blonde

GEORGIE FAME AND THE BLUE FLAMES – FAT MATTRESS

during the Redlands drug bust in 1967. It was Jagger who produced her "comeback" single, 'Something Better' in 1969, and later in the same year Marianne flew to Australia to star with him in 'Ned Kelly'. This never came about, however, as she took a drug overdose soon after her arrival and spent several days in a coma.

During the seventies, in between affairs with various aristocrats and distinguished members of the film and pop world, and treatment for heroin addiction, Marianne has continued to try and forge a successful stage career.

She also made another single in 1975, 'Dreamin' My Dreams' on NEMS, which showed that the rigours of the years had changed the voice of youthful innocence into something more akin to a young Marlene Dietrich. An attempt by Island to relaunch her career yet again with the album 'Broken English' met with critical acclaim but little success, although the single 'Ballad of Lucy Jordan' spent a short time the charts in 1980.

GEORGIE FAME AND THE BLUE FLAMES Clive Powell was a pianist from Leigh in Lancashire, who played in local groups before moving to London in 1959 and being "discovered" by impresario Larry Parnes. Parnes rechristened him, and after backing various singers including Marty Wilde and Vince Eager, Fame joined Billy Fury's backing band, The Blue Flames.

At the end of 1961, Fame formed his own Blue Flames with Colin Green (guitar), Mick Eve (sax), Tony Makins (bass) and Red Reece (drums), and moved from piano to organ. They became the first resident act at the Flamingo (q.v.) in Soho, and in 1963 were signed up by Columbia.

Their first three singles - 'Do The Dog', 'Do-Re-Mi' and 'Bend A Little' - got nowhere, but then 'Yeh Yeh' reached Number One in early 1965. Several further hits followed, as well as four EPs (one of them recorded live at the Flamingo) and three albums, of which 'Sweet Things' was a particular success.

Shortly after their second Number One, 'Get Away', Fame disbanded The Blue Flames in September 1966 to go solo. The group's personnel had been fairly flexible over the years, and the musicians who passed through the line-up were guitarist John McLaughlin, drummers Jon Hiseman and Mitch Mitchell, who later played with Graham Bond (q.v.) and Jimi Hendrix (q.v.) respectively, and percussionist Speedy Acquaye.

Fame then deserted the jazz-tinged R&B which had made him famous and headed for the more commercial fields of pop. His first venture was recording an album with The Harry South Big Band, and he continued to make regular chart entries, firstly for Columbia and later for CBS, having his third Number One with 'The Ballad Of Bonnie And Clyde' in 1967.

An alliance with Alan Price (q.v.) took Fame even closer to the cabaret graveyard, and although there was an abortive attempt to relive the days of The Blue Flames with an album for Island in 1974, he now spends most of his time writing jingles for TV commercials.

FAMILY Roger Chapman (vocals), John "Charlie" Whitney (guitar), Jim King (saxes), Ric Grech (bass) and Rob Townsend (drums) came together in 1967 from two Leicester bands, The Farinas (q.v.) and The Roaring Sixties (q.v.).

Advertising themselves with posters asking "Are you in the Family way?", they soon established themselves on the underground circuit, and after signing with Reprise in 1968 they made two highly acclaimed albums, 'Music From A Doll's House' - produced by Dave Mason from Traffic (q.v.) - and 'Family Entertainment'. They also had the dubious distinction of being the anonymous subjects of Jenny Fabian's book 'Groupie'.

In 1969 Jim King left, and was followed soon afterwards by Ric Grech, who was in Blind Faith (q.v.) before moving to America. Many further personnel changes followed in the seventies, but the group carried on regardless, revolving around the Chapman/Whitney songwriting partnership and Chapman's remarkable acetylene vocals ... which had once defeated Engelbert Humperdinck in a talent contest.

Among the musicians who passed through the group were guitarist John Weider, who had been with Eric Burdon and The Animals (q.v.) and later cropped up in Moonrider with Keith West (q.v.); guitarist Jim Cregan from Blossom Toes (q.v.), who went on to Cockney Rebel and Rod Stewart's (q.v.) band; bassist John Wetton, later in King Crimson (q.v.) and Uriah Heep; and keyboard player Tony Ashton, from Ashton, Gardner and Dyke.

The group made five further albums during the seventies, and had hit singles with 'No Mule's Fool', 'Strange Band', 'In My Own Time' and 'Burlesque'. They finally split up in 1974, due mainly to their failure to make headway in America. Chapman and Whitney stayed together in the moderately successful Streetwalkers, while Townsend joined Medicine Head. After the demise of Streetwalkers Chapman lay low for a couple of years, but returned in early 1979 with a solo album.

FAMILY DOGG The brainchild of American producer Steve Rowland, who had worked with Dave Dee, Dozy, Beaky, Mick and Tich (q.v.) among others. The group consisted of two girls and three boys, including Rowland, and their first single, 'Way Of Life', got to No.6 in 1969.

Despite several further singles on Bell, including 'When Tomorrow Comes Tomorrow', 'Jesus Loves Me', 'Brown Eyed Girl' and 'Sweet America', they couldn't repeat this success, and in 1970 Rowland sacked all the other members. He tried forming a new version of the group in 1976, but needn't have bothered.

Among the several girl singers who partnered Rowland was Christine Holmes, who did a stint hosting 'Crackerjack', called herself Kristine Sparkle for a few ghastly singles, and shortened the name to Kristine to do Impersonations on the 'Who Do You Do' TV series.

BARRY FANTONI A shaggy haired, hook-nosed cartoonist, writer and TV host who became quite a well-known face in the mid-sixties. He also made a couple of records for Fontana and wrote songs, one of which, 'Trafalgar Square', was recorded by The Good Time Losers (q.v.). The seventies saw him working as a freelance writer and illustrator once again.

DON FARDON AND THE SOUL MACHINE A long standing soul act with a good reputation in clubs up and down the country. When they stopped working together Fardon had a minor hit with 'Belfast Bay' and a Top Three with 'Indian Reservation' in 1970.

THE FARINAS A first-rate R&B group from Leicester whose Fontana singles included a version of the standard 'I Like It Like That'. They later evolved into The Roaring Sixties (q.v.) and then Family (q.v.).

CHRIS FARLOWE AND THE THUNDERBIRDS Farlowe (whose real name was John Deighton) started his singing career fronting the John Henry Skiffle Group, who reached the pinnacle of being All-England Skiffle Champions in 1957.

The early sixties saw him as a solo artist for Decca, and although none of his singles made any headway, it was during this period that he put together The Thunderbirds to back him on his live appearances. The group's first line-up in 1962 was Albert Lee (guitar), Dave Greenslade (keyboards), Bruce Waddell (bass) and Ian Mague (drums). Greenslade later played with Colosseum (q.v.), and Lee was with Head Hands & Feet in the early seventies before making a very successful move to California.

They were regulars at The Flamingo (q.v.), featuring blues, soul and R&B standards such as 'Stormy Monday Blues', 'Mr. Pitiful' and 'Midnight Hour', and were popular throughout the capital. Farlowe himself had a throaty, but undeniably powerful voice, and was rated by connoisseurs of the R&B scene as one of the country's top singers.

Despite this, and a change to the Columbia label, they had no record success until they moved again, this time to Immediate at the end of 1965. The Jagger/Richard song 'Think' was a minor hit for them, and in the summer of 1966 another song from The Rolling Stones (q.v.) 'Aftermath' album; 'Out Of Time', was a Number One.

This breakthrough led to the demise of The Thunderbirds, although Farlowe did reform them when things got sticky again, with Lee on guitar once more and Carl Palmer, later with Arthur Brown (q.v.) and Atomic Rooster (q.v.), on drums.

Farlowe did actually have minor hits in the year after 'Out Of Time' with 'Ride On Baby', 'My Way Of Giving', 'Moanin'' and 'Handbags And Gladrags', the latter written by Mike d'Abo from Manfred Mann (q.v.). He was unable to establish himself as a major artist, however, and after 'The Last Goodbye' album in 1968 he broke up The Thunderbirds yet again and retired from the music business to run a shop in North London selling military souvenirs.

In the early seventies he did brief stints with Colosseum (q.v.) and Atomic Rooster (q.v.) and in 1975 the re-release of some of his old Immediate material encouraged him to form a new band - again with Albert Lee - which did a nationwide tour and recorded a live album for Polydor.

FARON'S FLAMINGOES One of the more popular groups from the Merseybeat boom in their home town, but one which failed to make the grade on a national scale. They had two tracks on Oriole's 'This Is Merseybeat' album - 'Let's Stomp' and 'Talking 'Bout You' - and two singles for the same label, 'Shake Sherry' and 'Do You Love Me', the latter a cover of The Contours big US hit which bombed out when Brian Poole and The Tremeloes (q.v.) had the same idea.

The group split up at the end of 1963 when Bill 'Faron' Russley and guitarist Paddy Chambers joined The Big Three (q.v.), and their other guitarist Nicky Crouch joined The Mojos (q.v.).

GARY FARR AND THE T-BONES Farr, the blond-haired son of boxer Tommy Farr and brother of Ricky Farr who promoted the Isle Of Wight festivals in the late sixties, formed The T-Bones in Worthing during 1963.

A raw-sounding R&B outfit, they made their recording debut with 'I'm A Lover Not A Fighter' on Columbia in 1964. This was followed by an EP, 'Dem Bones Dem Bones Dem T-Bones', and further singles including 'Won't You Give Him One More Chance' and 'Give All She's Got', but despite their popularity in the clubs and several appearances on 'Ready Steady Go' (q.v.) the group never had any substantial record success.

The T-Bones included keyboard player Keith Emerson and bassist Lee Jackson, who later teamed up in The Nice (q.v.). Farr went on to a solo career after finishing The T-Bones in 1967, recording a single for Marmalade before going to the States and making an album for CBS.

In the late sixties the group was featured on the 'Rock Generation Vol.7' album released by the French Byg label.

FAT MATTRESS Neil Landon (vocals), Noel Redding (guitar), James Leverton (bass) and Eric Dillon (drums) were given a loud fanfare and a fat advance when they signed to Polydor in 1968, solely because Redding had been bassist in The Jimi Hendrix Experience (q.v.).

They made two albums - 'Fat Mattress' and 'Fat Mattress Two' - comprising druggy songs like 'Mr. Moonshine', 'Magic Forest' and 'She Came In The Morning', and featuring the vocal range of ex-session singer Landon.

Redding left the group halfway through recording the second album - much to the distress of the record company, no doubt - and moved to America and then Ireland, but doing little musically until he formed The Noel Redding Band in 1975.

FEDERALS—WAYNE FONTANA & THE MINDBENDERS

THE FEDERALS An early sixties instrumental group whose singles for Parlophone included 'Boot Hill' in 1963.

FEEL FOR SOUL Dave Quinton (vocals), Julian Revell (tenor sax), Chris Green (baritone sax), Norman Samways (trumpet), Keith Burbury (organ), Paul Moss (bass), Stewart Fuller (guitar) and Jeff Revell (drums) were from Norwich, and originally got together in 1966 as Dave Quinton and The Chequers.

They became Feel For Soul during the following year, and when Quinton left shortly afterwards he was replaced by Boz Burrell from Boz People (q.v.). By this time only Revell and Green remained from the original line-up as Ronnie Dearing (guitar) and Colin Clegg (bass) from Eyes Of Blonde, and Brian Tatum (organ) from The Baskervilles (q.v.) had come in, along with a succession of drummers.

When Burrell left, to hit the big time in the seventies with King Crimson (q.v.) and Bad Company, the group carried on as the backing band for visiting American acts, such as The Drifters. They kept this up, often under the name of The London All-Stars, until mid-1968 when they split.

SHANE FENTON AND THE FENTONES In the early sixties young Bernard Jewry was friendly with a local band who were starting to expand their horizons. When their vocalist had the misfortune to die, he became their singer, giving himself the slightly more commercial name of Shane Fenton and calling the group The Fentones.

They recorded for Parlophone from 1961-63, and although they never scored a major hit, 'I'm A Moody Guy', 'Walk Away', 'It's All Over Now' and 'Cindy's Birthday' were minor successes. The Fentones also made the lower reaches of the charts in their own right with the instrumentals 'The Mexican' and 'The Breeze And I', and they were featured playing 'It's Gonna Take Magic' in the Billy Fury film 'Play It Cool'.

Jewry returned to the music business in the seventies in the more successful guise of Alvin Stardust.

FERRIS WHEEL An outfit who worked the clubs in the late sixties and early seventies without making any great impact, despite recording singles for Philips: 'I Can't Break The Habit' and Polydor: 'Can't Stop Now'.

Their guitarist was Bernie Holland, who was later in Jody Grind (q.v.), and their vocalists at various times included Marsha Hunt (q.v.) and Linda Lewis, both of whom went on to solo careers.

MICKY FINN AND THE BLUE MEN A very good R&B group whose singles for the Oriole label included 'Please Love Me' and a version of Bo Diddley's 'Pills'. Jimmy Page was their guitarist for a short while prior to joining The Yardbirds (q.v.) in July 1966. Micky Finn is not connected with the gentleman of the same name who hit bongoes for Tyrannosaurus Rex (q.v.) later in the decade.

THE MICKEY FINN A heavy rock band featuring Mickey Waller on lead guitar, who recorded a few singles for the Direction label, including 'Garden Of My Mind' in 1967. Waller was a founder member of The Heavy Metal Kids in the seventies, and also played with Steve Marriott's All Stars.

THE FIRST GEAR Dave Walton (vocals), Raymond Wafer (guitar), Phil Birkenshaw (guitar, vocals), Michael Ryal (bass) and Ian Colling (drums) made up this group who recorded for Pye in the mid-sixties. Their first single was 'A Certain Girl' in 1965, and featured Jimmy Page on guitar. The follow-up was a cover of 'The In Crowd'. Both records were produced by Shel Talmy (q.v.).

THE FLAMINGO CLUB Situated in Wardour Street, Soho, the Flamingo - along with the nearby Marquee (q.v.) - became the focal point of London's soul and R&B scene after its opening in 1962. A Mecca for the capital's mods, as well as visiting coloured Americans, it featured mainly jazz-flavoured R&B, and regular favourites with the patrons included Georgie Fame and The Blue Flames (q.v.), Zoot Money's Big Roll Band (q.v.), Chris Farlowe and The Thunderbirds (q.v.), and Geno Washington and The Ram Jam Band (q.v.). The club was run by Rik and John Gunnell, and the former also owned an agency to which all these artists were signed.

THE FLEEREKKERS One of several instrumental groups who sprang up in the early sixties prior to the Merseybeat boom, they recorded a few singles for the Triumph and Piccadilly labels, of which 'Green Jeans' was a Top Thirty hit in the summer of 1960.

FLEETWOOD MAC Formed in July 1967 as Peter Green's Fleetwood Mac and signed immediately to Mike Vernon's Blue Horizon label, the group made their debut at the National Jazz and Blues Federation festival in August. Their initial line-up was Peter Green (guitar, vocals) from Shotgun Express (q.v.) and John Mayall (q.v.), Mick Fleetwood (drums) who had been with him in both those groups, Bob Brunning (bass) and Jeremy Spencer (guitar, piano, vocals). Brunning soon left, however, to be replaced by another ex-Mayall sideman, John McVie.

Fleetwood Mac were on the crest of a wave during the big blues boom of the time, and their first album, featuring a blend of classic American blues and original material, was a huge success in early 1968. They also made the lower rungs of the singles chart with 'Black Magic Woman' and 'Need Your Love So Bad'.

The second album, 'Mr.Wonderful', was another big seller later in the same year, but after the addition of guitarist Danny Kirwan had expanded their instrumental, vocal and compositional range even further, they began moving away from the twelve-bar format. 'Blues Jam At Chess', a double album recorded in Chicago with some of the giants of American blues, marked the end of this first phase in their career.

Phase two started on the highest possible note, when the plaintive instrumental 'Albatross' made Number One in January 1969. The equally mournful 'Man Of The World' was another huge hit, and then the Mac moved to Reprise for the adventurous 'Then Play On' album, which spawned another massive single in the remarkable 'Oh Well Parts 1 & 2'.

By now the group were among the biggest in the UK, but just when they were poised to crack open the American market as well, Peter Green suddenly left in May 1970. He recorded an album of what were basically instrumental jams, entitled 'End Of The Game', but then retired from the music business, became a grave digger and reportedly gave away most of his money and all his guitars.

There have been numerous rumours surrounding his escapades since then and his mental condition (certainly he has spent time in institutions). In 1972 he almost joined Stone The Crows (q.v.), and in 1978 he signed a solo contract, but nothing has come of this and it seems probable that one of the unique talents thrown up by British rock music is now lost forever.

Immediately after his departure the group had another Top Ten hit with Green's 'Green Manalishi', but have since spent nearly all their time in the States. Their albums in the early seventies - 'Kiln House', 'Future Games', 'Bare Trees', 'Penguin', 'Mystery To Me' and 'Heroes Are Hard To Find' - were all moderately successful across the Atlantic, but virtually ignored at home.

Pianist Christine Perfect, formerly with Chicken Shack (q.v.) and the wife of John McVie, played occasionally with the group during 1970, and then joined permanently after Jeremy Spencer had disappeared during an American tour in February 1971. It later transpired that Spencer had joined a religious group called the Children of God, and the following year he made an album called 'Jeremy Spencer And The Children Of God' for CBS. Later in the seventies he toured Europe with this band. He had also made another solo album for CBS while still with Fleetwood Mac.

Spencer was replaced by American guitarist Bob Welch, and in 1972 Kirwan departed to crop up again in 1975 as a solo artist on DJM. Further personnel changes followed, but by the end of 1973 the group had come to a virtual standstill. It was at this point that their manager sent out a bogus Fleetwood Mac, featuring vocalist Elmer Gantry (q.v.) and guitarist Kirby from Curved Air.

Legal action over rights to the name ensued, and after the group had won they returned to action as a Fleetwood/McVie/Perfect/Welch quartet with the 'Heroes Are Hard To Find' album in 1974.

Welch then embarked on a successful solo career, managed by Mick Fleetwood, and the American boy/girl duo Lindsay Buckingham and Stevie Nicks came in. With three strong writers in the group once again the group adopted a mellow, melodic style that is perfect for radio programming, and 'Fleetwood Mac' from 1975 and 'Rumours' from 1977 have both been absolutely colossal international best-sellers.

FLEURS DE LYS Bryn Haworth (guitar, vocals), Pete Sears (guitar), Gordon Raskell (bass) and Keith Guster (drums) were a popular London club band of the mid to late sixties. They started off recording for Immediate, for whom their singles included 'Moondreams' in 1965 (produced by Jimmy Page), and 'Circles' the following year. They later moved to Atlantic, recording 'Stop Crossing That Bridge' and 'Liar' in 1968 and 1969 respectively. They also did a little ditty called 'Gong With The Luminous Nose'.

Haworth returned in the mid-seventies as a solo artist on Island, while Sears went into session work (for Rod Stewart among others) before moving to San Francisco and joining Jefferson Starship. Other members at various times were Brian Potter and bassist Phil Sawyer, who joined The Spencer Davis Group (q.v.) in 1967.

THE FLIES An outrageous group who buzzed around between 1966 and 1968. At the Fourteen Hour Technicolour Dream (q.v.) in 1967 they appeared on stage wearing palm leaf skirts and capes, and sporting painted faces. The lead singer threw flour and water over the audience and then proceeded to urinate over them (far out, huh?).

Perhaps surprisingly, they were allowed into recording studios, and their singles included 'I'm Not Your Stepping Stone' for Decca in 1966 and the excellent 'The Magic Train' for RCA in 1968.

THE FLOWERPOT MEN Tony Burrows, Neil Landon and Perry Ford were three session singers who flung themselves on the flower power bandwagon in 1967, and were rewarded when 'Let's Go To San Francisco' on Deram got to No.4. The less flagrantly exploitative 'Am I Losing You' and 'Young Birds Fly' were not at all successful.

All three members had previously been involved in The Ivy League (q.v.), and in 1969 Landon joined Fat Mattress (q.v.) while Burrows fronted Edison Lighthouse.

WAYNE FONTANA AND THE MINDBENDERS Wayne Fontana, whose real name was Glyn Ellis, had been booked into a Manchester recording studio to record his first single for the Fontana label in 1963, when his backing group neglected to turn up. Luckily for him, session musicians Eric Stewart (guitar), Bob Land (bass) and Rick Rothwell (drums) were at the studio, so they backed him on the record and then became The Mindbenders.

The record in question, a version of 'Roadrunner', didn't happen, but 'Hello Josephine' later in that year and 'Stop Look And Listen' in early 1964 were minor hits, before their cover of Major Lance's 'Um Um Um Um Um' got to No.5 at the end of 1964.

PETER GREEN/FLEETWOOD MAC

FOOL-FREE

'Game Of Love' reached No.2, and was also a smash in the States, but when 'Just A Little Bit Too Late' and 'She Needs Love' were less successful the singer and the group blamed each other for their failure. They finally split up in early 1966.

Fontana made half a dozen singles and an album, 'Wayne One' over the next eighteen months, but only 'Come On Home' and 'Pamela Pamela' made the Top Twenty, although 'It Was Easier To Hurt Her' and 'Goodbye Bluebird' were minor hits.

Fontana's solo work definitely lacked the edge added by The Mindbenders, and after marrying a young girl fan he returned to the obscurity from which he had risen.

THE FOOL Simon Postuma and Marijke Koger were two designers from Amsterdam, who came to London in 1966 and teamed up with two British designers as The Fool. They designed the exterior of the Apple boutique for The Beatles (q.v.), and did the interior design for the homes of George Harrison and Paul McCartney.

They also designed stage clothes, for Cream (q.v.) and Procol Harum (q.v.) among others, and album sleeves, including work for The Hollies (q.v.) and The Incredible String Band (q.v.).

In 1967 they turned to recording in their own right, after causing a stir in the streets of the capital with their own court jester outfits, and made an album for Mercury. This album was produced by Graham Nash of The Hollies, and 'Lay It Down' and 'Shining Light' were released as singles. Musically they were interesting, if uncommercial, and featured a variety of instruments, including flute and bagpipes.

FORCE FIVE A mid-sixties group whose singles on United Artists included 'Yeah I'm Waitin'' and 'Don't Know Which Way To Turn'.

FORCE WEST A well-regarded Bristol group, whose singles for Decca in the mid-sixties failed to blow up much of a storm.

DEAN FORD AND THE GAYLORDS A very good Scottish group from Glasgow, comprising Dean Ford (vocals), Junior Campbell (guitar), Pat Fairlie (guitar), Graham Knight (bass) and Raymond Duffy (drums).

They were formed in 1963, and as well as touring throughout Britain they made several singles for Columbia, 'Twenty Miles', 'Mr. Heartbreak's Here Instead', 'Little Egypt' and 'He's A Good Face' among them.

None of these records got anywhere, however, and after Duffy had been replaced by Alan Whitehead they moved to CBS and became Marmalade (q.v.) in 1968.

FOREST Originally called The Foresters Of Walesky, this trio were together for two years before being signed by Harvest in 1969. Unfortunately they only got to record one album, named after themselves, of their gentle, swirling music.

THE FORTUNES Barry Pritchard (guitar), Glen Dale (guitar), David Carr (keyboards), Rod Allen (bass) and Andy Brown (drums) came from Birmingham in 1964. With their smart haircuts, well-tailored suits, beatific smiles, perfect harmony vocals and inoffensive pop ballads, they were a clean cut alternative to the sort of rough and rowdy R&B prevalent at the time.

Although their first single for Decca, 'Caroline', was adopted as the theme tune of the pirate radio station, they had to wait until mid-1965 for their first chart success. Their fourth single, 'You've Got Your Troubles', reached No.2, and was promptly followed by 'Here It Comes Again', which got almost as high.

'This Golden Ring' was their third successive Top Twenty entry in early 1966, but then the golden touch deserted them. The addition of two new members, singer-guitarists Shel Macrae and Rodney Bainbridge, and a move to United Artists did nothing to stop the rot, although 'The Idol', their first single for the new label, did arouse some interest.

In 1971, however, they joined the American Capitol label, and after 'Here Comes That Rainy Day Feeling Again' had been a Top Twenty hit in the States, they had further Top Ten successes at home with 'Freedom Come Freedom Go' and 'Storm In A Teacup'.

Since then they have been working mainly in cabaret, although their bank balances benefited when they were asked to record 'It's The Real Thing' for the Coca-Cola advert, and in 1974 they made an attempted comeback with a Lynsey De Paul number.

THE FOUNDATIONS Alan Warner (guitar, vocals), Colin Young (guitar, vocals), Tony Gomesz (organ), Pat Bourke (sax), Eric Allendale (trombone), Peter MacBeth (bass) and Tim Harris (drums) were a cosmopolitan mob from London, Barbados, Jamaica, Ceylon and Dominica.

An unabashed out-and-out pop group, they were managed by Tony Macauley, who also wrote their material. Between 1967 and 1969 they had half a dozen hit singles on Pye, including a Number One with 'Baby Now That I've Found You' and Top Tens with 'Build Me Up Buttercup' and 'In The Bad Bad Old Days'. They also had an album out featuring their hit singles.

They were obviously built on the foundations of someone else's talent, however, and had collapsed by the end of the decade.

THE FOUR JUST MEN A beat group from Manchester whose singles for Parlophone included 'Things Will Never Be The Same'.

THE FOUR PENNIES Lionel Morton (guitar, vocals), Mike Wilsh (guitar, piano), Fritz Fryer (guitar, bass) and Alan Buck (drums) came from Blackburn, Lancashire, and were originally called The Lionel Morton Four.

Morton had been in the choir of Blackburn cathedral, while the others had all been in various other bands. Bush had been with Johnny Kidd (q.v.) and Joe Brown, among others.

As well as being very adept musically, they also wrote most of their own material, and after 'Do You Want Me To' on Philips had been a minor hit in early 1964, the follow-up, 'Juliet', was a Number One.

They had further, less spectacular success with their own 'I Found Out The Hard Way', Leadbelly's 'Black Girl' and Buffy Sainte-Marie's 'Until It's Time For You To Go. They also made several EPs and two albums, 'Two Sides Of The Four Pennies' and 'Mixed Bag'.

When the hits dried up in 1966 the group moved into cabaret, but broke up shortly afterwards. Fritz Fryer formed Fritz, Mike and Mo, while Morton went solo and has often appeared on children's TV shows in the seventies. He was also married for a while to the actress Julia Foster.

FOUR PLUS ONE Vocalist Keith West (q.v.), Les Jones (lead guitar), John "Junior" Wood (rhythm guitar), Simon Alcot (bass) and Ken Lawrence (drums) recorded one single, 'Time Is On My Side', for Parlophone in 1965, before metamorphosing into The In Crowd (q.v.).

THE FOURMOST Brian O'Hara (lead guitar), Mike Millward (rhythm guitar, vocals), Billy Hatton (bass) and Dave Lovelady (drums) were part of the Merseybeat phenomenon, although they had a smoother sound than most of their Liverpool contemporaries, and had more of a "family entertainment" appeal with their comic stage routines.

They started life as The Four Jays and The Four Mosts, but became The Fourmost when Brian Epstein (q.v.) took over their management. Their first three singles on Parlophone, 'Hello Little Girl', 'I'm In Love' and 'A Little Lovin'', were all Top Twenty entries, and they had further minor hits with 'How Can I Tell Her?', 'Baby I Need Your Lovin'' and 'Girls Girls Girls' in 1964 and 1965.

Despite these successes, a lengthy residency at the London Palladium, and several EPs and albums, their progress was impeded by the ill-health of leader Mike Millward. He had to be replaced briefly by Bill Parkinson, and in 1966 he was forced to leave permanently and died soon afterwards

THE FOURTEEN HOUR TECHNICOLOUR DREAM Beginning on April 29th 1967, and running into the 30th, this mixed-media event at London's Alexandra Palace was run as a benefit for the underground newspaper International Times, which had just been raided by the London Vice Squad. Over ten thousand people turned up, and in the vast hall a stage was erected at each end, so that the forty-one groups who had offered their services could play two at a time throughout the event.

The featured groups included Pink Floyd, Soft Machine, John's Children, The Purple Gang, The Syn, Tomorrow, The Flies, The Crazy World Of Arthur Brown, The Social Deviants, The Pretty Things, Savoy Brown, Alexis Korner, Graham Bond and Champion Jack Dupree (q.q.v.), as well as poets like Barry Fantoni, Ron Geesin, Christopher Logue, Michael Horovitz and Yoko Ono, theatre groups, and even a fairground helter-skelter.

With light shows and drugs in abundance it was, in fact, a complete technicolour dream, and heralded the dawning of the psychedelic era in the UK.

FREDDIE AND THE DREAMERS Gnomelike Freddie Garritty (vocals), balding Roy Crewsdon (rhythm guitar), sunglasses-toting Derek Quinn (lead guitar), fat Pete Birrell (bass) and gormless Bernie Dwyer (drums) were undoubtedly one of the most motley-looking bunches ever to become "pop idols".

During the late fifties Garritty had sung part-time with a Manchester skiffle group called The Red Sox, and then with The John Norman Four and Crewsdon's group The Kingfishers. Freddie and The Dreamers evolved from the latter in 1959, but it was some time before Garritty was able to give up his milkman's round.

When groups caught on in the wake of The Beatles (q.v.), they had a two year run of hit singles, starting with 'If You Gotta Make A Fool Of Somebody', some covers of American hits and some co-written by group members. Their first album, 'Freddie and The Dreamers', was also a big seller.

They were actually very versatile, ranging from rock standards like 'Money' and 'Kansas City' through more sensitive ballads like 'I Understand' to comedy songs such as 'We Wear Short Shorts' and 'The Viper'. Almost inevitably, however, in view of their collective appearance and Garritty's high-pitched vocals, their staple diet was humour of a somewhat cheap variety. The diminutive, curly-haired, bespectacled Freddie was known to leap high in the air halfway through a number, yelping "Just a minute!", or just as suddenly drop his trousers.

When their chart success ran out after 1965 they turned to cabaret and pantomime, and during the seventies Garritty and Birrell have often appeared on children's television.

FREE Paul Rodgers (vocals), Paul Kossoff (guitar), Andy Fraser (bass) and Simon Kirke (drums) came together in May 1968. Fraser had been a teenage prodigy with John Mayall (q.v.), Kossoff and Kirke were both with the blues group Black Cat Bones (q.v.), and Rodgers came from Wild Flowers and Brown Sugar.

In their early days the group were encouraged by Alexis Korner (q.v.), who suggested their name and took them on tour with him, and by the end of the year they had signed with Island Records.

Playing hard-hitting blues and rock, Free were acclaimed as the new Rolling Stones (q.v.) and the individual members as heroes in their own right. Their first two albums, 'Tons Of

FREE AT LAST – GENESIS

Sobs' and 'Free', did not do them complete justice, but in the summer of 1970 'All Right Now' got to No.2 and their third album, the classic 'Fire And Water' which included an extended version of the single, was an equally huge success.

After a highly acclaimed appearance at the Isle of Wight festival later that year and further hits with the 'My Brother Jake' single and a live album in 1971, it looked as if the group would be unstoppable, but then they split up after a tour of Australia and the Far East.

Rodgers and Fraser formed their own bands, while Kossoff and Kirke recorded an album with American keyboard player John "Rabbit" Bundrick and Japanese bassist Tetsu. By the following year, however, they were back together again with the 'Free At Last' album and 'A Little Bit Of Love', which gave them their third hit single.

Fraser left again at the end of 1972, forming Sharks and then his own band, and was replaced by the afore-mentioned Tetsu and Rabbit. Kossoff was by now deeply immersed in drug problems, however, and much of 'Heartbreaker' was recorded without him. Nevertheless, the album was arguably their best since 'Fire And Water', and the hit single from it, 'Wishing Well', a lament to Kossoff's condition, was Free's finest moment.

At the end of 1973 the band broke up for good. Rabbit went into session work and backing bands; Tetsu joined The Faces (q.v.); Rodgers and Kirke joined Mick Ralphs from Mott The Hoople (q.v.) and Boz Burrell from King Crimson (q.v.) in the hugely successful Bad Company; and Kossoff made a solo album, 'Back Street Crawler', and then put together a band of the same name. His physical condition continued to deteriorate, however, and in 1976 he died during a plane flight to New York.

FREE AT LAST An early sixties blues group featuring Alexis Korner (q.v.), Graham Bond (q.v.) and Ginger Baker. It was from this group name that Korner christened Free (q.v.).

FREEDOM Formed in 1968, this heavy rock group recorded albums for Probe 'Freedom' and Vertigo 'Freedom Is More Than Just A Word' in the early seventies. Among the members was ex-Procol Harum (q.v.) drummer Bobby Harrison, who later became vocalist with Snafu.

WYNDER K. FROG A blues and jazz influenced group of the mid and late sixties led by keyboards man Mick Weaver from The Fairies (q.v.). Their Island albums were 'Out Of The Frying Pan' and 'Sunshine Superfrog', but they split up when Stevie Winwood left Traffic (q.v.) at the end of 1968, and Weaver joined the three remaining members for a brief spell as Capaldi, Wood, Mason and Frog. During the seventies he has become a ubiquitous session man and member of backing bands, including Frankie Miller's.

The other members of the group were Neil Hubbard (guitar), Alan Spenner (bass) and Bruce Rowlands (drums), who were in the Greaseband (q.v.) before and after, and Chris Mercer (sax) who also went into sessions.

RAYMOND FROGGATT Hailing from Birmingham, Froggatt put together his own eponymous band during the latter half of the sixties. They were a popular live act, especially in East Anglia, but never enjoyed any record success, although their 'Red Balloon' single had a fair amount of airplay.

During the seventies Froggatt has worked with numerous musicians for numerous record companies recording numerous albums - among them 'Bleach' (Bell), 'Rogues And Thieves' (Reprise) and 'Voice And Writing' (Polydor) - and his proclivities to country music have led him to spend some time in the States, but nothing he does seems to edge him any closer to success.

THE FRUIT EATING BEARS A Liverpool group who backed The Merseys (q.v.) in 1966, and then became an R&B group in their own right, managed by Chris Stamp and Kit Lambert, who also looked after The Who (q.v.).

Like The Pirates (q.v.), they enjoyed something of a renaissance with the advent of the New Wave, and reformed as a trio in 1977. They blew their credibility very badly, however, by appearing as contestants in the Eurovision Song Contest...although to be fair they did do very badly.

FUT The instigators of a bizarre record called 'Have You Heard The Word' c/w 'Futting' on the Beacon label in 1969, they were rumoured to be The Beatles (q.v.) and The Bee Gees (q.v.) combined.

THE GAMBLERS Jim Crawford (guitar), Alan George (keyboards), Ken Brady (sax), Tony Damond (trumpet, guitar), Alan Sanderson (bass) and Andy Mac (drums) came from Newcastle, and had their first taste of the big time when they backed Billy Fury in 1963.

Going it alone on the club/ballroom circuit, they made several singles for Decca and then Parlophone, of which 'It's So Nice' made the Top Thirty in the spring of 1964. Unfortunately for them the others, including versions of 'You've Really Got A Hold On Me' and 'Cry Me A River', didn't do so well.

GAME A mid-sixties mod group from Mitcham, Surrey. They were all youngsters (the drummer was only fourteen), and their manager was the coloured Cockney singer, songwriter and actor Kenny Lynch. Game recorded for Pye, including their single 'Gonna Get Me Someone', and made an appearance on Ready Steady Go (q.v.), but were lost in the end.

ELMER GANTRY'S VELVET OPERA Elmer Gantry (vocals), Colin Foster (guitar), John Ford (bass) and Richard "Hud" Hudson (drums) were a well-liked underground group of the late sixties, who were regular guests on John Peel's (q.v.) 'Top Gear'.

In 1967 they made an album for the Direction label featuring self-penned material such as 'Mother Writes' and the hard-rocking 'Flames', which was also a single. They shortened their name to Velvet Opera in 1969 for further singles, 'Volcano' on Direction and 'Anna Square Dance' on CBS.

Ford and Hudson later joined The Strawbs (q.v.) and then formed their own group. Gantry himself turned up again in 1974 fronting the bogus Fleetwood Mac (q.v.), an outfit sent out by the band's manager while the real members were out of action. This project was stopped short by litigation, but every cloud has a silver lining and the imposters stayed together as Stretch to have a hit with 'Why Did You Do It', a song written about the incident.

DAVID GARRICK Born Philip Darryl Core in Liverpool, he sang in a church choir and had four years operatic training, before naming himself after the eighteenth century actor and turning to the pop scene in 1965.

His first single was the dramatic 'Go', which was originally an Italian song called 'O Mio Seniori' and gave Gigliola Cinquetti a big hit in 1974. It didn't do so well for David, but his next two efforts, a version of The Rolling Stones' (q.v.) 'Lady Jane' and the catchy 'Dear Mrs. Applebee', were both minor hits on the Piccadilly label in 1966.

In the following year he had an album, 'A Boy Called David', which included his two hits along with covers of tracks like Ray Davies' 'Dandy' and the Mindbenders' (q.v.) 'A Groovy Kind Of Love'.

By now David, who was a good looking blond lad, was getting heavy coverage in the teeny magazines, but despite this his next single, 'Don't Go Out In The Rain Sugar', didn't happen, although it got played a lot on the pirate stations. Further singles, including 'I've Found A Love', 'Ave Maria', 'A Little Bit Of This (A Little Bit Of That)' and 'Maypole Mews', suffered a similar fate, and Garrick eventually disappeared from view.

GENESIS Peter Gabriel (vocals), Anthony Phillips (guitar), Tony Banks (keyboards), Mike Rutherford (bass) and John Mayhew (drums) were still at Charterhouse public school when they were discovered by Jonathan King (q.v.), who changed their name from Garden Wall to Genesis.

King got them a contract with Decca and

GERRY & THE PACEMAKERS — GREASEBAND

produced their two singles, 'Silent Sun' and 'A Winter's Tale' in 1967, and an album, 'From Genesis To Revelation', in 1968. None of these releases took off, and Decca dropped the band soon afterwards.

By now the group had left school to turn professional, but they struggled until Tony Stratton-Smith's Charisma label gave them a new contract in 1970. Their first album, 'Trespass', and its successor, 'Nursery Chryme', aroused only moderate interest, and after the former Phillips and Mayhew left to be replaced by Steve Hackett and Phil Collins respectively.

The group kept on slogging around the club circuit however, and their combination of grandiose, melodic music and Gabriel's theatrical flair built up a large following. By the time of 'Foxtrot' in late 1972, this following was big enough to put the album in the charts, and from then on Genesis never looked back with each album establishing them even further as a major international act.

In 1975, however, when the group were at a zenith in their career following the ambitious double album, 'The Lamb Lies Down On Broadway', Gabriel suddenly left to pursue a solo career. Against all expectations the rest of the group carried on from strength to strength, with Collins taking over the lead vocals, and even the departure of Hackett in 1977 has done little to dent their immense popularity.

The group's first album, 'How Do You Like It', was also a monster, staying on the charts for the latter part of 1963 and the first half of the following year. Further hit singles lasted until 1965, although they never made the coveted top spot again, and they also starred in 'Ferry Cross The Mersey', for which Marsden wrote the theme song.

Like Freddie and The Dreamers (q.v.), Gerry and The Pacemakers moved towards cabaret and pantomime when their time as pop stars ran out, but in 1967 Gerry went solo. He made a brace of singles for CBS, 'Please Let Them Be' and 'Gilbert Green', without success, and has appeared on children's television.

THE GIANT SUN TROLLEY Starting out as a psychedelic outfit in 1967, the group made several appearances at London's UFO (q.v.) club, before becoming The Hydrogen Jukebox and then The Third Ear Band (q.v.).

THE GIBSONS Arriving in London from Australia, this group put out one of 1966's better singles, the catchy 'Magic Box' on Major Minor. Despite its merits it was a miss, as were 'She's Not Like Any Girl' and 'Night And Day' in 1967, and 'Only When You're Lonely' in the following year.

THE GLASS MENAGERIE A late sixties group whose Polydor singles included 'Have You Forgotten Who You Are'. Everybody else has since forgotten who they were.

THE GODS This rock and blues band were omnipresent in the latter half of the sixties, but are not to be confused with the American group of the same name and vintage. The line-up included Ken Hensley (keyboards), Lee Kerslake (drums), Greg Lake (bass, vocals) and, in the early days, Mick Taylor (guitar).

Taylor joined John Mayall's Bluesbreakers (q.v.) in 1967, and when Lake went to King Crimson (q.v.) he was replaced by Paul Newton. When The Gods finally broke up, Kerslake, Hensley and Newton were all with Uriah Heep.

The Gods made two albums, 'Genesis' and 'To Samuel A Son', which were re-released in the seventies as a result of Heep's success.

THE GOOD TIME LOSERS They recorded the Barry Fantoni (q.v.) song 'Trafalgar Square' for Fontana in 1967, but both the record and the group were losers.

ERKEY GRANT AND THE EERWIGS An early sixties beat group whose Pye singles included 'I Can't Get Enough Of You' in 1963.

GRAPEFRUIT Pete Swettenham (guitar), his brother Geoff (drums) and John Perry (guitar) all joined Tony Rivers and The Castaways (q.v.) at the end of 1966, but a year later decided to form their own group.

A chance meeting with Terry Doran, the managing director of the Beatles' (q.v.) Apple company, led to an introduction to bass player and songwriter George Alexander, who became the fourth member of the group.

They were christened by John Lennon, signed by RCA, and launched amid terrific hoohah at the start of 1968. Their first single, 'Dear Delilah', made the Top Thirty, as did their third, 'C'mon Marianne', but further singles and two albums - 'Around Grapefruit' and the 'Deep Water'- failed to live up to expectations, although they included some fine music.

Pete Swettenham left in early 1969 to be replaced by Bobby Ware and Mike Fowler, but by the end of the year the group had broken up completely. In 1971 Alexander revived the group with the help of Harry Vanda and George Young from The Easybeats (q.v.), but the project only lasted for one Deram single, 'Sha Sha'. Perry returned to the limelight in 1977 with the New Wave band The Only Ones.

DORIAN GRAY Taking his name from the Oscar Wilde novel 'The Picture Of Dorian Gray', this gentleman recorded a Cook/Greenaway song, 'I've Got You On My Mind', for Parlophone in 1968.

THE GREASEBAND Originally formed as the backing band for Joe Cocker (q.v.) in Sheffield during 1964, their original line-up was Kenny Slade (drums), Alan Spenner (guitar), Henry McCullough (guitar), Tommy Eyre (keyboards) and Chris Stainton (bass).

Slade was replaced quite quickly by Bruce Rowlands, and when Eyre left after arranging their version of 'With A Little Help From My Friends', Stainton moved over to keyboards and Spenner onto the bass. They provided absolutely prime support for Cocker's vocal excesses and it was after ditching them in 1970 that his career started to take a turn for the worse.

Stainton stayed with Cocker (and in fact has been largely responsible for keeping his career alive for much of the seventies), while the remaining three went to work in the 'Jesus Christ Superstar' session band. There they met guitarist Neil Hubbard from Juicy Lucy (q.v.), and The Greaseband was reborn.

They made one fine album, 'The Greaseband',

GERRY AND THE PACEMAKERS Gerry Marsden (vocals, guitar), Les Maguire (piano), Les Chadwick (bass) and Freddie Marsden (drums) have the unique distinction of being the only artists ever to top the charts with their first three singles.

Gerry Marsden had begun his career with various Liverpool skiffle and rock'n'roll groups before forming his own group, The Mars Bars, with brother Freddie. In 1959 The Pacemakers were formed by the Marsden brothers and Les Chadwick, and with this line-up they went to Hamburg to play at the Top Ten club.

On their return they added pianist Les Maguire, and in 1962 were signed by Brian Epstein (q.v.) and Columbia Records. Their first two number ones were written by prolific hitsmith Mitch Murray- 'How Do You Do It' and 'I Like It' - and the hat-trick was completed by Rodgers and Hammerstein's 'You'll Never Walk Alone',from 'Carousel', which has since become a football terrace anthem.

GREAT WHITE IDIOT—KEEF HARTLEY BAND

for Harvest, and toured in America and Britain, but split up at the end of 1971 after a series of personnel changes. They did get back together in 1975 to record the 'Amazing Grease' album for the Good Ear label, but it was not a permanent project.

All the members have been in demand as session musicians, as well as playing with various bands. Rowlands was briefly in Fairport Convention (q.v.); McCullough joined Wings; and Spenner and Hubbard were with Chris Stainton's band and then Kokomo.

GREAT WHITE IDIOT This group was formed in 1969, but only played one gig. This was at the 100 Club in London's Oxford Street, and the group's original compositions were not well received by a largely black audience more interested in hearing soul music.

Various music business moguls had been enticed to see the group do their stuff, but by the time they arrived the audience had all but wrecked the club, which was now overrun with police.

Guitarist, singer and songwriter Kid Strange and drummer Pete DiLemma pondered this irony for a few years, and then in 1973 teamed up with bassist Stoner and violinist Urban Blitz in the almost equally ill-fated Doctors Of Madness.

THE GROUNDHOGS Initially a seven-piece R&B group founded in 1964 and known as John Lee's Groundhogs while backing bluesman John Lee Hooker (with whom they made an album for the Xtra label), their initial line-up included Tony McPhee (guitar), Pete Cruikshank (bass), John Cruickshank (harmonica, vocals), Bob Hall (piano) and Dave Boorman (drums).

They split up after a couple of years, but following periods with The John Dummer Blues Band (q.v.) and Hapshash And The Coloured Coat (q.v.), McPhee reformed the group with Pete Cruikshank, Ken Pustelnik (drums) and Steve Rye (harmonica, vocals). This line-up made 'Scratching The Surface' for Liberty, which perpetuated The Groundhogs blues heritage, and then Rye left.

Staying as a trio, the group then made 'Blues Obituary' in 1969 before switching to a heavier rock style and finding a much larger audience with 'Thank Christ For The Bomb' and 'Split'. In the wake of these albums, McPhee was hailed in some quarters as a new guitar hero for a short while in the early seventies.

They were unable to maintain their momentum, however, and from then on both their popularity and their albums deteriorated. Pustelnik left in 1972 being replaced by Clive Brooks from Egg, and after McPhee had made a solo album, 'The Two Sides Of Tony (T.S.) McPhee', in 1973 the band were broken up in the following year.

In 1975 McPhee launched a new version of The Groundhogs with himself as the only surviving member of the original band, but his music had been sadly left behind by changing fashions, and neither that group nor his subsequent Terraplane venture created much of a stir.

GROUP X An instrumental combo whose singles for Fontana included 'There Are Eight Million Cossack Melodies - And This Is One Of Them' and 'Crossbeat' in 1963

GRYPHON Originally called Happy Magazine (q.v.) this group included Colin Gibson from Skip Bifferty (q.v.) and drummer Alan White. They became Gryphon when they were joined by Skip Bifferty vocalist Graham Bell, but despite gaining a contract with Bell Records they were unable to record, thanks to an injunction taken out by Don Arden, Skip Bifferty's old manager.

Finding it impossible to work in Britain, the group either toured on the continent or survived on Alan White's income from session work with The Plastic Ono Band.

Eventually they recorded three tracks with Andrew Oldham (q.v.) for his Immediate label, but before any of them could be released Immediate was bought by...Don Arden. No doubt thoroughly choked off by now, the group threw in the towel in 1969.

White joined Ginger Baker's Airforce, then a group called Balls with ex-Move (q.v.) bassist Trevor Burton, and finally Yes (q.v.). The seventies saw Bell with Every Which Way and Bell & Arc, as well as solo, but without ever finding the stardom which was often predicted for him.

GUN A hard rock trio who had a Top Ten hit, 'Race With The Devil', on CBS in 1968. They also made an album of the same name, and further singles, including 'Hobo','Rupert's Travels' and 'Drown Yourself In The River', but were unable to repeat their success.

Focal point of the group were the Gurvitz brothers, guitarist Adrian and bassist Paul, and after Gun had fired their last shot this pair formed Three Man Army, and then Baker Gurvitz Army with Ginger Baker.

THE GURUS A mid-sixties group whose singles on United Artists included 'Come Girl' in 1966

GYPSY Robin Pizer (guitar, vocals), Rod Read (guitar, vocals), John Knapp (guitar, keyboards, vocals), David McCarthy (bass) and Moth Smith (drums) were originally called Legay (q.v.) before changing their name in 1968.

Their albums on United Artists included 'Gypsy' - after which Read was replaced by Ray Martinez - and 'Brenda And The Rattlesnake'. Among their singles were 'Brand New Car', 'Changes Coming' and 'Let's Roll'.

THE HABITS A London-based trio from the mid-sixties, their Decca singles included 'Elbow Baby', which was produced by Spencer Davis and Stevie Winwood from The Spencer Davis Group (q.v.).

HAIR A rock musical which originated in America and ran at the Shaftesbury Theatre in London from 1967 to 1974, 'Hair' became one of the landmarks of the hippy era, although after its initial notoriety it did rather decline to the status of staple fodder for Women's Institute coach parties.

Based loosely on the story of a boy's call-up to the US Army, the musical was very free form, with the emphasis on self-expression and even audience participation, rather than a set script.

There were some strong songs in it, however, and both the Broadway and the London cast albums sold well. It also yielded hit singles for Oliver - Oliver Tobias - in 'Good Morning Starshine', Nina Simone ('Ain't Got No, I Got Life'), Fifth Dimension ('Aquarius'), and innumerable covers.

Apart from Tobias, several other performers took their first steps to stardom with the cast of 'Hair', among them Marsha Hunt, Paul Nicholas, Elmer Gantry (q.v.), Sonja Kristina of Curved Air, and Julie Covington.

HAMILTON AND THE MOVEMENT A mid-sixties group whose membership ran into double figures, their singles, including 'I'm Not The Marrying Kind' on CBS in 1967, were produced by Bill Wyman of The Rolling Stones (q.v.). None of them made any impact on record buyers, however, and frontman Gary Hamilton later went on to play several leading roles in 'Hair' (q.v.).

HAPPY MAGAZINE A 1968 group featuring Colin Gibson from Skip Bifferty (q.v.) and drummer Alan White. They made two singles for Polydor, 'Satisfied Street' and 'Do Right Woman Do Right Man', before adding vocalist Graham Bell and becoming the decidedly unhappy Gryphon (q.v.).

HAPSHASH AND THE COLOURED COAT A late-sixties blues group who recorded a number of singles and albums on the Liberty label. Their guitarist was Tony McPhee of The Groundhogs (q.v.), and percussionist Mickey Finn was later in Tyrannosaurus Rex (q.v.). The group's first album used Art (q.v.) as session musicians.

HARMONY GRASS Formed out of Tony Rivers and The Castaways (q.v.) in 1968 they were, as the name suggests, a polished MOR vocal group. Their singles for RCA included 'Teach Me How' and Paul Simon's 'Cecilia', but only 'Move In A Little Closer' in early 1969 managed to reach the Top Thirty. They also made an album in the same year.

ROY HARPER Definitely one of the great originals in British music, Harper spent time in the RAF, mental hospitals and prison before coming to London in 1964 and joining the folk club circuit.

He made his first album, 'Sophisticated Beggar', for the Strike label and 1966 and 'Come Out Fighting Ghengis Smith' on CBS in 1967, the latter produced by Shel Talmy (q.v.).

It wasn't until 1968, however, when he came under the wing of Peter Jenner's Blackhill Enterprises, that he really established himself ...mainly through the medium of free concerts.

'Folkjokeopus' on Liberty followed in 1969 and he then signed to Harvest, making a series of albums in the seventies which have maintained a consistently high standard, using a variety of notable musicians and arrangers.

Despite acclaim from critics and fellow musicians (Led Zeppelin's 'Hat's Off To Harper is an ode to him) Harper has never really risen above the status of cult figure, and his career has been constantly hampered both by his own erratic temperament and by recurring ill-health.

RICHARD HARRIS Best known as an actor and film star, this fiery and controversial Irishman has also been a regular recording artist for Probe and ABC. He had a huge hit in the summer of 1968 with an epic rendition of Jimmy Webb's 'Macarthur Park', which he followed with an album of Webb songs, 'Yard Went On Forever'. His other albums include a collection of readings from the work of Khalid Gilbran.

THE KEEF HARTLEY BAND Born in Preston, Lancashire, this larger-than-life character started his career by replacing Ringo Starr in Rory Storm and The Hurricanes (q.v.) when the drummer joined The Beatles (q.v.).

Moving to London in 1964, Hartley spent nearly three years with The Artwoods (q.v.) before joining John Mayall's Bluesbreakers

ALEX HARVEY SOUL BAND—HERBAL MIXTURE

(q.v.). Having learnt the art of band leadership from Mayall, he then formed his own band in 1968, and they became a well-loved addition to the British blues scene. Hartley kept the group together for some five years, recording seven albums for the Deram label, although they never achieved mass popularity.

Among the ever-transient group members were bassist Gary Thain, who later joined Uriah Heep and died in 1976, guitarist Miller Anderson, trumpeter Henry Lowther, organist Mick Weaver from Wynder K. Frog (q.v.), vocalist Jess Roden, and pianist Pete Wingfield.

When Hartley folded the group in 1973 he went on the road with Mike Chapman (q.v.), and in the following year formed Dog Soldier with Miller Anderson.

THE ALEX HARVEY SOUL BAND Born in the docklands of Glasgow in February 1935, Harvey grew up in the Gorbals and in his late teens learned to play the guitar and then the trumpet. By the late fifties he was leading a skiffle group (he was actually crowned 'The Tommy Steele Of Scotland' in 1956), and with the passing of the skiffle craze he formed the Alex Harvey Soul Band, which lasted from 1958 until 1966.

The group's original line-up was two guitars, bass, drums, congas and timbales...definitely something original for the time. They built up a reputation in Scotland, graduated to backing visiting artists like Eddie Cochran and Gene Vincent, and by the mid-sixties were working the R&B circuit with the likes of Alexis Korner (q.v.), John Mayall (q.v.) and Graham Bond (q.v.).

In 1966, however, the group called it a day and returned home, leaving Alex to stay in London and get a recording contract in the unlikely guise of a ballad singer! Discovering that this was not where his destiny lay, he got a job in 1967 as resident guitarist at the 800 Club, playing six hours a night.

It was at this club that he was noticed by Derek Wordsworth, the musical director of 'Hair' (q.v.). He auditioned Alex for the show's group, and there he stayed until early 1972.

By this time Alex was hankering to get a group together again, and finding a bunch of likely lads in Glasgow's Tear Gas he moulded them into The Sensational Alex Harvey Band. By 1975 they were one of the country's top attractions, but in 1977 Alex was forced to leave through ill-health which has kept him rather quiet ever since.

His younger brother was Les Harvey, who was guitarist with Stone The Crows (q.v.).

HAYDOCK'S ROCKHOUSE The group formed in 1966 by ex-Hollies (q.v.) bassist Eric Haydock. They recorded a few singles, such as 'Cupid', for Columbia, but without success.

HEAVY JELLY A weird story this one! The London magazine 'Time Out' ran a bogus review in late 1968 as a joke, and so many people fell for it that not one, but two groups actually took advantage of the interest created.

First off the mark were Graham Bell, Mick Gallagher, Colin Gibson, Tommy Jacklin and Jon Turnbull...Skip Bifferty (q.v.) disguising their real identity to avoid contractual problems. Their single on Island, 'I Keep Singing That Same Old Song', was one of the longest ever made at 7 min. 49 secs., and apart from being a hit in Sweden also appears on the 'Nice Enough To Eat' sampler.

Guitarist John Morshead of Head Records used vocalist Jackie Lomax from Lomax Alliance (q.v.), bassist Alex Dmochowski and drummer Barry Jenkins from The Animals (q.v.) and The Nashville Teens (q.v.) for his effort, 'Time Out (The Long Wait)', which was released four months later.

HEDGEHOPPERS ANONYMOUS Ray Honeyball, Mick Tinsley, John Stewart and Leslie Dash were all in the RAF at Leighton Buzzard when they formed The Trendsetters in 1963. Six months later they became The Hedgehoppers, and when Jonathan King became their manager in 1965 he suggested their final name change.

Their first single for Decca was King's tongue-in-cheek protest song 'It's Good News Week', and it reached No.5 in the charts. Further singles during the following year- 'Dont Push Me, 'Baby You're My Everything' and 'Daytime' - failed to take off, and The Hedgehoppers were soon grounded.

THE HELLIANS A Worcestershire group who recorded 'Daydreaming Of You', produced by Kim Fowley, for Piccadilly in 1964. The line-up included guitarists Luther Grosvenor, who later played in Spooky Tooth (q.v.), and Dave Mason, who helped form Traffic (q.v.), as did drummer Jim Capaldi. Keyboard player Poli Palmer, later with Family (q.v.), was also in the group for a time.

THE JIMI HENDRIX EXPERIENCE James Marshall Hendrix was actually born in Seattle, Washington in 1942, but since he made his name after coming to Britain his inclusion here is fully justified.

He began playing guitar at the age of eleven, and was in various rock'n'roll bands during his teens before joining the US Paratroopers. After his discharge in 1963, following a parachute accident, he worked his way across the States with various R&B groups backing such stars as Little Richard, Wilson Pickett, The Isley Brothers and Ike and Tina Turner.

In 1964 he arrived in New York and went to Greenwich Village where he recorded with Curtis Knight, The Isley Brothers and Lonnie Youngblood. It was these early recordings which were to be so shamelessly exploited later in Hendrix's career.

Hendrix also formed his own group, Jimmy James and The Blue Flames, in 1965, and in the following year he was seen at the Cafe Wha by ex-Animals (q.v.) bassist Chas Chandler, who persuaded him to come to London.

On his arrival The Jimi Hendrix Experience was formed with bassist Noel Redding and drummer Mitch Mitchell, who ironically had just been fired from Georgie Fame's Blue Flames (q.v.), and the scene was set for instant sensation.

They made their debut in Paris at the end of 1966, and after Christmas their first single, 'Hey Joe', was released on Track, having been turned down by Decca...also one of the companies who turned down The Beatles! With his flamboyant appearance and extravagant guitar style, Hendrix was an instant smash on television, and 'Hey Joe' shot into the Top Ten.

Hendrix had everything going for him. A dynamic, sexually-charged image; considerable songwriting ability; and a mastery of the guitar's musical and technological potential which had probably never been surpassed in the rock medium. Fellow musicians, critics and the public were all stunned, and by the summer of 1967 - after further hit singles in 'Purple Haze' and 'The Wind Cries Mary', and the very successful 'Are You Experienced' album - Hendrix was the fastest-rising star in the country.

A performance at the Monterey Pop Festival, which has since assumed near-mythical status (and was partly captured on the 1970 Atlantic release 'Monterey - Otis Redding and The Jimi Hendrix Experience'), established him as the hottest property to hit the international music scene since the Fab Four. At the end of a remarkable year the second album, 'Axis Bold As Love', further cemented his standing as a composer and instrumentalist.

1968 was less happy, however. It began with Hendrix being arrested in Sweden for wrecking his hotel room, and continued with a tempestuous tour of America. In July Noel Redding walked out to form Fat Mattress (q.v.) and was replaced by Billy Cox, an old buddy from Hendrix's paratroop days, but in November the group disbanded completely.

Coinciding with this, the double album 'Electric Ladyland' came out. A mixture of songs and extended experimental pieces, recorded with the help of Al Kooper, Steve Winwood and Jack Casady among others, it came in for some critical flak, but nevertheless contains some of Hendrix's finest recorded moments.

In February 1969 The Experience reformed for a concert which was filmed and recorded at the Royal Albert Hall, although the album 'Experience: Original Soundtrack' was not released until 1973.

Hendrix then moved back to New York, turning in another epic performance at Woodstock in June, and forming The Band of Gypsies with Cox and drummer Buddy Miles. They recorded a live album at the Fillmore East on New Year's Eve 1969, but split up soon afterwards.

Since his return to the States Hendrix had suffered from various problems with the police, and was apparently also becoming increasingly disillusioned with public emphasis with ephemera - playing guitar with his teeth, guitar burnings, etc. - at the expense of his music.

'Cry Of Love', his last "proper" album, was a strong return to his song-based format, however, using Cox and Mitchell who also backed him for his last appearance at the Isle of Wight in August 1970. On September 18th he was found dead in his London apartment, the official cause of death being given as inhalation of vomit following barbiturate intoxication.

One of rock's most influential figures was gone, but his spirit was not allowed to rest in peace. The trickle of early recordings which had found unauthorised release while Hendrix was alive became a veritable deluge after his death, along with various official and unofficial live albums.

Most of these recordings were unworthy of the man's name, but a few, notably the two "doctored" by producer Alan Douglas - 'Crash Landing' and 'Midnight Lightning' - do him some justice. Ironically, Hendrix's biggest hit came posthumously, when 'Voodoo Chile' from 'Electric Ladyland' reached Number One in late 1970.

THE HEP STARS Actually Swedish, but regular visitors to these shores, they were formed in Stockholm in 1964. They achieved eight gold records in their native country, but were forced to break up after being declared bankrupt due to mishandling of their finances. Their pianist and songwriter Benny Andersson put his bank balance back in credit during the seventies as a member of Abba.

HERBAL MIXTURE Tony McPhee (guitar, vocals), Pete Cruickshank (bass) and Mick Meekham

HERD

(drums) made a couple of singles for Columbia in the mid-sixties. McPhee and Cruickshank were later in The Groundhogs (q.v.).

THE HERD Peter Frampton (guitar, vocals), Andy Bown (keyboards, vocals), Gary Taylor (bass, vocals) and Andrew Steele (drums) came together in early 1965 and were soon signed by Parlophone after building their reputation in the London clubs.

Their early singles, the self-penned 'Goodbye Baby' and 'She Was Really Saying Something' and the Jagger/Richard composition 'So Much In Love', were unsuccessful, and at the end of 1966 they moved to the Fontana label.

They were now managed by Ken Howard and Alan Blaikley, who also took over the writing of their singles, and after 'I Can Fly' had been another flop the heavily orchestrated 'From The Underworld' reached No.6 late in 1967.

The Herd has now been transformed from an 'underground' group into pop stars, and when Frampton was voted "The Face of '68" by Rave magazine their fame was assured. They had two more big hits in early 1968 with 'Paradise Lost' and 'I Don't Want Our Loving To Die' and made an album named after the former release, which allowed them to air their own compositional talent again, as well as their feel for jazz and humour.

Andrew Steele left for health reasons, and although he was replaced by Henry Spinetti (the younger brother of actor and film director Victor), the end was not far off. Frampton departed after 'Sunshine Cottage' had missed out, to form Humble Pie (q.v.) with Stevie Marriott from The Small Faces (q.v.).

The other members stayed together for one more single, 'The Game', and then went their separate ways, although in 1971 Taylor and Steele joined forces again in 1971 for 'You Got Me Hanging From Your Lovin' Tree' on the Charisma label.

Bown and Spinetti formed the short-lived Judas Jump (q.v.) with members of Amen Corner (q.v.), and Bown was later with folk-rock group Storyteller before going solo. Taylor became a radio DJ, but picked up his bass once more in 1975 to play with Fox; Steele went into session work; and Frampton formed Frampton's Camel and then found massive solo success after moving to the States.

HERMAN'S HERMITS – HOLLIES

HERMAN'S HERMITS Peter 'Herman' Noone was a singer and actor from Manchester who formed The Heartbeats - Keith Hopwood (guitar), Derek Leckenby (guitar), Karl Green (bass) and Barry Whitwarn (drums) - in 1963.

The following year Noone was seen by producer Mickie Most (q.v.) who took them under his wing and changed their name. Not surprisingly, in view of Most's Midas touch, they were an instant smash, and their first single, 'I'm Into Something Good', took them to the top of the charts.

This was followed by an almost uninterrupted run of hits which lasted until 1970, the first few covers of American successes, but all of them quite agonisingly winsome. The group hardly played on any of the records, in fact, but it mattered not one whit, as their appeal was based exclusively on the catchy pop material provided for them and Herman's toothy charm.

They also recorded numerous EPs and albums, although these were not such big sellers...presumably because of the teenybop nature of their audience. They were, however, quite vast in America during the mid-sixties...the most profitable British pop export after The Beatles (q.v.).

In 1970 they changed from Columbia to Most's RAK label, and shortly afterwards Herman went solo, reverting to his real name. He had Top Twenty entries with 'Lady Barbara' and David Bowie's (q.v.) 'Oh You Pretty Things', but has kept a low profile in recent years.

Jimmy Page and John Paul Jones, later with Led Zeppelin (q.v.), were actually Hermits on many of the group's hits.

THE HIGH NUMBERS Roger Daltry (vocals), Pete Townshend (guitar) and John Entwhistle (bass) were all at Acton County School together when they formed their first group in 1959. In the early sixties they added drummer Doug Sanden, calling themselves The Detours and then The Who (q.v.).

In 1964 they were discovered by publicist Peter Meaden, who took over their management. Meaden got them a contract with Fontana, gave them a mod image, and called them The High Numbers.

This enterprise lasted for one single, a rewrite of Slim Harpo's 'Got Live If You Want It' entitled 'I'm The Face', before Sanden was quite literally ousted from his drum stool by Keith Moon, Chris Stamp and Kit Lambert took over management, and the group became The Who once more.

Rumour alleges that the single sold a modest 500 copies, of which Meadon bought 250 and Entwhistle's grandmother two.

HIGH TIDE Tony Hill (guitar), Simon House (violin), Peter Pauli (bass) and Roger Hadden (drums) were a "progressive" group formed in the summer of 1969. They made two albums, 'Sea Shanties' and 'High Tide', for Liberty, which were much better received on the continent than at home. House later played with Hawkwind and David Bowie (q.v.).

THE HOLLIES Allan Clarke (vocals) and Graham Nash (guitar, vocals) had been a schoolboy duo called The Two Teens and then The Deltas before linking up with Tony Hicks (guitar, vocals) and Eric Haydock (bass) from another Manchester group, The Dolphins, and drummer Don Rathbone. They made their debut at Manchester's Oasis club in 1962, but Rathbone was soon replaced by Bobby Elliot from Shane Fenton and The Fentones (q.v.). Fenton himself was the group's manager for a while.

As was common practice in the late fifties and early sixties, the group's first few singles after signing with Parlophone in 1963 were covers of American hits. 'Just Like Me' made the Top Thirty, The Coasters' 'Searchin'' the Top Twenty, and Maurice Williams and The Zodiacs' 'Stay' the Top Ten. Over the next decade they were to use songs written specially for them and their own material, but their hit-making habit continued uninterrupted; and

THE HOLLIES

apart from The Beatles (q.v.) they were Britain's most consistently successful group in the sixties.

They had a smooth, polished sound and some strong songs, and although they often didn't play on their own records it was mainly so they could concentrate on their delicate vocal harmonies. In live appearances they were able to reproduce the sound of their records almost exactly.

In the summer of 1965 they had their only Number One, 'I'm Alive', but it wasn't until the following year that they started to make headway in America, where other (less worthy) exponents of British pop had been cornering the market for a couple of years.

In 1966 Haydock was sacked and went off to form Haydock's Rockhouse (q.v.). He was replaced by Bernie Calvert, another ex-member of The Dolphins. By now The Hollies were writing most of their own material and looking to expand their musical horizons, but it was difficult to break out of the pop mould in which they had been cast for so long.

Frustrated by this, and apparently not impressed by the group's plans for a 'Hollies Sing Dylan' album, Nash stayed in America after meeting David Crosby and Steve Stills during a tour. Crosby, Stills and Nash (and Young) went on to be the biggest group in the world in the early seventies, but whereas Nash's distinctive voice and facility with a good pop tune had made him the leading light of The Hollies, he has always looked rather out of his depth since leaving them. Undeniably successful, though, so he won't be complaining.

The future of The Hollies looked uncertain for a while, especially as they had some trouble replacing Nash. But eventually they recruited Terry Sylvester, who had previously been with Merseybeat groups The Escorts (q.v.) and The Swinging Blue Jeans (q.v.).

Thus reinforced, they turned to outside songwriters once again and resumed their chart-busting ways. 'Sorry Suzanne' and 'He Ain't Heavy He's My Brother' took them out of the sixties in fine style, but then the hits started to get thinner on the ground.

In 1971 Clarke left to make a solo album, 'My Real Name Is 'Arold', and was replaced by Swedish vocalist Michael Rickfors. He returned the following year, however, when the group signed to Polydor and had an American best seller with 'Long Cool Woman In A Black Dress'. In 1974 'The Air That I Breathe' was another huge international hit, and in 1978 a live recording of some of their hits also did very well.

Apart from this album and the collection of Dylan songs, The Hollies made seven albums during the sixties - 'The Hollies', 'In The Hollies Style', 'Stay With The Hollies', 'Would You Believe?', 'For Certain Because',

HONEYBUS – IDLE RACE

'Evolution' and 'Butterfly' - the popularity of which is some indication of the group's all-round ability and appeal.

HONEYBUS Pete Dello (vocals, guitar), Colin Hare (guitar), Ray Cane (bass) and Peter Kirchner (drums) made two exquisite records for the Deram label, 'Do I Figure In Your Life' and 'I Can't Let Maggie Go'. The former was an inexplicable miss, the latter got to No.8.

Both were written and produced by Dello, whose real name was Pete Blumsom. He then left, but the group carried on for a while, making no further impact. In 1970 Deram put out the 'Honeybus Story' album posthumously.

Dello continued to write, and in 1973 a girl called Leah made a single comprising two of his songs, 'Arise Sir Henry' and 'Uptight Basil', for GM Records.

THE HONEYCOMBS Denis D'Ell (vocals, harmonica), Martin Murray (lead guitar), Alan Ward (rhythm guitar), John Lantree (bass) and Honey Lantree (drums) were formed in North London during 1963 as The Sherabons. They were completely unremarkable except for having a female drummer in ex-hairdresser Honey, and what success they enjoyed was due almost entirely to the Howard/Blaikley songwriting team.

Their first single for Pye, 'Have I The Right', got to Number One in the summer of 1964 and was also a big hit in America. The group, however, promptly disappeared on a lengthy tour of Australia which did their career prospects no good at all.

On their return Murray was replaced by Peter Pye, and after minor hits with 'Is It Because' and 'Something Better Beginning' they made the Top Twenty again with 'That's The Way'. Further singles, including a quite monstrous version of 'Who Is Sylvia', were mercifully misses.

The group were also allowed to make a brace of albums, 'The Honeycombs' and 'All Systems Go', but after 1966 they slipped back into obscurity. Dennis D'Ell made an abortive comeback attempt during the seventies as a solo singer.

THE HOOCHIE COOCHIE MEN Originally The Cyril Davies R&B All Stars (q.v.), they were taken over and rechristened by Long John Baldry after Davies' death in 1964. They only lasted for about a year, during which time they recorded the 'Long John's Blues' album, and among their flexible line-up were pianist Ian Armit and vocalist Rod Stewart (q.v.).

NICKY HOPKINS This highly talented London-born pianist started his professional career with Screaming Lord Sutch's Savages and then joined The Cyril Davies R&B All Stars (q.q.v.).

Moving into session work, partly because his frail health couldn't stand the rigours of full-time group life, he was in constant demand, recording with many of the sixties top groups, including The Rolling Stones (q.v.), The Who (q.v.), The Kinks (q.v.) and The Easybeats (q.v.).

In 1967 he recorded an album entitled 'The Revolutionary Piano Of Nicky Hopkins' for CBS, and a Shel Talmy (q.v.) produced single as Nicky Hopkins and His Whistling Piano. The A-side of this little item was the Ray Davies' 'Mr.Pleasant', featuring Hopkins on piano accompanied by a drummer and an anonymous whistler.

In 1968 Hopkins was briefly with The Jeff Beck Group (q.v.), and when he couldn't stand it any more he moved to San Francisco, where he did further session work as well as playing with two of the city's leading combos, The Steve Miller Band and Quicksilver Messenger Service.

During the seventies Hopkins has toured on several occasions with The Rolling Stones. In 1973 he recorded an album for CBS with various other musicians under the collective title of 'Sweet Thursday', and the following year he made his second solo album for the same label, 'Tin Man Was A Dreamer'.

BRIAN HOWARD AND THE SILHOUETTES A group from Mitcham, Surrey, whose Fontana singles in the early sixties included a version of Chuck Berry's 'Back In The USA'.

THE HUMAN BEANS Dave Edmunds (guitar, vocals), John Williams (bass), and Tommy Riley (drums) were formed in Cardiff in 1966. They recorded a version of Tim Rose's 'Morning Dew' for Columbia in the following year, before developing into Love Sculpture (q.v.).

THE HUMBLEBUMS A Glaswegian folk duo of the late sixties, they were originally Billy Connolly and Tam Harvey. They recorded one album together for Transatlantic and were then joined by Gerry Rafferty in 1968. The trio soon became a duo once again when Harvey was dumped, and Connolly and Rafferty recorded a couple more albums as well as singles like 'Coconut Tree' and 'Saturday Roundabout Sunday'.

Eventually, however, the strain between Rafferty's serious songwriting aspirations and Connolly's flair as a comic and raconteur became too great, and they went their separate ways to illustrious solo careers.

HUMBLE PIE Steve Marriott (guitar, vocals) from The Small Faces (q.v.), Peter Frampton (guitar, vocals) from The Herd (q.v.), Greg Ridley (bass) from Spooky Tooth (q.v.), and drummer Jerry Shirley formed this heavy rock 'supergroup' in 1968.

Their first single on Immediate, 'Natural Born Boogie', was a big hit in the summer of 1969, but thereafter they found much more recognition in America, where they consequently spent most of their time.

They made two albums for Immediate - 'As Safe As Yesterday' and 'Town And Country' - before moving to A&M for a further seven albums, which became increasingly less subtle as the seventies wore on.

After their most successful albums, 'Rock On' and 'Performance - Rockin' At The Fillmore' - Frampton left to form his own band, and was replaced by Clem Clempson from Bakerloo (q.v.) and Colosseum (q.v.).

The group adopted a gospel-influenced sound, and in fact toured with the coloured girl vocal group The Blackberries. They went steadily downhill, however, and split up in 1975, after which Marriott formed Steve Marriott's All Stars.

THE DAVE HUNT BLUES BAND The resident group at The Crawdaddy (q.v.) in Richmond before The Rolling Stones (q.v.) took over in 1963, their guitarist was Ray Davies, who went on to form The Kinks (q.v.).

MARSHA HUNT Having sung with various groups, including Steampacket (q.v.) and Alexis Korner (q.v.) in the mid-sixties, this coloured lady was in the cast of 'Hair' (q.v.) and briefly with Ferris Wheel (q.v.) before going solo at the end of the sixties.

She formed two backing bands, White Trash and Her Pleasure, neither of which lasted very long, but had minor hits on Track with 'Walk On Gilded Splinters' in 1969 and 'Keep The Customer Satisfied' the following year. She also recorded an album, 'Woman Child'.

Nowadays her name is kept in the public eye mainly by American legal proceedings over her allegation that Mick Jagger is the father of her child.

THE HUSTLERS An early to mid-sixties beat group who recorded for both Philips and Mercury. Among their singles were 'Gimme What I want' on Philips in 1963, and 'Easy To Find' on Mercury in 1964.

IAN AND THE ZODIACS A Merseybeat group who were featured on the Oriole label's 'This Is Merseybeat' album. They also recorded an album, named after the group, and a few singles for Pye.

ICE A group who recorded a pair of singles for Decca in 1967, 'Anniversary' and 'Ice Man'.

THE IDLE RACE Jeff Lynne (guitar, vocals), Dave Pritchard (guitar), Greg Masters (bass) and Roger Spencer (drums) rose in 1967 from the ashes of Birmingham's Mike Sheridan and The Nightriders (q.v.).

A quite excellent "psychedelic" pop group,

IMAGE – IVY LEAGUE

they signed to United Artists when the label went independent, and although they never had a hit they made some memorable records.

Their singles were 'Imposters Of Life's Magazine', 'The Skeleton and The Roundabout', 'I Like My Toys', 'Days Of The Broken Arrows' and 'Come With Me'. They also made two albums - 'Idle Race' and 'The Birthday Party' - before Lynne left in 1971 to join The Move (q.v.) The rest of the group brought in David Walker and Mike Hopkins to make one more album, 'Time Is' on Regal Zonophone, but their guiding force was gone and they split up soon afterwards.

'The Birthday Party' and a single from it, 'Roundabout', were re-released in early 1976 to cash in on Lynne's success with the Electric Light Orchestra, and United Artists also put out a compilation album, 'On With The Show', on their budget Sunset label.

THE IMAGE They made a single called 'I Can't Stop Myself' for Parlophone in 1966.

THE IN CROWD Vocalist Keith West (q.v.), Les Jones (lead guitar), John "Junior" Wood (rhythm guitar), Simon "Boots" Alcot (bass) and Ken Lawrence (drums) were a mid-sixties R&B/soul group who had originally been Four Plus One (q.v.).

Their first Parlophone single, 'That's How Strong My Love Is', made the lower reaches of the charts in 1965, but after 'Stop Wait A Minute' had flopped Jones was ousted in favour of Steve Howe.

The group made a further single, 'Why Must They Criticise', and an album which was never released, before changing their name yet again to Tomorrow (q.v.).

THE INCREDIBLE STRING BAND Edinburgh folk singers Robin Williamson, Mike Heron and Clive Palmer pooled their talents in 1965, but after their first Elektra album in 1966 Palmer left, leaving Heron and Williamson to carry on as a duo.

Besides the obligatory guitars they were able to turn their hands to numerous bizarre and exotic instruments. Their music was gentle, but often complex, and their lyrics had a mystical and mythical flavour which was perfect for the times.

Their second album, 'The Five Thousand Spirits Or The Layers Of The Onion', created considerable interest in 1967, and in the following year they came up with 'The Hangman's Beautiful Daughter'. The definitive String Band album, it was also their biggest seller.

After an erratic double album, 'Wee Tam and The Big Huge', the line-up was expanded with the addition of girlfriends Licorice McKechnie and Rosie Simpson, on violin and bass respectively. From this point on, The Incredible String Band never recaptured the very special spirit of their earlier work, and further expansions of the line-up during the seventies only dissipated it even more.

In 1970 they launched the ambitious musical project, 'U', and with the addition of dancer and vocalist Malcolm le Maistre a permanent theatrical element was introduced into their act. As the seventies went by Heron, who was the superior musician and more straightforward songwriter of the two, assumed an increasingly dominant influence over the group's direction, and after their move to the Island label they started to bear more resemblance to a rock group than folkies.

Both Williamson and Heron made solo albums, 'Myrrh' and 'Smiling Men With Bad Reputations', which graphically illustrated how wide apart their musical ambitions had grown, and in 1974 the group split up.

Williamson moved to California, where he spent much of his time as an author, but in 1978 he returned to Britain with a new album and a group of American musicians.

Heron, meanwhile, formed Reputation with Le Maistre, and Graham Forbes (guitar) and John Gilston (drums) from the last String Band line-up. They made one album for the Neighbourhood label, and then Heron, Le Maistre and Gilston formed Heron in 1976. This also lasted for only one album, 'Diamond Of Dreams' on Bronze, before Heron returned to Scotland to concentrate on his songwriting.

INFLUENCE A Newcastle group whose members included John Miles (keyboards, guitar, vocals), Vic Malcolm (guitar) and Paul Thompson (drums). In the early seventies Thompson joined Roxy Music, and after several years of waiting Miles emerged as a solo star in 1975.

THE INTERNS A mid-sixties group from Cardiff who (surprise, surprise!) wore surgeons' outfits on stage. Among their singles for Philips and Parlophone was 'Don't You Dare'.

IVANS MEADS A mid-sixties group from Manchester who were managed by Mike Maxfield from The Dakotas (q.v.), they had an unusual vocals, organ, sax, bass and drums line-up. They were the first group to record for George Martin's production company, but neither P.F.Sloan's 'Sins Of The Family' in 1965, nor 'We'll Talk About It Tomorrow' in 1966 did anything for them.

THE IVEYS Pete Ham (guitar, vocals), Ron Griffiths (guitar, vocals), Tom Evans (bass) and Mike Gibbins (drums) came from South Wales. After building a local reputation they toured the country in 1966 as the backing group for David Garrick (q.v.). In 1968 they were signed to the newly-formed Apple label, but after their debut single, the self-penned 'Maybe Tomorrow', they became Badfinger (q.v.).

THE IVY LEAGUE They were formed in 1964 when John Carter and Ken Lewis from Carter-Lewis and The Southerners (q.v.) linked up with Perry Ford. Carter's real name was Shakespeare (really!), Lewis was James Hawker and Ford was Brian Pugh, and all were session singers and songwriters, specialising in a high-pitched vocal harmony sound.

They recorded for Piccadilly, and after 'What More Do You Want' had flopped they had successive hits in 1965 with 'Funny How Love Can Be', 'That's Why I'm Crying' and 'Tossing And Turning'. They also made an album, 'This Is The Ivy League', a bizarre mixture of their own material and songs like 'Floral Dance' and 'Don't Think Twice It's Alright'.

In January 1966 Carter left to be replaced by another sessionman, Tony Burrows, and soon afterwards Lewis made way for Neil Landon. The Ivy League kept on recording until the end of 1967, but only 'Willow Tree' was even a minor hit for them. They finally transmogrified into The Flowerpot Men (q.v.).

ROBERT WILLIAMSON AND MIKE HERON/THE INCREDIBLE STRING BAND

TONY JACKSON & THE VIBRATIONS — JOHN & JOHNNY

TONY JACKSON AND THE VIBRATIONS Tony Jackson was bassist with The Searchers (q.v.), but left to form The Vibrations when they were at the peak of their popularity. The group had three singles released by Pye, of which the first, 'Bye Bye Baby' was a modest hit.

In mid-1965 Jackson went completely solo, recording 'Stage Door' before moving to CBS for a few more singles which got nowhere.

JIMMY JAMES AND THE VAGABONDS Jimmy James sang with various R&B and soul combos in the early sixties, and then formed The Vagabonds in late 1965. They were favourites on the club scene and recorded several singles and an album, 'New Religion', for Piccadilly. They had to wait until 1968, and 'Red Red Wine' on Pye, however, before they saw even minor chart action. James carried on undeterred with numerous Vagabonds line-ups, and eventually had another hit in 1976.

JASON CREST A progressive rock band of the late sixties, their singles included Roy Wood's '(Here We Go Round The) Lemon Tree' and 'Turquoise Tandem' on Philips in 1968, and 'A Place In The Sun' in 1969.

PETER JAY AND THE JAYWALKERS Drummer Peter Jay put this seven-piece instrumental group together right at the start of the decade while at Great Yarmouth art school. Each member wore a different coloured suit, Jay had flashing lights inside his drum kit, and the highlight of their act was 'Can Can '62' in which the group showed off their terpsichorean talents.

They signed to Decca in 1962 and the above number was their debut single, and a minor hit. Their style became anachronistic almost overnight, however, with the advent of the Beat Boom. They worked steadily, particularly as a backing group on package tours, but further singles on Decca and Piccadilly (a version of 'Parchment Farm' amongst them) did nothing to advance their career.

The line-up of the group was changing constantly, but finished up as Jay, Tony Webster (guitar), Mac McIntyre (sax, flute), Lloyd Baker (piano, sax), Geoff Moss (acoustic bass), and Johnny Larke (bass). At the end of 1966, when Jay broke up the group and returned to Clacton, the other members all retired from professional music, except for McIntyre who went into PR work. Earlier in the year guitarist Terry Reid (q.v.) had been with them for a short while...his first full-time musical venture.

JETHRO TULL Ian Anderson (vocals), Chick Murray (guitar), John Evans (piano), Glenn Cornick (bass) and Barriemore Barlow (drums) were a Blackpool soul group called John Evans Smash, who moved south in 1967 to be closer to the centre of the action.

Unable to stand the impecunious circumstances in which they soon found themselves, all the members except for Anderson and Cornick soon returned home, leaving the remaining two in Luton, struggling to keep body and soul together.

With guitarist Mick Abrahams and drummer Clive Bunker, they formed Bag Of Blues who then became Jethro Tull, playing a "progressive" blend of rock, blues and jazz. Anderson had also learned to play the flute which was to become his trademark.

They recorded one single, 'Aeroplane' for MGM, which came out under the stupid name of Jethro Toe at the suggestion of Derek Lawrence, and then signed to Island Records.

With some thoroughly exciting music and an unmistakeable focal point in Anderson's Faginesque prancing, they made rapid progress on the club circuit and, like so many groups before and since, achieved their first major breakthrough at the National Jazz and Blues Festival.

Their second single, 'Song For Jeffrey', came out in September 1968, and at the end of the year their debut album, 'This Was', was an unexpected success. A power struggle between Anderson and Abrahams followed, resulting in Abrahams departure to form Blodwyn Pig (q.v.). Tony Iommi from Black Sabbath (q.v.) came in briefly, but the permanent replacement was Martin Barre.

In 1969 Tull had their first hit single, the Top Five 'Living In The Past', and their second album, the superb 'Stand Up', topped the album charts. Shifting to the new Chrysalis label they maintained their standards with 'Benefit', but then Cornick departed, to form Wild Turkey and later Paris with Bob Welch from Fleetwood Mac (q.v.), and the first golden era of Jethro Tull was over.

With Anderson now in complete control the group became little more than a vehicle for his ideas, and Evans and Barlow were summoned back from Blackpool to help execute them. 'Thick As A Brick', 'Passion Play', and 'War Child' were all complicated, wordy concept albums which lost the group ground in Britain, although by now they had established themselves internationally.

Later in the seventies a shift to something akin to folk rock with 'Songs From The Wood' and 'Heavy Horses' recaptured some of their popularity, and in 1978 the worldwide televising of a concert at Madison Square Gardens.

DAVID JOHN AND THE MOOD A mid-sixties R&B group from Preston, DJ was really one Miffy Charnley. They recorded three singles for Vocalion Pop and Parlophone, the first of which, 'To Catch That Man', was produced by Joe Meek in 1964.

JO JO GUNNE A late sixties heavy rock group whose Decca singles included 'Beggin' You Baby' in 1969. They have no connection with the much better-known American band of the same name.

JOHN AND JOHNNY John Banks and Johnny Gustafson formed this duo after leaving The Merseybeats

IAN ANDERSON/JETHRO TULL

JOHN'S CHILDREN — JUNCO PARTNERS

(q.v.) in 1966. They released one single, 'Bumper To Bumper' on Parlophone before Gustafson went solo. He later formed Quatermass, who made an album for Harvest in 1970, and played with various groups, including Roxy Music.

JOHN'S CHILDREN Andy Ellison (vocals), John Hewlett (guitar, bass), Geoff McLelland (guitar) and Chris Townson (drums) were one of the most controversial (and interesting) groups of the flower power/psychedelic era. Their main claims to fame were the temporary membership of guitarist Marc Bolan, and the poster campaign after his departure which showed the group naked except for strategically-placed flowers.

They started off in 1964 as a Surrey R&B combo called The Few, became Silence, and ended up in St.Tropez, where they were found by Simon Napier-Bell. Returning to London they recorded two singles for Columbia, 'The Love I Thought I'd Found' and 'Just What You Want, Just What You Get', before McLelland was sacked in early 1967 and Bolan came in.

Their third single was to have been 'Not The Sort Of Girl (You'd Take To Bed)', an anti-drug song which EMI declined to issue. A live album, subtly entitled "Orgasm", met with the same fate and was only issued in America, so the group moved to Track for their first single with Bolan, 'Desdemona'.

This release also attracted adverse attention and was banned by most radio stations, who objected to the line 'Lift up your skirt and fly'. An appearance at the Fourteen Hour Technicolour Dream festival (q.v.) featured Bolan balancing his guitar on his head, causing large quantities of ear-splitting feedback, but not the group playing in the nude, as had been threatened.

In June 1967 Bolan left, after a fuss about the production of "A Midsummer Night's Scene", which had been intended as their next single. As an alternative the B-side of 'Desdemona', 'Remember Thomas A Becket' was released, with a new mix and set of lyrics, as 'Come And Play With Me In The Garden'.

The group carried on for a while as a trio, and at the end of the year put out 'Go Go Girl', another Bolan song which was later remodelled as 'Mustang Ford' for Tyrannosaurus Rex (q.v.). After a tour of Germany, however, when they had their equipment stolen and reportedly drove through the streets of Hamburg in the altogether, they split up.

Hewlett went into publicity for Apple Records, and in the seventies became the manager of Sparks. Townson played with various groups, deputised for Keith Moon in The Who (q.v.), and then joined Jooks.

Ellison, meanwhile, went solo and made four singles. The wistful 'It's Been A Long Time' on Track was from the film 'Here We Go Round The Mulberry Bush'; 'You Can't Do That', the Beatles (q.v.) song, and 'Fool From Upper Eden', by George Alexander from Grapefruit (q.v.), were on CBS; and 'You Can't Do That' (re-released with a new B-side) was on Simon Napier-Bell's own label.

He then did some TV commercials and film stunt work, including one of the James Bond films, and wandered round Greece and Spain before taking up painting. At the end of 1974 Ellison and Townson met up with Hewlett again, who introduced them to ex-Sparks sidemen Martin Gordon and Sir Peter Oxendale. Together with ex-Nice (q.v.) guitarist David O'List they formed Jet, who made an album for CBS. By 1977 Ellison - still as energetic and daredevil as ever - and Gordon were fronting Radio Stars.

JOKERS WILD A Cambridge group from 1966/67 whose line-up included David Gilmour, who joined Pink Floyd (q.v.) after Syd Barrett's exit, drummer Willie Wilson, who was later with Quiver and then Sutherland Brothers & Quiver, and bassist Ricky Wills, who was with Cochise in the early seventies and part of the revamped Small Faces (q.v.) in 1977.

CASEY JONES AND THE ENGINEERS An early sixties R&B group from London, they had the distinction of including Eric Clapton for two weeks before he joined The Yardbirds (q.v.). Another member was guitarist Tom McGuinness, who was later in Manfred Mann (q.v.). They made one single, 'One Way Ticket' for Columbia in 1963.

CASEY JONES AND THE GOVENERS An early sixties group from Liverpool who spent most of their time in Germany, where they recorded two albums for the Golden 12 label. The first was 'Casey Jones and The Goveners' and featured rock standards such as 'Beautiful Delilah','Dr Feelgood' and 'Lucille', as well as some original compositions. The second, 'Don't Ha Ha', was more of the same, with 'Dizzy Miss Lizzy', 'Talkin' Bout You' and 'Too Much Monkey Business'.

DAVEY JONES AND THE KING BEES David Jones (vocals), Dick Underwood (guitar, harmonica), Roger Bluck (banjo), Frank Howard (bass) and Bob Allen (drums) got together in South London in late 1963, and played the R&B clubs for several months.

Eventually Jones contacted washing machine tycoon John Bloom with a view to management, and Bloom put him in touch with Les Conn. The group played at Bloom's wedding party, and although their music was largely ignored, Conn was sufficiently impressed to get them a contract with Decca. Their first single was 'Liza Jane' in May 1964, and for some reason was released under the name of Tome Jones and The Jonahs.

Over the next eighteen months they made several singles for various companies under various names, although it seems that the line-up remained intact. 'Catch That Man' and 'Liza Jane' were both issued on Vocalion as Davey Jones and The Kingbees; 'I Pity The Fool' on Parlophone as The Manish Boys (named after the Muddy Waters song); 'For Your Love' as Davey Jones and The Kingbees, but this time on Philips; 'Diggin' My Potatoes' and 'You've Got A Habit Of Leavin' on Parlophone as Davy Jones and The Mood and just Davy Jones respectively. These last two were produced, as was the earlier Parlophone single, by Shel Talmy (q.v.).

At the end of 1965 Jones moved on to Davie Jones and The Lower Third (q.v.), and in 1978, by which time Jones was slightly better known as David Bowie (q.v.), Decca reissued "Liza Jane".

DAVIE JONES AND THE LOWER THIRD Davie Jones (vocals), Dennis "T-Cup" Taylor (guitar), Graham Rivens (bass) and Phil Lancaster (drums) were formed in late 1965 after Jones had left The Kingbees (q.v.). Jones earlier exploits had not boosted his bank balance, and it was known for the group to be reduced to sleeping outside The Marquee (q.v.) in the ambulance which they used for transportation.

In 1966 they made one single for Pye, 'Can't Help Thinking About Me', before Jones became David Bowie (q.v.) and the group were renamed The Buzz. Soon afterwards Bowie went solo.

THE JOYSTRINGS A Salvation Army beat group led by Captain Joy Webb, who had two minor hits, 'It's An Open Secret' and 'Starry Night'. on Regal Zonophone in 1964. During the next three years they made further singles and EPs and two albums, 'Well Seasoned' and 'Carols Around The World', which were released to catch the Christmas market in 1966 and 1967 respectively.

The unexpected popularity of The Joystrings led to the formation of numerous Salvation Army rhythm combos up and down the country, most of whom got no further than playing local religious functions.

JUDAS JUMP A heavily hyped "supergroup" formed in 1969, who turned out to be less than super and not even a group for very long. Mike Smith (tenor sax), Allen Jones (baritone sax) came from Amen Corner (q.v.); Andy Bown (keyboards) and Henry Spinetti (drums) from The Herd (q.v.); and the line-up was completed by unknown Welsh vocalist Adrian Williams.

They managed two singles and an album, called 'Scorch', during their brief lifespan. Bown joined folk-rock group Storyteller and then went solo; Spinetti went into session work and various groups; the others seemed to disappear from the music scene.

JUICY LUCY This heavy rock band, formed at the end of the decade, were fronted by vocalist Paul Williams from Zoot Money's Big Roll Band (q.v.) and American steel guitarist Glen Campbell from The Misunderstood (q.v.). Other members at various times included drummer Keith Ellis, who was later with Spooky Tooth (q.v.) and Boxer; guitarist Neil Hubbard from The Greaseband (q.v.); and drummer Rod Coombes, who was also in Stealers Wheel, with Gerry Rafferty from The Humblebums (q.v.), and The Strawbs (q.v.).

In 1970 they had a Top Twenty hit with Bo Diddley's 'Who Do You Love', and another minor hit with 'Pretty Woman', both on the Vertigo label. They also recorded several albums for Vertigo, Polydor and Island, including 'Lie Back And Enjoy It', 'Pieces' and 'Get A Whiff Of This', before breaking up in 1975.

JUNCO PARTNERS A mid-sixties beat group from Newcastle who recorded for Columbia, and were part of the Robert Stigwood Agency.

JUNIORS EYES—KINKS

<u>JUNIORS EYES</u> A late sixties heavy rock band who recorded an album for Regal Zonophone in 1969, as well as singles like 'Woman Love' and 'Circus Days'. Featuring in the group were guitarist and vocalist Mick Wayne, who later spent a short while with The Pink Fairies, and guitarist Tim Renwick, who went on to Quiver and The Sutherland Brothers and Quiver.

<u>KALEIDOSCOPE</u> No relation to the American West Coast group of the same name, this Kaleidoscope was one of the more interesting groups to emerge from the psychedelic era in 1967. Led by vocalist and songwriter Peter Daltry, they were very *a la mode* in beads and kaftans, and featured regularly on John Peel's (q.v.) 'Top Gear', but never broke through to mass popularity.

Signed by Fontana, their debut single was 'Flight From Ayisha', which didn't make it despite a lot of play on the pirate stations. However, it did well enough for them to make an album, 'Tangerine Dream', which came out at the end of 1967, containing such delightful flights of fancy as 'Mr.Small The Watch Repairer Man', 'Further Reflections In The Room Of Percussion' and a fairytale entitled 'The Sky Children'.

Among their further singles were the catchy 'Jenny Artichoke', 'A Dream For Julie' in 1968 and 'Do It Again Jeffrey' and 'Balloon' in 1969. In the latter year they also made another album, 'Faintly Blowing'.

<u>KATE</u> A group put together in 1969 by drummer Viv Prince (q.v.) from The Pretty Things (q.v.). Among their singles for CBS was 'Shout It'.

<u>ACE KEFFORD STAND</u> A largely undistinguished venture undertaken by blonde bassist Chris "Ace" Kefford after his departure from The Move (q.v.). They did make a version of The Yardbirds' (q.v.) 'For Your Love' on Atlantic in 1969, and in 1976 Kefford made yet another abortive bid to recapture past glories with Rock Star.

<u>THE KESTRALS</u> A West Country vocal group whose line-up included Tony Burrows and Roger Greenaway. They both went on to become in-demand session singers, and Greenaway also formed a successful songwriting partnership with Roger Cook, with whom he had hits in his own right as David and Jonathan (q.v.). Burrows appeared in various session groups, including The Ivy League (q.v.), The Flowerpot Men (q.v.) and Edison Lighthouse.

<u>JOHNNY KIDD AND THE PIRATES</u> Londoner Fred Heath was vocalist and guitarist with his own rock'n' roll combo in the late fifties when a broken guitar string hit him in the eye before one performance, compelling him to go on stage sporting an eyepatch. Afterwards a female fan mentioned that he resembled the pirate Captain Kidd, and from then on he and his group became Johnny Kidd and The Pirates, with the eyepatch as their visual trademark.

Their raw rock'n'roll was something of an anomaly on the British music scene at the time, and their debut single, the self-penned 'Please Don't Touch', sold moderately well. A couple of flops followed, and then, after 'You Got What It Takes' had again been reasonably successful (despite being overshadowed by Marv Johnson's version), they came up with a *bona fide* rock classic in 'Shakin' All Over', which got to No.3 during the summer of 1960.

A second Top Twenty entry, 'Restless', and another minor hit, 'Linda Lu', came their way over the next few months, and then The Pirates went off to form The Tornadoes (q.v.). Kidd put together a new band with Mick Green (guitar), Johnny Spence (bass) and Frank Allen (drums), and carried on touring and recording.

They had a dramatic stage act, involving Kidd throwing swords which narrowly missed his guitarists, but they appeared to be heading for stagnation until they did a nifty hop onto the passing R&B bandwagon in late 1962.

'Shot Of Rhythm and Blues' gave them their first modest chart entry for two years at the start of 1963, and later in the year they were back in the big time with 'I'll Never Get Over You'. The earlier pattern was repeated.However, 'Hungry For Love' sneaked into the Top Twenty, 'Always And Ever' just made the Fifty, and after that...nothing.

Perhaps Kidd would have been able to revive his fortunes yet again when the flower power phase came along in 1967, but unfortunately he was killed in a car accident in October 1966.

The Pirates line-up had changed somewhat in the later stages, and new personnel included guitarist John Weider, who was later in Eric Burdon and The Animals (q.v.). Mick Green had a varied career after leaving, playing with the likes of Engelbert Humperdinck before joining Cliff Bennett (q.v.) in Shanghai in 1975. When this project foundered he reformed The Pirates with Spence and Allen, and they found new acceptance with the advent of the New Wave in 1977.

<u>DANNY KING AND THE ROYALS</u> When everything that moved in Liverpool had been signed up in 1963, record company scouts had to start looking further afield for new talent, and Danny King and The Royals were one of several "Brumbeat" groups signed to EMI at the time. King later formed The Mayfair Set...wishful thinking!

<u>JONATHAN KING</u> Bespectacled Cambridge undergraduate King leapt into the public eye in 1965 when 'Everyone's Gone To The Moon' on Decca got to No.4 in the charts.

It soon became obvious, however, that King's ambitions extended beyond mere pop stardom, and he embarked on a career of production, management and songwriting...while still finding time to have numerous hits both under his own name and various pseudonyms.

In the seventies he formed his own label, UK, which immediately found success with 10CC, and in 1978 stood for Parliament in the Epsom by-election...where, although losing his deposit, he made a much better showing than the other would-be pop politician, Screaming Lord Sutch (q.v.).

Nearly all of King's output, whether in his own right or with others, has been pop drivel of the most blatant and unashamed variety. He has to be admired, however, for his realisation of just how low mass taste is capable of sinking, and his astute exploitation thereof.

Among the monstrosities resulting from this awareness have been 'Johnny Reggae' by The Piglets, 'Jump Up And Down Wave Your Knickers In The Air' by St.Cecilia, and 'Loop-Di-Love' by Shag. Never a man to hide his light under a bushel, King has also been a regular broadcaster on television and radio.

<u>KING CRIMSON</u> Robert Fripp (guitar), Peter Giles (bass) and Mike Giles (drums), were a Bournemouth trio who made a pop-orientated album for Deram in 1968. In the following year Fripp and drummer Giles were joined by multi-instrumentalist Ian McDonald, bassist Greg Lake and lyricist/lighting engineer Pete Sinfield in King Crimson.

Astonishingly versatile and technically brilliant, they created an immediate sensation in London music circles, and after they had appeared at The Rolling Stones (q.v.) concert in Hyde Park their debut album for Island, 'In The Court Of The Crimson King', was a major critical and commercial success at the end of 1969.

Soon afterwards McDonald and Giles left during the group's first American tour, later making their own album on Island, and it became apparent that Fripp was the dominant force in the group. During the seventies he was the only constant factor in the line-up as King Crimson moved in an increasingly jazz-influenced direction.

Greg Lake left during the recording of the second album, 'In The Wake Of Poseidon', to form Emerson, Lake and Palmer; Sinfield departed after 'Lizard' and 'Islands', to make his own album, 'Still', and go into production; and McDonald, after guesting on the final Crimson album, 'Red' in 1974, joined ex-Spooky Tooth (q.v.) guitarist Mick Jones and several Americans in the multi-platinum Foreigner.

Among the musicians who passed through King Crimson over the years were bassist Boz Burrell from Boz People (q.v.), bassist John Wetton from Family (q.v.), drummer Bill Bruford from Yes (q.v.), and drummer Ian Wallace who later toured with Steve Marriott, Alvin Lee and Bob Dylan.

Fripp himself, who disbanded the group at the end of 1974, announced that he was retiring back to Dorset to prepare himself for the collapse of Western civilisation. He soon returned to active service, however, and has since involved himself in projects with Brian Eno from Roxy Music (q.v.), ex-Genesis (q.v.) vocalist Peter Gabriel, and Blondie.

<u>THE KINKS</u> Ray Davies (guitar, vocals), his younger brother Dave Davies (lead guitar), Pete Quaife (bass) and Mick Avory (drums), were an R&B group from Muswell Hill, London, who called themselves The Ramrods and The Ravens before manager Larry Page dressed them up in pink hunting jackets, called them The Kinks, and got them a contract with Pye.

Their first two singles in early 1964, Little Richard's 'Long Tall Sally' and 'You Still Want Me', were misses, and then Ray Davies began writing the group's material, with immediate success as 'You Really Got Me' shot to Number One.

Over the next three years they came up with a series of quite stunning singles, all produced by Shel Talmy (q.v.), including further chart-toppers in 'Tired Of Waiting For You' and 'Sunny Afternoon'. They were brilliantly observed vignettes of English life and manners, ranging from the satirical 'Dedicated Follower Of Fashion' to the poignant 'Waterloo Sunset', but - perhaps because Davies' inspiration was so ethnic - The Kinks never enjoyed the success in America that so many of their contemporaries had.

Their albums - 'The Kinks', 'Kinda Kinks', 'Kontroversy', 'Face To Face' and 'Something Else' - were mixtures of Davies' originals and standards like 'Long Tall Shorty', 'Dancing In The Streets', 'Milk Cow Blues' and 'Too Much Monkey Business', and all sold very strongly.

In 1967 Dave Davies had hits of his own with 'Death Of A Clown' and 'Susannah's Still Alive'.

KIPPINGTON LODGE — KREWCATS

but by 1968 the hits were getting harder to come by for The Kinks. 'Face To Face' had been probably the first concept album ever, and it was in this direction that Ray Davies subsequently moved with 'Village Green Preservation Society' and 'Arthur Or The Decline And Fall Of The British Empire', the latter album originally commissioned for a Granada TV production which was never made.

At the start of the seventies 'Lola' gave The Kinks their last big hit, and since then Davies has continued airing his views on life via albums for RCA and Arista, but The Kinks have been a mere shadow of their former selves ...and ironically become infinitely more popular in the States in the process!

In 1969 Pete Quaife left, being replaced by John Dalton, and in the following year the line-up was expanded by pianist John Gosling. They were also augmented for a short while by the brass section from The Mike Cotton Sound (q.v.). In fact the live side of The Kinks was considerably smartened up during the seventies, with frequent use of theatrical presentation... a far cry from their sixties heyday, when their shows were often a drunken shambles, punctuated by fights between group members.

In 1974 they formed their own Konk label, whose signings included female singer/songwriter Claire Hamill and Cafe Society, led by Tom Robinson, who has acknowledged Davies as one of his major inspirations.

KIPPINGTON LODGE Brinsley Schwarz (guitar), Nick Lowe (bass, vocals), Barry Landerman (keyboards) and Pete Whale (drums) were a late sixties group from Kent. Among their singles for Parlophone were 'Shy Boy', 'Rumours', 'Tell Me A Story', 'Tomorrow Today' and 'In My Life'. Landerman was replaced by Bob Andrews, and in the early seventies they became Brinsley Schwarz who, after a disastrous hype-ridden start, became one of the country's best-loved 'pub rock' groups.

KISS Terry Sealey (vocals), John Tuttle (sax, vocals), Dave Knowles (bass, vocals), Dave Smith-Howell (guitar, vocals) and Jimmy Jewell (drums) were from Norwich, and emerged from the ashes of The Alex Wilson Set in 1966.

During the late sixties they developed a sound not dissimilar to The Moody Blues (q.v.) and Yes (q.v.), and became quite popular on the continent, where they spent much of their time.

In 1969 they played support to The Moody Blues and so impressed drummer Graeme Edge that he produced a tape of their songs, most of which were written by Knowles. Reluctant to sign them to his own Threshold label because of their similarity to The Moodies themselves, he tried to find them a deal elsewhere. He failed, and shortly afterwards the group broke up.

THE KNACK A mid-sixties London mod group, named after the film, they recorded for both Decca and Pye, but spent most of their time working in Germany. They later became The Gun (q.v.).

BRIAN KNIGHT'S BLUES BY SIX A blues group who played the London clubs in 1963-4, including The Marquee (q.v.), their drummer for a short while was Charlie Watts, in between leaving Alexis Korner's Blues Incorporated (q.v.) and joining The Rolling Stones (q.v.).

TONY KNIGHT'S CHESSMEN A Decca recording outfit of the mid-sixties, their saxophonist was Lol Coxhill, who later played with Delivery (q.v.) and Kevin Ayers and The Whole World, before making several albums himself during the seventies.

THE KOOBAS A Liverpool group, who were formed as The Kubas after the Merseybeat boom had started, they made the obligatory trip to Hamburg and then became one of Brian Epstein's (q.v.) later signings. They appeared in 'Ferry Cross The Mersey' in 1965, toured with The Beatles (q.v.) later in the same year, and made several singles for Columbia and Pye - including 'I Love Her' and 'Take Me For A Little While' - as well as an album... but somehow avoided making any great impression on the general public.

ALEXIS KORNER A seminal influence on British blues and R&B during the sixties, and after, this colourful, cosmopolitan figure was born of mixed Greek/Turkish and Austrian parentage in Paris in 1928. Coming to England at the outbreak of the Second World War, he had several jobs after leaving school before starting his career as a professional musician in 1948, as a member of the blues group contained within The Chris Barber Jazz Band.

He then joined the skiffle group that was part of The Ken Colyer Band, and in 1953 formed a blues duo with Cyril Davies (q.v.). The pair rejoined Chris Barber in 1956, and stayed with him until 1961, although by the latter years they were busy with outside projects, running blues and folk evenings in various pubs and clubs.

In late 1961 Korner and Davies broke away and formed Blues Incorporated, a loose-knit aggregation of musicians and singers, who eventually got a residency at the Marquee club (q.v.) in Soho. As the popularity of Blues Incorporated and the kind of music they played spread, fans started literally travelling from all over the country to witness the "Blues Evenings", and in 1962 they recorded a live album, 'R&B From The Marquee', for Decca's Ace of Clubs label.

Numerous musicians and vocalists who were later to find fame and fortune sat in with Blues Incorporated during these sessions, including Paul Jones, Eric Burdon, Long John Baldry (q.v.), Mick Jagger, drummers Phil Seamen, Ginger Baker and Charlie Watts, bassists Jack Bruce and Lee Jackson, guitarist Brian Jones, organist Graham Bond (q.v.), and sax player Dick Heckstall-Smith.

Davies left to form his Rhythm and Blues All Stars (q.v.) at the end of 1961, and Korner kept on working the clubs over the next few years while his former acolytes reaped the financial rewards and public acclaim. In 1964 he made two more albums, 'Red Hot From Alex' for Trans-atlantic and 'At The Cavern' for Ace Of Clubs, but nothing else for the next three years, as he concentrated on touring and sessions... which included a stint in the house band on the children's TV show 'Five O'Clock Club'.

His touring at this point was done largely with bassist Danny Thompson and drummer Terry Cox, who were later in Pentangle (q.v.).

In 1967 he returned to recording with another pair of albums, 'I Wonder Who' for Fontana and 'Wednesday Night Prayer Meeting' The following year came 'New Generation Of Blues', his first album to concentrate on vocals, and a touring band which included vocalist Robert Plant, shortly before he joined Led Zeppelin (q.v.).

Korner then teamed up with Danish bluesman Peter Thorup, and together they formed New Church. This group nearly included Brian Jones, who had just left The Rolling Stones (q.v.), but Korner was reluctant to court the type of attention that having such a luminary in the line-up would attract, and encouraged Jones to form his own group instead. The group did, however, include bassist Colin Hodgkinson, who later led the jazz-rock trio Back Door. Ironically they were one of the groups on the bill at the Stones' Hyde Park concert, a few days after Jones' death.

New Church lasted until the end of 1970, at which point Korner and Thorup led the session group C.C.S. (Collective Consciousness Society) who had a series of hits on Mickie Most's (q.v.) RAK label, including versions of Led Zeppelin's (q.v.) 'Whole Lotta Love' (which became the theme for Top Of The Pops and Donovan's (q.v.) 'Walking'.

Returning to something closer to the style associated with him, Korner formed Snape, a short-lived venture with Thorup, and Mel Collins (sax), Ian Wallace (drums) and Boz Burrell (bass), all of whom had just left King Crimson (q.v.). Snape made one album, 'Accidentally Born In New Orleans', for Transatlantic in 1973.

Still very active, both as a musician and a broadcaster, the high esteem in which Korner is held is demonstrated by the stellar figures, such as Steve Marriott and Keith Richard, who continue to join him for recordings.

BILLY J. KRAMER AND THE DAKOTAS Kramer was born William Howard Ashton in Liverpool (his sister is Elkie Brooks (q.v.)), and he began his musical career as guitarist with The Coasters (q.v.). One night his guitar was stolen, so rather than stand around looking useless he sang...with such effect that he became the group's frontman, and changed his name to Billy J. Kramer.

Later in 1962 he was discovered by Brian Epstein (q.v.), who got rid of The Coasters and matched Kramer with Manchester group The Dakotas (q.v.). They had the good sense to make their debut single for Parlophone a Lennon/McCartney song, 'Do You Want To Know A Secret'. This record promptly reached No.2 in June 1965, and when they repeated the formula with 'Bad To Me' at the end of the summer, it went one better.

Their debut album, released in November 1963, also made the charts, and at the same time 'I'll Keep You Satisfied' was another Top Five entry. They broke with tradition for 'Little Children', their first single not to be a Lennon/McCartney song, but it was their second Number One in early 1964. A return to their staple source of material for 'From A Window' gave them another Top Ten hit in the summer, but it was to be their last success, apart from a version of 'Trains And Boats And Planes' by Burt Bacharach, which reached No.12 in the middle of 1965.

Although he was a good-looking lad in the Billy Fury mould, Kramer was not a particularly strong vocalist and an uncharismatic performer, and with the passing of the Merseybeat hue and cry, his popularity waned rapidly. In 1966 he and The Dakotas parted company, and after a couple of singles for Reaction - 'Sorry' and 'The Town Of Tuxley Toymaker' - he vanished into the obscurity of the variety club circuit.

THE KREWCATS Starting life in the late fifties as Marty Wilde's backing group, The Wildcats, they became The Krewcats and made several instrumental singles for HMV in the early sixties, of which 'Trambone' was a minor hit in 1961. Drummer Brian Bennett and bassist Brian "Licquorice" Locking joined The Shadows (q.v.) in late 1961 and 1962 respectively.

DENNY LAINE'S STRING BAND – LED ZEPPELIN

DENNY LAINE'S STRING BAND An interesting but comparatively short-lived outfit, whose use of amplified string instruments was probably the inspiration for the Electric Light Orchestra, formed in 1971 by Laine's fellow-Brummies Roy Wood and Jeff Lynne from The Move (q.v.).

Their Deram singles included 'Too Much In Love' and the superb 'Say You Don't Mind' in 1968, but they never found mass acceptance, despite several appearances on John Peel's (q.v.) 'Top Gear'.

Laine himself had been lead singer with The Moody Blues (q.v.), and during the seventies became Paul McCartney's right hand man in Wings. The group's drummer was the ubiquitous Viv Prince (q.v.).

THE LEAGUE OF GENTLEMEN Jonathan Kent (vocals), Ron Cleave (lead guitar), Ron Thomas (rhythm guitar), Joel James (sax), Jeff Bentley (bass) and Raymond Steadman (drums) were an early to mid-sixties soul band, who toured both in their own right and as the backing band for visiting Americans.

Frontman Kent was a dashing figure, resplendent in top hat and black cloak, but their recording career with Columbia and Planet was nothing like as eye-catching.

LED ZEPPELIN Jimmy Page had achieved near-legendary status as a session guitarist when he joined The Yardbirds (q.v.) in 1966, replacing bassist Paul Samwell-Smith. Page on bass was a palpably ridiculous waste, so guitarist Chris Dreja was swiftly moved over, leaving Page to share a formidable dual-guitar spearhead with Jeff Beck (q.v.).

Beck left soon afterwards, however, having suffered a breakdown during the group's American tour, but The Yardbirds soldiered on under the aegis of Mickie Most (q.v.) until the summer of 1968, when vocalist Keith Relf and drummer Jim McCarty left to form Together (q.v.). Chris Dreja went into photography, thus leaving Page high and dry to undertake the formation of a new group.

He first approached singer/guitarist Terry Reid, but Reid was under contract to Most as a solo artist. He did, however, mention Robert Plant, who had been with The Band Of Joy (q.v.) and was currently with Alexis Korner (q.v.). Plant himself recommended his old Band Of Joy colleague, drummer John Bonham, and Page recruited bassist and keyboard player John Paul Jones (real name John Baldwin), with whom he had done numerous sessions.

This line-up toured Scandinavia as The New Yardbirds, but on their return in October 1968 they became Led Zeppelin, at the suggestion of John Entwhistle and Keith Moon from The Who (q.v.). The legacy of Page's early connections still hung with them for a while, but this did them little harm, especially in America where The Yardbirds had been huge.

Their British debut was at the Marquee (q.v.), and after Peter Grant, an ex-wrestler who has himself become a legend as Zeppelin's manager, had negotiated a deal for them with Atlantic Records, they recorded their first album.

'Led Zeppelin', a compelling mixture of blues and hard-hitting rock, was an instant chartbuster on both sides of the Atlantic. The Page/Plant combination had become one of rock's most potent almost overnight, and Jones and Bonham were hailed as the world's premier rhythm section.

A lengthy tour of the States established their superstar status, and at the end of 1969 'Led Zeppelin II' topped both the British and American charts. A similar blend to their debut, it has since become one of the biggest perennial sellers of all time, although the group's uncredited "borrowing" of old blues classics has caused some controversy and ill-feeling.

Back at home, Zeppelin made an indelible impression with their performance at the Bath Festival, but throughout their careers they have been relatively infrequent visitors to the British concert stages. 'Led Zeppelin III' came out in November 1970 amidst a stir caused by the group's considerable (and not altogether impressive) use of more acoustic-flavoured material. It was another huge seller, however, as was 'Led Zeppelin IV' in 1971, which saw the group making more assured use of their diverse styles and yielded 'Stairway To Heaven', which was to take over from 'Whole Lotta Love' as their anthem.

By now acclaimed as the world's top group, Zeppelin have maintained their position and mystique by judiciously rationing their personal appearances and by rigid control over their recordings. Zeppelin have never released a single in this country, and have only made one (very early) TV appearance. They have also only given infrequent interviews.

Even demi-gods are not immune from the barbed quills of critics, however, and when 'Houses Of The Holy' came out in the spring of 1973, after a lengthy hold-up caused by the album artwork, it was roundly condemned and the group written off as a spent force.

This pessimistic opinion was largely confounded by subsequent live performances, and after founding their own record label, Swansong, Zeppelin produced one of their finest albums, the double 'Physical Graffiti' in 1975.

Other acts signed to the label include Bad Company and Dave Edmunds, and it is thriving, although Zeppelin themselves have been even quieter in recent years than previously. In 1975 a car accident put Plant out of action for some time, but the group were kept in the public eye with their film, 'The Song Remains The Same', a blend of footage from a 1973 concert and personal "fantasy" sequences, which was accompanied by a patchy soundtrack album. 'Presence', recorded with some speed after Plant's recovery, was also a less than perfect effort and Zeppelin have lain very low since. The sad death of John Bonham in September 1980 – while this book was being edited has thrown doubts upon a speculated tour in 1981.

JIMMY PAGE/LED ZEPPELIN

BARRY LEE SHOW – LOVE AFFAIR

THE BARRY LEE SHOW Formed in Aylsham, Norfolk, during 1963, they were originally known as Barry Lee and The Planets. Comprising Barry Lee, Mike Dyble, Tony Dyble, Angus Jarvis and Roger Reynolds, they toured the clubs for a couple of years with an act which ran the whole gamut from ballads through pop to soul, and eventually won a contract with EMI.

Changing their name to The Barry Lee Show they released three singles, as well as one solo effort by Lee, before changing to Pye for a further four singles as The Performing Lees.

In 1972 Barry Lee left to go solo, while the others carried on as The Brothers Lee and, having developed an act based on impressions and comedy, became quite successful as cabaret and TV performers.

THE MARK LEEMAN FIVE Mark Leeman (vocals), Alan Roskams (guitar), Terry Goldberg (organ), Dave Hyde (bass) and Brian Davison (drums) built up a good following in the London clubs during the mid-sixties, playing a mixture of R&B and jazz not dissimilar to that purveyed by the Graham Bond Organisation (q.v.).

Signed to Columbia, they had released one single produced by Manfred Mann, 'Portland Town', when Leeman was killed in a car crash in June 1965. 'Blow My Blues Away', recorded before his death, came out as a follow-up, and then Roger Peacock was brought in to front the group.

He lacked Leeman's *je ne sais quoi*, however, and after 'Follow Me' the group broke up in 1966. "Blinky" Davison then joined P.P.Arnold's backing group, The Nice (q.v.).

LEGAY Robin Pizer (guitar, vocals), Rod Read (guitar, vocals), John Knapp (guitar, keyboards, vocals), Dave McCarthy (bass) and Moth Smith (drums) made one single, 'No-one', for Fontana in 1969, before becoming Gypsy (q.v.).

LEGEND Micky Jupp (vocals, piano, guitar), Chris East (vocals, harmonica, twelve-string guitar), Steve Geere (string bass, vocals) and Nigel Dunbar (drums) were formed during 1968 in Southend by Jupp, who had been in The Orioles (q.v.) prior to disappearing from Southend for about three years.

This line-up recorded 'Legend' for Bell Records, a fine album of Jupp's acoustic blues songs like 'National Gas' and 'Twenty Carat Rocker', recorded in a session which lasted only nine hours. The group then did one gig at Staines in Middlesex, and then broke up.

The album was now due for release, so Jupp put together a new Legend, comprising ex-Orioles Mo Whitham (guitar) and John Bobin (bass), and Bill Fifield (drums). This line-up lasted for nearly two years from April 1969 and made yet another album called 'Legend'...this time on the Vertigo label and produced by Tony Visconti ...but another excellent record.

When Fifield left in mid-1971 to join T.Rex (q.v.) as Billy Legend, he was replaced by another ex-Oriole, Bob Clouter, who was himself replaced by Barney James shortly afterwards. With Clouter Legend made a third album, 'Moonshine', and actually had a hit in Italy with 'Life'. Unfortunately their tour of that fair land was a string of financial disasters and rip-offs, and soon after their return home Legend broke up for good in 1972.

Jupp lay low for several years, but put a new band together in 1975 to play the London pub circuit, where he enjoyed semi-mythical status as a result of the attention focused on Southend by the success of other local bands. In 1977 Stiff Records compiled an album of old Jupp material, and the following year the man made a new one, 'Juppanese'.

LEMON TREE A late sixties group who made a brace of singles for Parlophone in 1968. The first, 'William Chaukers Time Machine', was written by Ace Kefford (q.v.), and produced by another ex-Move (q.v.) man, Trevor Burton, and Andy Fairweather-Low from Amen Corner (q.v.). Fairweather-Low also produced the follow-up, 'It's So Nice To Come Home'.

GERRY LEVENE AND THE AVENGERS An early sixties Birmingham beat group, whose Decca singles included a version of 'Dr. Feelgood'. Their drummer was Graeme Edge, who went on to join The Moody Blues (q.v.).

LEVIATHAN The third British act to be signed to Elektra (after The Incredible String Band (q.v.) and Eclection (q.v.)), Leviathan made three singles during 1968 and 1969 - 'Remember The Times', 'The War Machine' and 'Flames'. Group members included Stuart Hobday, Roscoe Murphy and Brian Bennett, and they were the subject of BBC2 documentary, 'A Year In The Life', before splitting up due to managerial problems.

LINDISFARNE Alan Hull (vocals, guitar), Ray Jackson (harmonica, mandolin), Simon Cowe (guitar), Rod Clements (bass, violin) and Ray Laidlaw (drums) were formed during 1967 from various Newcastle area groups. Originally called Downtown Faction, they were also known as Brethren before signing with Charisma in 1968 and becoming Lindisfarne.

After spreading their brand of folk-rock to the masses with constant touring round clubs and colleges, and several festival appearances, their first album, 'Nicely Out Of Tune', got a very favourable reaction when it was released in 1969...although it didn't sell particularly brilliantly at the time.

The follow-up, 'Fog On The Tyne', was produced by Bob Johnston (who had worked previously with Bob Dylan and Simon & Garfunkel), and was to be the biggest album in the UK in 1971-2. In the wake of this spectacular success, the first album also picked up considerably, and in early 1972 'Meet Me On The Corner' and 'Lady Eleanor' (the latter a reissue from the debut) were both Top Five singles.

In the autumn of 1972 the third album, 'Dingly Dell', predictably charted and a single culled from it, 'All Fall Down', was a minor hit. It was a poor successor to their previous efforts, however, and early in the following year the group split in half.

Clements, Laidlaw and Cowe formed Jack The Lad, making a couple of albums for Charisma, while the others carried on as Lindisfarne and watched their popularity slowly evaporate. Hull also made two solo albums, 'Pipedream' and 'Squire'.

Obviously deciding that their whole was greater than some of their parts, they reformed with the original line-up in 1978, signing to Phonogram. Although arguably failing to recapture their early magic, they were nonetheless very well received.

THE LIVERPOOL SCENE An aggregation of leading Liverpool musicians and poets who formed in 1966 in a mixed-media project with the emphasis on satirical humour. They included poet Adrian Henri, and guitarists Andy Roberts and Mike Hart, and made several albums for RCA, 'St Adrian, Broadway And 3rd' among them.

They were regular favourites on John Peel's (q.v.) radio shows, with such memorable ditties as 'I've Got The Fleetwood Mac Chicken Shack John Mayall Can't Fail Blues', 'The Entry Of God Into Liverpool' and 'The Woo Woo'.

Roberts left in the early seventies to form Plainsong with ex-Fairport Convention (q.v.) vocalist Ian Matthews, and then made two solo albums, 'Andy Roberts And The Great Stampede' and 'Homegrown'. After the band's final demise Charisma compiled an album of their finest moments, entitled 'Recollections'.

LOCOMOTIVE A mid-sixties Birmingham band, they featured Chris Wood on sax and flute, who was a founder member of Traffic (q.v.) in 1967. The group carried on after his departure, and in 1968 had a Top Thirty hit with 'Rudy's In Love' on Parlophone. Further singles, among them 'Mr. Armageddon' in 1969, failed to emulate this achievement. Drummer Bob Lamb joined another Birmingham combo, The Steve Gibbons Band, in 1973.

LOMAX ALLIANCE Formed in 1967 by Jackie Lomax, who had been vocalist and guitarist with one of Liverpool's better groups, The Undertakers (q.v.). They made one single for CBS, 'See The People', but then Lomax began a solo career. At the end of 1967 he made 'Genuine Imitation Life' for CBS, and then signed to Apple under the aegis of George Harrison. His first single for them was the classic 'Sour Milk Sea', but it never took off, and although he has continued making albums for Warner Brothers and Capitol throughout the seventies he has never again come so close to a breakthrough.

LOOT Chris Bates (vocals), Bruce Turner (lead guitar), Dave Wright (rhythm guitar), Jeff Glover (bass) and Roger Pope (drums) were a late-sixties group from the Andover area, where Wright had been an early member of The Troggs (q.v.).

Signed by Troggs manager Larry Page to his Page One label, their debut single in 1968, 'She's A Winner', was produced by Troggs drummer Ronnie Bond. The follow-up was 'Try To Keep It A Secret'... which, judging by the sales, they did quite adequately.

LOS BRAVOS Mike Kogel (vocals), Tony Martinez (guitar), Manual Fernandez (organ), Miguel Vicens (bass) and Pablo Sanllehi (drums) were a Spanish group with a German singer, who came to Britain in 1966 attempting to reproduce the success they had enjoyed back home.

Their first single for Decca, 'Black Is Black', was a huge hit over the summer, and in the autumn 'I don't Care' also reached the Top Twenty. After that, however, further singles and an album named after their biggie didn't get anywhere. Several other Spanish groups tried to follow Los Bravos' British success, but fortunately the only long-term effect was a glut of wine waiters.

LOVE AFFAIR Steve Ellis (vocals), Rex Brayley (guitar), Morgan Fisher (keyboards), Mick Jackson (bass) and Maurice Bacon (drums) were brought together in late 1966 by Sid Bacon, so that his son Maurice would have someone to play with. They played the London clubs, including a residency at The Marquee (q.v.), and turned professional in mid-1967, at which point Fisher left (his mother insisted that he went to college) and was replaced by Lynton Guest.

Discovered by producer Muff Winwood, who had left The Spencer Davis Group (q.v.) to work for Island Records, they started recording a version of 'Everlasting Love', which had been a hit in America for soul singer Robert Knight.

Later in the year they re-recorded the song for CBS, using an orchestra instead of the group musicians, but CBS forgot to actually sign them due to an oversight! This error was hastily rectified when 'Everlasting Love' shot to No.1 at the start of 1968, and another Knight song, 'Rainbow Valley', reached No.5 in the June.

At this point Lynton Guest departed and Morgan Fisher returned, but the group had further chart successes with 'A Day Without Love', 'One Road' and 'Bringing On Back The Good Times' - all written by Philip Goodhand-Tait from The Stormsville Shakers (q.v.).

LOVE SCULPTURE – LULU & THE LUVVERS

The group's non-appearance on their records had been given controversial coverage in the Sunday papers.

By the end of 1969, however, their run of hits had come to an end, and early in the following year Steve Ellis left, to form Ellis with Zoot Money (q.v.) and then Widowmaker with Luther "Ariel Bender" Grosvenor from Spooky Tooth (q.v.). His replacement was Gus Eaden, a hippy gentleman whose recruitment was part of the group's effort to upgrade their credibility as L.A. Unfortunately Mr. Eaden's aspirations lay in the direction from which Love Affair had come, and he promptly had his hair cut!

A year later Bacon and Fisher went off to form Morgan, who made one album for RCA, "Nova Solis', and another which wasn't released in the UK until 1979. Mick Jackson also departed, returning home to Bradford to enter the car business. The group soldiered on, however, changing personnel with some regularity, but always finding work in cabaret and variety clubs. When Sid Bacon died in 1974, son Maurice took over the group's management.

Lynton Guest formed English Rose (q.v.) on his departure, but ended up in production and record company work, and in 1974 Morgan Fisher joined Mott The Hoople (q.v.). Between Fisher's exit and Guest's entry back in 1967, Love Affair's organist for a short while had been Peter Bardens from Shotgun Express (q.v.).

LOVE SCULPTURE Dave Edmunds (guitar, vocals), John Williams (bass, vocals) and Bob "Kongos" Jones (drums) came from Cardiff, and evolved from The Human Beans (q.v.) in 1968. At the end of the year they had a No.6 single with their seven minute, breakneck version of Khachaturian's 'Sabre Dance'.

They also made two albums for Parlophone, 'Blues Helping' and 'Forms And Feelings', and a further few singles, including 'In The Land Of The Few', before splitting up after an American tour. Edmunds has since concentrated, with notable success, on a solo career and production projects at his Rockfield Studios in Monmouthshire. At the end of 1970 he had a chart-topping single with his version of the old classic 'I Hear You Knocking'.

LUCAS AND THE EMPERORS Lester Middleton (guitar), Derek "Bugsy" Shepherd (organ), Bob Tuttle (bass) and Stuart Mackintosh (drums) made up Norwich group The Emperors, and they met coloured American serviceman Bruce MacPherson Lucas in 1963.

Lucas was a great showman, as well as a good soul singer, and the combination quickly became favourites with East Anglian audiences. The group mad a demo disc of 'Harlem Shuffle' which was never released, but when Lucas joined The Mike Cotton Sound (q.v.) in 1966 he did the number as a single with them.

The Emperors brought in another coloured American called Rocky to replace him, but only lasted a few months longer. Lucas himself put together several backing groups after leaving Mike Cotton, spent some time with Freddie Mack (q.v.), and eventually went into cabaret.

LULU AND THE LUVVERS Marie MacDonald McLaughlin Lawrie hailed from Glasgow, and became Lulu in early 1964 with The Luvvers - Ross Nelson (guitar), Jim Dewar (rhythm guitar), Alec Bell (keyboards), Jimmy Smith (saxes), Tony Tierney (bass) and David Miller (drums) - as her backing group.

Although only fifteen at the time, Lulu had a quite ludicrously powerful voice, which would have sounded much more appropriate emanating from a middle-aged negress! Not surprisingly, she attracted attention, and their first Decca single 'Shout', reached No.7 in mid-1964.

However, the next two records - Them's (q.v.) 'Here Comes The Night' and 'Satisfied' - only just crept into the Top Fifty, and Lulu and The Luvvers eventually split up. The Luvvers had their own single, 'House On The

LULU

FREDDIE MACK ROADSHOW – MANFRED MANN

Hill' in mid-1966, but then they disbanded. Dewar re-emerged in the seventies as bassist and vocalist with ex-Procol Harum (q.v.) guitarist Robin Trower.

Lulu, meanwhile, embarked on an increasingly bland solo career. She kept having hits of varying degrees on Decca, Columbia, Atco, Polydor and Chelsea; she appeared in the film 'To Sir With Love' in 1967, and had an American Number One with the theme song; she married, and later divorced, Bee Gee (q.v.) Maurice Gibb; and she had been a regular host and guest on TV variety shows. Her biggest record success in this country came in 1974 when 'The Man Who Sold The World', written and produced by David Bowie (q.v.), got to No.3.

THE FREDDIE MACK ROADSHOW This group was a first class soul package, consisting of anything up to a dozen musicians and two or three vocalists, who commenced operations in the mid-sixties. Led by coloured American Freddie Mack, they successfully toured clubs and discos and later became The Freddie Mack Extravaganza. In 1974 Mack, who had been dubbed Mr.Superbad (probably by himself), put together The Mighty Super Power Band.

PETE MACLAINE AND THE CLAN An early sixties beat group from Manchester, whose Decca singles included 'Yes I Do'.

THE MAGIC LANTERNS Emerging in 1966 they signed to CBS and had a minor hit with 'Excuse Me Baby'. The following year they went psychedelic, but disappeared after 'Auntie Greselda'.

THE MAJORITY A group who found particular favour among the upper echelons of British society, they played numerous debutante balls in the mid-sixties. Unfortunately their singles for Decca - 'Let The Joybells Ring', 'Hurt No More' and 'Rhapsody' among them - were not so high class.

MAN Formed in 1968 from Merthyr Tydfil's The Bystanders (q.v.), Man started out as a "progressive" band strongly influenced by American West Coast outfits like Quicksilver Messenger Service.

Their original line-up was Micky Jones (guitar, vocals), Clive John (keyboards), Ray Williams (bass) and Jeff Jones (drums), all from The Bystanders, and Roger "Deke" Leonard (guitar, vocals) from another South Wales group, The Dream. They made 'Revelation' for Pye and 'Two Ounces Of Plastic With A Hole In The Middle' for Dawn, but spent most of their time on the continent, particularly in Germany.

In 1970 Williams and Jeff Jones left, and were replaced by Martin Ace and Terry Williams, both of whom had been with The Dream. This line-up recorded 'Man' on United Artists and the limited edition 'Live At The Padgett Rooms Penarth' which at last began making some impact on the British market.

Although a perennially popular live band with consistent album sales, Man were always hampered by constant personnel changes through the seventies, with members coming and going with bewildering regularity. In 1975 they looked poised to reach new heights when ex-Quicksilver guitarist John Cipollina joined them for a British tour, but the result was less memorable than anticipated, and it is rumoured that Cipollina's guitar parts on the resulting live album, 'Maximum Darkness' were re-recorded by Mickey Jones.

After switching to MCA for 'The Welsh Connection' in 1976, they broke up early in the next year, apparently hampered by financial problems and disillusioned by their inability to expand on the audience they had garnered in the early seventies.

Leonard returned to a solo career, as did Micky Jones; Terry Williams joined Rockpile, with Dave Edmunds from Love Sculpture (q.v.); and Martin Ace formed The Flying Aces with his wife George.

MANFRED MANN South African jazz pianist Manfred Mann arrived in Britain in 1962, and soon formed The Mann Hugg Blues Brothers. The following year they recruited Mike Vickers (guitar, horns) and Dave Richmond (bass), and Manfred Mann was born.

Making their debut at The Marquee (q.v.) in March 1963, they soon replaced Richmond with Tom McGuinness from Casey Jones and The Engineers (q.v.), and in the July made their first single for HMV, the instrumental 'Why Should We Not'. This flopped, and vocalist Paul Jones (real name Paul Pond) was brought in, but the follow-up, 'Cock-A-Hoop', went the same way.

In early 1964 they finally cracked it when the self-penned '5-4-3-2-1-' got to No.5...

helped, no doubt, by the fact that it was used as the theme for Ready Steady Go (q.v.). This was swiftly followed by 'Hubble Bubble Toil And Trouble', again written by the group, which made the Top Twenty, and then in the summer they covered the Barry/Greenwich number 'Doo Wah Diddy Diddy'.

This record went to Number One on both sides of the Atlantic, setting them up for a long run of British success...although they never really capitalised on their opportunity in America. They had another Number One with 'Pretty Flamingo' in mid-1966, and their albums - 'The Five Faces Of Manfred Mann' and 'Mann Made' - blended the group's hits and standards like 'Smokestack Lightning' and 'Stormy Monday Blues', in the accustomed manner of the time, and sold very well.

During 1965 Mike Vickers left to go into film scores and TV commercials, so McGuinness moved to lead guitar and Jack Bruce from The Graham Bond Organisation (q.v.) came in on bass. The group were further augmented for a short while by a brass section which included trumpeter Henry Lowther.

In mid-1966, however, a far more traumatic upheaval occurred when Paul Jones departed in search of solo stardom. He made a good start, as 'High Time' and 'I've Been A Bad Bad Boy' both made the Top Ten, but thereafter he began to concentrate more on acting, and starred in the film 'Privilege' with model Jean Shrimpton. In the early seventies he formed a new blues group for the album and single 'Perfect Roadie' but this was a short-lived venture, and he is now well-established in the world of theatre, and has enjoyed reasonable success with The Bluesband.

Manfred Mann, meanwhile, were left with the unenviable task of replacing him. This they did with Mike d'Abo, from The Band Of Angels (q.v.), who both looked and sounded something like Jones. 'You Gave Me Somebody To Love', the first single with d'Abo and the last for HMV, was a very minor success by Mann's standards, but they soon resumed their Top Ten habits after moving to Fontana.

MARAUDERS—CATHY McGOWAN

In 1967 Bruce left and was replaced by Klaus Voorman, the German bassist from Paddy, Klaus and Gibson (q.v.), and not long afterwards they had their third Number One with Bob Dylan's 'Mighty Quinn'. Their albums - 'Soul Of Mann', 'As Is', 'Up The Junction' (the film soundtrack), and 'Mighty Garvey' - were doing less well, however, and the group members were anxious to do something a little more stimulating than churn out hit singles written by other people.

When they finally split up in June 1969, shortly after 'Ragamuffin Man' had given them their fifteenth Top Twenty hit, McGuinness formed McGuinness Flint with ex-John Mayall (q.v.) drummer Hughie Flint, and had two big hits with 'When I'm Dead And Gone' and 'Malt And Barley Blues'. D'Abo went solo, but had more success as a songwriter, before teaming up with Mike Smith from The Dave Clark Five (q.v.) as Smith D'Abo in 1976. Klaus Voorman resumed his Beatles (q.v.) connection with The Plastic Ono Band, and also did a fair amount of session work.

Mann and Hugg, back on their own once again, launched Manfred Mann Chapter Three, a jazz-rock band with a brass section who made two albums for Vertigo before splitting up. Mann then formed Manfred Mann's Earth Band, a more hard-rock orientated venture, which has built up a considerable international following.

THE MARAUDERS A R&B group from Stoke on Trent whose Decca singles included 'That's What I Want', which was a minor hit in the summer of 1963, and Little Richard's 'Lucille' in 1964

THE MARBLES A duo who reached No.5 in late 1968 with 'Only One Woman', a song written by The Bee Gees (q.v.). The follow-up, 'The Walls Fell Down', also made the Top Thirty. One of the pair, Graham Bonnet, was actually the Gibb brothers' cousin, and when The Marbles rolled off he began a solo career with some success on the continent and down under. He was married to actress and singer Adrienne Posta. In 1979 Bonnett became vocalist with Ritchie Blackmore's Rainbow.

MARK FOUR Kenny Pickett (vocals), Eddie Phillips (guitar), John Dalton (bass) and Jack Jones (drums) made a couple of singles - 'Hurt Me If You Will' for Decca in 1965, and 'Work All Day' for Fontana the following year. When Dalton joined The Kinks (q.v.) the group changed their name to Creation (q.v.).

MARMALADE Dean Ford (vocals), Junior Campbell (guitar, keyboards), Pat Fairley (guitar), Graham Knight (bass) and Alan Whitehead (drums) started life in the mid-sixties as Dean Ford and The Gaylords (q.v.), playing soul and Tamla Motown covers.

After becoming Marmalade and turning to out-and-out pop in 1967, they had their first Top Ten hit in mid-1968 with 'Little Things' on CBS. 'Wait For Me Marianne' sneaked into the Top Thirty, and early in 1969 they topped the charts with a cover of The Beatles' (q.v.) 'Ob-La-Di Ob-La-Da'.

When they moved to Decca at the end of the year they had several further successes, penned by Campbell, but then he left to go solo, making the Top Twenty with 'Hallelujah Freedom' and 'Sweet Illusion'.

In 1971 the group's "nice boys" image received a dreadful tarnishing when a Sunday newspaper exposed the hanky panky that went on during their tours, and soon afterwards they broke up. Ford tried to come back as a solo artist, without much joy, and in 1976 Knight and Whitehead reformed Marmalade with Sandy Newman (lead guitar, vocals) and Charlie Smith (guitar). They had a Top Ten entry with 'Falling Apart At The Seams'.

THE MARQUEE CLUB Run by Jack Barry, the Marquee started out as a jazz club, but moved to R&B when it changed location to Wardour Street in Soho and Alexis Korner (q.v.) began holding his blues sessions there. It was at The Marquee that The Rolling Stones (q.v.) played their first proper date, when Korner and his mates had gone off to do a radio session, and since then innumerable groups have had their first big break there. In the early seventies the club went through a leaner spell, but later recovered its prestige as a launching pad for punk and new wave groups. The Marquee organisation is also responsible for the annual Reading Festival, which evolved out of the National Jazz and Blues Federation festivals of the sixties.

BERYL MARSDEN A popular Merseybeat singer who was originally backed by The Crew, she made several singles in the early sixties, including 'I Know' and 'Who You Gonna Hurt', which was moderately successful. In 1966 she joined Shotgun Express (q.v.), and on the demise of this outfit formed She Trinity, an all-girl group. In 1976 she was still plugging away, touring with a group called The Gamblers (q.v.).

THE MASSED ALBERTS A trad jazz styled group with the emphasis on comedy, somewhat similar to The Temperance Seven (q.v.), they recorded a version of 'Goodbye Dolly (Gray)' for Parlophone in 1964.

JOHN MAYALL'S BLUESBREAKERS One of the three father figures of British R&B, along with Alexis Korner (q.v.) and Graham Bond (q.v.), Mayall put his first group together in Manchester during 1955, while at college after his demob. Called The Powerhouse Four, they comprised Bernie Watson (guitar), John McVie (bass) and Keith Robertson (drums), and after becoming The Blues Syndicate they arrived in London in 1961.

Almost inevitably they became involved with Korner's Blues Incorporated, and in March 1962 the first Bluesbreakers was formed, though only on a semi-pro basis, and with the fluctuating line-up which has always been a feature of Mayall's bands.

Never particularly interested in recording singles (although several were culled from his albums). Mayall made his first album for Decca. 'Mayall Plays Mayall', in 1964 with McVie, Roger Dean (guitar) and Hughie Flint (drums). It wasn't until the following year, however, that the group came to prominence when Eric Clapton joined from The Yardbirds (q.v.). The 'Bluesbreakers' album was recorded with him, and was a richly-deserved commercial success. By 1966, however, the graffiti announcing that "Clapton Is God" had begun to appear on the walls of the capital, and later in the year Clapton left to form Cream (q.v.) with another ex-Mayall man, bassist Jack Bruce.

'Blues Alone' was recorded in late '66 with Mayall overdubbing vocals, guitar, keyboards, bass and harmonica, assisted only by ex-Artwoods (q.v.) drummer Keef Hartley. After that it was back to ever-changing Bluesbreakers and further successful albums in 'A Hard Road', 'Crusade' and 'Bare Wires', as well as two live albums, 'Diary Of A Band Vols. 1 & 2'.

For all the fine music encapsulated on these albums, The Bluesbreakers (of which Mayall himself was undisputed boss...even to the extent of having the rest of the band crammed into the front of their van after gigs, while he slept on a bed in the back!) are generally remembered as a remarkable breeding ground for young musicians who later went on to great things.

Apart from those already mentioned, the lengthy rota of Mayall sidemen includes Jon Hiseman, Dick Heckstall-Smith and Tony Reeves, who all formed Colosseum (q.v.); guitarists Peter Green, who joined John McVie in Fleetwood Mac (q.v.), Mick Taylor, who was with Mayall for two years before joining The Rolling Stones (q.v.), and Jon Mark, who formed Mark-Almond with fellow Mayallite saxist Johnny Almond; drummers Mick Fleetwood, who also went on to Fleetwood Mac, and Aynsley Dunbar (q.v.); and bassist Andy Fraser, who was later in Free (q.v.).

In 1969 Mayall brought The Bluesbreakers to a halt and took a long vacation in Los Angeles, returning to make an album about his experiences there, 'Blues From Laurel Canyon', with Taylor on guitar and a rhythm section of Steve Thompson (bass) and Colin Allen (drums), who were both in Stone The Crows (q.v.) during the seventies.

Moving to Polydor, Mayall also started pursuing a jazzier direction with the 'Turning Point' album - the first he had made without a drummer - and it has been a kind of jazz/blues fusion that he has developed in his seventies albums since his move to the States in 1970.

Although perhaps not especially innovative in his own right, Mayall has nevertheless had a profound influence on the course of British rock music, and without him the sixties music scene would certainly have looked far different.

THE MAZE A mid-sixties group from Slough who began life as M.I.5, they broke up when vocalist Rod Evans and drummer Ian Paice joined Deep Purple (q.v.) in 1967.

CATHY McGOWAN With her fringe, toothy grin and dress sense she was the perfect female reflection of the mod generation, and so was plucked from obscurity to host 'Ready Steady Go' (q.v.)

JOHN MAYALL

ME & THEM – MIGHTY AVENGERS

She was frequently struck dumb with awe when talking to the groups on the show, and "super" and "fabulous" seemed to be the limit of her critical vocabulary (especially referring to The Dave Clark Five (q.v.)). Nevertheless, she was ideal for the show, and she became such a figurehead among teenage girls that Cathy McGowan fashions and make-up were not long appearing on the market. She later married actor Hywel Bennett, and when the marriage fell apart in 1975 she attempted to make a comeback. Though nothing like so disastrous as Simon Dee's, it was hardly spectacular.

ME AND THEM An early to mid-sixties beat group, whose Pye singles included Buddy Knox's death song 'I Think I'm Gonna Kill Myself' in 1964.

THE MEASLES An excellent, raw-sounding R&B group from Manchester, led by vocalist Red Hoffman, they made several singles for Columbia – 'Casting My Spell' and 'Night People' in 1965 among them – but never proved particularly contagious.

THE MERSEYBEATS Tony Crane (lead guitar, vocals), Aaron Williams (rhythm guitar), Billy Kinsley (bass) and John Banks (drums) were one of the best groups to be thrown up by the Merseybeat era. Although they concentrated on slow, romantic numbers for their singles, their EPs and albums showed much greater versatility and a capacity for honest-to-goodness rock'n'roll.

Formed by Crane and Kinsley, who had been in The Mavericks before, The Merseybeats made the Top Thirty with their first single for Fontana, 'It's Love That Really Counts' in 1963.

Early in the next year 'I Think Of You' went into the Top Five, after being given a glowing testimonial by The Beatles (q.v.) on 'Juke Box Jury', but then Billy Kinsley suddenly walked out. He was replaced by Bob Garner, who joined Creation (q.v.) in 1967, and then Johnny Gustafson from The Big Three (q.v.).

Carrying on regardless, they had further Top Twenty hits with 'Don't Turn Around' and the Bacharach/David song 'Wishin' and Hopin'' during 1964, and their debut album was also a good seller. With their good looks, frilly shirts and 'Free Love' inscribed on Banks' drum kit they incited a hysterical reaction from their predominantly female audience, and looked set for even greater glory.

However, 'Last Night', 'I Love You Yes I Do' and 'I Stand Accused' did only moderately well, 'Don't Let It Happen To Us' flopped completely, and in January 1966 – not long after Billy Kinsley had returned to the fold – The Merseybeats called it a day.

Aaron Williams retired from professional music; Banks linked up with Gustafson as John and Johnny (q.v.); and Crane and Kinsley became The Merseys (q.v.).

THE MERSEYS A duo formed by Tony Crane and Billy Kinsley in early 1966 after the demise of The Merseybeats (q.v.), they used another Liverpool group, The Fruit Eating Bears (q.v.), as their backing band.

They started famously when 'Sorrow' reached No.4 in the charts, and although the rest of their singles for Fontana – including 'So Sad About Us', 'Rhythm Of Love', and 'Cat' – were all misses, Crane and Kinsley stayed together on the cabaret circuit for several years.

After they had parted company in the seventies Crane formed his own eponymous group, while Kinsley hit the charts yet again with Liverpool Express.

METHUSELAH A late sixties band who made two albums for Elektra (only one of which was released), their line-up included guitarists John Gladwin and Terry Wincott, who later formed Amazing Blondel and made several albums on Island.

THE MIGHTY AVENGERS Tony Campbell (lead guitar, vocals), Mike Linnell (bass, lead vocals), Tony Machon (rhythm guitar) and Biffo Beech (drums) were a Rugby based group who had a minor hit

THE MERSEYBEATS

MIGHTY BABY – MOODY BLUES

on Decca in late 1964 with the Jagger/Richard song 'So Much In Love', which was produced by Andrew Loog Oldham (q.v.) and arranged by John Paul Jones in his pre-Led Zeppelin (q.v.) days. Unfortunately for them, two further versions of Jagger/Richard songs, 'Blue Turns To Grey' and 'Sleepy City', didn't even do that well.

MIGHTY BABY Formed in the late sixties from the remnants of The Action (q.v.), they made albums for Head Records and Polydor. Guitarist Martin Stone later fronted Chilly Willy and The Red Hot Peppers.

THE MIGIL FIVE Gil Lucas (piano), Lenny Blanche (bass) and Mike Felix (drums, vocals) started out in 1961 as a jazz trio. Seeing which way the wind was blowing, however, they added guitarist Red Lambert and switched to pop music securing a residency at Tottenham Royal Ballroom in 1963 as The Migil Four.

Their first single on Pye, 'Maybe', was a flop, but after they expanded to The Migil Five with the addition of sax player Alan Watson, on the recommendation of Kenny Ball, they had a No.7 hit with a blue beat version of 'Mockingbird Hill'.

This was followed by a Top Thirty entry, 'Near You', but further singles, an EP and an album named after their big hit did nothing, and in 1967 the group moved onto the cabaret circuit.

THE MINDBENDERS Eric Stewart (guitar, vocals), Bob Land (bass) and Ric Rothwell (drums) set out from Manchester in 1963 as Wayne Fontana's (q.v.) backing group. Dissatisfaction between singer and group eventually set in, however, and in early 1966 they went their separate ways.

Perhaps unexpectedly it was The Mindbenders who fared the better of the two parties. Their first single on the Fontana label, 'A Groovy Kind Of Love', reached No.2 on both sides of the Atlantic, and later in the year they had a minor hit with 'Can't Live Without You,Can't Live With You', and another Top Twenty entry, 'Ashes To Ashes'.

The rest of their singles and their two albums, 'The Mindbenders' and 'With Woman In Mind', were not so successful, and in 1968 Rothwell left the group to open an antique shop. Land retired from the music business for several years, but re-emerged with Racing Cars in the mid-seventies; and Eric Stewart concentrated on session work before forming Hotlegs, who scored with 'Neanderthal Man' and then developed into 10CC.

MR. TOAD A popular Norwich group of the late sixties, led by vocalist Keith Lamb, who emigrated to Australia in the early seventies, where he formed Hush, one of Australia's top groups. Bassist Alan Fish joined various groups, including Kiss (q.v.), Zoe and Poacher, before becoming part of Tony McPhee's reformed Groundhogs (q.v.) in 1977.

MISUNDERSTOOD American Glen Campbell (steel guitar), Greg Treadway (guitar), Tony Hill (guitar), Rick Brown (vocals), Steve Whiting (bass) and Rick Moe (drums) came together in 1966, and made two singles for Fontana. 'I Can Take You To The Sun' and 'Children Of The Sun', before breaking up the following year. Later in the sixties Hill was a member of High Tide (q.v.).

In 1969 Campbell reformed the band with Steve Hoard (vocals), Neil Hubbard (guitar), David O'List (guitar) from The Nice (q.v.), Chris Mercer (sax) from John Mayall (q.v.), Nic Potter (bass) and Guy Evans (drums). Evans had been with the original Van Der Graaf Generator (q.v.), and both he and Potter were to join the reformed line-up later that year.

This mob made two more singles for Fontana. 'Tough Enough' and 'Never Had A Girl Like You Before', and then Campbell, Mercer and Hubbard all went off to form Juicy Lucy (q.v.).

THE MOCKINGBIRDS Graham Gouldman, Kevin Godley, Bernard Basso and Steve Jacobson made up this mid-sixties Manchester group. Gouldman had previously been with The Whirlwinds (q.v.), and despite the fact that his songs were providing hits for other artists, notably The Hollies (q.v.) and The Yardbirds (q.v.), The Mockingbirds never had a success to call their own.

Their debut single for Columbia in 1965 was to have been 'For Your Love', but EMI didn't want them to do it, so The Yardbirds took it instead. In its place they released 'That's How It's Gonna Stay', which was followed over the next couple of years by 'I Can Feel We're Parting', 'You Stole My Love', 'One By One' and 'How To Find A Lover', for Columbia, Immediate and Decca.

When the group broke up at the end of 1966, Graham concentrated on songwriting and solo recordings, until in 1972 he joined Godley and fellow-Mancunians Eric Stewart (from The Mindbenders (q.v.)) and Lol Creme in 10CC.

THE MOJOS Stu James (vocals), Nicky Crouch (guitar), Terry O'Toole (piano), Keith Alcock (bass) and Bob Konrad (drums) were one of the top Merseybeat groups of 1963/64, after serving their apprenticeship in local clubs and ballrooms and in Hamburg.

After being signed by Decca they missed out with 'Forever', but then got to No.9 in early 1964 with 'Everything's Alright', which has since become regarded as something of a sixties classic.

They quickly fell away from this zenith, however, and after 'Why Not Tonight' and 'Seven Daffodils' had made the Top Thirty later in the year they had no further chart success, although they carried on making singles right up until 1967.

THE MOLES Like Fut (q.v.), The Moles were a mystery group. Their single, 'We Are The Moles' came out on Parlophone in 1968 and was produced by George Martin, so it was suspected that they might be The Beatles (q.v.). In fact they were Simon Dupree and The Big Sound (q.v.).

THE MOMENTS Steve Marriott (guitar, vocals), John Weider (guitar), Jimmy Winston (bass) and Kenny Rowe (drums) were a London band who covered The Kinks' (q.v.) 'You Really Got Me' in 1964. Marriott and Winston both went on to The Small Faces (q.v.); Weider was with Eric Burdon and The Animals (q.v.) and then Family (q.v.); and Rowe resurfaced in the seventies with Capability Brown.

ZOOT MONEY'S BIG ROLL BAND George Bruno (Zoot Money) came to London from Bournemouth, and formed his Big Roll Band in 1964. They played jazz and soul-tinged style of R&B, and quickly established themselves on the London club circuit, particularly at The Flamingo (q.v.).

They were also signed up by Decca, but after their first single, 'Uncle Willie', had bombed out they moved to Columbia. Despite their live popularity and Money's flair for showmanship (he loved dressing up and comic antics) they had to wait until mid-1966 after 'Bring It Home To Me', 'Please Stay', 'Something is Worrying Me', 'Many Faces Of Love', and 'Let's Run For Cover' had all failed - before 'Big Time Operator' gave them their

one and only taste of Top Thirty success.

As well as the singles, The Big Roll Band made a couple of albums - 'It Should Have Been Me' in 1965, and 'Zoot' in 1966. The actual line-up of the group was typically changeable, and among Money's sidemen were vocalist Paul Williams, who was in Juicy Lucy (q.v.) a few years later, guitarist Andy Somers, who went with Zoot to Eric Burdon and The New Animals (q.v.), and saxist Johnny Almond and drummer Colin Allen, both of whom became John Mayall (q.v.) alumni.

In 1967 The Big Roll Band metamorphosed into Dantalion's Chariot (q.v.), which gave Money plenty more opportunity to dress up. In the early seventies, after his stint with Burdon, Money formed Ellis with ex-Love Affair (q.v.) vocalist Steve Ellis, and has since worked on various sessions and backing groups.

THE MONOTONES An early to mid-sixties beat group from Southend whose singles for Pye included 'What Would I Do?' in 1964.

THE MONTANAS A harmony group who had a little uccess with 'Ciao Baby' on Pye in 1967, but failed to follow it up.

MOOCHE Formed in the Chelmsford/Sudbury area during the late sixties, the line-up included Brian Tatum (organ, vocals) from The Baskervilles (q.v.), and Dave Wenthropp (sax, vocals) who joined Supertramp in the early seventies.

Mooche built up a strong following in East Anglia, appeared on Radio One Club, and made one single - 'Hot Smoke And Sassafras' for Pye in 1969.

THE MOODY BLUES Denny Laine (guitar, vocals), Mike Pinder (keyboards), Ray Thomas (horns, vocals), Clint Warwick (bass) and Graeme Edge (drums) were formed in Birmingham during 1963, after Laine had left Denny and The Diplomats (q.v.).

The following year they moved to London, and having won a residency at the Marquee (q.v.) they were signed by Decca. Their first single, the sprightly 'Loose Your Money', didn't get very far, but in early 1965 the slower, almost stately 'Go Now' went to No.1.

They attempted to emulate this feat with 'I don't Want To Go On Without You', but it wasn't in the same class... sounding quite maudlin, in fact...and was only a minor hit. 'From The Bottom Of My Heart' made the Top Thirty in the summer, but after a version of Buddy Holly's 'Everyday' had just sneaked into the Fifty at the end of 1965, things went from bad to worse for the Moodies.

After their big hit they had toured America with The Beatles ('Go Now' was a hit over there too) and made an album 'The Magnificent Moodies', but now they were on an alarming downhillslide which even the arrival of new manager Brian Epstein (q.v.) couldn't halt.

Finally Laine (real name Brian Hines) and

MOONTREKKERS—MITCH MURRAY'S MONKEYS

Warwick (real name Clint Eccles) both left in 1966, and were replaced by another Brummie, bassist John Lodge, and guitarist Justin Hayward, who had been a solo artist with Parlophone.

Their arrival gave no immediate reversal to The Moody Blues declining fortunes, and 'Boulevard De La Madelaine', 'Life's Not Life', 'Fly Me High' and 'Love And Beauty' were all stiffs. In 1967, however, the group embarked on a drastic change of direction, acquiring a grandiose, quasi-classical sound characterised by Pinder's mellotron, replete with "meaningful" and poetic lyrics.

The first album in this new guise was 'Days Of Future Past', recorded with the London Symphony Orchestra, which included 'Nights In White Satin', their first Top Twenty hit for three years

Successive albums - 'In Search Of The Lost Chord', 'On The Threshold Of A Dream', 'To Our Children's Children's Children', 'A Question Of Balance', 'Every Good Boy Deserves Favour' and 'Seventh Sojourn' - continued this pattern, establishing them as one of the world's major groups. To some, the whole concept of the group might have been laughably overblown, but to many they assumed the status of Messiahs.

They also had a run of hit singles with songs taken from their albums, the most successful being 'Question' in 1970, by which time The Moodies were able to form their own record label, Threshold.

After 1973 the group stopped touring and recording, and although there was no announcement of a split it appeared they were defunct, especially when all five members embarked on their own projects between 1974-76. However, with the possible exception of Hayward and Lodge's Bluejays, these ventures were notably unimpressive and unsuccessful, and in 1977 they regrouped to make 'Octave', which went some way towards reclaiming their earlier elevated position.

THE MOONTREKKERS An early sixties instrumental group, their singles included 'Night Of The Vampire', which was a minor hit on Parlophone in 1961, and 'Moondust' on Decca in 1963.

THE MOQUETTES A mid-sixties mod outfit who blended R&B and beat music, they got a recording contract with Columbia, and among their singles was 'Right String Baby But The Wrong Yo-Yo'.

MICKIE MOST Born in Aldershot (his real name is Michael Hayes), the precocious Mr.Most formed The Most Brothers during the skiffle era with Alex Murray (the man who produced 'Go Now' for The Moody Blues (q.v.)), before emigrating to South Africa in 1959.

While there he led The Minutemen, who became the country's leading group by the simple expedient of making copies of American hits. This did at least teach Most the art of production, however, and when he returned to England in 1962 he wasted no time finding groups and singers to work with, and soon embarked on a career of quite extraordinarily consistent hit-making which continues unabated today.

His first moment of glory was with The Animals (q.v.), and having thus established himself he has since worked with an enormous list of artists, who include The Nashville Teens (q.v.), Hermans Hermits (q.v.), The Yardbirds (q.v.), Jeff Beck (q.v.), Donovan (q.v.), Lulu (q.v.) and Rod Stewart (q.v.) in the sixties, and Mud, CCS, Suzi Quatro, Hot Chocolate, Smokie and Racey during the seventies, after the formation of his own RAK label.

In 1963 Most actually made a single in his own right, 'Mr Porter' for Decca, but ironically it was only a very minor hit. In the mid-seventies he became a nationally-recognised figure after his appearances as a panellist on the 'New Faces' TV talent show

MOTT THE HOOPLE Mick Ralphs (guitar), Verden Allen (keyboards), Peter "Overend" Watts (bass)

and Dale "Buffin" Griffin (drums) from the Herefordshire group Silence combined with itinerant vocalist/pianist Ian Hunter in June 1969 to form Mott The Hoople.

Their first album for Island was to have been called 'Talking Bear Mountain Picnic Massacre Disaster Dylan Blues' in acknowledgement to their strong Bob Dylan influence, but ended up as plain old 'Mott The Hoople'

Over the next three years they built up a large live following with their exuberantly frenetic stage act (it was one of their performances which caused the ban on rock music at the Albert Hall) and made three more albums with producer/manager Guy Stevens.

By 1972, however, they had run out of impetus and even broke up briefly, but were encouraged to continue by David Bowie (q.v.), who wrote and produced their first hit single, 'All The Young Dudes'.

Thus revived, Mott went from strength to strength after Hunter had emerged as their frontman and main songwriter. They made two first-class albums, 'Mott' and 'The Hoople', and became widely acclaimed on both sides of the Atlantic.

In 1973, however, Ralphs left to reappear in Bad Company, and was replaced by ex-Spooky Tooth (q.v.) guitarist Luther Grosvenor (by now calling himself Ariel Bender), and then by David Bowie's (q.v.) old guitarist Mick Ronson. At the end of 1974 Hunter also departed, embarking on a rather disappointing solo career, and although the remaining members brought in new people and struggled on for a while as Mott, the group was lost without its guiding force.

THE MOVE Carl Wayne (vocals), Roy Wood (guitar), Trevor Burton (guitar), Ace Kefford (bass) and Bev Bevan (drums) formed The Move in 1965 as a kind of Birmingham "supergroup". In 1966 they moved to London with manager Tony Secunda, and soon took over The Who's (q.v.) Tuesday night residency at The Marquee (q.v.). By the end of the year they had a contract with Deram, and at the start of 1967 their first single, 'Night Of Fear' got to No.2.

This song was written by Roy Wood, as were the string of hit singles which followed it - 'I Can Hear The Grass Grow', 'Flowers In The Rain' (the first record to be played on Radio 1), 'Fire Brigade' and 'Blackberry Way' (their only Number One) - and the group were quickly established as a major chart act.

Not only did Wood have an uncanny knack for writing utterly commercial, but timelessly enjoyable hit singles, but the group had a gift for courting publicity. They attracted attention by smashing up TV sets on stage, and in 1968 they publicised 'Flowers In The Rain' with postcards of Prime Minister Harold Wilson naked in his bath. Wilson was not amused, and served an injunction on the group and their manager which resulted in all the royalties from the record going to charity.

For all their success, the group were remarkably unstable. They changed record labels from Deram to Regal Zonophone and then to Harvest, recording two albums for Zonophone - 'The Move' and 'Shazam'- and one for Harvest - 'Message From The Country' - in addition to their singles.

The personnel of the group also changed regularly. Ace Kefford (q.v.) was the first to go in 1968, forming his own group, and Trevor Burton moved onto bass. Early in the following year Burton also left, to appear later in Balls with ex-Moody Blues (q.v.) vocalist Denny Laine, and then The Steve Gibbons Band. He was replaced by another Brummie, Rick Price.

Ever since 'Fire Brigade' in early 1968, Wood had handled the vocals on Move singles himself, so it was hardly surprising that Carl Wayne eventually departed at the end of 1970, heading for a career as a tuxedoed crooner in the chicken-in-the-basket palaces of the North and Midlands.

In his place came guitarist and vocalist Jeff Lynne from The Idle Race (q.v.), and the hits continued with 'Brontosaurus' and 'Tonight'. By now, however, Wood and Lynne were feeling restricted by the "pop group" image with which the group were irrevocably saddled in this country, and in 1972 they formed The Electric Light Orchestra to run parallel to The Move.

Later in the year The Move finally stopped moving, and at the same time Wood left ELO to Lynne and Bevan, and conjured up Wizzard. In 1973 Wizzard had two consecutive Number Ones with 'Angel Fingers' and 'See My Baby Jive', and Wood had several other successes, both with them and under his own name, but since 1975 he has been keeping a very low profile. ELO, meanwhile, have gone on to be one of the world's biggest groups.

THE MOVING FINGER They developed from the long-standing Norwich group, Gary Freeman and The Contours, who had been one of East Anglia's top groups, employing several of the area's best musicians and numerous changes of musical direction.

In 1966 the group became The Anglians, and recorded a single as such, before ending up as Moving Finger in 1968. They recorded for Mercury, with 'Jeremy The Lamp' and 'Higher And Higher' among their singles, and continued working well into the seventies, mostly on the continent.

THE MULESKINNERS An early sixties R&B group formed at Twickenham art school, their singles for Fontana included a version of Howlin' Wolf's 'Back Door Man' in 1965. Their original keyboard player was Ian MacLagen, who went on to join Boz People (q.v.) and then The Small Faces (q.v.).

MITCH MURRAY'S MONKEYS An early sixties group who recorded for Pye, their leader went on to become a successful songwriter with numerous hits to his credit, including Gerry And The Pacemakers' (q.v.) first two Number Ones.

'N' BETWEENS—NOCTURNES

THE 'N' BETWEENS Formed in the Wolverhampton area by Noddy Holder (guitar, vocals), Dave Hill (guitar), Jim Lea (bass) and Don Powell (drums), they made a single called 'You Better Run', produced by Kim Fowley for Columbia in 1966. They later became Ambrose Slade (q.v.) and then Slade.

THE NASHVILLE TEENS Art Sharp (vocals), John Allen (guitar), Pete Shannon (guitar), John Hawkens (piano), Ray Phillips (bass) and Barry Jenkins (drums) were an excellent R&B/rock group formed in Weybridge, Surrey, during 1962.

In 1963 they spent several months in Hamburg and then backed Bo Diddley on a British tour, where they were spotted by Mickie Most (q.v.), who was on the tour with The Minutemen. He produced their first single for Decca, a version of John D. Loudermilk's 'Tobacco Road' which featured the double vocal attack of Sharp and Phillips with some great stomping piano from Hawkens.

This record went swiftly into the Top Ten in the middle of 1964, and was soon followed there by another Loudermilk composition, 'Google Eye'. The Teens certainly looked set for great things, for they certainly had the capacity to back up their record success on stage, but Decca put surprisingly little muscle behind them, and after 'Find My Way Back Home', 'This Little Bird' and 'The Hard Way' had been minor hits, they faded away from the chart scene.

They kept on working, however, backing visiting Americans like Chuck Berry and Carl Perkins, and making the occasional single, right up until 1969. Several personnel changes took place, and among their later guitarists was Mick Dunford, who joined Renaissance (q.v.) in 1973. Barry Jenkins left the group in 1966 and joined Eric Burdon and The Animals (q.v.), while John Hawkens has since played with various bands, including Vinegar Joe and The Strawbs (q.v.).

In 1974 New World Records put out a compilation of Nashville Teens recordings, which included several of their singles as well as some previously unreleased material.

THE NATURALS Ricki Potter (vocals), Curt Cresswell (guitar), Bob O'Neale (harmonica), Mike Wakelin (bass) and Roy Heather (drums) came from Harlow, and were previously known as The Blue Beats (q.v.). As The Naturals they recorded for Parlophone, and had a Top Thirty hit in the summer of 1964 with The Beatles' (q.v.) song 'I Should Have Known Better'. Their other singles - 'It Was You' and 'Blue Roses' among them - got nowhere.

NERO AND THE GLADIATORS A stomping instrumental combo from the early sixties, they had two minor hits on Decca in 1961 with 'Entry Of The Gladiators' and 'In The Hall Of The Mountain King'. Their guitarist was Richie Blackmoor, who formed Deep Purple (q.v.) later in the sixties.

THE NERVE A Hampshire group who recorded for Larry Page's Page One label in the late sixties. Their singles included 'Magic Spectacles', 'It Is' and 'Piece By Piece' in 1968, the first two being produced by Troggs (q.v.) vocalist Reg Presley.

THE NEW VAUDEVILLE BAND Formed in 1966 by Henry Harrison, who had been the drummer with Cops'n' Robbers (q.v.), they modelled themselves on a twenties/thirties jazzy sound...as might be deduced from their name. It was quite novel, and they enjoyed some success for a while. 'Winchester Cathedral' reached No.4 at the end of 1966, 'Peek A Boo' was No.7 and 'Finchley Central' No.11 in 1967, and 'Green Street Green' was a minor hit at the end of the year. It was a fairly limited idea, though, and it was not surprising that the public tired of it quite quickly.

NEW YORK PUBLIC LIBRARY A group which had a single produced by Mickie Most (q.v.), 'I Ain't Gonna Eat My Heart Out Anymore' on Columbia in 1966. Sadly for them it was one of his rare efforts which didn't work out.

THE NEWS A Norwich-based group who started out in the early sixties as The Continentals, backing coloured American serviceman Milton. After his return to the States they carried on with an ever-changing line-up, and in 1966 landed a record contract with Decca, at which point they became The News.

With the personnel of Andy Fields (piano, vocals), Ivan Zagni (guitar), Harvey Platt (bass) and Denny Royal (drums) they made two unsuccessful singles, 'The Entertainer' and 'I Count The Tears', before Fields left. He was replaced by Peter Miller from Peter Jay and The Jaywalkers (q.v.), but the group broke up shortly afterwards.

THE NICE Keith Emerson (keyboards) and Lee Jackson (bass, vocals) had been with Gary Farr and The T-Bones (q.v.), and Emerson was in the short-lived V.I.P.s (q.v.), before they teamed up with David O'List (guitar) and Brian "Blinky" Davison (drums) in 1967, as the backing group for P.P.Arnold (q.v.).

The group played their own set before backing her, and went down so well that in the October they went off on their own, signing to manager Andrew Oldham's (q.v.) Immediate label.

Coming on strong with the beads and bells at the height of flower power and psychedelia, they released their first album, 'The Thoughts Of Emerlist Davjack', which included two lengthy tracks, 'Rondo' and 'War And Peace', which indicated the style of revamped classics which was to become their trademark.

O'List, probably feeling overshadowed by Emerson, left soon afterwards to crop up again in the seventies in Jet, with Andy Ellison from John's Children (q.v.), and The Nice carried on as a trio. 'Ars Longa Vita Brevis' in 1968 was a blend of Emerson's ambitious tendencies and rather dubious arrangements of songs like Dylan's 'She Belongs To Me' and Tim Hardin's 'Hang Onto A Dream'. They also had a Top Thirty single with 'America' from 'West Side Story', which composer Leonard Bernstein prevented from being released in the States.

'Nice' in 1969 saw them concentrating almost exclusively on the quasi-classical bit, and was their breakthrough album in chart terms. Their position was further enhanced when they joined Charisma after Immediate had folded, and put out 'Five Bridges Suite' and 'Elegy'.

This latter album was actually released posthumously, for The Nice had broken up in late 1970 when Emerson formed Emerson Lake and Palmer with Greg Lake from King Crimson (q.v.) and Carl Palmer from Atomic Rooster (q.v.).

Jackson and Davison both launched their own bands, Jackson Heights and Every Which Way, but when these were less than successful they recruited Swiss keyboard wizard Patrick Moraz for a sub-Nice endeavour, Refugee. Although much vaunted when they first appeared in 1974, Refugee didn't last long, and Jackson and Davison were left in the lurch once again when Moraz went off to join Yes (q.v.).

PAUL NICHOLAS In 1964, at the tender age of 16, Nicholas played piano with Screaming Lord Sutch and The Savages (q.v.), but then moved into drama and in 1967 joined the original London cast of 'Hair' (q.v.), in the starring role of Claude. He stayed there for about two years, then went on to play the title role in 'Jesus Christ Superstar', and followed this with a role in another rock musical, 'Grease'.

During the seventies he has moved into the film world with appearances in 'Stardust', 'Tommy' and 'Lisztomania', as well as having several chart successes as a pop singer.

THE NIGHT TIMERS A popular London club act, formed in 1964 by coloured American vocalist Herbie Goins, who had previously been with Alexis Korner's Blues Incorporated (q.v.). They played a mixture of R&B, blues and soul, and made several singles for Parlophone - 'The Music Played On' and 'Incredible Miss Brown' among them - and even got to record an album, 'Number One In Your Heart', in 1967. As well as Goins, The Night Timers were also fronted by another American, Ronnie Jones.

NIRVANA Patrick Campbell-Lyons and Alex Spyropoulos were a late sixties duo who played a multitude of instruments between them, and recorded for the Island label. They put out several delightful, dreamy singles, including 'Tiny Goddess', 'Darling Darene', 'Girl In The Park', 'Pentecostal Hotel' and 'Rainbow Chaser', which was a small hit for them in mid-1968.

They also released two albums, 'The Story Of Simon Simopath' and 'All Of Us', before moving to Phonogram for two more, 'Songs Of Love And Praise' and 'Local Anaesthetic'. In 1973 Campbell-Lyons made a solo album, 'Me And My Friend', for Sovereign.

NIX NOMADS A popular early sixties R&B group, whose singles for HMV included 'You're Nobody Till Somebody Loves You' in 1964. They were led by vocalist Nick Wymer, who briefly joined The Fairies (q.v.) in 1965 and then returned to Ipswich to form St.Willy Cool School.

THE NOCTURNES A mid-sixties Birmingham group, whose bassist John Camp joined Renaissance (q.v.) in 1973.

OLA & THE JANGLERS—ANDREW LOOG OLDHAM

O

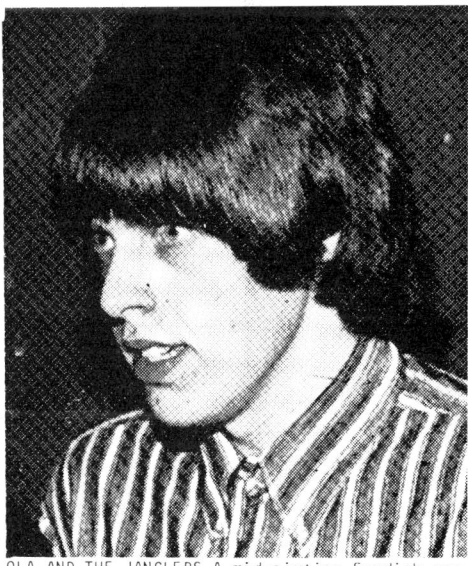

OLA AND THE JANGLERS A mid-sixties Swedish pop group, whose catchy singles were enormously popular back home, but cut little ice in Britain. In 1968 Ola went solo, and his singles included 'What A Way To Die' on Transatlantic.

ANDREW LOOG OLDHAM Starting his career at the beginning of the sixties as a singer masquerading under the name of Sandy Beach (a name which was later modified for Sandy Shaw (q.v.)), Oldham soon realised that his gifts lay in other directions and moved into publicity work.

He was publicist for The Beatles (q.v.) in their early days, but in April 1963 he dropped that to manage The Rolling Stones (q.v.) while still in his early twenties. Oldham's attention grabbing flair was instrumental in The Stones rapid rise to notoriety, but he still found time to discover and nurture other artists, such as Marianne Faithfull (q.v.).

In 1966 he launched his own record company, Immediate, which was very successful for a time with signings which included The Small Faces, Chris Farlowe, Amen Corner, P.P.Arnold and The Nice (q.q.v.). In the following year, however, Oldham parted company with The Stones, and in 1969 Immediate went bankrupt.

OTHERS—MIKE PATTO & THE BREAKAWAYS

After this setback Oldham disappeared to America for several years, but re-emerged later in the seventies to do some production work with Donovan (q.v.) and Humble Pie (q.v.) among others. In 1976 NEMS bought up the old Immediate catalogue, having some success with reissues, and when Oldham became their American director Immediate was relaunched.

In 1966 Oldham made one last entry into the performing side of the business when he formed The Andrew Loog Oldham Orchestra for a one-off single on Decca. As Phil Spector was Oldham's idol, it isn't surprising that the A-side was a version of The Crystals hit 'Da Doo Ron Ron', with Mick Jagger vocalising.

ORANGE BICYCLE R.J.Scales (vocals), Wilson Malone (keyboards, vocals), Bernie Lee (guitar) John Bachini (bass) and Kevin Curry (drums) were a psychedelic era group with the emphasis on vocal harmonies. In 1967 they had a French chart-topper with 'Hyacinth Threads', but that and future singles - 'Competition', 'Early Pearly Morning', 'Jenskadajka' and a version of The Rolling Stones' (q.v.) 'Sing This Song Altogether' - didn't happen at home

In 1968 they moved to Parlophone, for whom they recorded 'Last Cloud Home' and 'Golden Slumbers/Carry That Weight', a cover of The Beatles (q.v.) song which lost out in competition with the version by Trash (q.v.). In 1970 they made an album, produced by John Peel (q.v.), which included versions of Bob Dylan's 'Tonight I'll Be Staying Here With You', Denny Laine's (q.v.) 'Say You Don't Mind', and four songs by Elton John and Bernie Taupin, one of which - 'Take Me To The Pilot' - was Orange Bicycle's last single.

THE ORIOLES Mickey Jupp (piano, vocals), Dougie Sheldrake (guitar), Ada Baggerly (bass) and Tony Diamond (drums) were a Southend R&B group formed in 1963, who built a fanatical following in local clubs like The Shades and The Cricketers playing standards like 'Right String Baby But The Wrong Yo-Yo', 'Brand New Cadillac' and 'Money'.

In 1964 Diamond was replaced by Bob Clouter, who played with Stan Webb from Chicken Shack (q.v.) in the early seventies. Despite their local fame and general excellence, however, The Orioles never managed to get a record contract.

In the autumn of 1965 Jupp put together a new line-up with Barry Scanling (guitar), John Bobin (bass), Clouter and Mo Whitham (guitar), who had lost the chance to join Lulu and The Luvvers (q.v.) when he refused to have his tattoos removed! The group broke up shortly afterwards when Jupp was imprisoned for non-payment of maintenance to his ex-wife.

Three years later Jupp returned to Southend and formed Legend (q.v.), which eventually comprised all the latter Orioles apart from Scanling.

OSCAR A mid-sixties singer who achieved some notoriety with a single called 'Over The Wall We Go' on the Reaction label. This ditty had a chorus which went "Over the wall we go, all coppers are 'nanas", and Oscar appeared on television dressed in prisoners' uniform to promote it. The single never made the charts, but the chorus won some popularity as a street gang chant.

The record had been written and produced by David Bowie (q.v.), who also produced it and sang on one line. A further single by Oscar, 'Club Of Lights', made even less impression.

THE OTHERS Paul Stewart (vocals), John Stanley (lead guitar), Bob Freeman (rhythm guitar), Ian McLintock (bass) and Nigel Baldwin (drums) were a worthy R&B group, formed during the mid-sixties at Hampton Grammar School in Middlesex.

In 1964 they made 'Oh Yeah' for Fontana, which became a minor R&B classic although it failed to make the charts. The group later became Sands, and recorded a Bee Gees (q.v.) composition entitled 'Mrs Gillespie's Refrigerator'.

THE OUTCASTS Ronnie Lane (guitar, vocals), Steve ? (guitar), Ben Chimes (organ), Alan Hunt (bass) and Kenny Jones (drums) were an early sixties group from Barry in South Wales. Lane, Hunt and Jones all went on to The Pioneers (q.v.) before Lane and Jones became Small Faces (q.v.).

THE OUTLAWS Best known as the backing group for Mike Berry, who had hits in 1963 with 'Don't You Think It's Time' and 'Tribute To Buddy Holly', they also made a few instrumental singles on HMV in their own right. 'Swingin' Low' and 'Ambush' were minor hits in 1961, but the others, including 'Law And Order', were not. One of their guitarists was Ritchie Blackmore, who later formed Deep Purple (q.v.).

THE OVERLANDERS Paul Arnold, Laurie Mason, and Peter Bartholomew formed The Overlanders in 1963 as a folky vocal trio. They made a whole string of singles for Pye, including versions of 'Yesterday's Gone' and 'Along Came Jones', but it wasn't until 1965, after the addition of Terry Widlake (bass) and David Walsh (drums), that they had any success.

In the December of that year they cut a cover version of The Beatles (q.v.) 'Michelle' produced (like all their other singles) by Tony Hatch. This went hotfoot to Number One, prompting the release of an EP and an album, both of which featured the song. It was to be their only taste of the big time, however, and in October 1966 Arnold left, to be replaced by Ian Griffiths.

THE PACK Rob Grodway (guitar, vocals), Andy Rickell (guitar, harmonica), Roger Hartley (guitar), Brian Gregg (bass) and Bob Duck (drums) came out of Wiltshire in the mid-sixties. Gregg had earlier been Heinz Burt's replacement in The Tornadoes (q.v.), and in 1965 the group had a modest hit on Columbia with the Lovin' Spoonful's 'Do You Believe In Magic', produced by the ubiquitous Mickie Most (q.v.).

PADDY, KLAUS AND GIBSON Paddy Chambers, Klaus Voorman and Gibson Kemp joined forces in Liverpool during the mid-sixties, and their singles on Pye included 'No Good Without You Baby' in 1966

Voorman was a German student who had befriended The Beatles (q.v.) during their residency in Hamburg. His ex-girlfriend became engaged to Stuart Sutcliffe (the Beatle who stayed behind in Germany), and after his death was also engaged to Gibson Kemp, who at that time was with Rory Storm and The Hurricanes (q.v.).

Voorman came to England in 1965, and as well as playing with the trio he did design work, including the cover of The Beatles' 'Revolver' album. When Paddy, Klaus and Gibson split up in 1967 he replaced Jack Bruce as bassist for Manfred Mann (q.v.), and was later with John Lennon in The Plastic Ono Band.

PANAMA LIMITED One of many "progressive" group signed to EMI's Harvest label at the end of the sixties, their 'Panama Limited Jug Band' album was produced by John Peel (q.v.).

THE PAPER DOLLS A somewhat anachronistic girl vocal trio, with blonde wigs and matching satin dresses, they recorded several middle-of-the-road singles for Pye, of which 'Something Here In My Heart' reached No.11 in mid-1968.

THE PARAMOUNTS Gary Brooker (keyboards, vocals) Robin Trower (guitar), Chris Copping (bass) an Barrie "B.J." Wilson (drums) were formed in Southend during 1962, specializing in black American R&B *a la* James Brown and Ray Charles.

Signed by Parlophone in 1963, they made half a dozen singles and one EP, but despite their natty outfits, complete with suede boots and waistcoats, and the fact that The Rolling Stones (q.v.) described them as "the best R&B group in England", they were not especially successful. 'Poison Ivy' reached the Top Forty early in 1964, but the others - 'Little Bitty Pretty One', 'I'm The One Who Loves You'. 'Bad Blood', 'Blue Ribbons' and 'You Never Had It So Good' - all missed out.

In 1963 Copping had left to go to college, and was replaced by Diz Derrick. By 1966 The Paramounts, who had done quite a bit of work in their early days backing singers like Marty Wilde when they visited Southend, were reduced to backing Sandie Shaw (q.v.) and Chris Andrews on tours of the continent.

Eventually they packed it in, but after Brooker had formed Procol Harum (q.v.) to play the songs he had written with lyricist Keith Reid, and had a No.1 hit with 'A Whiter Shade Of Pale' in the summer of 1967, all the old Paramounts apart from Derrick were gradually reunited.

PATCHES A south coast group, discovered by ex-Roulette (q.v.) Dave Courtney, who became their manager and fixed up recording sessions through the auspices of his old boss, Adam Faith. The resulting single, 'Living In America', sold a grand total of 55 copies, after which the group (not surprisingly) split up. Their vocalist, Leo Sayer, stayed with the Courtney/Faith management team, however, and became one of the country's most successful solo singers in the mid-seventies.

THE PATHFINDERS Ian Crawford-Clews (vocals), Fraser Watson (lead guitar), Ronald Leahy (organ), Colin Hunter-Morrison (bass) and Timi Donald (drums) were one of the Glasgow area's favourite groups when they were discovered and managed by ex-Shadow (q.v.) Tony Meehan in early 1968.

By the April of that year they had been signed by Apple, who renamed them White Trash. This became shortened to Trash (q.v.), however, as the BBC found the full name unpalatable.

MIKE PATTO AND THE BREAKAWAYS A Norwich R&B group who toured the East Anglian circuit in the early sixties, they went through numerous personnel changes, but these counted for little, as the group was definitely singer Patto's baby. He was a good vocalist, in the same mould as Georgie Fame (q.v.) and Zoot Money (q.v.), with a strong stage presence, and after The Breakaways had become The Bluebottles, he moved down to London to join the National Youth Jazz Orchestra.

PEDDLERS—PINK FLOYD

He then had a spell with The Bo Street Runners (q.v.) and Chicago Line Blues Band (q.v.) in 1966, before forming Timebox (q.v.) which developed into Patto at the turn of the decade.

This latter group - which comprised Ollie Halsall (guitar), Chris Holmes (piano), Clive Griffiths (bass) and John Halsey (drums) - signed to the Vertigo label after switching to a heavier style, and made two albums, 'Patto' and 'Hold Your Fire', before moving to Island for 'Roll 'Em, Smoke 'Em, Put Another Line Out'.

They finally split up in 1973 after failing to find themselves a wider audience, after which Patto had a brief spell with Spooky Tooth (q.v.) before reuniting with Halsall in Boxer. This venture also foundered, and Patto's activities became restricted to occasional appearances with impromptu bands like Hinkley's Heroes and Dick and The Firemen. In March 1979 he died of throat cancer after a long illness.

THE PEDDLERS Roy Phillips (keyboards, guitar, vocals), Tab Martin (bass) and Trevor Morais (drums) were a very polished jazz/pop trio whose career spanned a decade. Phillips and Martin had both been with The Tornadoes (q.v.) in the early sixties, while Morais had drummed for Rory Storm and The Hurricanes (q.v.) and Faron's Flamingoes (q.v.).

During their time together they recorded about a dozen albums for Philips, CBS and EMI. In 1965 they had a minor hit with 'Let The Sunshine In'; at the end of 1969 'Birth' made the Top Twenty, and at the beginning of the following year 'Girlie' was another modest success. These latter two singles launched their 'Birthday' album into the album charts.

Although they had originally started out as a jazz-flavoured R&B group in the mid-sixties, The Peddlers moved increasingly towards a slicker style aimed at the cabaret circuit, and made regular guest appearances on TV variety shows.

After they had split up in the mid-seventies Morais joined Decca recording group Quantum Jump.

JOHN PEEL Born John Ravenscroft in Liverpool, he went to America in the early sixties after leaving the army, and got his first experience as a radio disc jockey...apparently on the strength of sharing his hometown with The Beatles (q.v.)!

Returning to England several years later he managed Misunderstood (q.v.) for a while, and then joined the pirate radio (q.v.) ship Radio London. His 'Perfumed Garden' late night show soon acquired considerable influence as he played music, most of it by British or American "underground" bands, that no other radio show was picking up on.

When the pirates were closed down, Peel joined Radio One and kept up his good work on 'Top Gear', which was instrumental in bringing many artists to a wider audience...notably Marc Bolan. At the end of the sixties formed his own record label, Dandelion, which included Kevin Coyne, Bridget St.John, Principal Edwards Magic Theatre (q.v.) and Medicine Head among its signings. He also produced albums for Panama Limited, Toe Fat and Orange Bicycle (q.v.), and wrote a regular column, again entitled 'The Perfumed Garden', for the underground newspaper International Times.

In the seventies he pushed his pen for less esoteric organs - Disc & Music Echo, and then Sounds - and his influence appeared to be waning, until he repeated his ground-breaking activities of the mid-sixties when the punk/new wave era arrived in 1977. This actually meant a complete volte-face so far as the contents of his programme went, but while he lost much of his old audience he rapidly acquired an equally large new one.

PENTANGLE Jacqui McShee (vocals), John Renbourn (guitar), Bert Jansch (guitar), Danny Thompson (bass) and Terry Cox (drums) were looked on as something of a folk-rock "supergroup" when they formed in 1967. Renbourn and Jansch were two of the folk world's most respected solo artists, while Thompson and Cox were busy sessionmen in the jazz and blues fields, and had spent some time with Alexis Korner (q.v.).

Signing to Transatlantic their albums were produced by Shel Talmy (q.v.), and after 'The Pentangle' and 'Sweet Child' had been well received, 'Basket Of Light' gave them their biggest commercial success in 1969 aided by the TV drama serial 'Take Three Girls', which used it as the title track. They also had minor hit singles with 'Once I Had A Sweetheart' and 'Light Flight'.

During the early seventies stagnation set in as it became apparent that their lofty aim of a complete musical *pot-pourri* was not going to be fully realised. The group broke up in 1973, and the individual members returned to their previous activities.

PETER AND GORDON Peter Asher met Beatle (q.v.) Paul McCartney through his actress sister Jane, who was McCartney's girlfriend, and when he formed a duo with his old school chum Gordon Waller in 1964, the fab one gave them one of his songs to record. 'World Without Love' was released on Columbia and shot to Number One, and before they went their separate ways in 1967 Peter and Gordon were to have six more hits.

'Nobody I Know', another Lennon/McCartney ditty, went Top Ten in mid-1964, and in the following spring their lush, romantic version of Buddy Holly's 'True Love Ways' reached No.2. Their other successes included covers of the Teddy Bears' hit 'To Know Him Is To Love Him' and Barbara Lewis' American hit 'Baby I'm Yours'.

They also recorded several EPs and albums, and were even more popular in America than at home. When they split up in 1967 Asher went into production work for Apple, and in the seventies he moved to Los Angeles where he soon found tremendous success as a manager and producer - notably with James Taylor and Linda Ronstadt. Waller, meanwhile, made several abortive attempts to launch a solo career, but the closest he came to recapturing the headlines was in the seventies, when he incorporated an impersonation of Elvis Presley into the role of Judas in the Tim Rice/Andrew Lloyd Webber rock musical 'Joseph And His Amazing Technicolour Dream Coat'.

MARK PETERS AND THE SILHOUETTES A six-piece Merseybeat outfit whose performance of 'Some day (When I'm Gone From You)' was included on Oriole's 'This Is Merseybeat' album in 1963.

THE PINEAPPLE CHUNKS A London group who recorded a version of The Beatles' (q.v.) 'Drive My Car' for Mercury in 1967.

PINK FLOYD Roger "Syd" Barrett (guitar, vocals) Roger Waters (bass, vocals), Rick Wright (keyboards) and Nick Mason (drums) started playing together during the mid-sixties in an R&B group called The Abdabs (q.v.). In late 1965 they became The Pink Floyd Sound, named after a blues record of Barrett's by Pink Anderson and Floyd Council, playing standards like 'Roadrunner' and 'Louie Louie' of howling feedback.

They were on the verge of breaking up when they were spotted in early 1966 by promoter Peter Jenner and underground guru John "Hoppy" Hopkins, who became their managers. Shortening their name to Pink Floyd and playing Barrett's own bizarre compositions, accompanied by a light show and odd antics like sawing up wood on stage, they soon became the darlings of the burgeoning underground movement, appearing regularly at London's new clubs.

They signed with Columbia, and in 1967 their first single, 'Arnold Layne', was released. The quaint tale of a young man whose hobby was stealing women's undergarments from washing lines, it was banned by Radio London, but made the Top Twenty anyway. A couple of months later 'See Emily Play' reached No.6, and the nation's living rooms were disorientated by the sight of Pink Floyd on the telly, sitting on cushions surrounded by drapes.

Their debut album, 'Piper At The Gates Of Dawn', was a tremendous success during the summer of 1967, comprising quaint Syd Barrett ditties like 'Matilda Mother', 'The Gnome' and 'Bike', and a lengthy, spacy piece entitled 'Interstellar Overdrive'.

Unfortunately, as Pink Floyd's reputation increased, so did Barrett's consumption of LSD. He became increasingly bizarre and unpredictable, and in February 1968 was replaced by Dave Gilmour, an old school friend of Waters who was with a Cambridge band called Jokers Wild (q.v.). Barrett meanwhile, became a recluse, emerging to make two solo albums,

JOHN PEEL

PINKERTONS ASSORTED COLOURS—EARL PRESTON & THE T.T.S

'The Madcap Laughs' and 'Barrett', in 1969/70 with the aid of other Floyd members, but resisting all attempts to get him back in the studio thereafter.

Floyd's second album, released in the summer of 1968, was 'Saucerful Of Secrets'. It had only one Barrett song, 'Jugband Blues', and the rest of the album developed the more complex "cosmic rock" which had received its first airing with 'Interstellar Overdrive' and was to become the distinctive Pink Floyd style.

The half-live, half-studio double album 'Ummagumma', 'Atom Heart Mother', 'Meddle' and two soundtracks for films by French film director Barbet Schroeder, 'More' and 'Obscured By Clouds', further expanded their audience over the next few years. They were also a hugely popular live attraction, making up for their lack of personal magnetism with highly sophisticated sound equipment (they were one of the first acts to use a stereophonic and then a quadrophonic PA system) and effects which at various times included crashing aeroplanes, gigantic flying pigs and puppet theatre.

In 1973 they released 'Dark Side Of The Moon', which has stayed in the album charts almost ever since. After this zenith the group's records and tours have become increasingly more sporadic as the basic motivation for carrying on seems to have deserted them. In 1978 both Gilmour and Wright recorded solo albums.

It is certainly indisputable that Pink Floyd have never been the same since Barrett's sad departure, though whether this has been for better or for worse is a matter of personal opinion. The group members themselves certainly seem to have missed him, and their 1976 album 'Wish You Were Here' is largely taken up by 'Shine On You Crazy Diamond', a lament for the errant guitarist.

PINKERTONS ASSORTED COLOURS Samuel "Pinkerton" Kemp (autoharp, vocals), Tony Newman (guitar), Tom Long (guitar), Barrie Bernard (bass) and Dave Holland (drums) came from Rugby, where they were formed in 1964 as The Liberators.

After being discovered by Fortunes (q.v.) manager Reg Calvert they changed their name, adopted bright pink stage jackets, and in early 1966 had a Top Ten hit with their first Decca single, 'Mirror Mirror', which was written by Tony Newman.

'Don't Stop Loving Me Baby' just made the Top Ten later in the year, but further singles for Decca and Pye got nowhere ...a situation which even the abbreviation of their name to Pinkerton's Colours and the substitution of Ian Colman for Barrie Bernard could do nothing to improve.

THE PIONEERS They lined up as George ? (vocals), Terry Newman (guitar), Ronnie Lane (guitar), Alan Hunt (bass) and Kenny Jones (drums). Lane and Jones had previously been with Hunt in The Outcasts (q.v.), and went on to The Small Faces (q.v.) in 1965.

PIRATE RADIO Pirate radio was a quintessential part of the mid-sixties pop scene. The stations were operated from ships anchored outside the three mile limit, or from Martello towers in the Thames estuary, and were largely financed by advertising. Offering a much wider, and more intensive, range of pop music than the BBC, they were enormously popular until the Labour government's Marine Offences Act forced most of them off the air in mid-1967.

The original pirate station was Radio Veronica, which operated off the coast of Holland from 1964 onwards, but the biggest were Radio Caroline and Radio London. There were many others, however, and even Screaming Lord Sutch (q.v.) got in on the act with Radio Sutch, which broadcast extracts from the still notorious 'Lady Chatterly's Lover' every hour.

With the demise of the pirates, many of the DJs - including John Peel (q.v.), Tony Blackburn

Kenny Everett and Dave Lee Travis - went to work for 'legitimate' stations like Radio One or Radio Luxembourg.

THE PLASTIC DREAMBOAT A late sixties group from Norwich, led by vocalist Roger Moon. In the early seventies Moon formed folk-rock group Storyteller, who made two albums for Transatlantic, and then went to America, where he made two solo albums, neither of which was released in Britain. The first, 'Nobody Knows My Name', was produced by Peter Frampton, who also played lead guitar on it. Returning to Norwich in 1977 he formed a new group which was variously known as Fly By Night Removals, The Flys and Yah Boo Sucks.

PLASTIC PENNY Mick Grabham (guitar), Paul Raymond (keyboards), Tony Murray (bass) and Nigel Olsson (drums) collaborated with session singer Brian Keith to have a No.6 hit in 1968 with 'Everything I Am' on the Page One label. The group then recorded an album without Keith, 'Two Sides Of A Penny', and in 1970 Page One put out a sampler of their material called 'Heads I Win - Tails You Lose'.

After this generally undistinguished episode was over, Grabham helped form Cochise and then joined Procol Harum (q.v.) in 1973; Paul Raymond was with Chicken Shack (q.v.) and then Savoy Brown (q.v.); Tony Murray joined The Troggs (q.v.), and Nigel Olsson was with The Spencer Davis Group (q.v.) for a while before drumming with Elton John's backing group.

THE PLEBS An early to mid-sixties beat group who recorded a version of 'Bad Blood' for Decca in 1964. Guitarist Mick Dunford reappeared in 1973 with Renaissance (q.v.).

THE POETS George Gallacher (vocals), Hume Paton (lead guitar, vocals), Tony Myles (rhythm guitar), John Dawson (bass) and Alan Weir (drums) were a Glasgow group signed up by Andrew Loog Oldham (q.v.) in 1964.

After decking them out in corduroy suits with velvet collars and frilly shirts, Oldham produced their first single for Decca, 'Now We're Thru', which made the lower rungs of the charts at the end of the year. Their later singles for Decca and Oldham's own Immediate label didn't advance their cause any further.

BRIAN POOLE AND THE TREMELOES Butcher's son Brian Poole formed his backing band The Tremeloes in Dagenham during 1959 with Ricky West (lead guitar), Alan Blakely (rhythm guitar), Alan Howard (bass guitar) and Dave Munden (drums). Poole wore thick black-rimmed spectacles like Buddy Holly, and the group's music was in something like Holly's style.

After some radio appearances in 1961 they signed with Decca in the following year, releasing their first single, 'Lost Love', and an album entitled 'Big Hits Of '62'...which was just that, an uninspired collection of cover versions.

In 1963, with Beatle mania sweeping the country, the group underwent a change of image, and Poole swapped his Buddy Holly specs for contact lenses. Many people actually thought they were a Merseybeat group, and after 'Keep On Dancing' had missed out, their version of The Isley Brothers' 'Twist And Shout' raced to No.4 in the summer of 1963.

This was followed over the next two years by several successful covers of other people's hits. The Contours' 'Do You Love Me' hit the top spot later in 1963, Roy Orbison's 'Candy Man' got to No.6 in early '64, and an old Crickets' song, 'Someone Someone' was No.2 a few months later. After some more minor success

with 'Twelve Steps To Love', 'I Want Candy' and The Browns' 'Three Bells', however, Poole parted company with The Tremeloes at the start of 1966. He had a brief and unrewarding try at a solo career, and then returned to his butcher's shop. The Tremeloes (q.v.) carried on regardless, becoming even more successful on their own than they had been with Poole.

THE POOR SOULS Chick ? (lead guitar), Hud ? (rhythm guitar), Doug Martin (bass) and Johnny Casey (drums, vocals) were a mid-sixties group from Dundee, who actually spent most of their time based in Norwich. Originally known as The Johnny Hudson four, they landed a record contract as The Poor Souls, and their singles included 'When My Baby Cries'.

THE POTATOES In 1966 they recorded a single, 'The Bend' c/w 'Do The Bend', for Fontana. Both sides were written by successful songwriters and managers Ken Howard and Alan Blaikley.

JIMMY POWELL AND THE FIVE DIMENSIONS Jimmy Powell was a raucous R&B singer who created a stir, but not too many sales, with two great singles on Decca in 1962 - 'Sugar Babe' and a vocal version of Elias and the Zig Zag Jive Flutes hit 'Tom Hark'.

The following year he formed The Five Dimensions, who briefly included Rod Stewart (q.v.) playing harmonica. The group made a couple of singles for Pye in 1964, 'That's Alright' and 'I've Been Watching You', and were regulars at the Crawdaddy (q.v.).

When The Five Dimensions broke up in 1965, Powell formed various new backing bands under the name of The Dimensions, working mainly in the Midlands clubs. In 1966 they recorded 'I Can Go Down' for the Strike label, and later in the sixties one of the Dimensions' line-ups was featured a few times in the ITV soap opera 'The Newcomers'.

KEITH POWELL AND THE VALETS One of several Birmingham beat groups signed by Columbia in 1963, their singles included a version of Chuck Berry's 'Too Much Monkey Business'.

THE PREACHERS An early sixties London-based R&B group with Peter Frampton on lead guitar. They were managed by Rolling Stones (q.v.) bassist Bill Wyman, and recorded 'Hole In My Soul' for Columbia in 1965 before turning to a poppier direction and becoming The Herd (q.v.).

THE PRECIOUS FEW Pete Reynolds (vocals), Brian Crook (lead guitar), Roger Pymer (bass) and Chris Bell (drums) joined forces in Norwich during 1967, where Crook, Bell and Pymer had been in The Versions (q.v.). They played a mixture of pop and Motown material, and in 1968 made a cover of Gary Puckett and The Union Gap's 'Young Girl', which sold moderately well. Another single on Pye, 'The Pleasure Of You', flopped dismally, and in early 1969 the group broke up.

EARL PRESTON AND THE T.T.S A popular Merseybeat

combo formed in 1962, they failed to make it nationally despite singles for Fontana, which included a version of 'Do You Love Me' in 1963 and 'Watch Your Step' in 1964. They were also on Oriole's 'This Is Merseybeat' album, and in 1966, when Preston had formed The Realms, he was on Ember's 'Live At The Cavern'.

THE PRETTY THINGS During the early sixties, guitarist Dick Taylor was attending Sidcup Art College and used to jam in break periods with fellow student Keith Richard. Taylor also played in a group called Little Boy Blue and The Blue Boys, fronted by one Mick Jagger, so when Jagger and Richard formed The Rolling Stones (q.v.) Taylor joined them on bass.

When the Stones turned professional, however, Taylor opted out in favour of completing his art course. When he finished his studies in 1963 he teamed up with another Sidcup artist, singer Phil May, and formed The Pretty Things with the addition of bassist John Stax and rhythm guitarist Brian Pendleton. They had no permanent drummer at first, but when they signed with Fontana at the end of the year, they recruited Viv Prince (q.v.).

The Pretty Things were undoubtedly the wildest. At a time when The Rolling Stones were considered shocking and a threat to the moral fibre of the nation, The Pretty Things were like something out of a nightmare, with hair that was actually long - even by later standards - and even wilder R&B music. They created a tremendous furore, but never got as huge as they should have been...perhaps they were just too over the top for mass public acceptance.

Their debut single, 'Rosalyn', was a minor hit in June 1964, and later in the year 'Don't Bring Me Down' (not the same song as The Animals (q.v.) hit) reached No.10...it was to be their biggest success. The self-penned 'Honey I Need' made the Top Twenty in early 1965, to

PRETTY THINGS—P.J. PROBY

be followed by an excellent debut album, which featured R&B classics like 'Roadrunner', 'Big City' and 'Don't Lie To Me', as well as Bo Diddley's 'Pretty Thing', from which they had borrowed their name.

For some reason The Pretties never went to America - which was crying out for them - but did go to Australasia for a disastrous tour, in the course of which Prince - who had always been the wildest of a wild bunch - got the elbow. He was briefly replaced by Mitch Mitchell, who joined The Jimi Hendrix Experience (q.v.) a year or so later, and then by Skip Alan, who had previously done session work and led The Skip Alan Trio (q.v.).

'Cry To Me', 'Midnight To Six Man', 'Come See Me' and Ray Davies' 'A House In The Country' were all minor hits in late 1965 and through 1966, and in early 1966 a second album, 'Get The Picture', which had been made before Prince's departure, fared disappointingly. By mid-1967 the R&B scene was fading fast, Skip Alan had left to be supplanted by Twink from The Fairies (q.v.), and The Pretty Things had well and truly missed the boat.

After swiftly recording the 'Emotions' album - which jumped on the psychedelic bandwagon with numbers like 'Growing In My Mind' and 'Tripping' - to fulfil their contract with Fontana, Stax and Pendleton both quit, and it looked as if the group was finished.

At this point May and Taylor made drastic changes, bringing in Wally Allen and John Povey from Bern Elliott and The Fenmen (q.v.), signing with Harvest, and writing what was the first "rock opera", 'S.F. Sorrow'. Released in 1968, it gave Pete Townshend the inspiration to write 'Tommy' for The Who (q.v.), but made an undeservedly weak impact on the general public.

Taylor and Twink then left, and Skip Alan returned for the harder rock of 'Parachute'. This was another worthy album which got overlooked, and 1971 the group packed up in disgust. Phil May went off to Greece, and Alan joined a group called Sunshine. One night Alan and the group's manager, Bill Shepherd, were driving in Alan's car when 'Parachute' came on the radio.

Suitably stunned, Shepherd vowed to get the group back together again. He succeeded, and in 1973 'Freeway Madness' was released by Warner Brothers, with a line-up of May, Alan, Povey, guitarist Peter Tolson from Eire Apparent (q.v.) and Black Cat Bones (q.v.), and bassist Stuart Brooks.

Again the album was not a big seller, and the group was on the brink of another dissolution, when long-time Pretty Things fans Led Zeppelin (q.v.) stepped in and signed the group to their Swansong label. With two albums for the label, 'Silk Torpedo' in 1974 and 'Savage Eye' in 1976, proper tours and TV appearances, the group were a respected outfit once more, but in 1977 Phil May left to go solo, and The Pretty Things were finally no more.

THE ALAN PRICE SET Clive Burrows (sax, flute), Steve Gregory (sax, flute), John Walters (Trumpet), Ray Slade (bass) and Ray Mills (drums) were the group that Alan Price put together on his departure from The Animals (q.v.) in 1965.

Their first single, 'Any Day Now', was a flop, but in early 1966 they had a Top Ten hit with 'I Put A Spell On You', and went on to have four more Top Twenty entries before The Set was disbanded in 1968.

Perhaps surprisingly, as Price was such an accomplished songwriter, only 'The House That Jack Built' of these was actually penned by him.'I Put A Spell On You' was an old Screamin' Jay Hawkins number, 'Hi-Lili-Hi-Lo' was from the musical 'Lili', 'Simon Smith And His Amazing Dancing Bear' was by Randy Newman, and 'Don't Stop The Carnival' by American jazzman Sonny Rollins.

They also had a happy-go-lucky air which was a far cry from Price's work with The Animals, although the group's albums, 'The Price To

Play' and 'Price On His Head' featured more bluesy material.

When The Set broke up Price further expanded his audience by teaming up with Georgie Fame (q.v.). He has also made several solo albums in the seventies, been seen on television, and wrote the music for the film 'O Lucky Man'. John Walters from The Set subsequently hung up his trumpet and became the producer of John Peel's (q.v.) radio show.

THE PRIMITIVES A raw, long-haired R&B group in a similar vein to The Pretty Things (q.v.), they recorded several singles for Pye in the mid-sixties, including 'You Said' and 'Help Me'. Their great moment of glory, however, came when they had their hair cut on Eamonn Andrews' Sunday night TV chat show.

VIV PRINCE One of the great looners of the British rock scene, Prince started out in the early sixties drumming with The Dauphin Street Trad Band. He then moved on to Carter-Lewis and The Southerners (q.v.) before joining The Pretty Things (q.v.) in 1963.

Although The Pretties were the most notorious group around, Prince was crazy even by their standards. He hit the headlines quite early in their career by being the first rock star to fall victim of a drug bust, and ended up being sacked by The Pretty Things after an Australasian tour in 1965 when his antics included getting thrown off a plane for being drunk and disorderly, crawling round the stage during the set drinking whisky from his boots, and finally setting fire to the stage.

Prince then made a solo single for Columbia, 'The Light Of The Charge Brigade' c/w 'Minuet For Ringo', formed The Bunch Of Fives (q.v.), played a few dates with The Who (q.v.) as a stand-in for rival arch-ligger Keith Moon, briefly joined Denny Laine's String Band (q.v.), and was chosen for the first incarnation of The Jeff Beck Group (q.v.), but failed to make it as far as the first rehearsal.

He could usually be found, in some state of narcotic or alcoholic disrepair, either jamming or propping up the bar in fashionable London clubs. In 1969 he formed Kate (q.v.), but little has been heard of him since, except when he was beaten up by Hell's Angels in 1973.

PRINCIPAL EDWARDS MAGIC THEATRE A group whose membership fluctuated around the twelve or thirteen mark, they were formed in the late sixties at Exeter University (their name was inspired by the head of the university) and were a multi-media enterprise, with drama, dance and lightshows accompanying their music. John Peel (q.v.) featured them regularly on

Top Gear, and eventually signed them to his Dandelion label, for whom they made the 'Round One' album. They then moved to CBS for 'Soundtrack' before splitting up to go their many different ways.

P.J. PROBY Born James Marcus Smith in America, he made demo discs for Elvis Presley in the late fifties and early sixties, appeared in several Westerns, and toured the States under the pseudonym of Jet Powers.

He came to Britain with his new name after being discovered by TV producer Jack Good, who first displayed him on a Beatles (q.v.) TV spectacular in 1964. A flamboyant character, who wore his long hair in a ponytail and dressed in tight velvet trousers, fancy shirts and buckled shoes, he also had a strong, throbbing voice to go with the image, and his Decca debut single, 'Hold Me' went to No.3 in the summer of 1964.

Over the next four years he had numerous hits, small and large, on Decca and Liberty, including 'Somewhere' and 'Maria' taken from the musical 'West Side Story', and his debut album in 1965 was also a commercial success.

Proby was always a controversial figure, however, and trouble followed him throughout his career. He started off by upsetting theatre managers by refusing to take the stage without being paid first, and followed this by splitting his trousers during a performance. He was given the benefit of the doubt as to whether this was an accident, but when the same thing happened on the next two nights the Rank/ABC organisation decided (not unreasonably) that it wasn't, and banned him from their venues, as did BBC Television.

With a fine sense of ironic humour, Proby's next single was 'I Apologise', which reached No.11 in the spring of 1965. His next headline-grabbing stunt was to proclaim that Welsh singer Tom Jones was rubbish, and challenge him to a singing match. The contest never took place, and by 1968 Proby was bankrupt.

Jack Good came to the rescue with the offer of the starring role of Cassio in Good's rock musical version of 'Othello', 'Catch My Soul'. In 1978 he was playing Elvis Presley in another good musical, 'Elvis On Stage', but after leaving the production he was receiving publicity he would rather have done without, with court appearances for bankruptcy and on charges of assaulting his girlfriend.

PROCOL HARUM – REDCAPS

PROCOL HARUM Formed in April 1967 to perform the songs of pianist/vocalist Gary Brooker, who had previously been with The Paramounts (q.v.), and lyricist Keith Reid, the original line-up of Procol Harum was Brooker, Matthew Fisher (organ), Ray Royer (guitar), Dave Knights (bass) and Bobby Harrison (drums).

Their first single on Deram, 'A Whiter Shade Of Pale', was the biggest hit of that magical summer, with its surreal lyrics and almost classical tune, but ironically it gave Procol more headaches than rewards. The group were not ready to go on tour to back up their unexpected success, and they found themselves the centre of controversy when drummer Bill Eyden revealed that he (along with other session men) had actually played on the record.

Over the summer Procol tried to sort themselves out, firing Royer and Harrison (who later formed Freedom (q.v.)) and bringing in ex-Paramounts Robin Trower and Barrie Wilson, and signing with Regal Zonophone, 'Homburg', another classic single, reached No.6 at the end of the year at the same time as their debut album was released, but it was the last substantial recognition Procol would get in their own country for several years.

The group found much greater acclaim in America, and subsequently spent much of their time there. After two excellent albums, 'Shine On Brightly' and 'A Salty Dog', Knights and Fisher both left in March 1969, and when organist/bassist Chris Copping took the places of both of them, the original Paramounts line-up had become Procol Harum. Knights went into management with Legend (q.v.), and Fisher took to production, as well as making a couple of solo albums during the seventies.

With this contraction of their line-up, Procol's sound became somewhat rockier, dominated more by Trower's guitar than the organ which had always been their trademark. In mid-1971, however, Trower left for a highly auspicious solo career, and Copping was able to concentrate on the keyboards as Alan Cartwright came in on bass. Trower was replaced by Dave Ball, who later backed Long John Baldry (q.v.), who in turn made way for ex-Plastic Penny (q.v.) and Cochise guitarist Mick Grabham.

Throughout the seventies Procol produced a string of albums - including one recorded live in Canada with the Edmonton Symphony Orchestra - and had an occasional minor hit single, a revamped version of 'Conquistador' from their debut album among them. Always well-respected, but never really either gaining or losing ground in terms of their audience, they eventually made a quiet exit in 1977.

THE PURPLE GANG Peter "Lucifer" Walker (vocals), Geoffrey Bowyer (piano, washboard), Christopher Joe Beard (guitar), Dee Jay Robinson (mandolin) and Tony Moss (bass) made one of the best singles of the psychedelic era for Transatlantic in 1967, entitled 'Granny Takes A Trip', it was the story of an old lady going to Hollywood to break into movies. Unfortunately it was banned by the BBC because of the title's drug connotations.

The group made one further single, 'Kiss Me Goodnight Sally Green', and an album, 'The Purple Gang Strikes', and then broke up. Peter Walker later became a Tory cabinet minister... no he didn't!..he became a warlock (really!).

THE QUARE FELLOWS A mid-sixties group from Halifax whose members sported dyed blonde hair and outrageous clothes, they made the front cover of one of the national music papers, and then promptly disappeared.

TOMMY QUICKLY A Liverpool singer from the Merseybeat era, he is best remembered as the artist who was dropped by Beatles' manager Brian Epstein (q.q.v.). In 1963-4 he made three singles for Pye, 'Tip Of My Tongue', 'Wild Side Of Life', a version of the Josh MacRae hit which got into the Top Thirty, and 'Humpty Dumpty'.

Epstein recruited the Remo Four (q.v.) as his backing group, and with them Quickly toured the country and made three further singles, 'Forget The Other Guy' on Pye, and 'Prove It' and 'Simple As That' on Piccadilly. Unfortunately for Quickly, he really didn't have the talent for stardom...or for Epstein.

THE QUIET FIVE They had minor hits in 1965 with 'When The Morning Sun Dries The Dew', and in 1966 with a version of Paul Simon's 'Homeward Bound'. Both were on Parlophone, as was a cover of The Rolling Stones' (q.v.) 'I Am Waiting' later in 1966.

QUIK Signed by Deram in 1967, they made three singles, 'Love Is A Beautiful Thing', 'King Of The World' and 'I Can't Sleep'.

THE QUOTATIONS A heavy rock group formed by ex-Big Three (q.v.) and Merseybeats (q.v.) bass guitarist Johnny Gustafson. They recorded for Decca.

RARE AMBER A sinister-looking blues outfit, who recorded an album for Polydor in 1969. The album sleeve depicted the five group members holding a black mass ceremony, while the actual record contained some good blues playing on several original compositions, plus others by B.B.King and Otis Spann.

THE RATS A mid-sixties R&B group from Hull, their singles included Willie Dixon's 'Spoonful' and 'I Gotta See My Baby' on Decca in 1965, and a version of 'Parchment Farm' on Oriole. Their guitarist was Mick Ronson and their drummer was Mick "Woody" Woodmansey. Ronson later played with another Hullite, Michael Chapman (q.v.), and in the early seventies they both joined The Spiders From Mars with David Bowie (q.v.). Ronson then made a couple of solo albums, and played with Mott The Hoople (q.v.), Ian Hunter and Bob Dylan's Rolling Thunder Review, as well as doing production for several people. Woodmansey tried to keep The Spiders going for a while after Bowie's "retirement", and then formed U Boat in 1976.

CHRIS RAVELL AND THE RAVERS This group recorded a single called 'I Do' for Decca in 1963. Ravell's real name was Chris Andrews, and he went on to have hits under his own name with 'Yesterday Man' and 'To Whom It Concerns'. He was also a fairly successful songwriter, penning hits for Sandie Shaw (q.v.) and Adam Faith, among others.

READY STEADY GO ITV's mid-sixties pop show came on the air early on Friday evenings, with the slogan "The weekend starts here". Hosted by mod dolly Cathy McGowan (q.v.) and disc jockey Keith Fordyce, the recipe of the programme was non-stop live action, and all the top groups of the era appeared on it...along with many who didn't make it. Although it has been off the air for more than a decade now, its flair and energy have never been rivalled in televised pop.

THE REDCAPS A hard-rocking outfit who started off in Birmingham in the early sixties, they landed a record contract with Decca, and their singles included Chuck Berry's 'Talkin' 'Bout You' and The Isley Brothers 'Shout' in 1963. This latter single was vastly superior to the

TERRY REID – ROLLING STONES

version by Lulu and The Luvvers (q.v.), but for some reason the Scots had the hit. In late 1977 The Redcaps vocalist, Dave Walker, was briefly in Black Sabbath in place of Ozzy Osbourne.

TERRY REID After having his first professional experience with Peter Jay and The Jaywalkers (q.v.), singer/guitarist Reid was signed by producer Mickie Most (q.v.) as a solo artist in 1966. After recording two singles, 'The Hand Don't Fit The Glove' and 'Better By Far', which both flopped, he was approached by Jimmy Page with a view to joining the nascent Led Zeppelin (q.v.). Unable to accept because of his contractual obligations to Most, Reid suggested Robert Plant instead.

In 1968 Reid formed a trio with Keith Webb (drums) and Pete Solley (keyboards), who later formed Snafu with ex-Procol Harum (q.v.) drummer Bobby Harrison, and then joined Procol themselves in their latter stages. Reid went with them to America to record 'Bang Bang You're Terry Reid', which featured several of his own songs alongside versions of 'Bang Bang', 'Summertime Blues', 'Season Of The Witch' and 'Something's Gotten Hold Of My Heart'. Neither this, nor the subsequent 'Superlungs' from 1969, were released in this country, and the only impact Reid made here was when Arrival (q.v.) had a hit with a version of his 'Friends'.

Reid has since spent nearly all his time in America, and has made only three albums in the seventies, 'River' in 1973, 'Seed Of Memory' in 1976, and 'Rogue Waves' in 1979.

KEITH RELF While fronting The Yardbirds (q.v.) Relf recorded three solo singles in a more mellow mood. 'Mr.Zero', a Bob Lind song, and 'Shapes In My Mind' were both on Columbia in 1966, and 'No Life Child' was released on Plexium in 1968 under the name of Keith Dangerfield. After The Yardbirds broke up, Relf formed Renaissance (q.v.), then briefly joined Medicine Head, and finally formed Armageddon in 1975. In 1978 he was killed at his home by an electric shock.

THE REMO FOUR An early to mid-sixties Liverpool group who at various times backed singers Johnny Sandon and Tommy Quickly (q.v.), their pianist was Tony Ashton, who formed Ashton, Gardner and Dyke in the early seventies, and then joined Family (q.v.).

RENAISSANCE When vocalist Keith Relf (q.v.) and drummer Jim McCarty left The Yardbirds (q.v.) they formed Renaissance with Relf's sister Jane (vocals), John Hawken (keyboards) from The Nashville Teens (q.v.), and Louis Cennamo (bass), a session musician who had also spent brief periods with The Chicago Line Blues Band (q.v.) and The Herd (q.v.).

Making their debut in 1969, the group took a completely different direction to The Yardbirds, specializing in strong harmony vocals with music that had a classical feel to it. They made one very pleasant album for Island, but then all the original members left. A new line-up of Annie Haslam (vocals), Mick Dunford (guitar, vocals), John Tout (keyboards), John Camp (bass, vocals) and Terence Sullivan (drums) carried on the musical tradition of their predecessors, and became very big in the States...a popularity which finally spread to Britain around 1976.

THE RIOT SQUAD A six-piece beat and R&B group formed in the mid-sixties, they undertook a nationwide tour with The Kinks (q.v.) in 1965, and between 1965 and 1967 made several singles for Pye. Among these were 'Anytime', 'Nevertheless', 'Gonna Make You Mine', 'Cry Cry Cry', 'I Take It We're Through' and 'It's Never Too Late To Forgive', but none of them charted.

The only time that The Riot Squad managed to reach a wider audience was when they appeared in a couple of episodes of the popular TV hospital series, 'Emergency Ward Ten', but unfortunately for them the role didn't involve their music.

Although the group originated in Liverpool, they went through several personnel changes in the course of their career. Mitch Mitchell, who was later with Georgie Fame and The Blue Flames (q.v.) and The Jimi Hendrix Experience (q.v.), was their drummer for a while, and keyboard player Jon Lord from The Action (q.v.) was with them before forming Deep Purple (q.v.).

TONY RIVERS AND THE CASTAWAYS This group began as a hard-hitting R&B outfit from Dagenham in Essex. They recorded one single in this vein, 'Shake Shake Shake' on Columbia in 1963, but then gradually developed into a harmony group. Among their many singles were 'Life's Too Short' and a cover of The Beach Boys 'God Only Knows' on Columbia, in 1964 and 1966 respectively; 'Girl From Salt Lake City' on Immediate in 1966; and 'Pantomime' and 'I Can Guarantee You Love' on Polydor in 1968.

At the end of 1968 they became Harmony Grass (q.v.). The Castaways had gone through numerous personnel changes over the years, and in 1966 they briefly contained Geoff and Pete Swettenham and John Perry, who went on to form Grapefruit (q.v.).

THE ROADRUNNERS A semi-pro Portsmouth band formed by the Shulman brothers, Ray, Derek and Phil, their manager changed their name to Simon Dupree and The Big Sound (q.v.) in 1966. There was also a Merseybeat group around by the same name.

THE ROARING SIXTIES A Leicester group, previously called The Farinas (q.v.), who made a single called 'We Love The Pirates', about pirate radio stations (q.v.), for Marmalade in 1966. They then evolved into Family (q.v.).

THE ROCKIN' BERRIES Chris Lea (vocals) Geoff Turton (guitar, vocals), Chuck Botfield (guitar), Roy Austin (bass) and Terry Bond (drums) began their career in 1961 as a Birmingham rock'n'roll group. They worked in Germany during 1962-3, and then toured with P.J.Proby (q.v.) on their return to England.

They had been signed by Decca during 1963, but their first two singles, 'Wah Wah Woo' and 'Little Bitty Pieces', flopped and it wasn't until they signed with Piccadilly in 1964 that they had their first minor chart success with 'I Didn't Mean To Hurt You'.

During the Proby tour the group met up with American freak Kim Fowley, who played them a song by The Tokens called 'He's In Town'. The Rockin' Berries recorded it, and it went to No.3 at the end of the year. They had a few more successes over the next year or so, the most notable being 'Poor Man's Son', another song pinched from an American group (this time The Reflections), which made No.5 in mid-1965. Their debut album 'In Town' also did well, although the second, 'Life Is Just A Bowl Of Berries', which contained oddities like 'Iko Iko' and 'The Laughing Policeman', did not.

The Berries' big hits had a distinctive falsetto vocal sound, and it was in fact Turton, not Lea, who took the lead on these songs. He later went solo under the name of Jefferson, leaving the rest of the group to become more of an all-round variety act, with the emphasis on comedy and impressions. They continued to make singles in the late sixties, but concentrated on pantomime, TV and cabaret work.

THE ROCKIN' JAYMEN Another early sixties Birmingham group signed up by EMI in 1963.

THE ROCKIN' VICKERS Harry Feeney (vocals), Alex Hamilton (guitar), Ken Whatsisname (guitar), Pete Moorhouse (bass) and Ciggy Shaw (drums) came from Blackpool, and were originally known as Rev.Black and The Rockin' Vicars.

A wild bunch, very popular in the North, they recorded for Decca, and their singles included 'I Go Ape' in 1964...which resurfaced a decade later on the double compilation album 'Hard Up Heroes'. In 1966 they switched to CBS for further singles like Ray Davies' 'Dandy' and 'It's Alright'. For a while their bass player was Ian "Lemmy" Kilminster, who was later in Hawkwind before forming Motorhead.

THE ROLLING STONES Britain's biggest-ever group, excepting The Beatles (q.v.), and introduced for a while (not without justification) as "the greatest rock'n'roll group in the world", The Rolling Stones actually had their beginnings in a Dartford primary school in the early fifties. Mick Jagger and Keith Richard were fellow-pupils there, and when they met up again by accident a decade later, they discovered that they shared a love of obscure American blues and R&B music.

Jagger was at the London School of Economics by now, and Richard was at Sidcup Art College, and they joined forces with Richard's colleague guitarist/bassist Dick Taylor to form Little Boy Blue and The Blue Boys in their spare time. When Alexis Korner (q.v.) started running his blues evenings at The Marquee (q.v.) in 1962, the boys became regular visitors to the club and even sat in on some of the sessions, with Jagger singing and playing harmonica, and Richard on guitar. It was here that they met Brian Jones.

Jones had been a pupil at Cheltenham Grammar School where, despite being twice suspended (once for leading a revolt against prefects, and once for organising a protest against the wearing of mortar boards), he had obtained nine O Levels and two A Levels. Declining to go to university, he had taken several jobs, including bus conductor and coalman, and played with a local group called The Ramrods. After meeting Korner in Cheltenham he had come up to London, hoping to form his own group.

Together they rehearsed their new group, while still joining in the Korner sessions, and when Korner had to miss an evening at the Marquee to do a BBC programme in June 1962, The Rolling Stones deputised for their first-ever gig. The line-up was Jagger, Richard, Jones, Ian Stewart (piano) and Tony Chapman (drums). Dick Taylor, who had been playing bass, had left a couple of weeks earlier to concentrate on his studies, so the group were looking for a new bass player. The job eventually went to Bill Wyman (real name Perks), whose main qualification was the fact that he owned a large amplifier at a time when The Stones were desperately short of equipment.

The group also needed a new drummer, and after trying out several people, including Mick Avory, who later joined The Kinks (q.v.), and Carlo Little, who had been with Screaming

ROLLING STONES

Lord Sutch (q.v.), they finally persuaded Korner's drummer, Charlie Watts, to join them.

After playing regularly at The Flamingo (q.v.) and The Marquee, and various other London clubs and pubs, The Stones landed a residency at The Crawdaddy (q.v.) in Richmond, and it was here that things really started happening for them. Although they were still pretty rough musically, playing blues and R&B covers, they had definite charisma, and soon the hip London scene was flocking down south of the river for their Sunday afternoon performances. Among those who came along were The Beatles (q.v.), and their ex-publicist, Andrew Loog Oldham (q.v.). Oldham, in concert with his current boss, businessman Eric Easton, became the group's managers, and promptly got them a contract with Decca, who were still kicking themselves for having turned down the Fab Four.

By the end of 1963 they had been in the charts twice, with Chuck Berry's 'Come On' and 'I Wanna Be Your Man', which was donated to them by The Beatles; they had been on tour with one of their heroes, Bo Diddley; and they had dropped pianist Ian Stewart, who was considered by Oldham to be visually unsuitable, but stayed on to play on their records and be their road manager.

Oldham, meanwhile, was working overtime on the group's image. Whereas The Beatles were being promoted as "the lovable moptops", every mother's sons and every girl's dream date, The Stones were the exact opposites. Their long hair and scruffy clothes were designed to antagonise the older generation, and although they were actually quite intelligent they went out of their way to play up the "morons" image. On 'Juke Box Jury' they were morose and uncooperative; they were banned from numerous hotels for being improperly dressed; BBC radio banned them temporarily for turning up late to two shows; and they had several brushes with TV producers, notably on 'Sunday Night At The London Palladium', when they were the only act ever to refuse to join the cast on the revolving stage for the grand finale.

The final insult to public decency came in 1965, when Jagger, Wyman and Jones all appeared in court for urinating against the wall of a filling station. To parents they had become a complete anathema, and the kids loved them for it.

From 1964 onwards the hits came thick and fast. Buddy Holly's 'Not Fade Away' reached No.3, Bobby Womack's 'It's All Over Now' gave them the first of eight Number Ones, and Willie Dixon's 'Little Red Rooster' emulated it. They also came out with a debut album, comprising epic covers of classics like 'Route 66', 'King Bee' and 'Walking The Dog', which was a runaway smash success.

1964 also saw them commencing their assault on the American market, and they recorded their great 'Five By Five' EP at Chess Records in Chicago, the home of so much of their inspiration. Apart from that their first tour of the States was moderately disastrous - especially their first TV appearance, wherein host Dean Martin lampooned them unmercifully - but the Yanks were soon to come round.

Jagger and Richard had been writing songs together for some time and other artists, notably Marianne Faithfull (q.v.) had been having some success with them, but it wasn't until early 1965 that The Stones started using their material for their own A sides. The decision finally to do so was fully justified, however, when 'The Last Time' gave them their third consecutive Number One in the UK and went Top Ten in America.

Through 1965 and 1966 The Stones continued a punishing touring schedule, conquering virtually the entire globe in the process, and had a tremendous run of international chart successes. They consistently challenged The Beatles position as the world's most popular group, and the Jagger/Richard songwriting team (which went under the pseudonym of Nanker/Phelge on their early B-sides) rivalled Lennon and McCartney as a prime source of material for lesser groups. The albums - 'No.2', 'Out

ROULETTES—PAUL & BARRY RYAN

Of Our Heads' and 'Aftermath' - were also huge sellers.

1967 was not a happy year for them, however. It saw The Stones splitting up with Oldham, who had played such a crucial role in their meteoric rise to infamy and fortune; flirting miserably with psychedelia; and ultimately almost coming to an abrupt end.

It started off well enough. 'Let's Spend The Night Together' went to No.3 at home and Number One in America (after being retitled 'Let's Spend Some Time Together' for the benefit of sensitive TV producers), and 'Between The Buttons' was another chart-topping album. But the final moments of the album, with Jagger giving a mock impression of TV's famous P.C. Dixon, were to prove ironic.

In February the drug squad raided Redlands, Keith Richard's country home, and arrested Jagger and Richard, along with art dealer Robert Fraser. The case came up on May 10th, and on the same day Brian Jones was also busted ...giving rise to strong suspicion that The Stones were being deliberately singled out after their years of conspicuously flouting authority.

The first case resulted in Richard being sentenced to a year's imprisonment, and Jagger to three months. The Who (q.v.) rushed out a single of 'The Last Time' and 'Under My Thumb', promising to keep The Stones music alive with further singles, but fortunately this was not necessary as the pair were swiftly released pending appeal, following an unprecedented public outcry (led by The Times!) against the severity of the sentences.

With typical Stones defiance, their next single was 'We Love You', which featured harmony vocals from Lennon and McCartney, and started with the clanging of prison gates. The jail sentences were later reduced to fines in the appeal court. In the October Jones also received a heavy prison sentence - nine months - which was again quashed on appeal in favour of a £1000 fine.

At the end of the year they released 'Their Satanic Majesties Request' and had their first real taste of critical disapproval. Not only was its acid consciousness miles removed from what was generally thought of as "Stones Music" ...it was a pretty pathetic effort by anybody's standards. It was also known that Jagger was branching out into films with a starring role in Nicholas Roeg's 'Performance', and the group had not toured since 1966. The future looked grim.

In May 1968, however, the first Stones single for nearly a year, 'Jumping Jack Flash', showed them to be back to their masterful best, and at the end of the year they celebrated the release of 'Beggars Banquet' with a lavish banquet. The album was probably The Stones finest hour, containing classics like 'Street Fighting Man' and 'Sympathy For The Devil', but it was later revealed that Brian Jones had made virtually no contribution to the recording at all.

Since the group's inception Jones had really been their musical leader, as well as a strong rival to Jagger in the public popularity stakes. By far the most proficient musician among them, he played harmonica, sitar, dulcimer, recorders and various keyboards as well as guitars, and in effect the early Stones sound was his sound.

But he was also the hardest living of the five...which took a bit of doing. By the time he moved to London he had fathered two children, the first by a fourteen year old schoolgirl, and he went on to sire at least four more. Between 1963 and 1965 he could invariably be found in fashionable clubs until the early hours of the morning, and as his drug consumption increased he changed from being the snappiest dresser in the group to wandering around cloaked in various weird and wonderful garments which he often topped off with a woman's hat.

Twice busted, in 1967 and again in May 1968, Jones also spent some time in hospital and suffered severe mental strain as a result of this police harassment and his deteriorating relationship with the rest of the group. By the time 'Beggars Banquet' was recorded he was virtually incapable of playing a musical instrument, and on June 9th 1969 he was sacked by The Stones...although press reports glossed things over by blaming musical differences for his departure. The Stones replaced him with Mick Taylor, from John Mayall's Bluesbreakers (q.v.) and prepared to start gigging again.

Jones, meanwhile, having considered joining Alexis Korner's new group, New Church, went down to his newly-purchased home in Sussex, Cotchford Farm the former home of A.A.Milne, to start searching for musicians to join in his next venture.

Sadly this project never even began, for on July 3rd Jones was found dead in his swimming pool after going for a midnight swim. Rumours circulated that he had committed suicide, while friends felt that he might have had one of his frequent asthma attacks. The coroner's report stated that he had died by misadventure while under the influence of drink and drugs. In 1971 the Rolling Stones label released an album of Moroccan folk music, 'The Pipes Of Pan At Joujouka', which Jones had recorded in Morocco shortly before his death.

Two days after this, The Stones went ahead with their scheduled free concert in Hyde Park, which was Mick Taylor's debut with the group. As a tribute to Jones, Jagger began the concert by reading an extract from Shelley's 'Adonais' and releasing several thousand white butterflies over the heads of the quarter million strong crowd. The next day he flew out to Australia to start work on the filming of 'Ned Kelly'.

In his absence 'Honky Tonk Women', another slice of the Stones at their strutting, greasy peak, topped both the British and American charts, and on his return they set out on a long tour of America. At the end of the tour 'Let It Bleed' was released, to great acclaim, but the tour itself was strife-ridden, and ended up in disaster with the ill-judged free concert at Altamont Speedway, where a negro youth called Meredith Hunter was stabbed to death by Hells Angels as the climax to a day of savage violence.

This, after The Stones' dabbling in dope, devilry and destruction on the previous few albums, tarnished their reputation somewhat, and this was worsened when they moved into tax exile in the South of France and formed their own record company.

During the seventies The Stones fell into the superstar routine of annual albums and infrequent tours, and started hanging out with the upper echelons of chic society and the aristocracy. Only Keith Richard's penchant for falling foul of various countries' anti-narcotics laws has kept their street credibility alive, although the quality of their albums and the sheer spectacle of their live performances maintained their position at the top of the rock'n'roll tree.

In 1970 'Performance' was finally put on general release, and 'Memo From Turner' from the film's soundtrack gave Jagger a minor solo hit. The following year Jagger, Wyman and Watts together with regular Stones sideman Nicky Hopkins (q.v.) and American guitarist Ry Cooder had a thoroughly uninspired album called 'Jamming With Edward' released on the Stones label, and later in the decade Wyman made a couple of solo albums, 'Monkey Grip' and 'A Stone Alone'.

At the end of 1974 Mick Taylor left, forming a short-lived band with ex-Cream (q.v.) bass guitarist Jack Bruce, and after trying out almost every guitarist in the western hemisphere his place was taken by Ronnie Wood from The Faces (q.v.). 'Black And Blue', recorded with several different guitarists, was disappointing by Stones' standards, but after a rather weak live set, 'Some Girls' in 1978 showed that they still packed a fair punch.

THE ROULETTES Russ Ballard (guitar), Pete Salt (guitar), John Rodgers (bass) and Bob Henrit (drums) were originally formed in 1963 as the backing group for Adam Faith. In 1964 Rodgers was killed in a car accident and replaced by 'Mod' Rogan, but thereafter the group's line-up stayed constant until they split at the end of 1967.

As well as backing Faith on several of his records, the first two of which were hits, and making the 'On The Move' album with him, they also had several singles in their own right, and an album, 'Stakes And Chips', in 1965. None of their singles, among them 'Bad Time', 'Melody' and 'Long Cigarette' on Parlophone, and 'Rhyme Boy Rhyme' and 'Help Me To Help Myself' on Fontana, made the charts.

When the group disbanded Ballard and Henrit joined Unit Four Plus Two (q.v.) for a few months before forming Argent (q.v.). In the latter stages of the Roulettes' existence they had been helped out by pianist David Courtney, who re-emerged in 1974 as co-songwriter and producer for Leo Sayer. In the following year he also made his own album for EMI.

ROUNDABOUT This group was formed in late 1967 by ex-Searchers (q.v.) drummer Chris Curtis. He had become a vocalist, and recruited ex-Artwoods (q.v.) keyboard player Jon Lord, ex-Outlaws (q.v.) guitarist Ritchie Blackmore, Dave Curtis (bass) and Bobby Clark (drums). Clark was considered unsuitable soon after the group's inception, and was replaced by Ian Paice from The Maze (q.v.).

Things soon fell apart, however, and Lord went off to Germany for a while, but on his return he contacted Blackmore and Paice again, and they reformed Roundabout with vocalist Rod Evans, who had also been in Maze, and bassist Nick Simper, who had been with Johnny Kidd and The Pirates (q.v.) and Screaming Lord Sutch (q.v.), and had worked with Lord in the backing group for The Flowerpot Men (q.v.).

This line-up rehearsed for a month, went to Denmark to do some gigs and TV work, and became Deep Purple (q.v.) when they got back to England.

EARL ROYCE AND THE OLYMPICS A Merseybeat group whose singles for Columbia and Parlophone included a version of 'Que Sera Sera' in 1964. They also appeared in 'Ferry Cross The Mersey'.

THE RUBBER BAND Jack Chapman (organ, vocals), Phil Drewery (bass, vocals) and Harry Rix (drums) comprised this Peddlers (q.v.) style trio, who were formed in 1965. During their career they backed several top singers, appeared on Radio One, and toured all over the country and on the continent, but never recorded. In the late sixties they changed their name to Skinn, and then split up in 1970. In 1976 Chapman was killed in a car accident.

RUPERT'S PEOPLE A psychedelic group formed in 1967 by vocalist Rod Lynton, they also included Adrian Curtis and keyboard player John Tout, the latter joining Renaissance (q.v.) in 1973. They recorded for Columbia through 1967-8, and among their singles were 'A Reflection Of Charles Brown', 'A Prologue To A Magic World' (which was based on 'Alice Through The Looking Glass'), and 'Dream On My Mind'.

PAUL AND BARRY RYAN The identical twin sons of fifties singer Marion Ryan, they were signed by Decca in 1965 and given the full pop star treatment. Their long hair was cut into a neat mod style, they were dressed in bright shirts and white suits, and they were given some dreadful slushy pop songs (most of them by Les Reed) to record. Over the next two years they had several minor hits, but only 'Don't Bring Me Your Heartaches', 'Have Pity On The Boy' and 'I Love Her' made the Top Twenty.

In 1968, with even this moderate level of success slipping away from them, the twins packed up as a recording duo. Barry carried on as a solo artist, while Paul turned to song writing. It was a pity they hadn't taken this

ST. LOUIS UNION — SIMON SCOTT

step earlier, because Barry's first single for MGM which was Paul's song 'Eloise' reached No.2. He went on to have two more small chart entries with 'Love Is Love' and 'Hunt', but has only been heard of again when 'Eloise' was reissued in 1976, and when he married some fabulously wealthy foreign bint in 1978.

ST.LOUIS UNION Tony Cassidy (vocals), Keith Millar (guitar), Alex Kirby (sax), David Tomlinson (organ), John Nichols (bass) and Dave Webb (drums) came from Manchester, and got a recording contract with Decca after winning the Melody Maker Beat Group Contest in 1965. At the beginning of 1966 their debut single, The Beatles' (q.v.) 'Girl' got into the Top Twenty, but later singles — 'Behind The Door' and 'East Side Story' among them — passed unnoticed.

CRISPIAN ST. PETERS Having changed his name from the substantially less memorable Peter Smith, this arrogant young gentleman burst onto the scene in early 1966 with 'You Were On My Mind'. It was a very strong song, a huge hit in America for We Five during the previous year, and would probably have been a hit whoever recorded it. St.Peters was so elated when it reached No.2, however, that he made the presumptuous boast that he was better than anyone else on the pop scene, including Elvis Presley and The Beatles (q.v.).

His immodesty was amply rewarded when, after another big hit with 'Pied Piper' and a minor one with 'Changes' later in 1966, he sank without trace.

THE ST.VALENTINE DAY MASSACRE This group came about in 1967 as a result of The Artwoods (q.v.) deciding to change their image. As the Massacre they wore Bonnie and Clyde style outfits — very chic at the time with the success of the film — with pin stripe suits and wide brimmed hats. They recorded 'Brother Can You Spare A Dime' for Fontana, but it was a flop, and the group faded faster than the shine on their natty shoes.

THE SALLYANGIE A pleasant contemporary folk duo consisting of Sally Oldfield and her young brother Mike, they recorded for Transatlantic and made an album and a single, 'Two Ships' in 1969.

Mike then became guitarist and bassist with Kevin Ayers and The Whole World, before retiring into the studio to compile the massively successful 'Tubular Bells'. Sally carried on less spectacularly as a solo folkie, and finally got her breakthrough in early 1979 when 'Mirrors' reached the Top Twenty.

THE SAVAGE ROSE A seven piece Dutch group, who got together in 1968, they comprised four boys and three girls. They were particularly popular in their own country and in Germany, and made some headway in Britain...largely because of female lead vocalist Anisette, who was not unattractive to man, and had a strong voice similar to Julie Driscoll's (q.v.).

They recorded several albums for Polydor — 'Savage Rose', 'In The Plain', 'Travellin'' and 'I'm Satisfied' — before moving to RCA in the early seventies for 'Refugee'. Polydor also put out a double compilation set as No.15 in their 'Pop History' series.

SAVOY BROWN Starting out in 1966 as one of the many groups thrown up by the British blues boom, they went on to have considerable and sustained success in America without really meaning anything at home. Originally known as The Savoy Brown Blues Band, they have gone through innumerable changes of personnel over the years, the only constant factors being guitarist Kim Simmonds and his brother Harry, who manages the group.

Among those who have passed through Savoy Brown are vocalist Chris Youlden, who made a couple of solo albums, 'City Child' and 'Nowhere Road', for Deram after his departure; Paul Raymond (keyboards), Andy Silvester (bass and Stan Webb (guitar), all from Chicken Shack (q.v.); and Lonesome Dave (guitar, piano, vocals), Roger Earl (bass) and Tone Stevens (drums), who formed Foghat, another band to strike boogie gold in the great American Mid-West, while remaining virtually unknown back in Blighty.

All the groups UK releases have been on Decca, and in the sixties they were: 'Shake Down' in 1967, 'Getting To The Point' in 1968, and 'Blue Matter' and 'A Step Further' in 1969.

THE SCAFFOLD Roger McGough, Mike McGear and John Gorman joined forces at Liverpool arts laboratory in the mid-sixties, presenting a very individual brand of music, poetry and wit. McGough was, and still remains, one of the country's most successful poets; McGear was the best singer, and was soon discovered to be Paul McCartney's younger brother; and Gorman was the most overt loony of the three.

After building a reputation at arts festivals and colleges, The Scaffold were signed by Parlophone in 1966. 'Two Days Monday' and 'Goodbat Nightman' both flopped, but in 1967 they moved to Columbia and had a No.4 hit with the jolly singalong 'Thank U Very Much. This formula was repeated with even greater success by 'Lily The Pink', which topped the charts at the end of 1968, and they also had several minor hits.

They made several albums, including 'Live At The Queen Elizabeth Hall', 'Lily The Pink', 'McGough And McGear', 'Sold Out' and 'Fresh Liver'. This latter, recorded for Island, was their last before they teamed up with some ex-members of The Bonzo Dog Doo Dah Band (q.v.) and various other odd characters as Grimms in 1973. Grimms was a very loose set-up, and while still performing with them McGear made a solo album, produced by brother Paul, and several singles, of which 'Leave It' was a minor hit in 1974. In 1979 Roger McGough made an album of his own poetry set to music for Island.

SIMON SCOTT A young man with dark, sultry good looks rather in the mould of Cliff Richard or the early Elvis, Scott came to England in 1962 from Darjeeling in India. A couple of years later he was signed up by Parlophone and subjected to an enormous publicity campaign, which even extended to sending plaster busts immortalising his handsomeness to influential

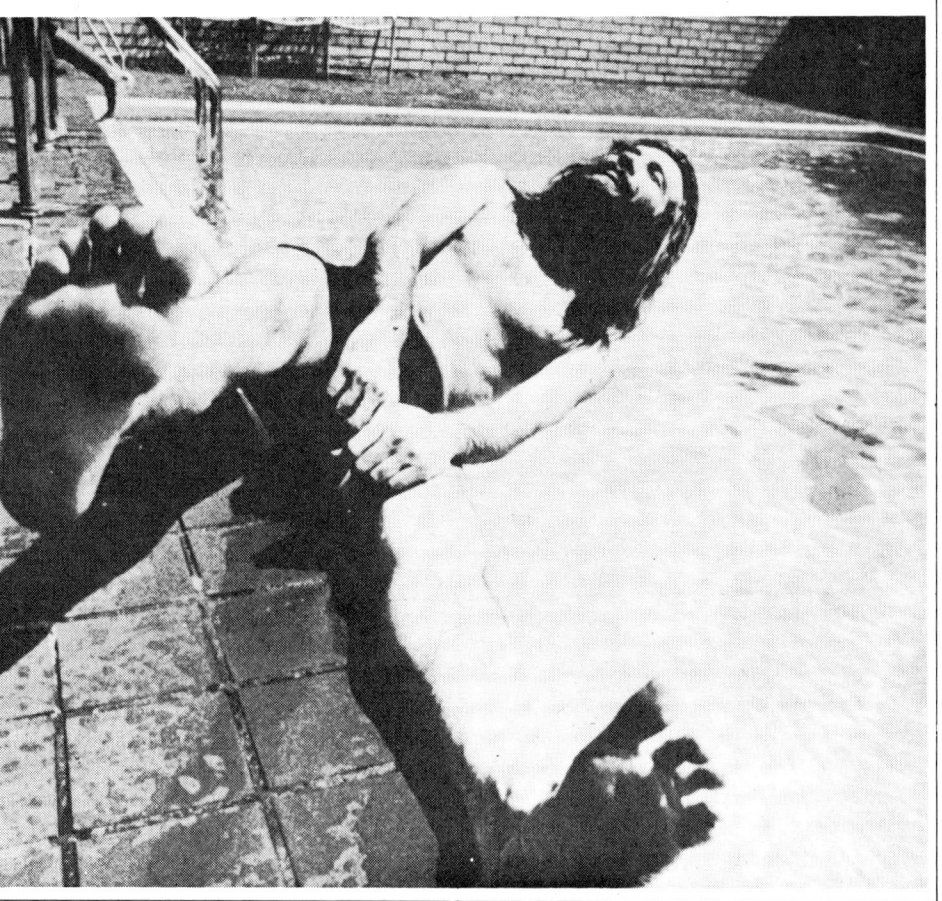

SEARCHERS—SHADOWS

people in the music business. He was heavily featured in 'Fabulous' pop magazine, but apart from a minor hit with 'Move It Baby' he flopped disastrously...leaving some unfortunate to count the cost.

THE SEARCHERS Mike Pender (lead guitar), John McNally (rhythm guitar), Tony Jackson (bass, vocals) and Chris Curtis (drums) were the biggest of the Merseybeat groups, with the exception of The Beatles (q.v.), although they never really cracked the American market in the manner of some of their contemporaries.

Formed in 1960, they worked for a while as the backing group for Johnny Sanden, but when Sanden formed The Remo Four (q.v.) they carried on alone, and spent some time in Hamburg. On their return to Liverpool they were spotted by Pye producer Tony Hatch, and also taken under the wing of manager Tito Burns.

The group's sound was closer to what was later dubbed "country rock", with tight vocal harmonies, and in mid-1963 their debut single - a cover of The Drifters' 'Sweets For My Sweet' - made short work of getting to Number One. This was followed by 'Sugar And Spice', which reached No.2, and after 'Sweet Nothin's' (which had been recorded for Philips while they were in Germany) had been a minor hit, 'Needles And Pins' gave them another chart topper at the end of the year.

In early 1964 The Searchers suffered an unexpected setback when Tony Jackson (q.v.) left to form his own group, The Vibrations. Mike Pender took over the lead vocals, Frank Allen from Cliff Bennett's Rebel Rousers (q.v.) joined on bass, and although the group's sound changed slightly, taking on a more dramatic tone, they continued to have big hits for the next couple of years.

The Shirelles' 'Don't Throw Your Love Away' gave them their third (and final) Number One soon after Jackson's departure, and Jackie de Shannon's 'When You Walk In The Room' went to No.3 at the end of the year. All the early Searchers singles, in fact, were borrowed from other artists, although they did feature self-penned material on their albums - 'Meet The Searchers', 'Sugar And Spice', 'It's The Searchers' and 'Sounds Like The Searchers'. It wasn't until 'He's Got No Love' in the summer of 1965 that they used one of their own songs for an A-side, and when they did it reached No.12...their last substantial hit.

As the Beat Boom died away so did The Searchers audience, and in mid-1966 Chris Curtis left. He put out one solo single, 'Aggravation', did some production for Pye, and formed his own group, Roundabout (q.v.), without much joy. The rest of the group replaced him with John Blunt and disappeared onto the cabaret circuit, although they carried on making singles for a while.

In 1974 they made a comeback single, 'Solitaire', for RCA, but it was completely overshadowed by Andy Williams' hit version. In 1979, with the line-up now Pender, McNally, Allen and Billy Adamson (drums), the group were surprisingly signed up by the predominantly new-wave Sire label.

THE SEEKERS Judith Durham, Athol Guy, Keith Potger and Bruce Woodley came over from Australia in 1964, bearing with them a brand of folk/pop music which won them instant popularity. Their dominant feature was the crystaline voice of Miss Durham, and their clean cut, decidedly square image made them the darlings of mums and dads and TV producers everywhere.

They made a string of successful singles and albums, and had chart toppers with 'I'll Never Find Another You' and 'The Carnival Is Over' in 1965, which were both written for them by ex-Springfield (q.v.) Tom Springfield.

When they split up in 1968 three of the members went back Down Under, leaving Keith Potger to form The New Seekers. After he had left this mob also became very popular in the seventies, although they were possibly even more nauseatingly winsome than the first lot.

THE SHADOWS

DENNY SEYTON AND THE SABRES An early sixties rock group, whose singles for Mercury included 'Tricky Dicky', 'Short Fat Fanny' and 'The Way You Look Tonight', which was a minor hit in 1964.

THE SHADOWS Hank Marvin (guitar) and Bruce Welch (rhythm guitar) from Newcastle skiffle group The Railroaders joined up with Terry "Jet" Harris (bass) and Tony Meehan (drums) from the London-based Vipers in the late fifties.

Backing rock'n'roll singer Cliff Richard, who was being promoted as Britain's answer to Elvis Presley, they were called The Drifters at first, but changed to The Shadows when the American Drifters came along. They played on Cliff's records, and in 1959 began recording in their own right for Columbia. 'Feelin' Fine' and 'Jet Black', the latter an instrumental, were recorded as The Drifters, and then came another vocal effort, 'Saturday Dance', as The Shadows.

They didn't emulate Richard's chart success, however, until mid-1960, when an instrumental called 'Apache' took them to the top of the charts. Thereafter they stuck with instrumentals, and had a lengthy string of hits which lasted right up until 1967, and included four more Number Ones. With their distinctive, tremeloed guitar sound and their neat little dance steps, they were the most imitated group in the country until The Beatles (q.v.) came along. Such was their influence that guitarists up and down the country even took to wearing thick rimmed glasses like Marvin.

In 1961 the group appeared with Cliff Richard in his film 'The Young Ones', and then in September Tony Meehan left to become a record producer for Decca. One further single featuring Meehan, 'Wonderful Land', was released, and while it was at the top of the charts Jet Harris also left the group.

Harris recorded two solo singles for Decca, 'Besame Mucho' and 'The Man With The Golden Arm', which both got into the hit parade, and an EP, before teaming up with Meehan again. At the start of 1963 they topped the charts with 'Diamonds', and had further huge hits with 'Scarlet O'Hara' and 'Applejack', but at the end of the year tragedy struck when Jet Harris was seriously injured in a car accident. He has resurfaced periodically since - he was in The Jeff Beck Group (q.v.) for a very short while in 1967 - but he never completely recovered from the accident, and was last heard of living in a caravan. Meehan formed The Tony Meehan Combo and had a minor hit in early 1964 with 'Song Of Mexico', but then returned to production.

Meanwhile, back in The Shadows, the duo had been replaced by Brian "Licquorice" Locking and Brian Bennett from The Krewcats (q.v.). The group carried on having big singles like 'Guitar Tango', 'Foot Tapper' and 'Atlantis', as well as albums which stayed on the charts for an eternity - 'The Shadows', 'Out Of The Shadows', 'The Shadows Greatest Hits' and 'Dance With The Shadows'. A year after joining, Locking left to become a Jehovah's Witness and John Rostill came in.

With the music scene turned upside down by the Beat Boom, The Shadows dominant position inevitably suffered, but most of their singles continued to make the Top Twenty, even after they started singing again on '(Next Time I See) Mary Anne'. The hits finally ground to a halt in 1967, and although they were kept in the public eye by their appearances on Cliff Richard's shows, they broke up in 1969.

Marvin and Welch then teamed up with John Farrar on bass in Marvin, Welch and Farrar, a sort of sub-Crosby, Stills and Nash enterprise. They recorded several albums, and were also regular faces on Cliff's TV specials. After they split up, Farrar went into song-

SHAKEDOWN SOUND – SMALL FACES

writing and production where he had huge success with Olivia Newton-John, who had been engaged to Welch at one point.

In 1973 Marvin and Welch reformed The Shadows, and they represented Britain in the 1975 Eurovision Song Contest. They didn't win, but 'Let Me Be The One' was their first Top Twenty entry for eight years. In 1977 EMI released a compilation album of their twenty greatest hits, which was advertised on TV and sold very well, and in 1978 they reunited with Cliff Richard, whose career was also taking a turn for the better, and played a one-off concert at the London Palladium. The album of this event was a big success in early 1979, and at the same time The Shadows had a taste of their old instrumental glory with an adaptation of 'Don't Cry For Me Argentina' from the musical 'Evita'.

In 1975 John Rostill had been found electrocuted at his home.

THE SHAKEDOWN SOUND Jess Roden (vocals), Mick Ralphs (guitar), Verden Allen (organ), Pete "Overend" Watts (bass) and Dale "Buffin" Griffin (drums) came from Hereford in the mid-sixties. Roden went on to sing with several other bands, including The Alan Bown Set (q.v.) before forming his own band in the seventies.

The others became Silence, and at the end of the decade they moved to London, where they were discovered by producer Guy Stevens and teamed up with singer/pianist Ian Hunter as Mott The Hoople (q.v.).

THE SHAKERS A Merseybeat group from the early sixties, and one of many groups to record a version of the classic 'Money'.

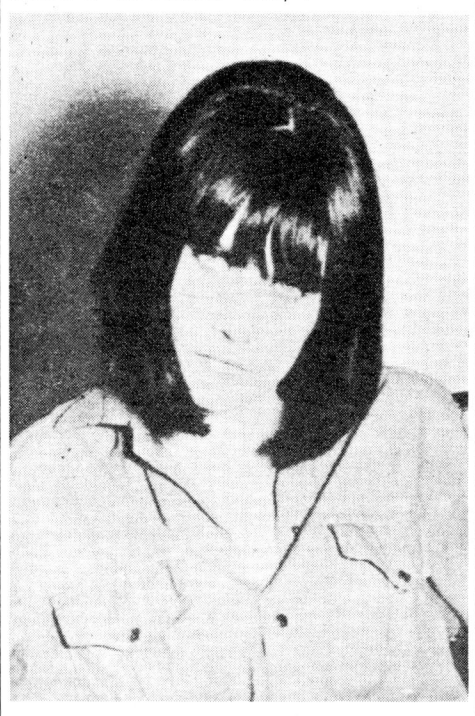

SANDIE SHAW Sandra Goodritch was a factory worker in Dagenham, Essex and a great fan of Adam Faith and The Roulettes (q.v.), when one night in 1964 she plucked up the courage to visit Faith in his dressing room. Once there she sang for him and his manager, Eve Taylor, and was instantly signed up.

Having had her name changed to Sandie Shaw, this tall girl with model's features was given a Chris Andrews' song 'As Long As You're Happy Baby' as her debut release on Pye. It flopped, but at the end of 1964 a version of Bacharach and David's 'There's Always Something There To Remind Me' hastened to Number One. Thereafter she toured the country, appeared several times on 'Ready Steady Go' (q.v.) - where she rivalled Cathy McGowan (q.v.) as the archetypal mid-sixties chick - and earned considerable publicity with her gimmick of singing in bare feet.

'Girl Don't Come' and 'I'll Stop At Nothing' both Andrews songs, were further big singles for her in early 1965, her debut album sold well, and 'Long Live Love' gave her a second Number One in the June.

The hits just kept on coming, and she made a second album, entitled 'Me', but her career was going off the boil when she was chosen to represent Britain in the 1967 Eurovision Song Contest. Her song was a bouncy little item called 'Puppet On A String', and after she had become only the second Briton to win the contest it topped the charts.

In the following year she had her own TV series, 'The Sandie Shaw Supplement', but had only one further Top Ten hit, with 'Monsieur Dupont' in the spring of 1969. By that time she had married fashion designer Jeff Banks, and when she had a baby she gracefully retired from the music business. In 1975 she attempted a comeback as a rock singer, performing her own material.

THE SHE TRINITY An all-girl three-piece formed by Beryl Marsden (q.v.) in 1967, they recorded for Columbia and their singles included 'Hair', 'Wild Flower' and 'I Fought The Law'.

THE SHEFFIELDS A mid-sixties R&B group from (wait for it!) Sheffield, their singles for Pye included 'It Must Be Love', 'Got My Mojo Working' and 'Bags Groove' in 1964.

MIKE SHERIDAN AND THE NIGHTRIDERS Mike Sheridan (vocals), Dave Pritchard (guitar), Greg Masters (bass) and Roger Spencer (drums) were one of Birmingham's top bands, and among the several local outfits signed by Columbia in 1963. After two unsuccessful singles they were joined by guitarist Roy Wood and cut two more flops, after which they became Mike Sheridan's Lot. Two more failures followed, and then Sheridan left in 1966 to go solo. He eventually formed a duo with Rick Price, who later joined The Move (q.v.). Roy Wood also left, actually to form The Move, and the remaining three stuck together as The Nightriders for one last single on Polydor, 'It's Only The Dog', before adding guitarist Jeff Lynne and becoming Idle Race (q.v.).

SHORTY AND THEM An early to mid-sixties R&B group from Newcastle who made a few singles for the Fontana label.

SHOTGUN EXPRESS Formed in late 1966 in London as a touring R&B package show, they worked the clubs and ballrooms for just a few months before going their separate ways again. The vocalists were Rod Stewart (q.v.) and Beryl Marsden (q.v.), and the backing was provided by The Peter B's (q.v.).

Apart from touring, the group made two singles for Columbia, 'I Could Feel The Whole World Turn Around' and 'Funny 'Cos Neither Could I'. On their demise Stewart joined The Jeff Beck Group (q.v.), Marsden formed She Trinity, and of The Peter B's, guitarist Peter Green and drummer Mick Fleetwood joined John Mayall's Bluesbreakers (q.v.) for a short while before forming Fleetwood Mac (q.v.), bassist Dave Ambrose joined The Brian Auger Trinity (q.v.), and Bardens, the keyboard player and group leader, had spells with Love Affair (q.v.) and The Mike Cotton Sound (q.v.) before forming Village (q.v.).

THE SILKIE Sylvia Tatler (vocals), Mike Ramsden (guitar, vocals), Ivor Aylesbury (guitar) and Kevin Cunningham (string bass) were four Hull University students who played contemporary folk music and were signed up by Brian Epstein (q.v.). Their mid-1965 debut single for Fontana was 'Blood Red River', and a few months later they got into the Top Thirty with a cover of The Beatles' (q.v.) 'You've Got To Hide Your Love Away', which was actually produced by Lennon and McCartney.

They then toured the country and made an album, 'The Silkie Sing The Songs Of Bob Dylan', but further singles, including 'Keys To My Soul' and 'Born To Be With You' (which had been a big hit for The Chordettes ten years earlier), got nowhere, and they faded back onto the folk club circuit.

SIREN Kevin Coyne (guitar, vocals), John Chichester (lead guitar), Dave Clague (bass), Nick Cudworth (piano) and various drummers formed Siren in Bradford in the late sixties. Moving to London they signed with John Peel's (q.v.) Dandelion label, releasing two singles in 1969, 'The Stride' and 'Mandy Lee', and an album. In 1971 they made another album, 'Strange Locomotion', with Mick Gratton replacing Chichester on lead guitar, and then split up. Coyne stayed with Dandelion for 'Case History', and then moved to Virgin to make a series of remarkable albums, based largely on his experiences as a psychiatric and social worker, which have never really been given the recognition they deserve.

SKID ROW An Irish blues and rock group of the late sixties and early seventies led by guitarist Gary Moore. They had a good following in the clubs, but their albums for CBS failed to create any great impact. Their vocalist at one point was Phil Lynott, who went on to form Thin Lizzy, where Moore later rejoined him.

SKIP BIFFERTY Having sung with various Newcastle groups, including The Chosen Few (q.v.), since 1963, Graham Bell formed the flower-power group Skip Bifferty in 1967 with Micky Gallagher from The Chosen Few, Colin Gibson, Tom Jacklin and Jon Turnbull. They travelled down to London, and after a gig at the Marquee (q.v.) they were signed by manager Don Arden, who got them a contract with RCA.

They made several fine singles - 'On Love', 'Happy Land' and 'Man In Black' - which got a fair amount of airplay but failed to crack the charts, and an album featuring tracks like 'Jeremy Carabine' and 'Gasboard Underdog'. Critical acclaim and several appearances on John Peel's (q.v.) 'Top Gear' didn't help to provide the crucial breakthrough, and during 1968 the group started falling out with Arden. Eventually they sneaked off to record for Island as Heavy Jelly (q.v.), and soon afterwards they split up.

During the seventies Bell sang with Every Which Way, and formed Bell and Arc, which also included Gallagher and Turnbull. In the mid-seventies Gibson joined Snafu with ex-Freedom (q.v.) vocalist Bobby Harrison.

THE SMALL FACES Steve Marriott (guitar, vocals), Ronnie "Plonk" Lane (bass, vocals), Jimmy Winston (organ) and Kenny Jones (drums) were four mods who came together in London in 1965. Lane and Jones had previously been together in several groups, while Marriott and Winston both came from The Moments (q.v.). Marriott had also been a child actor on TV and in Lionel Bart's musical 'Oliver'.

Before The Moments Marriott had led The Moonliters and The Frantics, and even had two solo singles, 'Give Her My Regards' in 1963 and 'Tell Me' in early 1965. Since the top mods were called "faces" and all of this new group stood less than 5'6" in their socks, it seemed natural that they should be dubbed The Small Faces.

Signed up by manager Don Arden and Decca, they had been together for only a few weeks when 'Watcha Gonna Do About It' went into the Top Twenty. The follow-up, 'I've Got Mine', flopped completely, but 'Sha La La La Lee' put them back on course by reaching No.3. Thereafter they released a string of excellent singles, all written by the group, on Decca and then Immediate, and four albums - 'Small Faces', 'From The Beginning', 'There Are But Four Small Faces' and the classic 'Ogden's Nutgone Flake'.

As sharp and as pugnacious musically as

SMILE – SOFT MACHINE

THE SMALL FACES

they were visually, The Small Faces never rested on their laurels, with the result that some of their singles bombed out somewhat. 'Tin Soldier' was recorded with P.P.Arnold (q.v.) and was one of the first-ever singles in a picture sleeve; 'Itchycoo Park' was one of the first records to use phasing; 'Lazy Sunday' had a great cockney music hall flavour; and 'The Universal' was actually recorded on a mono cassette recorder!

In late 1965 Jimmy Winston left, recording 'Sorry She's Mine' for Decca before returning to his earlier acting career and joining the cast of 'Hair' (q.v.). His place was taken by Ian MacLagen from Boz People (q.v.). Soon afterwards the group all had acting roles in the film 'Dateline Diamonds'.

Late in 1968, apparently frustrated by the group's inability to break away from their "pop group" tag, Steve Marriott left to form Humble Pie (q.v.). The other three carried on with Ron Wood and Rod Stewart (q.v.) from The Jeff Beck Group (q.v.) as The Faces (q.v.).

In 1969 'Afterglow', from 'Ogden's Nutgone Flake', was a minor posthumous hit, and Immediate put together a definitive anthology, 'The Autumn Stone'. In 1976, after 'Itchycoo Park' and 'Lazy Sunday' had been successfully re-issued, Marriott, MacLagen and Jones reformed The Small Faces with Ricky Wills on bass. They made an album for Atlantic, but did little justice to the memory of a great group.

SMILE A late sixties group who had a single called 'Earth' in 1969. The personnel included guitarist Brian May and drummer Roger Taylor, who formed Queen in the early seventies.

WHISTLING JACK SMITH Smith was really Billy Moeller, the brother of Unit Four Plus Two (q.v.) vocalist Tommy Moeller. In 1967 he reached No.5 in the charts with the novelty single 'I Was Kaiser Bill's Batman' on Decca, but it was later revealed that the whistling on the record was actually done by a session man!

THE SMOKE Mick Rowley (vocals), Mal Luker (guitar), John "Zeke" Lund (bass) and Geoff Gill (drums) got together in 1967. Their debut Columbia single, 'My Friend Jack', contained the line "My friend Jack eats sugar lumps", and since the consumption of sugar lumps impregnated with LSD was a popular pastime among hippies, the record was banned by the BBC. Nevertheless, it reached the lower echelons of the charts, and was a huge hit on the continent.

After following up with 'If The Weather's Sunny' they switched to Island, where they appeared to alternate between The Smoke and Chords Five (q.v.). As The Smoke they made 'It Could Be Wonderful' and 'Utterly Simple', the latter a Dave Mason song, produced by Mason himself and Jeff Beck (q.v.). They underwent numerous personnel changes, but were still going in the early seventies.

THE SNOBS Sporting buckled shoes and powdered wigs, The Snobs put out one great single, 'Buckle Shoe Stomp', on Decca in 1964. Recorded live it had a stomping beat and some fine raucous vocals, but wasn't a hit. In this country the group played mostly debutante balls, but they found a wider audience in Scandinavia. The line-up of the group is unknown, but in a photo taken of them at a London film premiere one of them, beneath his wig, looks remarkably like Marc Bolan.

THE SOFT MACHINE Formed in Canterbury during 1966, the original line-up of the group was Robert Wyatt (drums, vocals), who had been in the local Wilde Flowers (q.v.), Kevin Ayers (bass, vocals) from nearby Herne Bay, Mike Ratledge (keyboards), a local boy who had got bored with life at Oxford University, and Daevid Allen (guitar), an Australian hippy. Their influences were avant garde jazz and R&B, and they had some difficulty in deciding on a name. They were The Bishops Of Canterbury, Dingo Virgin and The Four Skins, and then just The Four Skins, when guitarist Larry Nolan joined for a short while. Finally Ratledge suggested Soft Machine, taken from the book by William Burroughs.

During a visit to Majorca, Allen and Ayers met an eccentric American millionaire called Wes Brunson who generously financed the group, and when they returned to London in early 1967 The Soft Machine started getting gigs at the UFO club (q.v.). This led to a management contract with Mike Jeffries, who lined them up for a three day recording session with Giorgio Gomelsky.

The group spent the time rehearsing Kevin Ayers' songs, but when Jeffries refused to pay for the tapes Gomelsky hung onto them, and a few years later they were released by the French label Byg, as Volumes 7 & 8 of their 'Rock Generation' series. Next to pick up on the group was Kim Fowley, and he produced the Soft Machine's first and only single, 'Feelin' Reelin' Squeelin'', which he had written with Ayers.

This record was released by Polydor in mid-1967, but a week after it came out the record company flipped the record over, making another Ayers song, 'Love Makes Sweet Music', the A-side. It actually made the lower rungs of the Radio London chart.

After appearing at the Fourteen Hour Technicolour Dream (q.v.), where Daevid Allen took the stage wearing a coal miners hat with the light on and Kevin Ayers sported a cowboy hat with giant glider wings, they went to France and got involved in a production of Picasso's

SONS OF FRED—SPRINGFIELDS

play, 'Desire Attrape La Queue'. This was the start of what was to be a very happy relationship with French audiences for the group.

Unfortunately, when they tried to get back to England, Allen was refused entry because his visa had expired and his passport was out of date. He stayed in France, and shortly afterwards put together the first version of Gong. His place was taken by Andy Somers from Dantalion's Chariot (q.v.), and the group took off on a long tour of America with The Jimi Hendrix Experience (q.v.) and Eire Apparent (q.v.).

Somers didn't stay long, but while in America the other three recorded an album for Probe in New York, which eventually got a release in the States (but not at home) in late 1968.

The group split up at the end of the tour, but a couple of months later reformed with ex-Wilde Flower Hugh Hopper taking over from Ayers. Ayers went on to record a memorable solo album, 'Joy Of A Toy', and then formed The Whole World, with a youthful Mike Oldfield on guitar, and an ageing Lol Coxhill on saxes. They made one album, 'Shooting At The Moon', before Ayers reverted to solo status for a string of albums during the seventies, which made him a cult figure if never a star.

With Hopper, Soft Machine recorded 'Volume Two', which got a British release on Probe in 1969, and was reissued in 1973 as a double set together with the first album. Thereafter the group broke away from Mike Jeffries, and began moving increasingly away from rock in the direction of avant garde jazz.

Elton Dean (alto sax), Lyn Dobson (flute and soprano sax), Nick Evans (trombone) and Mark Charig (cornet) were added for a British tour, at the end of which Evans and Charig were forced out for financial reasons. The remaining five recorded their first album for CBS, the double 'Soft Machine Third', which came out in January 1970. A month later Dobson left, but the group were enjoying their greatest period of public interest, and after they had become the first rock group to appear in the BBC Promenade Concerts, the album actually charted.

'Four' followed in 1971, but then in September Wyatt left to form Matching Mole (taken from the French for "soft machine" - machine molle). This outfit recorded two albums for CBS, but then in 1974 Wyatt fell out of an upstairs window at a party and broke his back, leaving himself paralysed from the waist down. While in hospital he wrote a considerable body of new material and, having changed from drums to keyboards, made two albums for Virgin Records, and even had a Top Thirty single with a version of The Monkees 'I'm A Believer'.

With his departure the Softs lost their last semblance of alleviating humour. They became a serious, experimental, wholly instrumental group, and of course their popularity fell away drastically. Hugh Hopper left in 1972, recording the solo '1984', as did Elton Dean, and when Ratledge also departed in 1976 Soft Machine existed in name only. A line-up which bore no relation to the original group carried on for a while, but to an increasing lack of public response.

In 1977 Charly Records put out the Gomelsky tapes under the title 'Soft Machine - At The Beginning'.

SONS OF FRED A Great Yarmouth group of the mid sixties who recorded for Columbia and Parlophone without notable success. Among their singles was 'Sweet Love' in 1965.

THE SORROWS Don Maughn (vocals), Philip Witcher (lead guitar), Wez Price (rhythm guitar), Philip Packham (bass) and Bruce Findlay (drums) were a mid-sixties R&B group from Coventry who recorded for Piccadilly.

Their main asset was the powerful voice of Maughn, and after appearing on Ready Steady Go (q.v.) their third single, 'Take A Heart', was a Top Thirty hit in the autumn of 1965. Their other singles - 'I Don't Wanna Be Free', 'Baby', 'You've Got What I Want', 'Let The Live Live', 'Pink Purple Yellow And Red' and 'Let Me In' - and an album named after their hit single were less successful, and they split up around late '66/early '67. Maughn then changed his name to Don Fardon (q.v.) and formed his own group.

THE SOUL AGENTS An excellent Southampton R&B group, led by organist Don Shinn, who were popular in the clubs and recorded a few singles for Pye, including versions of Willie Dixon's 'The Seventh Son' and 'I Just Wanna Make Love To You'. Their gimmick - in common with Sandie Shaw (q.v.) - was playing in bare feet.

The group had several line-ups, one of which backed Rod Stewart (q.v.) for a time, and when they finally split up in 1968 the last incarnation - Ian Duck (guitar), Dave Glover (bass) and Roger Pope (drums) - became Hookfoot. Shinn went into session work, which included playing on James Taylor's Apple album.

SOUNDS INCORPORATED Alan Holmes (flute, sax), Griff West (sax), John St.John (guitar), Barrie Cameron (keyboards), Wes Hunter (bass) and Tony Newman (drums) not only backed many top visiting American rock stars during the early sixties, they were also a popular instrumental group in their own right.

They had a strong, rocking sound, led by their two saxes, and in 1964 had two minor hits on Columbia with 'The Spartans' and 'Spanish Harlem'. Their other singles for Decca, Columbia and Polydor included 'William Tell' and 'My Little Red Book', and they also made two albums for Columbia.

In 1964 they were signed by manager Brian Epstein (q.v.), and through this connection played on 'Good Morning Good Morning' from The Beatles (q.v.) 'Sgt.Pepper', and also opened their show at Shea Stadium in New York.

When the group finally faded out most of the members went into sessions, but Tony Newman joined the Jeff Beck Group (q.v.), and in the seventies was with David Bowie (q.v.) before forming Boxer with Mike Patto (q.v.) in 1975.

SOUTHERN SOUND A mid-sixties group whose singles for Columbia included 'Just The Same As You' in 1966.

THE SPECTRES Mike Rossi and Alan Lancaster were schoolboy guitarists who formed a group in 1962 with John Coghlan on drums, and two others on keyboards and bass. They played some sports club dances around their South London homes featuring rock'n'roll standards, a few ballads, and later on a Lancaster composition, 'You Are My Girl'.

As the group became more serious Rod Lynes replaced the original keyboard player, and they called themselves The Spectres. They played some holiday camp dates, backed some visiting American singers, and built up a following at the Cafe Des Artistes in Earls Court, where they met bassist Rick Parfitt, who was with a group called The Highlights.

Some time later Parfitt actually joined the group, and in 1966 they were signed by Piccadilly, for whom they made three singles - 'I (Who Have Nothing)', a cover of Shirley Bassey's hit, 'Hurdy Gurdy Man' and 'We Ain't Got Nothin' Yet', which had just been a big American hit for The Blues Magoos. In early 1967 they became Traffic Jam (q.v.).

SPECTRUM A pop group formed around 1967 and signed by RCA, their singles included 'Portobello Road' in 1967, 'Little Red Boat By The River' in 1968, and 'Glory' and 'Free' in 1969. They were still soldiering on in 1974 when they made an album, 'The Light Is Dark Enough', also on RCA.

THE SPINNERS Mick Groves, Tony Davis, Cliff Hall and Hugh James make up this very polished and professional folk group, which formed in Liverpool in 1968. Very versatile, featuring anything from gentle ballads to spirituals, they are perennial favourites with cabaret and TV audiences. Their albums, of which there have been many, included 'Family Of Man', 'Folk At The Phil', 'More Folk At The Phil' and 'Not Quite Folk' in the late sixties.

SPOOKY TOOTH Mike Harrison (piano, vocals), Luther Grosvenor (guitar), Greg Ridley (bass) and Mike Kellie (drums) evolved into Spooky Tooth out of Art (q.v.) with the addition of American keyboard player/vocalist Gary Wright.

Starting out in 1967, they made two fine albums for Island, 'It's All About' in 1968 and 'Spooky Two' in 1969, as well as a single of The Band's 'The Weight'. They featured regularly on John Peel's (q.v.) 'Top Gear', and enjoyed considerable critical acclaim, but never reached the wider audience that they deserved.

Ridley left after making the second album to join Humble Pie (q.v.), and was replaced by Andy Leigh. With this line-up the group collaborated with French electronics wizard Pierre Henry on the experimental 'Ceremony', but regarding it as a dismal failure and feeling generally fed up with things, Spooky Tooth broke up in February 1970.

Wright went off to form Wonderwheel, who made two albums for A&M, but later in the year Harrison, Grosvenor and Kellie reformed the group with Steve Thompson (bass) from John Mayall's (q.v.) group, and John Hawken (keyboards) from The Nashville Teens (q.v.) and Renaissance (q.v.). They made 'The Last Puff' (which just about sums up the album) with help from Greaseband (q.v.) men Alan Spenner and Henry McCullough, and then folded yet again.

Grosvenor made a solo album, 'Under Open Skies', joined Stealers Wheel and then Mott The Hoople (q.v.), the latter under the name of Ariel Bender; Kellie did session work and played with Frampton's Camel; Thompson joined Stone The Crows (q.v.) and Hawken reunited with his old Renaissance colleagues in Illusion; while Harrison made two solo albums, 'Mike Harrison' and 'Smokestack Lightning'.

In September 1972, seeing that their solo careers weren't exploding with quite the impact they might have hoped for, Harrison and Wright (who had been the original Spooky's prime motivators) formed yet another new line-up, with drummer Bryson Graham and guitarist Mick Jones from Wonderwheel, and bassist Ian Herbert who had played on Harrison's first solo album.

Spooky Tooth ground on for two more years in increasingly uninspired fashion, making three more albums - 'You Broke My Heart So I Busted Your Jaw' and 'Witness' for Island, and 'The Mirror' for Good Ear - and going through numerous personnel changes. Among those who came and went were Mike Kellie (who later cropped in new wave combo The Only Ones), vocalist Mike Patto (q.v.) and bassist Keith Ellis, who went on to form Boxer, and bassist Chris Stewart from Eire Apparent (q.v.).

Ironically, when they finally gave up in despair in late 1974, Wright immediately found enormous solo success in his home country, while Mick Jones, after a lengthy silence, formed the platinum-selling Foreigner with ex-King Crimson (q.v.) keyboard player Ian McDonald and several Americans. In 1976 Island put out a compilation album, 'The Best Of Spooky Tooth'.

THE SPOTNIKS An early sixties instrumental group from Sweden, led by guitarist Bo Winberg, The Spotnicks wore spacesuits on stage and used equipment connected by radio waves. This gimmickry apart, they released a batch of singles and EPs, and three albums, between 1962 and 1965, and had modest hits with 'Orange Blossom Special', 'The Rocket Man', 'Hava Nagila' and 'Rocket Man', all on the Oriole label.

THE SPRINGFIELDS Tom and Dusty Springfield (their real name was O'Brien) and Tim Field made up this early sixties folksy trio. After minor hits on Philips with 'Breakaway'

DUSTY SPRINGFIELD – STEELEYE SPAN

THE SPRINGFIELDS

and 'Bambino', Field left in 1962 and was replaced by Mike Hurst, whose real name was Mike Longhurst-Pickworth.

In the following year they hit the charts with 'Island Of Dreams', 'Say I Won't Be There' and 'Come On Home', but then split up. Tom, who had written much of the trio's material, concentrated on this and on production, as did Hurst, while Dusty (q.v.) carried on as a solo artist.

DUSTY SPRINGFIELD When The Springfields (q.v.) broke up in 1963, Dusty drastically reorganised her image with a new hairdo and clothes, and a switch from folk to soul and big ballads, and went on to become Britain's most popular female singer of the mid-sixties.

A combination of a great voice and carefully chosen songs gave her a string of hit singles which lasted right up until 1970, and included a Number One with 'You Don't Have To Say You Love Me' in 1966. She also made several big-selling albums, including 'A Girl Called Dusty' and 'Everything Is Coming Up Dusty'.

In the early seventies she moved to America, where she had also had several hits, but kept a low profile apart from occasional session work. In the late seventies she attempted a comeback, via two albums for Phonogram, but despite considerable interest from the media it never really took off.

STACKWADDY John Knail (vocals), Mick Stott (guitar), Stuart Banham (bass) and Steve Revell (drums) were a wild, raucous R&B group from Manchester, who first started playing together in 1965. They built up a reputation on the club circuit (or at least, at those clubs where they weren't banned), thanks partly to Knail's predilection for throwing bottles at his audience or physically assaulting them when dissatisfied with the level of appreciation forthcoming. Before he ended up in jail, Stackwaddy managed to make two albums. The first, featuring stuff like Bo Diddley's 'Roadrunner' (which was also released as a single), was on John Peel's (q.v.) Dandelion label, while the second, delicately entitled 'Bugger Off', was on Polydor.

FREDDIE STARR AND THE MIDNIGHTERS An early sixties Merseybeat group whose singles included 'It's Shakin' Time' for Decca in 1963. Starr was a good looking lad with his hair combed in a quiff, but he was little more than a pale imitation of rock'n'roller Billy Fury, and the group failed to make the grade. In the seventies Starr found fame as an impressionist on ITV's 'Who Do You Do', which led to his own TV series and even a Top Ten hit with 'It's You' in 1974.

STATUS QUO Mike Rossi (guitar, vocals), Rick Parfitt (guitar, vocals), Rod Lynes (organ, vocals), Alan Lancaster (bass) and John Coghlan (drums) were called The Spectres (q.v.) and Traffic Jam (q.v.) before becoming Quo Vadis, and then very quickly Status Quo, at the end of 1967.

Moving to Pye and acquiring a pop image with smart trousers and frilly shirts, they had a big hit early in 1968 with Rossi's 'Pictures Of Matchstick Men'. Over the next three years they followed this with 'Ice In The Sun', 'Down The Dustpipe' and 'In My Chair'. They also made four albums - 'Picturesque Matchstickable Messages', 'Status Quotation', 'Ma Kelly's Greasy Spoon' and 'Dog Of Two Head' - but as they were labelled as a singles group at a period when the singles and albums markets were poles apart, their long-players didn't do particularly well.

In 1971, tired of this pop image, Status Quo faded out of the picture. They took two years off to grow their hair and allow their denims to fade, and then burst back in early 1973 without Lynes, but with a new record contract with Vertigo, and Rossi now calling himself Francis instead of Mike. They also had a new, heavied-up style, and since then (without apparently developing one iota) they have attained and maintained a position as one of the country's top bands. In 1974 they had a Number One single with 'Down Down', and in 1973 Pye compiled a selection of their older material for their 'Golden Hour' series.

THE STEAM PACKET A package R&B show which toured clubs and ballrooms for a year between autumn '65 and autumn '66. Their three-strong vocal line-up of Long John Baldry (q.v.), Rod Stewart (q.v.) and Julie Driscoll (q.v.) was backed by The Brian Auger Trinity (q.v.).

When they split up, Baldry turned to big ballads for chart success; Stewart joined Shotgun Express (q.v.); and Driscoll and the Trinity joined forces some time later. No records by Steampacket were put out at the time, but in 1977 Charly released 'Steampacket - The First Supergroup'.

STEELEYE SPAN The popular face of folk-rock, along with Fairport Convention (q.v.), Steeleye Span were formed in 1969 by ex-Fairport bassist Ashley Hutchings, who originally wanted to call the group Middlemarch Wait. The other members were two duos who were well-known on the folk club circuit in their own right, Maddy Prior and Tim Hart, and Gay and Terry Woods. They played a delightful form of electric folk, using uncommon instruments like dulcimer and autoharp as well as more regular ones, and their first album was 'Hark The Village Wait' for RCA.

CAT STEVENS–ROD STEWART

After recording the album Gay and Terry Woods left to resume their duo activities, and their places were taken by another well-known folkie, Martin Carthy (who had originally suggested the group's name) and violinist Peter Knight. This line-up went on the road for the first time, and made two albums - 'Please To See The King' and 'Ten Man Mop Or Mr.Reservoir Butler Rides Again' - which concentrated on updating traditional material. They also performed in the play 'Corunna', written for them by Keith Dewhurst, at London's Royal Court Theatre, before Hutchings became disenchanted at the way the group were heading, and went off to start again with The Albion Country Band.

Rick Kemp, a bassist from Hull who had been working with Michael Chapman (q.v.) came in, and Martin Carthy, who had wanted a multi-instrumentalist as the replacement, went out. In came Bob Johnson on lead guitar, whose prior experience had been with P.J.Proby (q.v.) and Paul Raven (Gary Glitter), and gradually the rock side of Steeleye's character became increasingly predominant.

They recorded a string of successful albums for Chrysalis, one of which was produced by Ian Anderson from Jethro Tull (q.v.) and another by Wombles mastermind Mike Batt, and had hit singles with 'Gaudete' and 'All Around My Hat'. Despite their great popularity, the watered-down rock versions of beautiful traditional songs, which they were now performing, were a far cry from the ideals with which Steeleye began. Apparently the group members themselves realised it, and in early 1978 they disbanded.

<u>CAT STEVENS</u> Born Steven Georgiou of Greek parentage in Soho, London. In July 1947, he arrived on the pop scene in 1966, after being discovered by ex-Springfield (q.v.) Mike Hurst while still at Hammersmith College.

Signed by Deram, his first single, 'I Love My Dog', got into the Top Thirty at the end of the year, and in early 1967 he had two major hits with 'Matthew And Son' and 'I'm Gonna Get Me A Gun', both self-penned songs with enthusiastic string arrangements. His debut album, 'Matthew And Son', was a best-seller; his songs were getting recorded by other artists - notably 'Here Comes My Baby' by The Tremeloes, and 'The First Cut Is The Deepest' by P.P.Arnold (q.q.v.); he was voted "Brightest Hope" in a music paper poll, and his Mediterranean good looks made him a favourite with the ladies. In fact, young Mr.Stevens looked set for a very successful run.

By the end of 1967, however, he was getting dissatisfied with his "pop star" appeal. His songwriting and arranging were getting more adventurous, and as a result less commercial, and 'A Bad Night' and 'Kitty' were only minor hits at the end of 1967. In 1968 his second album, 'New Masters', was also less successful, and then he was suddenly struck down by TB and forced to retire for nearly two years.

In 1970 he re-emerged with a batch of more introspective, philosophical material which he had written while in hospital, and caught the crest of the singer/songwriter wave. At the end of the year he had a Top Ten hit with 'Lady d'Arbanville', about an ex-girlfriend, model Patti d'Arbanville, and established his new, mellower acoustic style. This was continued with a string of albums for Island in the early seventies - 'Mona Bone Jakon', 'Teaser And The Firecat', 'Tea For The Tillerman', 'Catch Bull At Four' and 'Foreigner' - which made him one of the world's top solo artists, although his reputation has diminished in recent years as his appearances have become less frequent and his albums more spiritually-orientated.

<u>AL STEWART</u> Born in Glasgow, Stewart had played guitar with various groups in the Bournemouth area (including one with DJ Tony Blackburn) before moving to London as a solo singer/songwriter. His first album, 'Bedsitter Images' on CBS, came out in 1967, and was followed in 1969 by 'Love Chronicles', on which Jimmy Page played guitar, and which attracted some controversy by the epic 17-minute title track's use of the word "fucking".

His early albums were largely documentations of his personal love life, but after his fourth album, 'Orange' in 1972, he began writing more grandiose material using historical events and figures for inspiration. After moving to RCA he found fame and fortune in America with albums like 'Modern Times' and 'Year Of The Cat', although he remains a cult figure in this country.

<u>ROD STEWART</u> Born on January 10th 1945, Roderick David Stewart's early ambitions of stardom lay on the football field, and in fact he was an apprentice with Brentford F.C. before going to art college. In the early sixties he bummed round France and Spain with folk singer Wizz Jones, and when the pair were deported back to England for vagrancy, he got his first professional job as harmonica player with Jimmy Powell and The Five Dimension (q.v.) in 1964.

He was next with Long John Baldry (q.v.) and The Hoochie Coochie Men (q.v.), and at the end of 1964 had his first solo single, 'Good Morning Little Schoolgirl' on Decca. He also acquired his nickname "Rod The Mod", and when Baldry put together Steampacket (q.v.) in 1965 Stewart went with him. This group didn't have any records released during their brief lifespan, but Rod had a second solo single, 'Day Will Come', for Columbia. This was followed by 'Shake', also on Columbia, and 'Come Home Baby' on Decca, which was produced by Mick Jagger.

When Steampacket split up in 1966 he joined Shotgun Express (q.v.), with whom he made two singles for Columbia. In 1967 he recorded a version of 'Little Misunderstood' for Immediate, and in the same year made two singles under the name of Python Lee Jackson, 'In A Broken Dream' and 'The Blues'. The former reached No.3 when it was rereleased in 1972, and both records were re-issued in 1975. Around this time Stewart was also doing some session work for albums comprising covers of current hits.

After the demise of Shotgun Express Stewart made his first major leap towards international stardom as vocalist with The Jeff Beck Group (q.v.). The combination of his gravelly blues voice and Beck's fiery guitar work was a truly powerful one, and was particularly well received in America. He stayed with Beck until mid-

STONE THE CROWS — SULLIVAN JAMES BAND

1969, making 'Truth' and 'Beckola', and then joined The Faces (q.v.) with Beck's old bassist Ron Wood.

While with The Faces Stewart continued to pursue his solo career, which led to some complications as he was a solo artist with Mercury while The Faces were with Warner Bros. The Faces live performances established him still further as a showman of the first order, making especial play of his Scottish ancestry, while his albums - blending his own songs with well chosen material by other writers - were more successful, both artistically and commercially, than those by the whole group.

This disparity led to inevitable friction, which was heightened when 'Maggie May' from his third solo album, 'Every Picture Tells A Story', topped the charts on both sides of the Atlantic. Eventually Stewart went off on his own completely, leaving The Faces to slide into non-existence.

Since then his albums - 'Never A Dull Moment', 'Smiler', 'Atlantic Crossing', 'A Night On The Town' and 'Blondes Have More Fun' - and successive singles have made him into one of rock's biggest-selling artists. His tangled love life (including a celebrated relationship with Swedish film star Britt Ekland) and his transformation from "one of the lads" into an international jet-setter have made him the gossip columnists' delight, although threatening to erode his immensely strong grassroots following, but the consistent quality of his recorded and live work have more than staved off this danger.

STONE THE CROWS Maggie Bell (vocals), Les Harvey (lead guitar), John McGinnis (keyboards), Jim Dewar (bass) and Colin Allen (drums) were a Scottish heavy rock/blues group called Power, who toured clubs and airforce bases in Europe before being signed and renamed by Led Zeppelin (q.v.) manager Peter Grant. The group were signed by Polydor, but after 'Stone The Crows' and 'Ode To John Law' McGinnis and Dewar left in early 1971. Dewar, who had been with Lulu and The Luvvers (q.v.) in the mid-sixties, went on to play with ex-Procol Harum (q.v.) guitarist Robin Trower.

They were replaced by Ronnie Leahy (keyboards) and Steve Thompson (bass), the latter having previously been with Allen in John Mayall's (q.v.) group. Together they made 'Teenage Licks', by which time the group looked like breaking into the big time, and Maggie Bell was being widely acclaimed as Britain's top female vocalist. In 1972, however, Les Harvey, the younger brother of Alex Harvey (q.v.), was electrocuted onstage at Swansea, halfway through the recording of 'Continuous Performance'. Ex-Thunderclap Newman (q.v.) guitarist Jimmy McCulloch was eventually recruited in his place, but in mid-1973 the group split up.

McCulloch went on to join Paul McCartney's Wings, and Maggie Bell, who had had a long career singing with Glasgow dance bands before forming Power, took up a solo career which promised more than it actually achieved.

DANNY STORM AND THE STROLLERS Danny Storm was a good-looking lad who had a minor hit in 1962 with a sentimental ballad called 'Honest I Do' on Piccadilly. The Strollers were the backing group he used on tour.

RORY STORM AND THE HURRICANES Probably the most popular Merseybeat group never to make any national impact, they started off in the late fifties as a skiffle group called The Raving Texans, but became The Hurricanes when they took up rock'n'roll after the turn of the decade.

Storm himself was renowned on Merseyside for his wild stage act, and the group featured on Oriole's 'This Is Merseybeat' album. They also recorded a single version of 'Dr.Feelgood' for the same label at the end of 1963, and in the following year did a cover of 'America' for Parlophone, which was the first record to be produced by Brian Epstein (q.v.).

Their main claim to fame, however, was that Ringo Starr was their drummer before being pinched by The Beatles (q.v.). His successors behind the kit included Keef Hartley (q.v.) and Gibson Kemp, who went on to play with Paddy, Klaus and Gibson (q.v.). In 1973 Rory Storm committed suicide.

ROB STORME AND THE WHISPERS A Midlands-based beat group from the early sixties who recorded several singles for Pye. Storme himself later formed The Rob Storme Group, whose singles included a cover of The Beach Boys' 'Here Today' for Columbia in 1966.

THE STORMSVILLE SHAKERS A mid-sixties beat group fronted by keyboard player/vocalist Philip Goodhand-Tait, they made two albums with coloured American vocalist Larry Williams. They also made a few singles of their own for Parlophone, but Goodhand-Tait had much greater success as a songwriter, notably for The Love Affair (q.v.). He also recorded a number of solo albums for DJM and Chrysalis during the seventies.

THE STRAWBS Dave Cousins (acoustic guitar, banjo, vocals), Tony Hooper (acoustic guitar, vocals) and Ron Chesterman (double bass) started out in the mid-sixties as a bluegrass group called The Strawberry Hill Boys. They were joined at various times by banjoists Arthur Phillips and Talking John Berry, and gradually moved towards contemporary folk.

In 1967 they were joined by female singer Sandy Denny, and went to do a residency at The Tivoli in Copenhagen. While there they recorded an album, 'All Our Own Work', which was finally released in Britain by the Hallmark label in 1974. Back down to a trio again, they recorded their first "proper" album for A&M in 1969. 'The Strawbs' consisted entirely of material written by Cooper and Hooper, and included 'The Man Who Called Himself Jesus'.

For a while the group was augmented by classically trained cellist Clare Deniz, but she soon left, as did Chesterman to join Noel Murphy and Davy Johnstone in Draught Porridge. After 'Dragonfly' in 1970 The Strawbs became more rock-orientated with the addition of rhythm section John Ford and Richard "Hud" Hudson from Elmer Gantry's Velvet Opera (q.v.), and a young keyboards wizard from the Royal Academy of Music called Rick Wakeman.

'Just A Collection Of Antiques And Curios', recorded live at the Queen Elizabeth Hall', introduced them to a wider audience, which was solidified by 'From The Witchwood' in 1971. Wakeman then left to join Yes (q.v.) and was replaced by Blue Weaver from Amen Corner (q.v.) Hooper also left, dissatisfied with the group's increasingly commercial approach, after 'Grave New World' had given The Strawbs their first chart album in early 1972. His replacement was Dave Lambert, an old friend of Cousins.

Later that year Cousins made a solo album, 'Two Weeks Last Summer', and at the end of the year The Strawbs had their first singles success with 'Lay Down'. A few months later the singalong 'Part Of The Union' reached No.2, but its composers were Hudson and Ford, not Cousins. The almost inevitable clash of egos resulted, and after 'Bursting At The Seams' had been The Strawbs biggest selling album, the pair left to go it alone.

By now the group's direction was irretrievably confused between pop, rock and folk, and although they carried on to make several more albums with steadily-changing personnel, their popularity slumped alarmingly.

STUDIO SIX A Glasgow group formed in 1966, their singles for Polydor over the next year or so were 'When I See My Baby', 'Bless My Soul (I've Been And Gone And Done It)', 'Times Were When' and 'Strawberry Window'. They broke up in 1968.

THE SULLIVAN JAMES BAND A mid-sixties Ipswich group who recorded a few singles for Parlophone. They were an offshoot of Nix Nomads (q.v.) and St.Willy Cool School, although Nick Wymer, who had fronted both these groups, was not with them.

DAVE COUSINS/THE STRAWBS

SCREAMING LORD SUTCH & THE SAVAGES – TASTE

SCREAMING LORD SUTCH AND THE SAVAGES One of the most colourful personalities of the era, David Sutch burst forth in the early sixties with leopard skins, large bull horns, monster feet and two-foot-long hair. His act was a mixture of horror rock and slapstick humour, much of it "borrowed" from other performers, notably Screamin' Jay Hawkins, but great entertainment nevertheless.

In their early days The Savages - whose first line-up was Scratch And Scrape Bailey (guitar extraordinary), Hopping Ken, Rupert Pain (bass), Freddie Fingers (piano), Little Slasher Carlo (drums) and Leo The Flea - also sported leopard skins, and would carry Sutch onstage in a black coffin, from which he would crawl screaming. A single on this subject, 'Till The Following Night' was released by HMV in 1961, coupled with a version of 'Good Golly Miss Molly'.

Advertisements for the group warned that "those of a nervous disposition are advised to keep away", and onstage anything could happen ...including Sutch crashing through a grand piano while trying to leap from the stage into the orchestra pit! The group travelled to dates in an ambulance with a large pink plastic crocodile on top of it, though this practice was halted after an amazed motorist drove into a ditch while watching the crocodile open and close its mouth as the ambulance wended its way through the quiet country lanes of Devon.

In 1963 came Sutch's second single, 'Jack The Ripper' on Decca. It wasn't a hit, but was very popular on the video juke boxes of the time, where for a shilling Sutch could be seen performing the song while stalking young maidens, clad in a top hat and long black cloak, clutching a large butcher's knife. This was followed by 'I'm A Hog For You' coupled with 'Monster In Black Tights', which was Sutch's version of the current hit, 'Venus In Blue Jeans'.

1964 brought a change of label to Oriole, and 'Dracula's Daughter' followed by 'She's Fallen In Love With The Monster Man'. April 1965 saw Sutch as the subject of a BBC TV documentary called 'Sutch's Life', and later that year he caused a further sensation by standing as a parliamentary candidate for Stratford-Upon-Avon. For this escapade he formed his own party, the National Teenage Party, whose aims included the lowering of the voting age from 21 to 18, and the abolition of dog licences. He collected a grand total of thirty three votes, and lost his deposit.

Shortly after this he changed his name to Lord Sutch by deed poll, but while he continued to tour and make headlines consistently he only made one more single during the sixties, a version of 'Train Kept A-Rolling' for CBS. The Savages were eventually disbanded, having included such luminaries as guitarist Ritchie Blackmore, who went on to Deep Purple (q.v.), organist Matthew Fisher, who joined Procol Harum (q.v.), pianist Paul Nicholas (q.v.), and session drummer Carlo Little.

Despite his theatrical flair and eye for publicity, Sutch lacked the vocal ability to back up his antics, but in the early seventies he got to record two albums for Atlantic, 'Lord Sutch And Heavy Friends' and 'Hands Of Jack The Ripper', on which he received support from the likes of Blackmore, Little, Jimmy Page, John Bonham, Jeff Beck (q.v.), Nicky Hopkins (q.v.), Noel Redding and Keith Moon.

Soon afterwards he was in the news again, when he had the gall to accuse Alice Cooper of copying his style, and in 1973 he was booked to appear at a grand scale rock'n'roll revival concert at Wembley Stadium. To promote the event he dyed his hair green and paraded through the streets of London accompanied by several unclad young ladies waving banners. The outcome was a court appearance for all concerned, and as much publicity as he could possibly have hoped for.

Later in the decade he got married, after having an operation to enable him to father children, and went back on the road with a new version of The Savages.

SVENSKE A blond-haired duo from Bournemouth, they called themselves Svenske after friends had remarked that they looked Swedish, as that is the native translation of the word. Their debut single for Page One in 1966 was a pleasant ditty called 'Dream Magazine', which featured a church organ in the backing. The boys claimed that the record would go to Number One, and that their only problem would be writing B-sides, as all their songs were good enough to be top sellers. Sadly for them the public did not share their generous assessment of their talents, and neither 'Dream Magazine' nor the later 'You' sold in any great quantities.

THE SWINGING BLUE JEANS Ray Ennis (lead guitar, vocals), Ralph Ellis (rhythm guitar, vocals), Les Braid (bass) and Norman Kuhlke (drums) got together during 1959, and played at Hamburg's Star Club as The Bluegenes. With the advent of Merseybeat they were inevitably signed, by HMV, and after 'It's Too Late Now' had just made the Top Thirty in mid-1963 and 'Do You Know' had flopped, their cover of Chan Romero's 'Hippy Hippy Shake' reached No.2 at the start of 1964.

The follow-up, 'Good Golly Miss Molly', was a bit too much of a hoary old chestnut even by then, and only got to No.11. The group were getting plenty of exposure, however, and being promoted as rivals in fashion to The Beatles (q.v.) with their leather waistcoats and blue jeans. 'You're No Good' accordingly hit the Top Three later in the year, but then their hour of glory was suddenly over. They made an album, 'Blue Jeans A-swinging', comprising numbers like 'Tutti Frutti' and 'Long Tall Sally', and continued making singles for HMV right up until their demise in 1967. Only 'Don't Make Me Over' in 1967 was even a minor hit, however.

Ralph Ellis did the sane thing and left in 1964, right after The Swinging Blue Jeans had had their big hits. He was replaced by Terry Sylvester from The Escorts (q.v.), who replaced Graham Nash in The Hollies (q.v.) when the Blue Jeans broke up.

THE SYMBOLS A mid-sixties group who played the ballrooms with a Beach Boys-inspired surfing sound, they were in fact a very pale imitation of the real thing, and their singles for Parlophone and Columbia - which included 'See You In September' - were not big sellers.

THE SYN A flower power group formed in 1967, they were descendants of The Syndicats (q.v.). They made two singles for Deram, 'Created By Clive' and 'Flowerman', the latter being coupled with 'Fourteen Hour Technicolour Dream', a homage to the festival (q.v.). Among the group's personnel were bassist Chris Squire and guitarist Peter Banks, who helped form Yes (q.v.) in the following year.

THE SYNDICATS A mid-sixties R&B group, whose early line-up was Steve Howe (guitar) with S. Truelove, P.Driscoll and K.Driscoll. Howe left in 1965 to join The In Crowd (q.v.), and various personnel changes in the group's career saw Pete Banks and Chris Squire coming in, as well as guitarist Mick Stubbs, who cropped up in the seventies with Home.

Their singles included Chuck Berry's 'Maybelline' in 1964, and 'Howlin' For My Baby' and 'On The Horizon' in 1965, all on Columbia. The group shortened its name to The Syn to be more *au fait* in 1967.

THE TAGES A good Swedish five-piece group who were hailed as their homeland's answer to The Beatles (q.v.) in the mid-sixties. Unfortunately for them their live work and records in this country - 'Halcyon Days' on MGM among them - went virtually unnoticed.

TAKE FIVE An early sixties group from Southport, specializing in modern jazz and featuring vibraphonist Ollie Halsall. Halsall later took up the guitar, and was with Timebox (q.v.) and Mike Patto (q.v.).

SHEL TALMY A highly respected American producer, who came to England in the early sixties and produced all their early hits for The Who (q.v.) and The Kinks (q.v.), as well as working with Chad and Jeremy, The Bachelors, Creation, Manfred Mann, The Easybeats, Amen Corner, Nicky Hopkins and Pentangle (q.q.v.), among many others.

In the early seventies he became a partner in Talmy Franklin book publishers, whose best sellers included such literary milestones as 'Groupie', 'The Happy Hooker' and 'All Night Stand'. He also wrote his own novel, 'The Ichabod Deception', which was published in 1975. In the following year he returned to record production (which gives some idea how well his book did), and has since worked with Ralph McTell and ex-Creation guitarist Eddie Phillips.

TANGERINE PEEL A late sixties five-piece whose recordings included a single, 'Never Say Never Again' on MGM in 1969, and a pleasant sounding album, 'Soft Delights' on RCA in 1970. Their singer and songwriter was Mike Chapman (q.v.), who went on to write numerous hits, for people like Sweet, Mud and Suzi Quatro, in partnership with Nicky Chinn.

TASTE Rory Gallagher (guitar, vocals) came from

KING SIZE TAYLOR & THE DOMINOES – TEN YEARS AFTER

Cork in Southern Ireland, and after leaving school at an early age spent some time touring the country with The Fontana Showband. Quickly tiring of the kind of music they were playing, he broke away in 1965 with the rhythm section from the band, Norman Damery and Eric Kittringham, to form Taste. In mid-1966 they came to England, and spent the next two years touring the UK and the continent, gradually laying the groundwork for Gallagher's "guitar hero" status.

When Taste finally won a contract with Polydor, Damery and Kittringham had been replaced by Richard McCracken (bass) and John Wilson (drums). It made no difference, though as Taste were essentially a vehicle for Gallagher's blues guitar playing. They made four albums - 'Taste', 'On The Boards', 'Live At The Isle Of Wight' and 'Live' - before Gallagher decided to go solo in late 1970. Quite why is a mystery, since all he did was get in a new rhythm section, and carry on doing exactly what he'd been doing before.

KING SIZE TAYLOR AND THE DOMINOES One of the first Merseybeat groups in existence, known as The James Boys during the skiffle era, they spent much of the early sixties in Hamburg. Their act revolved around standards like Larry Williams' 'Dizzy Miss Lizzy', Chuck Berry's 'Memphis', 'Slippin' and Slidin'', 'Hello Josephine' and 'Studpidity', the latter coming out as a single on Decca in 1963. They made several more singles, and an EP called 'Teenbeat 2' in early 1965.

Apart from Taylor himself, the group comprised two guitarists and a drummer, who for a time was Gibson Kemp, formerly with Rory Storm and The Hurricanes (q.v.) and later with Paddy, Klaus and Gibson (q.v.). Taylor, who played sax as well as singing, went on to record as a solo artist for Polydor when the Dominoes packed up, but in 1967 he returned to his former trade as a butcher.

TEA AND SYMPHONY A "progressive" group from Birmingham, who made the 'Asylum For The Musically Insane' album for Harvest in 1969. Guitarists Dave Carroll and Bob Wilson joined The Steve Gibbons Band in 1973.

THE TEA TIME FOUR An early sixties R&B group from Kings Lynn in Norfolk, fronted by singer and rhythm guitarist Raymond "Boz" Burrell. The group had a good reputation on the local circuit, and often gave the top-line bands they supported a hard time. They had several line-up changes during their career, and included bass players Fats Dean and Bernard Barton, and guitarist Mike Prior, among others. In 1965 the group moved down to London, and with the addition of organist Ian MacLagen became Boz People (q.v.).

THE TEMPERENCE SEVEN Whispering Paul McDowell (vocals), Cephas Howerd (trumpet), Joe Clark (clarinet), Alan Swainton Cooper (pedal clarinet), Phillip Harrison (banjo), Colin Bowles (piano and harmonica), Clifford Bevan (tuba), Brian Innes (drums) plus A.N.Other were nine professional men who got together in 1955 to play their own brand of 1920s jazz, with singer McDowell adding the final touch of authenticity by singing through a megaphone.

When asked why they were called The Temperence Seven when there were nine of them, the reply was that they were usually "one over the eight". Their music was actually both witty and sophisticated, and in 1961 their debut single, an arrangement of 'You're Driving Me Crazy' on Parlophone, shot to the top of the charts. This was followed by further Top Twenty success in the same year with 'Pasadena', 'Hard Hearted Hannah/Chilli Bom-Bom' and 'The Charleston'. They also made three albums in the same year - 'Temperence Seven Plus One', 'Temperence Seven 1961' and 'Temperence Seven'.

During their career the group made numerous TV appearances, and also performed in the Spike Milligan/John Antrobus play 'The Red Sitting Room'. The group eventually split up when McDowell departed to become a satirist, but in the seventies they reformed with a new vocalist.

TEN FOOT FIVE An Andover group who recorded 'Baby's Back In Town' for Fontana in 1965. The group included guitarist Chris Britton and bassist Pete Staples, who joined The Troggs (q.v.) later in that same year.

TEN YEARS AFTER Alvin Lee (guitar, vocals), Chick Churchill (keyboards), Leo Lyons (bass) and Ric Lee (drums) started out together in the mid-sixties as The Jaybirds, backing The Ivy League (q.v.). They then became Blues Yard, and finally rode the late sixties blues wave as Ten Years After. Originating in Nottingham, the group's main claim to fame (some might say only claim to fame) was Alvin Lee's speed-of-light guitar work.

Signed by Decca, they made 'Ten Years After' in 1967 and 'Undead' in 1968, and then became international superstars almost overnight, as a result of their appearance at the Woodstock festival, and their prominently featured role in the subsequent movie performing their "anthem", 'Goin' Home'.

Thereafter the group spent most of their time abroad, particularly in the States, but their albums in the late sixties and early seventies - 'Stonedhenge', 'Ssshh', 'Cricklewood Green' and 'Watt' - continued to make the British charts, and they even had a Top Ten single in mid-1970 with 'Love Like A Man'.

Eventually Alvin Lee became tired of their endless touring schedule and the limited range imposed on them by post-Woodstock public expectations, and from 1973 until the group's final demise in 1975, he became increasingly involved in outside activities. He made the 'On The Road To Freedom' album with American gospel singer Mylon LeFevre and a live double album, 'In

THEE — TORNADOES

Flight', and later formed his own group, Alvin Lee & Co. Chick Churchill also made a solo album, 'You And Me', but after the group's demise he and the two other members both went to work in other areas of the music business.

THEE A four-piece mid-sixties group, managed by Andrew Loog Oldham's (q.v.) chauffeur Reg King, their singles for Decca included the Jagger/ Richard song 'Each And Every Day' in 1965.

THEM Van Morrison (vocals, harmonica, sax) formed Them in Belfast during 1963, after several years in local semi-professional groups and a tour of Britain and the continent with an R&B group called The Monarchs. The original line-up was Ray Elliott (organ), Jim Armstrong (guitar), Alan Henderson (bass) and David Harvey (drums), although they didn't last long, and the more settled line-up (or as settled as Them were ever likely to be) was Henderson, Billy Harrison (guitar), Jackie McAuley (organ) and Patrick McAuley (drums).

As an all-out R&B band they had few equals, and after performing regularly at Belfast's only R&B venue, the Old Sailors Maritime Dance Hall, they brought their raw sound and rebel image to London in 1964, and were soon signed by Decca.

They were produced by illustrious American Bert Berns (who had done 'Hang On Sloopy' for The McCoys and 'Under The Boardwalk' for The Drifters, as well as co-writing 'Twist And Shout'), and after 'Don't Start Crying Now' had flopped, Them hit the Top Ten (thanks partly to a startling appearance on Ready Steady Go (q.v.)) with Big Joe Williams' 'Baby Please Don't Go'. The flip side was Morrison's own 'Gloria', which has since become a rock classic.

The follow-up to this success was Berns' 'Here Comes The Night'. It reached No.2 in the spring of 1965, but was to be the group's last chart entry. The McAuley brothers left and went home to Ireland, being replaced by Peter Bardens (keyboards) and Ronnie Millinck (drums) but from that point onwards the line-up became very loose, and the group's remaining singles - Van's own 'One More Time', 'It Won't Hurt Half As Much', 'Mystic Eyes' and 'Call My Name', and Paul Simon's 'Richard Cory' - were often recorded with just Van and various session men (who sometimes included Jimmy Page).

There were two albums, 'Them' and 'Them Again', and an EP, but in June 1966 the group finally broke up after an unhappy tour of America, and Morrison returned to Ireland to lick his wounds. Henderson kept the name alive, however, with the recruitment of Keith McDowell (vocals), Jim Armstrong and David Harvey, and they made four albums which were never released in the UK before splitting up once and for all.

In 1967 Major Minor released a double-sided single 'The Story Of Them', which had actually been recorded in 1964 and told the story of the group's early days in Belfast. Decca have also disinterred Them's past with three compilation albums, 'The World Of Them', 'Them, Featuring Van Morrison' and 'Rock Roots'.

Morrison himself, meanwhile, had gone to New York at the invitation of Bert Berns, and in 1967 had a Top Ten single in the States with 'Brown Eyed Girl' on Berns' own Bang label. He did several other sessions, which were subsequently released as 'Blowin' Your Mind' and later as 'This Is Where I Came In', but at the end of the year Berns died of a heart attack. This left Morrison free to sign with Warner Brothers, for whom he recorded the classic 'Astral Weeks' in 1968. This was followed by another brilliant work, 'Moondance' in 1969, and a string of albums through the seventies which have enhanced Morrison's status as one of the finest singers and writers in rock music.

THE THIRD EAR BAND American Richard Coff(viola, violin) and Britons Paul Minns (oboe), Ursula Smith (cello) and Glenn Sweeney (percussion) began life in 1967 as The Giant Sun Trolley, and were also known as The Hydrogen Jukebox before becoming the Third Ear Band. They played hypnotic, largely improvised music with a strong oriental flavour, and made two albums for Harvest, 'Alchemy' in 1969 and 'Third Ear Band' in 1970, the latter comprising four extended pieces inspired by the different elements. In 1972, without Coff and Smith, but with the addition of cellist Paul Buckmaster, guitarist Denim Bridges and ex-High Tide (q.v.) violinist Simon House, they composed and recorded the soundtrack music for Roman Polanski's 'Macbeth'.

THOUGHTS A group led by vocalist Paul Dean who recorded a version of Ray Davies' 'All Night Stand' for Planet in 1966.

THREE GOOD REASONS A mid-sixties group whose singles for Parlophone included a version of The Beatles' (q.v.) 'Here There And Everywhere' in 1966. In the same year they had a minor hit on Mercury with 'Nowhere Man'.

THUNDERCLAP NEWMAN Speedy Keen was a songwriter who used to hang around Track's offices in the late sixties, and eventually Pete Townshend put together a studio group with Keen on drums, himself on bass, sixteen-year-old Jimmy Mc-Culloch on guitar, and a plump, bespectacled ex-post office engineer and Bix Beiderbecke fanatic called Andy Newman.

Their first single was Keen's 'Something In The Air', a brilliant record which perfectly captured the changing mood of the times and hastened to Number One in the middle of 1969.

This runaway success caught Thunderclap Newman on the hop, however, as they were unprepared for any touring. The line-up was hastily expanded by pushing Keen to the front and bringing in Jim Avery (bass) and Jimmy McCulloch's younger brother Jack on drums, but they were a thoroughly ill-assorted outfit, almost doomed from the start. Accordingly, after a minor hit with 'Accidents' and an album called 'Hollywood Dream', they broke up in mid-1970.

Andy Newman made a solo album called 'Rainbow' in 1971; Jimmy McCulloch joined Stone The Crows (q.v.) and then Wings; and Keen also made a couple of solo albums without recapturing his magic touch.

TIMEBOX Mike Patto (vocals), Pete "Ollie" Halsall (guitar), Chris Holmes (piano), Clive Griffiths (bass) and John Halsey (drums) formed Timebox in 1966, but were not signed by Deram until two years later. They were given the old Four Seasons American hit 'Beggin'' to record, and it became a minor hit. The group were not happy with this style, however, and after 'Baked Jam Roll In Your Eye' in 1969 they changed their musical direction and became Patto (q.v.).

TINTERN ABBEY A group whose singles for Deram included 'Beeside' in 1967.

T.N.T. The group who took over from The Nice (q.v.) as P.P.Arnold's (q.v.) backing group in 1967. Eddie Phillips, the guitarist from Creation (q.v.), gave the group a distinctive sound by playing lead on a bass guitar.

TOBY TWIRL A psychedelic pop group whose singles for Decca included 'Harry Faversham' and 'Utopia Daydream' in 1968.

TOE FAT After finally phasing out The Rebel Rousers in the late sixties, Cliff Bennett (q.v.) took time out for the hair on his head and chin to grow, and then turned heavy with Toe Fat. They made two albums, 'Toe Fat' and 'Toe Fat 2', produced by John Peel (q.v.), whose lack of impact can perhaps be partly attributed to the gross sleeve designs. The group also featured keyboard player Ken Hensley from The Gods (q.v.), prior to that worthy forming Uriah Heep.

THE TOGGERY FIVE A Manchester group who were runners-up to The Bo Street Runners (q.v.) in the Ready Steady Go (q.v.) R&B Group Contest of 1964, they nevertheless landed a contract with Parlophone. Among their singles were the dramatic death song, 'I'm Gonna Jump', and an Andrew Oldham (q.v.)/Keith Richard composition, 'I'd Much Rather Be With The Boys'.

TOMORROW Vocalist Keith West (q.v.), Steve Howe (guitar), John "Junior" Wood (bass) and Twink (q.v.) on drums made up one of the best groups of the psychedelic era, who would undoubtedly have gone much further had it not been for a confusion of interests.

West, Howe and Wood had all been with The In Crowd (q.v.), while Twink had come from The Fairies (q.v.), but at the same time as Tomorrow were in existence West was working on the 'Teenage Opera' project with Marc Wirtz...in fact the idea originally was for all four members to have parallel solo careers. After he had struck big with 'Excerpt From A Teenage Opera', the group were often billed as Tomorrow featuring Keith West, which tended to draw in large teenybop crowds who weren't too appreciative of the group's usual stuff.

Their singles for Parlophone were 'My White Bicycle' and a version of The Beatles' (q.v.) 'Revolution', and they also made an album comprising such delights as 'Real Life Permanent Dream', 'Auntie Mary's Dress Shop' and 'Strawberry Fields Forever'. This album was re-released by Harvest in 1977.

Eventually the group just faded away as the members became involved in other things. Howe formed Bodast (q.v.), Twink joined The Pretty Things (q.v.), Wood was briefly with The Jeff Beck Group (q.v.), and West moved into production.

THE TORNADOES Alan Caddy (lead guitar), George Bellamy (rhythm guitar), Roger Lavern (keyboards), Heinz Burt (bass) and Clem Cattini (drums) were formed in 1961 by producer Joe Meek, and after backing Billy Fury for a while shot to Number One in late 1962 with their first single for Decca, the instrumental 'Telstar', which was also the first record by a British group to top the American charts.

'Globetrotter' followed into the Top Five, and 'Robot' and 'Ice Cream Man' made the Top Twenty during 1963, but thereafter The Tornadoes faded, and were wiped out by Merseybeat. They kept recording singles for Decca and Columbia until their final demise in 1966, and also made three EPs and an album, 'Away From It All'. They went through various personnel changes, and at one time included Roy

TRADER HORN — TRAFFIC

Phillips (keyboards, guitar) and Tab Martin (bass), who later formed The Peddlars (q.v.). Drummer Cattini went on to become an in-demand session musician.

Bassist Heinz was the blond-haired token sex symbol of the group, and in mid-1963 he left to go solo. Over the next three years he made a series of singles for Decca and Columbia, of which 'Just Like Eddie' (a tribute to Eddie Cochran) reached No.5, and 'Country Boy', 'You Were There', 'Questions I Can't Answer' and 'Diggin' My Potatoes' were minor hits. He also put out an EP and an album, and in 1977 Decca put together a compilation album, 'Remember Heinz'. He retired from the business in the late sixties, after appearing in a couple of pop films, but cropped up again in 1976 as an actor in a TV play.

TRADER HORN A late sixties folk duo with Judy Dyble, from Fairport Convention (q.v.), and Jackie McAuley from Them (q.v.) and Belfast Gypsies (q.v.). Judy was replaced by Saffron Summerfield, but after about eighteen months the pair went their separate ways, with Saffron going back to working the folk clubs of Britain and the continent as a solo performer. Trader Horn made an album for Pye, and their singles included 'Sheens' in 1969.

TRAFFIC Stevie Winwood (guitar, keyboards, vocals), Dave Mason (guitar, vocals), Chris Wood (sax, flute) and Jim Capaldi (drums) were formed in early 1967 after Winwood had left The Spencer Davis Group (q.v.). The others also came from the Birmingham area, Mason and Capaldi having been with Deep Feeling (q.v.) and Wood with Locomotive (q.v.).

The group spent several months in Berkshire, pioneering the "getting it together in the country" syndrome, and during this period their eagerly-awaited Island debut, 'Paper Sun', went to No.5 in the charts. Not surprisingly, the single was in the psychedelic vein, as were the next two, 'Hole In My Shoe' and 'Here We Go Round The Mulberry Bush', which also made the Top Ten.

Their first album, 'Mr.Fantasy', amply fulfilled Traffic's promise with songs like 'No Face No Name No Number', 'Coloured Rain' and 'Heaven Is In Your Mind', but at the end of 1967 Dave Mason left the group. He was back again within a few months, however, to help record 'Traffic', but in December 1968 the group split up completely, leaving 'Last Exit' as their legacy.

Winwood joined Blind Faith (q.v.), while the remaining members formed Mason, Wood, Capaldi and Frog, with keyboard player Wynder K.Frog (q.v.), and made one album for Island. Mason then headed for America, where he launched a solo career with the fine 'Alone Together'. Wood also went to America and toured with Dr. John, while Capaldi did some session work, including Mason's first album.

In 1970 Winwood, Wood and Capaldi met up again in Ginger Baker's Airforce, and soon reformed Traffic to make 'John Barleycorn Must Die', which took an almost folk-rock direction. A few months later bassist Ric Grech, from Family (q.v.), Blind Faith (q.v.) and Airforce, came in, and was soon followed by American drummer Jim Gordon and percussionist Rebop, which left Capaldi free to move to the fore as vocalist. Mason also returned for a British tour, and this line-up was captured for posterity on the live 'Welcome To The Canteen'.

After Mason's return to the States, Traffic moved into the area of funky rock, where they stayed for the rest of their days together. After 'Low Spark Of High Heeled Boys' Gordon left, as did Grech, and in their places came America's top Muscle Shoals sessionmen, David Hood (drums), Roger Hawkins (bass) and Barry Beckett (keyboards). They recorded 'Shootout At The Fantasy Factory' and did a European tour during which 'On The Road' was made.

In 1974 Traffic went back down to a quartet

TRAFFIC JAM — TROGGS

with Winwood, Capaldi, Wood and black bassist Rosko Gee, but after 'When The Eagle Flies' and a British tour they came off the road for the final time. Capaldi continued the solo career which he had begun in 1972 with 'Oh How We Danced', and had a No.4 hit in 1975 with the old Roy Orbison song 'Love Hurts'. Winwood went into hibernation until 1977, when he also made a solo album.

TRAFFIC JAM Mike Rossi (guitar, vocals), Alan Lancaster (guitar), Rod Lynes (organ), Rick Parfitt (bass) and John Coghlan (drums) changed their name from The Spectres (q.v.) to Traffic in 1967, However, since Stevie Winwood had a head's start on them with this name they became Traffic Jam, and recorded 'Almost There But Not Quite' for Piccadilly before metamorphosing yet again into Status Quo (q.v.).

TRAMLINE A late sixties group whose solitary album for Island, 'Moves Of Vegetable Centuries' included the Winwood/Capaldi composition 'Pearly Queen'.

TRASH Ian Crawford-Clews (vocals), Fraser Watson (lead guitar), Ronald Leahy (organ), Colin Hunter-Morrison (bass) and Timi Donald (drums) started out during the mid-sixties as The Pathfinders (q.v.), and by 1968 were one of Glasgow's top groups. Discovered by ex-Shadow (q.v.) Tony Meehan, they came down to London, where they were signed by Apple and renamed White Trash by Apple's "house hippy" Richard DiLello.

However, when they put out their first single, 'Road To Nowhere', the BBC refused to play it because they found the name offensive. Their name was accordingly shortened and the record got a fair bit of airplay, and became a hit in Holland.

In 1969 Trash embarked on a British tour backing Marsha Hunt (q.v.), and then had a minor hit with a version of The Beatles (q.v.) 'Golden Slumbers/Carry That Weight'. By now, though, Apple was becoming increasingly chaotic, and soon afterwards Trash split up. Timi Donald went on to play with various groups, including Blue, and Ronnie Leahy has done time with Stone The Crows (q.v.), Alvin Lee & Co. and the short-lived Jack Bruce Band.

THE TREKKAS A mid-sixties group whose singles included 'Please Go' on Planet in 1965.

THE TREMELOES When Brian Poole (q.v.) decided to go solo in 1966, his backing group The Tremeloes carried on without him. Alan Blakely (guitar, keyboards, vocals), Ricky West (guitar) and Dave Munden (drums) replaced bassist Alan Howard with Chip Hawkes (bass, vocals), and after 'Blessed' and 'Good Day Sunshine' had both flopped on Decca, they signed with CBS in 1967 and had a run of chart successes which lasted four years.

Cat Stevens' (q.v.) 'Here Comes My Baby' went to No.4, and this was followed by a Number One with 'Silence Is Golden'. Their debut album, 'Here Come The Tremeloes', also sold well, and several of their later hits were written by the group. They were an unashamed, good-time pop group, who were naturally looked down on by "serious" music lovers, but they developed ideas above their station. In the early seventies they decried all their previous work as rubbish, and their fans as morons. Despite the probable truth of this statement, they promptly lost their following, and an attempt to gain credibility via the 'Master' album fell predictably flat.

Chip Hawkes eventually left to make a solo album in Nashville, leaving the others to tout their "rubbish" round the cabaret circuit.

TRENDSETTERS LTD. A mid-sixties instrumental combo from Bournemouth, complete with brass section, who recorded for Parlophone and spent much of their time backing visiting American soul artists like Ben E. King.

THE TRIDENTS An early sixties R&B group who featured Jeff Beck (q.v.) on lead guitar. Beck replaced Eric Clapton in The Yardbirds (q.v.) in 1965.

THE TROGGS Reg Presley (real name Ball) (vocals), Chris Britton (guitar), Pete Staples (bass) and Ronnie Bond (drums) came from Andover in Hampshire, and did much to liven up the charts in the latter half of the sixties.

Anybody with the nerve to call himself Presley was not to be instantly dismissed, and sure enough, after 'Lost Girl' had flopped on CBS in early 1966, The Troggs (who were originally called The Troglodytes) made No.2 with a Chip Taylor song, 'Wild Thing', on Fontana.

They were brash, completely without subtlety, and specialised in raw rock songs with suggestive lyrics...and the great British public took Reg and his boys to their hearts. 'With A Girl Like You' reached Number One in the summer of 1966, and after moving to manager Larry Page's Page One label 'I Can't Control Myself' stopped only one place short of that. Both songs were penned by naughty Reg, and the latter was banned in Australia and virtually banned by the BBC, thanks to the line "Her slacks are low and her hips are showing".

Both their albums, 'From Nowhere' and 'Trogglodynamite', got into the album Top Ten, and 1967 - although less successful than the previous year - saw them hitting the Top Ten with 'Anyway That You Want Me' and 'Love Is All Around', and the Top Twenty with 'Give It To Me' and 'Night Of The Long Grass'.

Chris Britton apparently wanted to leave the group around this time, having become disenchanted with being a pop star, but Page made him hang on to the bitter end...which finally came in early 1969, by which time The Troggs hour of glory was well and truly passed.

Page One put out 'Cellophane', a "best of" anthology, and The Troggs went their separate ways. Presley had a solo single, 'Lucinda Lee', as did Ronnie Bond in 'Anything For You'. Chris Britton went one better and actually made an album, 'As I Am', although it didn't cause much of a stir. The group also left behind them (inadvertently) a tape of themselves in the studio, trying to come up with another hit without the guidance of Larry Page and giving a wonderful demonstration of the richness of West Country vocabulary...the tape has since become something of a collectors' item in music business circles.

In 1972 The Troggs reformed with Presley and Bond as the only surviving members, and since then they have toured consistently, although preferring to stick to clubs and colleges rather than follow many of their contemporaries into cabaret. They have also made the occasional record, and have remained as *risqué* as ever. Their version of the Beach Boys 'Good Vibrations' replaced the line "I love the purple cloak she wears" with "I love the dress she almost wears", and prompted one music paper wag to suggest that their version should have been retitled 'Good Vibrators'.

The Troggs touring schedule even took them over to the States, where 'Wild Thing' had been a Number One, and in 1979 they signed with the Max's Kansas City label in New York.

TRUTH-UGLIES

TRUTH A north country group who had a Top Thirty hit in early 1966 with The Beatles' (q.v.) 'Girl'...although St.Louis Union (q.v.) had the bigger-selling version. The group were together for four years in all, during which time Groundhogs (q.v.) guitarist was briefly a member, and after their demise vocalist Steve Jameson made several records as a solo artist. In 1974 he assumed the name of Nosmo King, and entered the Top Thirty again with 'Goodbye Nothing To Say'.

CY TUCKER A Merseybeat singer whose singles included 'My Prayer' in 1964, on which he was backed by Earl Preston's group The TTs (q.v.).

TUESDAY'S CHILDREN A pop group of the mid to late sixties who recorded singles for both Columbia and Mercury without making much impression.

TWICE AS MUCH David Skinner and Stephen Rose were two ex-public schoolboys who wrote songs and sang together. In 1966 they approached Andrew Loog Oldham (q.v.) to play him some of their material, and he signed them to his Immediate label. They were given a Jagger/Richard song, 'Sittin' On A Fence', for their first single, and it went into the Top Thirty. The follow-up, their own 'Step Out Of Line', did not do so well, but after making an album called 'That's All' it was, and the duo went their separate ways. In the early seventies Skinner popped up again as the keyboard player with pub rock group Uncle Dog, and then in 1979 he joined the re-formed Roxy Music.

TWINK Johnny Alder grew up in the Colchester area, and in 1963 became the drummer with a local group called Dane Stephens and The Deep Beats, who changed their name to The Fairies (q.v.) when they got a recording contract in 1964.

When The Fairies vanished in 1967 Twink (as he was now known) joined Tomorrow (q.v.), but while still with them he became involved with The Pretty Things (q.v.), whom he eventually joined for the recording of the 'S.F. Sorrow' album. By this time Twink had established a reputation as an arch-looner, and after leaving The Pretty Things in 1969 he formed the first, "unofficial" version of The Pink Fairies with two gentlemen of similar inclinations, Mick Farren from The Deviants (q.v.) and Steve Peregrine Took from Tyrannosaurus Rex (q.v.)...their name came from the pink velvet jacket which was Twink's trademark. While still playing with their respective groups, the three got into the habit of turning up at each others gigs, and causing such a disturbance that the Bryan Morrison agency eventually banned any of the groups from appearing together.

Also in 1969, Twink recorded an album, 'Think Pink', with the assistance of a whole host of people, including "Junior" Wood from Tomorrow, Took, and the three other Deviants, Duncan Sanderson, Russell Hunter and Paul Rudolph. A mixture of self-penned songs, poems and instrumentals, which featured Twink singing as well as drumming, it was eventually released by Polydor in 1970.

Meanwhile The Deviants had split up after an American tour, and when Farren returned to London the first Pink Fairies got together properly (if it can be so called). They played on Farren's solo album, 'Mona', but the nearest they got to actually performing was when they went to Manchester...but without bothering to take any instruments, which caused some confusion amongst the audience.

Deciding that he wanted a group who would actually play music, Twink contacted the other Deviants, who were still in America, and on April 5th 1970 the quartet made The Pink Fairies first live appearance at The Roundhouse. In the same year they had a single, 'The Snake', and an album, 'Never Never Land', out on Polydor.

By mid-1971, however, Twink was suffering from "personal problems" which prohibited communication with the rest of the group, and also made it hard for him to play his drums. In the June he suddenly announced that he was leaving both the group and the country, and promptly disappeared. Rumours about his fate abounded, but a few months later he returned and made a few guest appearances with the group.

In 1972 he formed Stars with ex-Pink Floyd (q.v.)guitarist Syd Barrett and bass guitarist Jack Monk from Delivery (q.v.).The past record of this line-up made a long term association unlikely, however, and indeed they lasted for only half a set before Barrett walked offstage, never to return.

In 1974 Twink got married, and soon afterwards was reported to be putting together a group called Glider. This came to nothing, as did a projected group called Fallen Angels in 1976, but in mid-1977 Twink finally got back into action as lead vocalist with The Rings, who had a single called 'I Wanna Be Free' on the Chiswick label. He then recorded one further single,'Do It '77'as Twink and the Fairies, before retiring to Germany.

TYRANNOSAURUS REX Mark Feld was born in Hackney, North London, in September 1947, and began his career in show business as a child actor, appearing in the TV series 'Orlando'. After featuring in 'Town' magazine as one of the capital's leading mods, he signed a recording contract with Decca, who were going to call him Mark Bowland until he changed it to Marc Bolan. He made two singles for them, 'The Wizard' and 'The Third Degree in 1965 and 1966 respectively, and even went on the TV show 'Thank Your Lucky Stars'.

In late 1966 came 'Hippy Gumbo'on Columbia, and he then spent a few short, but eventful months with John's Children (q.v.) before forming Tyrannosaurus Rex in early 1968. Originally the group was going to have five or six members, but after losing all their equipment almost at once, it was reduced to an acoustic duo comprising Marc and Steve Peregrine Took (percussion and backing vocals). Steve's last two names came from Tolkien's 'Lord Of The Rings', which was very apt in view of the mythical, fantastical subject matter of most of Tyrannosaurus Rex's early songs.

The duo started gigging at London's Middle Earth club, and were soon receiving almost fanatical support from DJs John Peel (q.v.) and Jeff Dexter, which helped them to build up a tremendous following among the hippy population. Bolan sang his strange songs in a very nasal voice, and their first single on Regal Zonophone, 'Deborah', was a minor hit, as were 'One Inch Rock' and 'King Of The Rumbling Spires'.The first two were later reissued as a double A-side in 1972, when they reached No.7 in the charts.

The first two albums, 'My People Were Fair And Wore Stars In Their Hair' and 'Prophets Seers And Sages', were more of the same acoustic fare and sold well, but for 'Unicorn' in 1969 the group's instrumental sound was considerably expanded. Took then left to form The Pink Fairies, and was replaced by Micky Finn from Haphash and The Coloured Coat (q.v.). Together they made the much more electric rock orientated 'Beard Of Stars', their last album for Regal Zonophone, which pointed the way Bolan was to follow to superstardom.

In late 1970 their first album on Fly, 'T.Rex', was released along with 'Ride A White Swan', which hastened up the charts to No.2. The combination of catchy boogie and Bolan's teen appeal was an instant smash, and for over two years Bolan was to be the hottest pop property in the country, enjoying eleven successive Top Ten singles, including four Number Ones.

The group's line-up was expanded by bassist Steve Currie, drummer Bill Legend from Legend (q.v.), and guitarist Jack Green. The albums 'Electric Warrior' and 'The Slider'were highly successful, and wild scenes took place at T.Rex concerts as Bolan - together with David Bowie (q.v.) ushered in the glitter age.

Eventually it all became too much, however. T.Rex's attempts to capture the American market were fairly disastrous, the quality of their records (and their popularity) was dropping, and Bolan's state of health was in decline at the same time. He had his own label by now, distributed through EMI, but by the end of 1973 T.Rex singles were struggling to reach the Top Twenty. Moreover, Bolan had been divorced from his wife June, who in many eyes had been instrumental behind the scenes in his rise to the top.

At the end of 1975, after T.Rex had been declared defunct, Bolan announced that his girlfriend, coloured American singer Gloria Jones, was expecting his child, and that he was expecting to make a comeback. He was having no further truck with drugs, was looking much fitter, and had put together a completely new T.Rex, which included Ms.Jones on keyboards. The 'Futuristic Dragon' album in early 1976 and an accompanying British tour didn't exactly restore Bolan to his former prominence, but it showed there was still life in him, and in 1977 the line-up was refurbished yet again for the 'Dandy In The Underworld' album. Before his career could gather its old momentum, however, Bolan was tragically killed in a car crash in September 1977.

THE UFO CLUB Run in conjunction with the underground newspaper International Times, the UFO operated from a basement in Tottenham Court Road. It opened in December 1966, and quickly became a focal point for the burgeoning underground movement and the drastically-changing music scene. All the top groups of the psychedelic era - Pink Floyd, Soft Machine,Tomorrow, The Crazy World Of Arthur Brown, The Move, Family (q.q.v.), etc. - appeared there, along with established acts like The Jeff Beck Group (q.v.) and various multi-media events. The club was eventually closed in October 1967.

THE UGLIES Variously known as The Uglies, The Uglys and The Ugly's, but not to be confused with the American group of the same name, they came from Birmingham in the mid-sixties, led by vocalist Steve Gibbons. Changes in the group's personnel were frequent, and among

UNDERTAKERS – VAN DER GRAAF GENERATOR

those passing through were Trevor Burton from The Move (q.v.), drummer Keith Smart who went on to join Roy Wood's Wizzard, and keyboard player Richard Tandy, later in the Electric Light Orchestra. Another keyboard man with the group was Jimmy O'Neill, who later spent periods with The Mindbenders (q.v.) and The Walker Brothers (q.v.).

In the mid-sixties they made several singles for Pye, including 'Wake Up My Mind', 'It's Alright', 'A Good Idea' and Ray Davies' 'End Of The Season'. None of them got a look at the charts, but the group were still alive and kicking at the end of the decade, when they made 'And The Squire Blew His Horn' for CBS, and 'I See The Light' for MGM. Gibbons later made a solo album on Wizard Records, 'Short Stories', and in 1973 formed The Steve Gibbons Band.

THE UNDERTAKERS Jackie Lomax, Bugs Pemberton, Chris Huxton, George Nugent and Brian Jones (not the Rolling Stone (q.v.)) made up one of Merseyside's better groups of the early sixties. They used to arrive at gigs in a hearse, and appeared on stage (and on TV) in black frock coats, black trousers and top hats. Their singles for Pye during 1963-4 were 'Mashed Potatoes', 'What About us' and 'Just A Little Bit', which was a minor hit. They then shortened their name to The 'Takers for 'If You Don't Come Back'.

The group's outstanding features were Brian Jones' fine sax playing and Jackie Lomax's incredible vocal range, and after the group had broken up Lomax formed Lomax Alliance (q.v.) before embarking on a solo career.

UNIT FOUR PLUS TWO Pete Moules (vocals) Tommy Moeller (guitar, vocals), Howard Lubin (guitar, vocals) and David Meikle (guitar, vocals) were a Hertfordshire folk group called Unit Four who decided to beef up their sound with the addition of Rod Garwood (bass) and Hugh Halliday (drums) in 1964.

Their first single for Decca, 'The Green Fields' was a minor hit, but 'Sorrow And Pain' flopped before another song written by Tommy Moeller and Brian Parker (who had been with the group in their very early days), the beautiful 'Concrete And Clay', swept to Number One in the spring of 1965.

'You've Never Been In Love Like This Before' got into the Top Twenty shortly afterwards, and Unit Four Plus Two also made an EP and an album, but of their further singles for Decca and Fontana, only 'Hark', 'You've Got To Be Cruel To Be Kind' and 'Baby Never Say Goodbye' were even minor successes, and by 1967 the times had well and truly passed the group by. In their latter days, Russ Ballard (guitar) and Bob Henrit (drums) from The Roulettes (q.v.) were members for a few months.

THE UNTAMED A mid-sixties group led by Lindsay Muir, who were groomed by producer Shel Talmy (q.v.) to follow in the footsteps of The Who (q.v.), but never quite made it. Their singles between 1964 and 1966 were 'So Long' on Decca, 'Once Upon A Time' on Parlophone, 'I'll Go Crazy' on Stateside', 'It's Not True' (written by Pete Townshend) and 'Daddy Long Legs' on Planet.

THE URCHINS A group whose Polydor singles included 'I Made Her That Way' in 1967.

VAN DER GRAAF GENERATOR Formed by singer/songwriter Peter Hammill while at Manchester University in 1967, the original members were Hammill (guitar, vocals), Nick Pearne (organ) and Chris Smith (drums). This line-up was short-lived, and was soon replaced by Hammill, Hugh Banton (organ), Keith Ellis (bass) and Guy Evans (drums). Again the group split up without recording, but when Hammill started recording a solo album for Mercury in 1968, Banton and Evans helped out, along with Dave Jackson (sax) and Nick Potter (bass), and eventually 'Aerosol Grey Machine' became Van Der Graaf Generator's debut album.

The group then joined Charisma, and made 'The Least We Can Do Is Wave To Each Other' and 'H to He Who Am The Only One' in 1969 and 1970. They acquired a strong following, especially on the continent, but Potter left during the recording of 'H To He', and after 'Pawn Hearts' the group split up once more in 1972.

The Van Der Graaf albums had been getting increasingly ambitious, complex and psychotic, so it was hardly surprising that when Hammill went off on a solo career which pursued the same direction he didn't exactly take the pop world by storm. He made five solo albums for Charisma, and then in 1975 Van Der Graaf reformed with him, Banton, Jackson and Evans,

PETER HAMMILL

VANITY FAYRE – WARRIORS

and the 'Godbluff' album. The small but committed body of fans were ecstatic...the vast majority remained unmoved.

VANITY FAYRE A middle-of-the-road pop group who recorded for Larry Page's Page One label in the late sixties. They offered catchy, vacuous pop, and had hits with 'I Live For The Sun', 'Early In The Morning' and 'Hitchin A Ride'.

THE VERSIONS Malcolm Hooper (vocals), Roy Crook (guitar), Roger Pymer (bass) and Chris Bell (drums) were the last line-up of long standing Norwich group, Malcolm and The Jet Blacks. In 1966 they changed their name to The Versions, and reached the final of the Melody Maker beat group contest, playing a mixture of pop and Tamla Motown. They made a demo of 'Bad Time', but got just that, and when Hooper departed the rest of the group became The Precious Few (q.v.).

VILLAGE Formed in 1969 by ubiquitous keyboards player Peter Bardens. They recorded for Head Records, but numerous recording sessions resulted in just one single, 'Long Time Coming'. The group supported Chicago at the Royal Albert Hall and toured on the continent, but split up in February 1970. Bassist Bruce Thomas then joined Quiver, while Bardens recorded a solo album for Transatlantic, 'The Answer', before forming On and then Camel.

THE V.I.P.s Mike Harrison (piano, vocals), Luther Grosvenor (guitar, vocals), Greg Ridley (bass) and Mike Kellie (drums) made up this mid-sixties quartet from Carlisle, which also included keyboard wizard Keith Emerson for a very short while before he formed The Nice (q.v.). They made two singles for Island, 'I Wanna Be Free' in 1966 and 'In A Dream' in 1967, and then became Art (q.v.) and subsequently Spooky Tooth (q.v.).

THE WACKERS An early to mid-sixties beat group whose singles included 'Love Or Money' for Piccadilly in 1964, and 'The Girl Who Wanted Fame'.

WAINWRIGHTS GENTLEMEN A group from the latter half of the sixties who included Ian Gillan on vocals, who later joined Episode Six (q.v.) and Deep Purple (q.v.), and drummer Mick Tucker and vocalist Brian Connolly, who were half of Sweet during the seventies.

THE WALKER BROTHERS Scott Engel, John Maus and Gary Leeds first met during their student days in California, although they didn't form The Walker Brothers until 1964. Scott and John were both ex-child actors; Scott had been with The Routers, who had an American Top Twenty hit in 1962 with the instrumental 'Let's Go'; John played guitar in a group with his sister; and Gary had drummed with Elvis Presley and P.J. Proby (q.v.). In fact it was after touring Britain with Proby that Gary suggested the trio should try their luck over here.

They arrived in early 1965 and soon got signed up by Philips. Their debut single was the up-tempo 'Pretty Girls Everywhere', with John on lead vocals, and although it received a fair amount of airplay, it didn't make the charts. The follow-up, 'Love Her', was a slower, more romantic number, with Scott's deeper tones taking the lead part. It reached No.20 in mid-1966, and established the style which the group were to follow.

Over the next year, 'Make It Easy On Yourself' and 'The Sun Ain't Gonna Shine Anymore' both topped the charts, and 'My Ship Is Coming In' got to No.3. All were throbbing big ballads and the good-looking trio became the nation's number one pin-up boys. At first they had played instruments on stage, Gary playing drums Scott bass and John guitar, and for a while they were joined by ex-Uglies (q.v.) keyboard player Jimmy O'Neill. As their fame grew, however, Scott and John concentrated on singing and tantalising the young ladies, while Johnny B. Great and The Quotations provided the backing.

'Take It Easy', 'Portrait', 'Images' and the compilation 'Walker Brothers Story' were all big-selling albums between 1965 and 1967, and '(Baby) You Don't Have To Tell Me' and 'Another Tear Falls' were Top Twenty hits in 1966. Due to contractual problems Gary was unable to play on the group's records, so in 1966 he formed a parallel outfit called Rain and made two singles for his other company, CBS. 'You Don't Love Me' and 'Twinkie Lee' were both Top Thirty hits.

By mid-1967 the Walker Brothers' gradually dwindling record sales and Scott's apparent moodiness were causing problems, and after the EP 'Solo Scott - Solo John', they called it a day. John promptly made a solo single, 'Annabella', which gave him a Top Thirty success, but only Scott managed to have any lasting success as a solo artist.

He had hits in 1968/9 with 'Jackie', 'Joanna' and 'Lights Of Cincinatti', and (thanks largely to TV appearances) had four very successful albums - 'Scott 1-3' and 'Songs From His TV Series' - over the two years after the Brothers split up. These albums consisted largely of Scott's own songs and compositions by Jacques Brel, and kept up his image of mean, moody magnificence.

He continued recording albums at regular intervals in the seventies for Philips and CBS, but his staple audience had grown out of idol-worship, and they didn't do terribly well. In 1976 the Brothers reunited, made an album called 'No Regrets' for GTO, and had their first Top Ten entry for nearly a decade with the Tom Rush-penned title track.

WARM DUST One of the many "progressive" groups starting out in the late sixties, Warm Dust had their first single, 'Sticks And Stones' on the Immediate label. In the early seventies they made a single, 'It's A Beautiful Day', and a double album, 'It Came To Pass', for Trend, and then 'Peace For Our Time' for Phonogram. Their personnel included Paul Carrack (keyboards) and Tex Comer (bass) who were with Ace in the mid-seventies.

WARM SOUNDS A duo who had a Top Thirty hit in mid-1967 with 'Birds And Bees' on the Deram label, Barry Younghusband and Denver Gerrard were less successful with 'Nite Is A-Comin'' on Deram, and 'Sticks and Stones' on Immediate. Denver Gerrard later made an album, 'Sinister Morning', for Decca's budget-line "progressive" label, Nova.

THE WARRIORS Jon Anderson (vocals), Anthony Anderson (vocals), Michael Brereton (lead guitar), Rodney Hill (rhythm guitar), David Foster (bass) and Ian Wallace (drums) were a beat group from Accrington who made one single, 'You Came Along' for Decca in 1964.

THE WALKER BROTHERS

WASHINGTON D.C.s—WHO

In 1968 Anderson formed Yes (q.v.), and during the seventies Wallace has been an in-demand session musician and played with Alexis Korner (q.v.), King Crimson (q.v.), Steve Marriott, Alvin Lee and Bob Dylan.

THE WASHINGTON D.C.s A group whose singles for CBS included 'Seek And Find' in 1966, produced by ex-Yardbird (q.v.) Paul Samwell-Smith.

GENO WASHINGTON AND THE RAM JAM BAND Geno Washington was one of several black American servicemen who stayed in England after their discharge to form soul bands. Geno and his Ram Jam Band were one of the most popular acts on the British club circuit in the mid-sixties, featuring a set packed full of soul classics like 'Midnight Hour', 'Ride Your Pony', 'Respect' and 'Land Of 1000 Dances'.

They recorded for Piccadilly, and although they never had a big hit they enjoyed minor successes in 1966/7 with 'Water', 'Hi Hi Hazel' 'Que Sera Sera' and 'Michael'. Their albums were much bigger sellers, however, and 'Hand Clappin', Foot Stompin', Funky Butt Live' and 'Hipsters Flipsters Finger Poppin' Daddies' both went high in the album charts. Their third album was 'Shake A Tail Feather Baby'.

After an absence of several years, Geno returned in 1975 with a shaven head and an album on the DJM label.

THE WATERPROOF SPARROWS A psychedelic boogie band from 1967, they featured percussionist Steve Peregrine Took, who later became half of Tyrannosaurus Rex (q.v.).

JOHN L.WATSON AND THE WEB Lennie Wright, Kenny Beveridge, Tom Harris, Tony Edwards, John Eaton and Dick Lee came from the South coast, and recruited coloured American vocalist John L. Watson after moving up to London. They were a popular soul outfit in the clubs and ballrooms for several years before climbing aboard the "progressive" bandwagon with the 'Fully Interlocking' album on Deram in 1968. They then made two overt bubblegum singles, 'Baby Won't You Leave Me Alone' and 'Monday To Friday', which did better on the continent than at home, and went serious again for the 'Theraphosa Blondi' album in 1970. They shortened their name to The Web for these recordings.

CARL WAYNE AND THE VIKINGS An early to mid-sixties beat group from Birmingham who made a couple of singles of Beatles (q.v.) songs before Wayne became lead vocalist with The Move (q.v.).

PAT WAYNE AND THE BEACHCOMBERS Another of the Birmingham beat groups signed by Columbia in 1963, their singles included a version of Chuck Berry's 'Roll Over Beethoven'.

KEITH WEST After first making his mark as vocalist with R&B group The In Crowd (q.v.), West fronted Tomorrow (q.v.) in 1967. Round about the same time he met up with composer Mark Wirtz who was working on a planned "teenage opera", and as a result West put out a single on Parlophone entitled 'Excerpt From A Teenage Opera', which went to No.2 in the charts.

Not surprisingly, this aroused considerable interest, and there was much talk of a full-scale opera with many artists, including Cliff Richard, showing keen interest in the project. However, the next "highlight" from the work, 'Sam', was only a minor hit and West's involvement ceased. Wirtz went on to make a couple more singles, '(He's Our Dear Old) Weatherman' and 'Mrs. Raven', before the idea dwindled completely. West stated later that the whole concept of the opera was a publicity hoax.

After Tomorrow had broken up, West made one further single for Parlophone, the excellent 'On A Saturday', before moving into production. In 1975 he returned to performing, in better voice than ever, with the short-lived Moonrider who made just one album for Anchor.

WEST COAST DELEGATION A Deram recording group whose singles included 'Reach For The Top' in 1967. The "West Coast" in question was probably Somerset.

WHEELS Brian Rossi, Herbie Armstrong, Tito Tinsley, Rod Demick and Victor Catling formed Wheels in Belfast during the early sixties, but later based themselves in Blackpool.

Another rough and ready R&B combo, their debut single for Columbia in 1965 was an aptly chosen cover of Them's (q.v.) 'Gloria'. This was followed by the very similar 'Bad Little Girl', and after changing their name to Wheels-A-Way, to avoid confusion with Mitch Ryder's Detroit Wheels, they made one further single, 'Kicks'. They then split up.

Rossi stayed in Blackpool as a solo singer. Demick and Armstrong made two albums together, 'Looking Through' on A&M and 'Little Willie Ramble' on MAM, before Demick joined Bees Make Honey and Armstrong headed for a succesful career in sessions, which he interrupted in 1975 to play with Fox.

THE WHIRLWINDS An early sixties beat group from Manchester, led by Graham Gouldman, they made 'Look At Me' for HMV in 1964 before he went off to form The Mockingbirds (q.v.).

THE WHO Roger Daltry (vocals), Pete Townshend (guitar) and John Entwhistle (bass) first started playing together in 1959, while all three were pupils at Acton County Grammar School. In the early sixties, by which time Townshend was at art college, they added drummer Doug Sanden and became The Detours. At first they played a whole variety of material, but in 1963 they turned their attention to R&B and changed their name to The Who. Playing the clubs, pubs and youth clubs of the capital they gradually acquired a large following among London's growing mod army, and when publicist Peter Meadon became their first manager he played up this aspect of their appeal. He also got them a contract with Fontana and renamed them The High Numbers (q.v.).

One single, 'I'm The Face', came out of this, and then Sanden was ousted by Keith Moon, and Meadon by Chris Stamp and Kit Lambert. Stamp and Lambert reverted the group's name to The Who but kept their nascent image as supermods, spending a great deal of money on gear which included Townshend's famous Union Jack jacket. They also encouraged Townshend in his writing, and after signing with Brunswick The Who's first single in early 1965 was one of his compositions, 'I Can't Explain'. It went into the Top Ten, as did 'Anyway Anyhow Anywhere' a few months later, and The Who were away.

They produced a violent sound on stage and on record, which the mods loved, and the effect was enhanced (and promotion assisted) by the group's habit - especially Townshend and Moon - of smashing up their equipment at the end of a set. A further dimension was added to this aggressive stance when The Who declared publicly that they couldn't stand each other. Rumours soon flying that Daltry was due to be kicked out and replaced by Boz Burrell from Boz People (q.v.).

By now 'My Generation' was in the process of giving The Who their biggest-ever hit single, reaching No.2 in December 1965 just as their debut album of the same name went into the album charts. The song was, and remains, the anthem of the mod generation...a full tilt rocking sound, Daltry stuttering the words like a blocked pillhead, and Townshend's controversial lyrics, which included the line "Hope I die before I get old".

In early 1966 the group moved to the Reaction label and 'Substitute', built along similar lines to 'My Generation', went almost as high in the charts. At this point in time the group were attracting extensive coverage in all the media, including the Observer, appearing regularly on 'Ready Steady Go' (q.v.), and were among the hottest rock properties in the country. In an attempt to cash in Brunswick released two singles from the album, 'The Kids Are Alright' and 'A Legal Matter', but they were only minor hits as the group refused to promote them. The next two Reaction singles, 'I'm A Boy' and 'Happy Jack', both went into the Top Three, however, although Brunswick's departing shot, 'La La Lies', got nowhere. At the end of 1966 The Who's second album, 'A Quick One', was yet another big seller. It was also a unique Who album, as it contained songs by all four members of the group, and in the lengthy 'A Quick One While He's Away', a mini rock opera, Townshend gave a hint of what was to come later.

After this they joined Stamp and Lambert's new Track label, but after 'Pictures Of Lily' had reached No.4 in May 1967 (despite being on the subject of masturbation) they found big hit singles harder to come by in this country. They did, however, start to make inroads into the American market, and in the June of that year they went there for the first time to appear at Monterey. After their return came the celebrated Rolling Stones (q.v.) court case, in which Mick Jagger and Keith Richard were jailed for drug offences. The Who, despite the fact that Entwhistle was away on his honeymoon, issued a single of 'The Last Time' and 'Under My Thumb' within 48 hours, to help pay court costs. They also promised to keep the Stones music alive during the pair's incarceration with similar offerings, but this proved unnecessary as they were released on appeal within a few days...which was probably just as well, as the single was only a very minor hit.

In the following month The Who went back to the States for their first tour, and also did some recording over there. 'I Can See For Miles' was yet another Top Ten hit after they had come back, and in early 1968 'The Who Sell Out' was on the market...a bizarre affair with fake commercials and jingles from Radio London between the tracks. It remains The Who's worst selling album.

1968 was a quiet year for them. The group spent much of the time touring Australasia and America, and produced only two singles, 'Dogs' and 'Magic Bus', both of which only just made the Top Thirty. The year closed with Track issuing the 'Direct Hits' compilation. Those who thought that The Who were on their way out, however, couldn't have been more wrong.

In April 1967 'Pinball Wizard' reached No.4 and provided a great introduction to 'Tommy', Townshend's full-scale rock opera, which burst forth at the end of the following month. Despite the many monstrous "concept albums" and other operas which it spawned, and despite the ludicrous over-exposure it has received on record, stage and film, 'Tommy' remains one of rock music's major works...and one which has been a burden to Townshend ever since.

Besides Townshend, Entwhistle also made a considerable contribution to the group's fund of material, and shortly after 'Tommy', Track released a compilation of his tracks, 'John Entwhistle And The Who: The Ox'.

Townshend's difficulty in following his *tour de force* became more apparent when the next group album turned out to be 'Live At Leeds' in mid-1970. Certainly one of the best live albums ever, and a very popular one, it was nonetheless essentially a stop-gap. It was then rumoured that Townshend was working on another opera/concept, but 'Who's Next' in 1971 turned out to be their first straightforward album since 'My Generation'. It was also a superb album, their biggest commercial success, and contained the epic 'Won't Get Fooled Again', which was edited down to give them their first Top Ten single in over two years.

It was then solo time. Townshend's 'Who Came First' was strongly influenced by his conversion to the teachings of Indian mystic Meher Baba; Entwhistle came up with 'Whistle Rhymes'; and Daltry made an album of songs by David Courtney and Leo Sayer, which gave him a Top Five single with 'Giving It All Away'.

Rumours of a break-up (which have been

WHY NOT—DERRY WILKIE & THE SENIORS

heard consistently throughout The Who's life) were soon scotched, however, by 'Quadrophenia', another "concept" album based on the life of a mod in the mid-sixties which was even more ambitious than 'Tommy'. Because of its greater complexity and lack of any obvious anthems it was largely overlooked and underrated at the time of its release, but hindsight has shown its merits to be greater than was originally suspected.

By now The Who's combined activities were becoming more sporadic, partly because of Townshend's increasing reluctance to keep up a heavy touring schedule, so all four members became more involved in their own projects.

Daltry was the one who remained most clearly in the public eye. He made a second solo album, 'Ride A Rock Horse', formed his own record company, the short-lived Goldhawk Records, and got into the film world. This started with the title role in Ken Russell's extravagant film version of 'Tommy', and was followed by another in the same director's 'Lisztomania'.

Keith Moon also ventured into the movies with small roles in 'That'll Be The Day' and 'Stardust', and made his own album, the thoroughly uninspired 'Two Sides Of The Moon'. Most of his time, however, was spent being his own inimitable self...the greatest ligger and looner the rock world has ever seen.

Entwhistle made two further solo albums, 'Rigor Mortis Sets In' and 'Mad Dog', forming groups for each project, the second of which - John Entwhistle's Ox - even went on a tour of Britain. He also sifted through old material to compile the thoroughly worthwhile 'Odds And Sods' album in 1974, and did production for other people.

Townshend also involved himself with other acts, including John Otway and Wild Willy Barrett, as well as taking an interest in the various manifestations of 'Tommy', but on the whole he seemed to have trouble finding the inspiration and motivation to carry on. The first Who album for over two years, 'The Who By Numbers' in 1975, reflected this sombre mood and was unjustly dismissed in many quarters. It did, however, give them a rare Top Ten hit with 'Squeezebox', and a short tour of British football stadiums showed the group to be still capable of producing a rare magic on stage, despite (or perhaps because of) continuing reports of internal friction.

Another lengthy hiatus followed before 'Who Are You' in 1978. It was not one of The Who's finest hours, but it was to be one of their biggest sellers, especially in the States, partly because its release coincided with the untimely, but perhaps less than unexpected death of Keith Moon. The future of the group was put in jeopardy for a while, but the remaining members decided to carry on (although considering changing the group's name) and brought in ex-Faces (q.v.) drummer Kenny Jones. At the same time they were working on a film version of 'Quadrophenia' and an account of the group's history, 'The Kids Are Alright'.

WHY NOT After spending a few years at an exclusive Sussex boarding school, Oliver Tobias returned to his native Switzerland and formed Why Not? in the mid-sixties. They were a hard rock outfit, with Tobias on lead vocals, lead guitar and harmonica.

When they split up Tobias (full name Oliver Tobias Freitag) came back to England to study drama at London's East Fifteen school. In 1968 he landed the lead role of Berger in the London version of 'Hair' (q.v.) and subsequently toured Italy, Holland and Israel with the show. He then toured Germany as Judas in 'Jesus Christ Superstar', and by the late seventies had established himself with title roles in the TV series 'Arthur Of The Britons' and 'Luke's Kingdom', and the film 'The Stud'.

WILD FLOWERS A semi-pro band from Middlesborough who came down to London in March 1967 in search of fame and fortune, they included

THE WHO

vocalist Paul Rodgers, who found it with Free (q.v.) and Bad Company, bassist Bruce Thomas, who didn't find it with Village (q.v.) or Quiver but did with Elvis Costello and The Attractions, and guitarist Mick Moody, who didn't find it with Snafu and is still looking for it with Whitesnake.

WILD UNCERTAINTY A mid-sixties group whose singles included 'Man With Money' for Planet in 1966.

THE WILDE FLOWERS The legendary Canterbury group which gave birth to both Soft Machine (q.v.) and Caravan (q.v.), they started in 1964 with a line-up of Brian Hopper (guitar, sax), Richard Sinclair (rhythm guitar), Hugh Hopper (bass) and Robert Wyatt (drums), playing a mixture of modern jazz, rock'n'roll and R&B.

Vocalists Kevin Ayers and then Graham Flight came and went, and in 1965 Sinclair was replaced by Pye Hastings, with Richard Coghlan coming in on drums and Wyatt taking over the lead vocals. This line-up lasted for a year until Wyatt left for the Soft Machine and Hastings became vocalist-in-chief.

By this time the group was writing their own material, but wielding a bias towards soul music, which was popular at the time. A further personnel change occurred in 1967 when Richard Sinclair's cousin David joined on keyboards and Dave Lawrence replaced Hugh Hopper on bass. This only lasted another six months, however, before Brian Hopper and Lawrence left, Richard Sinclair came back to play bass, and the whole lot became Caravan.

DERRY WILKIE AND THE SENIORS A group who began life in Liverpool during 1958, fronted by the acrobatic, sensual West Indian Derry Wilkie. They were the first Merseyside group to play in Germany, and also the first to record when a single was released by Fontana in 1961.

When Wilkie was joined on vocals by Freddie Starr (q.v.) the group became Howie Casey and The Seniors, Casey being the group's leader and sax player. Wilkie left shortly afterwards to form The Pressmen, and when the group split up Starr formed The Midnighters. Casey joined

WINSTONS FUMBS — YARDBIRDS

Kingsize Taylor and The Dominoes (q.v.), and in the mid-seventies was very busy as a session musician as well as playing with Paul McCartney's Wings.

WINSTONS FUMBS The group formed by keyboard player Jimmy Winston following his departure from The Small Faces (q.v.). They made a single for RCA, 'Real Crazy Apartment' in 1967, and when they broke up Winston returned to his original career of acting, appearing in 'Hair' (q.v.).

WISHFUL THINKING A Scandinavian group managed by Jonathan King (q.v.) who came to this country in 1968 on the crest of a big publicity campaign. Photos and badges of the group were dispatched to all and sundry, but while they made a few pleasant pop singles for Decca the hopes behind their big push clearly lived up to their name.

THE YARDBIRDS Keith Relf (q.v.)(vocals, harmonica), Andrew "Top" Topham (lead Guitar), Chris Dreja (rhythm guitar), Paul Samwell-Smith (bass) and Jim McCarty (drums) formed The Yardbirds in 1963 out of The Metropolitan Blues Quartet, playing a mixture of blues and R&B covers

Topham was soon replaced by Eric Clapton from Casey Jones and The Engineers (q.v.), and when The Rolling Stones (q.v.) finished their residency at The Crawdaddy (q.v.) in Richmond, The Yardbirds took over and began to build their reputation as "the most blueswailing Yardbirds". They also toured the continent backing American bluesman Sonny Boy Williamson, an alliance captured for posterity on a live album released by Fontana in 1965.

In 1964 the group made two singles for Columbia, 'I Wish You Would' and 'Good Morning Little Schoolgirl. The latter was a minor hit at the end of the year, by which time they had made their debut album, 'Five Live Yardbirds'. Recorded at The Marquee (q.v.) the album contained standards like Chuck Berry's 'Too Much Monkey Business', The Isley Brothers 'Respectable', Howlin' Wolf's 'Smokestack Lightning', 'Got Love If You Want It' and 'I'm A Man'. It established The Yardbirds as one of the country's top R&B groups, had Clapton as a guitarist of major stature.

Early in 1965, however, they suddenly went in a more commercial direction with Graham Gouldman's 'For Your Love'. The single reached No.2 in the charts, but Clapton was totally opposed to the group's move away from the blues and in the March left to join John Mayall's Bluesbreakers (q.v.). The group auditioned for a new guitarist, and came up with another potential hero in Jeff Beck (q.v.) from The Tridents (q.v.).

With Beck firmly installed they hit the No.2 spot again with 'Heart Full Of Soul', another Gouldman song which was also their second American Top Ten entry. The 'Five Yardbirds' EP came next, with one side devoted to 'My Girl Sloopy', which was a version of The McCoys' 'Hang On Sloopy', and then two more big singles - 'Evil Hearted You'/'Still I'm Sad' and 'Shapes Of Things', the former written by Graham Gouldman yet again and the last two by the group.

The Yardbirds' first studio album, released in the summer of 1966, was a brilliantly adventurous effort made up entirely of original material, and 'Over Under Sideways Down' gave them their fifth Top Ten hit in just over a year. Paul Samwell-Smith then left, however, to become a producer working with Cat Stevens (q.v.) among others, and his place was taken by session guitarist Jimmy Page.

The group appeared in Antonioni's 'Blow Up' with this line-up, before Dreja took over on bass leaving Page to join Beck in a formidable dual-guitar frontline. 'Happenings Ten Years Time Ago', backed by the quite startling 'Psycho Daisies' was only a very minor hit, however, despite an appearance on 'Top Of The Pops' to promote it. Soon afterwards Beck suffered a breakdown during the group's ninth tour of America, and eventually he left in early 1967.

The Yardbirds struggled on for another year, forming an alliance with Mickie Most (q.v.) which resulted in two flop singles, 'Little Games' and 'Goodnight Sweet Josephine', and an album named after the former which was an unsatisfactory assortment of half-finished recordings. This album was only released in America, as was 'Live Yardbirds', a very late recording made in New York which was withdrawn almost immediately after its release in 1971.

The Yardbirds were now in a sorry state of disarray after their greatness of two years previously, and in July 1968 they finally threw in the towel. Relf and McCarty formed the folk duo Together (q.v.) and then Renaissance (q.v.); Dreja took up photography full time; and Page, who was left with the group's name, formed The New Yardbirds, who soon turned into Led Zeppelin (q.v.).

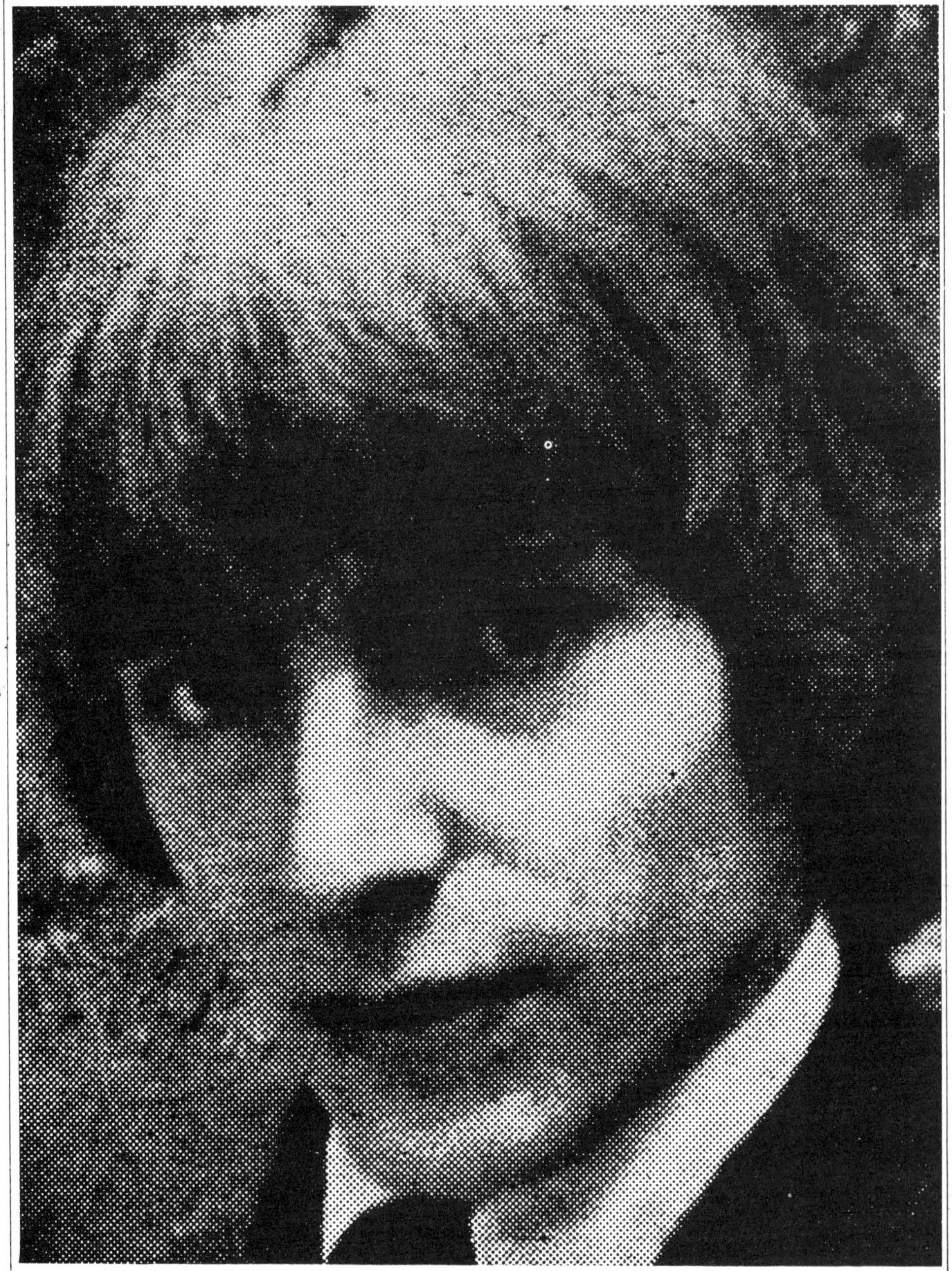

YES—ZOMBIES

YES Jon Anderson (vocals), Peter Banks (guitar), Tony Kaye (keyboards), Chris Squire (bass) and Bill Bruford (drums) were formed in 1968, and signed to Atlantic after establishing their credentials at The Marquee (q.v.). Anderson had previously been with The Warriors (q.v.), and Squire and Banks came from The Syn (q.v.).

The group wrote complex songs and gave them lavish arrangements, and their two albums in the sixties - 'Yes' and 'Time And A Word' - were less than satisfactory. After Banks had left to form Flash and been replaced by Steve Howe from Tomorrow (q.v.), however, they made what probably remains their finest hour on vinyl, 'The Yes Album'.

This release provided Yes with their breakthrough in the UK and made them the darlings of the music press for a while. Tony Kaye then departed to form Badger, and in his place came technical genius Rick Wakeman from The Strawbs (q.v.). From that point onwards, Yes have made a string of huge-selling albums which placed them among the world's top groups, but Anderson's lyrical conceits have often been ludicrously unfathomable and unwieldy while the group's arrangements could be accused of sacrificing feel for virtuosity. The double 'Tales From Topographic Oceans' has been the prime example of these tendencies.

Since, from the outside at least, the group appears to be dominated by Anderson it is not surprising that Yes have gone through several personnel changes over the years. Bill Bruford left after 'Close To The Edge' in 1972, complaining that the group had all spontaneity rehearsed out of it, and joined King Crimson (q.v.). His place was taken by Alan White from The Plastic Ono Band.

Rick Wakeman, who had already established a parallel solo career with 'The Six Wives Of Henry VIII', was also unhappy with 'Tales' and left to concentrate on his own projects in 1974. Wakeman and the others had also been at loggerheads over non-musical matters. Big Rick was the only band member who wasn't a health food addict or vegetarian, in fact he was something of a beer-and-skittles man at heart, and the others weren't impressed by his onstage boozing.

Before Swiss keyboard player Patrick Moraz joined them from Refugee, he was asked whether he was a vegetarian and replied "If necessary". Such unprincipled grovelling did him little good, however, and he only got to record one album with Yes, 'Relayer' in 1975. Wakeman returned to the fold for 'Going For The One' in 1977, and in the interim the other four members decided that the world would be the richer for a solo album from each of them.

Steve Howe's 'Beginnings', Chris Squire's 'Fish Out Of Water', Alan White's 'Ramshackle' and Jon Anderson's 'Olias Of Sunhillow' were accordingly unleashed...but the course of western civilisation was not altered perceptibly.

THE YOUNG IDEA Douglas MacCrae-Brown and Tony Cox were a duo who recorded for Columbia around 1967. Their singles included a version of The Lemon Pipers' 'Green Tambourine' and The Beatles'(q.v.) 'With A Little Help From My Friends', which reached No.10. This was also the title of the group's album in 1968, which featured several original songs. Cox later went into production

YOUNG TRADITION Peter Bellamy and Royston Wood started out singing unaccompanied traditional folk songs and sea shanties around the folk clubs. After a while they were joined by Heather Wood (no relation), and after signing with Transatlantic they made three albums in the late sixties, 'The Young Tradition', 'So Cheerfully Round' and 'Galleries', and an EP, 'Chicken On A Raft'. After they had gone their separate ways in 1969 Transatlantic also put out two compilations, 'Young Tradition Sampler' and 'Galleries Revisited'.

After a much-heralded farewell concert at Cecil Sharpe House, the home of the English Folk Song and Dance Society, Peter Bellamy went solo and made several albums, Royston Wood also spent a while on his own before joining various other folk groups, including the Albion Country Band formed by ex-Fairport Convention (q.v.) and Steeleye Span (q.v.) bassist Ashley Hutchings, and Heather Wood went to America.

THE ZEPHYRS John Peeby (guitar), John Hinde (bass), Marc Lease (organ) and John Carpenter (drums) were a London group from the mid-sixties, who recorded for Columbia and were produced by Shel Talmy (q.v.). They had a minor hit with their second single, a version of Bo Diddley's 'I Can Tell', but didn't make much impression with their others, among them a cover of Jimmy Justice's hit 'A Little Bit Of Soap' and 'Let Me Love You Baby'. Their guitarist later on was Pete Gage, who returned in the early seventies with Vinegar Joe.

ZERO ONE A mid-sixties outfit whose singles for Columbia included 'Dusty' in 1965.

THE ZOMBIES Colin Blunstone (vocals), Rod Argent (keyboards), Paul Atkinson (guitar), Chris White (bass) and Hugh Grundy (drums) made some of the most immaculate pop records of the mid-sixties, without ever receiving the recognition they deserved in this country.

Formed in St.Albans in 1962, with Paul Arnold their original bass player, they won the Evening News beat group competition in 1963 and received a great deal of publicity through their collective possession of 50 O Levels.. More to the point they also had a fine songwriter in Rod Argent and a strong vocalist in Colin Blunstone, and their first single for Decca, the dramatic 'She's Not There', reached No.12 in the UK and No.2 in America in late 1964.

The follow-up, 'Leave Me Be', flopped, and after 'Tell Her No' just squeezed into the Top Thirty in early 1965 The Zombies' British chart success was over for good. They made several more singles for Decca, including 'She's Coming Home', 'Whenever You're Ready' and 'Is This The Dream', as well as an album called 'Begin Here', which comprised R&B standards like 'Roadrunner' and 'I Got My Mojo Working', and a lush version of George Gershwin's 'Summertime', alongside the group's own material.

In 1967, finally fed up with their lack of artistic independence and Decca's wretched efforts to establish the group, The Zombies moved to CBS. Decca issued 'Goin' Out Of My Head' after their departure, and CBS put out 'Friends Of Mine' and 'Care Of Cell 44', but the group split up at the end of 1967. The superb 'Odyssey and Oracle' album was released posthumously, and 'Time Of The Season' taken from it was a huge American hit in early 1969.

These events prompted lavish offers for The Zombies to reform, but they declined... leaving the field open for various bogus aggregations to step in. Rod Argent formed Argent (q.v.), and Blunstone re-recorded 'She's Not There' as Neil McArthur before reverting to his real name for a solo career. In 1970 Decca re-released the 'Begin Again' album as 'The World Of The Zombies', and in 1976 a compilation of their early material came out in the 'Rock Roots' series. CBS also got maximum mileage out of their material with 'Time Of The Zombies' and the 'History Of...' double album in 1973.

INDEX

D'Abo, Mike; A BAND OF ANGELS, MANFRED MANN
Abrahams, Mick; JETHRO TULL, BLODWYN PIG
Ace, Martin; MAN
Acutt, John; THE FAIRIES
Adamson, Billy; THE SEARCHERS
Alan, Skip; THE SKIP ALAN TRIO, THE PRETTY THINGS
Alcock, Keith; THE MOJOS
Alcot, Simon "Boots"; FOUR PLUS ONE, THE IN CROWD
Alder, Johnny; (See Twink)
Alexander, George; GRAPEFRUIT
Alexander, Mervyn; JOHNNY CARR AND THE CADILLACS
Allen, Bob; DAVEY JONES AND THE KING BEES
Allen, Colin; ZOOT MONEY'S BIG ROLL BAND, DANTALLION'S CHARIOT, JOHN MAYALL, STONE THE CROWS
Allen, Daevid; THE SOFT MACHINE
Allen, Frank; CLIFF BENNET AND THE REBEL ROUSERS, THE SEARCHERS
Allen, Frank; JOHNNY KIDD AND THE PIRATES
Allen, Jeff; THE BEATSTALKERS
Allen, John; THE NASHVILLE TEENS
Allen, Rod; THE FORTUNES
Allen, Verden; THE SHAKEDOWN SOUND, MOTT THE HOOPLE
Allen, Wally; BERN ELLIOTT AND THE FENMEN, THE PRETTY THINGS
Allendale, Eric; THE FOUNDATIONS
Almond, Johnny; ZOOT MONEY'S BIG ROLL BAND, JOHN MAYALL
Ambrose, Dave; THE PETER B'S, BRIAN AUGER TRINITY
Amey, Ian "Tich"; DAVE DEE, DOZY, BEAKY, MICK AND TICH
Amoo, Eddie; THE CHANTS
Anderson, Ian; JETHRO TULL
Anderson, Jon; THE WARRIORS, YES
Anderson, Miller; THE KEEF HARTLEY BAND
Andersson, Benny; THE HEP STARS
Andrews, Chris; (See Ravell, Chris)
Andrews, Tim; TIM ANDREWS
Anisette; THE SAVAGE ROSE
Anthony, Barron; THE BARRON KNIGHTS
Anthony, David (See Dickens, Charles)
Appice, Carmine; JEFF BECK
Arbus, Dave; EAST OF EDEN
Argent, Rod; THE ZOMBIES, ARGENT
Armit, Ian; THE HOOCHIE COOCHIE MEN
Armstrong, Herbie; WHEELS
Armstrong, Jim; THEM
Arnold, Pat; P.P. ARNOLD
Arnold, Paul; THE OVERLANDERS
Art; HAPSHASH AND THE COLOURED COAT
Asher, Peter; PETER AND GORDON
Ashton, Tony; THE REMO FOUR, FAMILY
Ashton, William Howard; THE COASTERS, (See Kramer, Billy J.)
Atkinson, Paul; THE ZOMBIES
Auger, Brian; BRIAN AUGER TRINITY
Austin, Roy; THE ROCKIN' BERRIES
Avery, Jim; THUNDERCLAP NEWMAN
Avory, Mick; THE KINKS
Ayers, Kevin; THE WILDE FLOWERS
Aylesbury, Ivor; THE SILKIE

Babbington, Roy; DELIVERY, SOFT MACHINE
Bachini, John; ORANGE BICYCLE
Bacon, Maurice; LOVE AFFAIR
Baggerly, Ada; THE ORIOLES
Baggot, Martin; THE APPLEJACKS
Bailey, Steve; ASHKAN
Bailey, Scratch And Scrape; SCREAMING LORD SUTCH AND THE SAVAGES
Bainbridge, Rodney; THE FORTUNES
Baker, Butch; THE BARRON KNIGHTS
Baker, Ginger; FREE AT LAST, ALEXIS KORNER, THE GRAHAM BOND ORGANISATION, CREAM, BLIND FAITH
Baker, John; A BAND OF ANGELS
Baker, Keith; BAKERLOO
Baker, Lloyd; PETER JAY AND THE JAYWALKERS
Baldry, Long John; LONG JOHN BALDRY, ALEXIS KORNER, CYRIL DAVIES' RHYTHM AND BLUES ALL STARS, THE HOOCHIE COOCHIE MEN, THE STEAM PACKET, BLUESOLOGY
Baldwin, Nigel; THE OTHERS
Ball, Dave; PROCUL HARUM, LONG JOHN BALDRY
Ball, Reg; (See Presley, Reg)
Ballard, Russ; THE ROULETTES, ARGENT, UNIT FOUR PLUS TWO
Ballinger, Dave; THE BARRON KNIGHTS
Banham, Stuart; STACKWADDY
Banks, John; THE MERSEYBEATS, JOHN AND JOHNNY
Banks, Tony; GENESIS
Banks, Peter; THE SYNDICATS, THE SYN, YES, BLODWYN PIG
Banton, Hugh; VAN DER GRAAF GENERATOR
Barber, Chris; ALEXIS KORNER
Bardens, Peter; THE CHEYNES, THEM, THE PETER B'S, SHOT-GUN EXPRESS, LOVE AFFAIR, VILLAGE
Barlow, Barriemore; JETHRO TULL
Barre, Martin; JETHRO TULL
Barrett, Roger "Syd"; THE ABDABS
Bartholomew, Peter; THE OVERLANDERS
Barton, Bernard; THE TEA TIME FOUR
Barton, Gordon; ANDWELLA'S DREAM
Batchelor, Dave; DREAM POLICE
Bates, Chris; LOOT
Beach, Sandy; (See Oldham, Andrew Loog)
Beck, Jeff; JEFF BECK, THE TRIDENTS, THE YARDBIRDS
Beckett, Barry; TRAFFIC
Beech, Biffo; THE MIGHTY AVENGERS
Bell, Alec; LULU AND THE LUVVERS
Bell, Chris; THE VERSIONS, THE PRECIOUS FEW
Bell, Graham; THE CHOSEN FEW, SKIP BIFFERTY, HEAVY JELLY, GRYPHON
Bell, Madeline; BLUE MINK
Bell, Maggie; STONE THE CROWS
Bellamy, George; THE TORNADOES
Bellamy, Peter; YOUNG TRADITION
Belshaw, Brian; BLOSSOM TOES
Bender, Ariel; SPOOKY TOOTH, MOTT THE HOOPLE
Bennett, Brian; LEVIATHAN
Bennett, Brian; THE KREWCATS, THE SHADOWS
Bennett, Cliff; CLIFF BENNETT AND THE REBEL ROUSERS, TOE FAT
Bentley, Jeff; THE LEAGUE OF GENTLEMEN
Berg, Ron; BLODWYN PIG
Bernard, Barrie; PINKERTONS ASSORTED COLOURS

Berry, Dave; DAVE BERRY AND THE CRUISERS
Berry, Talking John; THE STRAWBS
Berryman, Peter; THE BASKERVILLES
Best, Pete; THE BEATLES, THE PETE BEST FOUR
Bevan, Bev; DENNY AND THE DIPLOMATS, THE MOVE
Bevan, Clifford; THE TEMPERENCE SEVEN
Beveridge, Kenny; JOHN L. WATSON AND THE WEB
Bidwell, Dave; CHICKEN SHACK
Birch, Dyan; THE EXCELLES, ARRIVAL
Bird, Tony; BUMBLEY HUM
Birkenshaw, Phil; THE FIRST GEAR
Birrell, Pete; FREDDIE AND THE DREAMERS
Bishop, Rex; BLUESOLOGY
Black, Cilla; CILLA BLACK
Blackmore, Richie; SCREAMING LORD SUTCH AND THE SAVAGES, THE OUTLAWS, ROUNDABOUT, NERO AND THE GLADIATORS, DEEP PURPLE
Blaikley, Mick; BLOSSOM
Blakely, Alan; BRIAN POOLE AND THE TREMELOES, THE TREMELOES
Blanche, Lenny; THE MIGIL FIVE
Bluck, Roger; DAVEY JONES AND THE KING BEES
Blunstone, Colin; THE ZOMBIES
Bobin, John; THE ORIOLES, LEGEND
Bogart, Tim; JEFF BECK
Bolan, Marc; JOHN'S CHILDREN, TYRANNOSAURUS REX
Bolder, Trevor; DAVID BOWIE
Bond, Graham; FREE AT LAST, ALEXIS KORNER, THE GRAHAM BOND ORGANISATION, PETE BROWN
Bond, Ronnie; THE TROGGS
Bond, Terry, THE ROCKIN' BERRIES
Bonham, John; BAND OF JOY, LED ZEPPELIN
Bonnett, Graham; THE MARBLES
Botfield, Chuck; THE ROCKIN' BERRIES
Bourke, Pat; THE FOUNDATIONS
Bowie, David; THE BUZZ, DAVID BOWIE, (See Jones, David)
Bowles, Colin; THE TEMPERENCE SEVEN
Bown, Alan; THE ALAN BOWN SET
Bown, Andy; THE HERD, JUDAS JUMP
Bowyer, Geoffrey; THE PURPLE GANG
Boyle, C; THE BEAT MERCHANTS
Boyle, Gary; BRIAN AUGER TRINTIY
Braden, Gerry; THE BYSTANDERS
Brady, Ken; THE GAMBLERS
Braid, Les; THE SWINGING BLUE JEANS
Brayley, Rex; LOVE AFFAIR
Brereton, Michael; THE WARRIORS
Bridges, Denim; THE THIRD EAR BAND
Britton, Buddy; BUDDY BRITTON AND THE REGENTS
Britton, Chris; TEN FOOT FIVE, THE TROGGS
Britton, Geoff; EAST OF EDEN
Brooker, Gary; THE PARAMOUNTS, PROCUL HARUM
Brooks, Clive; THE GROUNDHOGS
Brooks, Elkie; ELKIE BROOKS
Brooks, Stuart; THE PRETTY THINGS
Broughton, Edgar; THE EDGAR BROUGHTON BAND
Broughton, Steve; THE EDGAR BROUGHTON BAND
Brown, Andy; THE FORTUNES
Brown, Arthur; ARTHUR BROWN
Brown, Pete; PETE BROWN
Brown, Rick; BRIAN AUGER TRINITY
Brown, Rick; MISUNDERSTOOD
Brown, Sandra; SANDRA BROWN AND HER BOYFRIENDS
Brown, Stuart; BLUESOLOGY
Bruce, Jack; ALEXIS KORNER, THE GRAHAM BOND ORGANISATION, CREAM, MANFRED MANN
Bruford, Bill; YES, KING CRIMSON
Brummell, Beau; BEAU BRUMMELL ESQ.
Brunning, Bob; FLEETWOOD MAC
Bruno; BRUNO
Bruno, George; (See Money, Zoot)
Buck, Alan; THE FOUR PENNIES
Buckingham, Lindsay; FLEETWOOD MAC
Buckmaster, Paul; THE THIRD EAR BAND
Bundrick, John "Rabbit"; FREE
Bunker, Clive; JETHRO TULL
Burbury, Keith; FEEL FOR SOUL
Burdon, Eric; ALEXIS KORNER, THE ANIMALS
Burke, Ciaron; THE DUBLINERS
Burrell, Boz; THE TEA TIME FOUR, BOZ PEOPLE, FEEL FOR SOUL, KING CRIMSON, ALEXIS KORNER
Burrows, Clive; THE ALAN PRICE SET
Burrows, Tony; THE KESTRALS, THE IVY LEAGUE, THE FLOWERPOT MEN
Burt, Heinz; THE TORNADOES
Burton, Trevor; THE MOVE, THE UGLIES
Butler, Geezer; EARTH
Byron, Dennis; AMEN CORNER

Caddy, Alan; THE TORNADOES
Callaghan, John; BUMBLEY HUM
Calvert, Bernie; THE HOLLIES
Cameron, Barrie; SOUNDS INCORPORATED
Camp, John; THE NOCTURNES, RENAISSANCE
Campbell, Eddie; THE BEATSTALKERS
Campbell, Glen; THE MISUNDERSTOOD, JUICY LUCY
Campbell, Junior; DEAN FORD AND THE GAYLORDS, MARMALADE
Campbell, Tony; THE MIGHTY AVENGERS
Campbell-Lyons, Patrick; NIRVANA
Cane, Ray; HONEYBUS
Cann, John; ANDROMEDA, ATOMIC ROOSTER
Capaldi, Jim; THE HELLIANS DEEP FEELING, TRAFFIC
Cardew, Cornelius; AMM
Carlo, Little Slasher; SCREAMING LORD SUTCH AND THE SAVAGES
Carpenter, John; THE ZEPHYRS
Carr, David; THE FORTUNES
Carr, Johnny; JOHNNY CARR AND THE CADILLACS
Carrack, Paul; WARM DUST
Carroll, Dave; TEA AND SYMPHONY
Carter, John; CARTER LEWIS AND THE SOUTHENERS, THE IVY LEAGUE
Carthy, Martin; STEELEYE SPAN
Casey, Johnny; THE POOR SOULS
Cash, Phil; THE APPLEJACKS
Cassidy, Tony; ST. LOUIS UNION
Catling, Victor; WHEELS
Cattini, Clem; THE TORNADOES
Cennamo, Louis; THE CHICAGO LINE BLUES BAND, THE HERD, RENAISSANCE

Chadwick, Les; GERRY AND THE PACEMAKERS
Chaman, Clive; JEFF BECK
Chambers, Paddy; FARON'S FLAMINGOES
Chambers, Paddy; PADDY, KLAUS AND GIBSON, THE ESCORTS
Chandler, Chas; THE ANIMALS
Chapman, Jack; THE RUBBER BAND
Chapman, Mike; TANGERINE PEEL
Chapman, Mike; MIKE CHAPMAN
Chapman, Roger; FAMILY
Chapman, Tony; THE ROLLING STONES
Charig, Mark; THE SOFT MACHINE
Charnley, Miff; (See John, David)
Cherrell, Harry; BUMBLEY HUM
Chesterman, Ron; THE STRAWBS
Chichester, John; SIREN
Chimes, Ben; THE OUTCASTS
Churchill, Chick; TEN YEARS AFTER
Cipollina, John; MAN
Clague, Dave; SIREN
Clapton, Eric; CASEY JONES AND THE ENGINEERS, THE YARDBIRDS, JOHN MAYALL, CREAM, BLIND FAITH
Clark, Bobby; ROUNDABOUT
Clark, Dave; THE DAVE CLARK FIVE
Clark, Joe; THE TEMPERENCE SEVEN
Clarke, Allan; THE HOLLIES
Clarke, Mark; COLOSSEUM
Clarke, Pete; THE ESCORTS
Cleave, Ron; THE LEAGUE OF GENTLEMEN
Clegg, Colin; FEEL FOR SOUL
Clements, Rod; LINDISFARNE
Clempson, Clem; BAKERLOO, HUMBLE PIE, COLOSSEUM
Cliff, Peter; DAVE BERRY AND THE CRUISERS
Clouter, Bob; THE ORIOLES, LEGEND
Cluskey, Con; THE BACHELORS
Cluskey, Dec; THE BACHELORS
Clyde, Jeremy; CHAD AND JEREMY
Cocker, Joe; JOE COCKER
Coff, Richard; THE THIRD EAR BAND
Coghlan, John; THE SPECTRES, TRAFFIC JAM, STATUS QUO
Coghlan, Richard; THE WILDE FLOWERS
Colling, Ian; THE FIRST GEAR
Collins, Frank; THE EXCELLES, ARRIVAL
Collins, Mel; ALEXIS KORNER
Collins, Phil; GENESIS
Colman, Ian; PINKERTONS ASSORTED COLOURS
Comer, Tex; WARM DUST
Connolly, Billy; WAINWRIGHTS GENTLEMEN
Connolly, Billy; THE JUMBLEBUMS
Cook, David; THE EVERONS
Cooke, Roger; DAVID AND JONATHON, BLUE MINK
Coombes, Rod; JUICY LUCY
Cooper, Alan Swainton; THE TEMPERENCE SEVEN
Cooper, Colin; THE CLIMAX CHICAGO BLUES BAND
Copping, Chris; THE PARAMOUNTS, PROCOL HARUM
Core, Philip Darryl; (See Garrick, David)
Cornick, Glenn; JETHRO TULL
Cotton, Mike; THE MIKE COTTON SOUND
Coughlan, Richard; WILDE FLOWERS, CARAVAN
Coulam, Roger; BLUE MINK
Courtney, David; THE ROULETTES
Cousins, Dave; THE STRAWBS
Covington, Julie; HAIR
Cowe, Simon; LINDISFARNE
Cox, Billy; THE JIMI HENDRIX

EXPERIENCE
Cox, Terry; ALEXIS KORNER, PENTANGLE
Cox, Tony; THE YOUNG IDEA
Coxhill, Lol; TONY KNIGHT'S CHESSMEN, DELIVERY
Coyne, Kevin; SIREN
Crane, Don; THE DOWNLINERS SECT
Crane, Tony; THE MERSEYBEATS, THE MERSEYS
Crane, Vincent; ARTHUR BROWN, ATOMIC ROOSTER, PETE BROWN
Crawford, Jim; THE GAMBLERS
Crawford-Clews, Ian; THE PATHFINDERS, TRASH
Crogan, Jim; BLOSSOM TOES, FAMILY
Cresswell, Curt; THE BLUE BEATS, THE NATURALS
Crewsdon, Roy; FREDDIE AND THE DREAMERS
Crook, Brian; THE VERSIONS, THE PRECIOUS FEW
Crook, Roy; THE VERSIONS, THE PRECIOUS FEW
Crouch, Nicky; FARON'S FLAMINGOES, THE MOJOS
Cruikshank, Pete; HERBAL MIXTURE, THE GROUNDHOGS
Cudworth, Nick; SIREN
Cuffley, John; THE CLIMAX CHICAGO BLUES BAND
Cunningham, Kevin; THE SILKIE
Currie, Steve; TYRANNOSAURUS REX
Curry, Kevin; ORANGE BICYCLE
Curtis, Adrian; RUPERT'S PEOPLE
Curtis, Chris; THE SEARCHERS, ROUNDABOUT
Curtis, Dave; ROUNDABOUT, BODFAST
Curtis, Lee; LEE CURTIS

D'Ell, Denis; THE HONEYCOMBS
D'mond, Duke; THE BARRON KNIGHTS
Dale, Glen; THE FORTUNES
Dalton, John; MARK FOUR, CREATION, THE KINKS
Daltry, Peter; KALEIDOSCOPE
Daltry, Roger; THE HIGH NUMBERS, THE WHO
Damery, Norman; TASTE
Damond, Tony; THE GAMBLERS
Daneski, G.; THE BEAT MERCHANTS
Dash, Leslie; HEDGEHOPPERS ANONYMOUS
Davani, Dave; DAVE DAVANI AND THE D MEN
Davidson, Lenny; THE DAVE CLARK FIVE
Davies, Cyril; ALEXIS KORNER, THE CYRIL DAVIES RHYTHM AND BLUES ALL STARS
Davies, Dave; THE KINKS
Davies, Megan; THE APPLEJACKS
Davies, Ray; THE DAVE HUNT BLUES BAND, THE KINKS
Davies, Trevor "Dozy"; DAVE DEE, DOZY, BEAKY, MICK AND TICH
Davis, Spencer; THE SPENCER DAVIS GROUP
Davis, Tony; THE SPINNERS
Davison, Brian; THE MARK LEEMAN FIVE, THE NICE
Dawson, John; THE POETS
Dean, Elton; THE SOFT MACHINE
Dean, Fats; THE TEA TIME FOUR
Dean, Paul; PAUL DEAN AND THE SOUL SAVAGES, THOUGHTS
Dean, Roger; JOHN MAYALL
Dearing, Ronnie; FEEL FOR FREE
Dee, Kiki; KIKI DEE
Deighton, John; (See Farlowe, Chris)
Dello, Pete; HONEYBUS
Demick, Rod; WHEELS
Deniz, Clare; THE STRAWBS
Denny, Sandy; THE STRAWBS, FAIRPORT CONVENTION
Derrick, Diz; THE PARAMOUNTS
Dewar, Jim; LULU AND THE LUVVERS, STONE THE CROWS
Diamond, Tony; THE ORIOLES
Diamonde, Dick; THE EASYBEATS
Dickens, Charles; CHARLES DICKENS
DiLemma, Pete; GREAT WHITE IDIOT
Dillon, Eric; FAT MATTRESS
Dinney, Lester; THE BASKERVILLES
Dmochkowski, Alex; THE ANIMALS HEAVY JELLY
Dobson, Lyn; THE SOFT MACHINE
Donald, Timi; THE PATHFINDERS, TRASH
Donaldson, Pat; THE ZOOT MONEY BIG ROLL BAND, DANTALLIONS CHARIOT
Donnelly, Albie; THE CLAYTON SQUARES
Donovan; DONOVAN
Douglas, Carl; CARL DOUGLAS AND THE BIG STAMPEDE
Dower, Dave; THE CHEROKEES
Dreja, Chris; THE YARDBIRDS
Drew, Ronnie; THE DUBLINERS
Drewery, Phil; THE RUBBER BAND
Driscoll, Julie; THE STEAM PACKET, THE BRIAN AUGER TRINITY
Driscoll, K.; THE SYNDICATS
Duck, Bob; THE PACK
Duck, Ian; THE SOUL AGENTS
Duffy; COPS 'N' ROBBERS
Duffy, Raymond; DEAN FORD AND THE GAYLORDS
Dummer, John; THE JOHN DUMMER BLUES BAND
Dunbar, Aynsley; JOHN MAYALL, JEFF BECK, THE AYNSLEY DUNBAR RETALIATION
Dunbar, Nigel; LEGEND
Dunford, Mick; THE PLEBS, THE NASHVILLE TEENS, RENAISSANCE
Durham, Judith; THE SEEKERS
Dwight, Reg; BLUESOLOGY
Dyble, Judy; FAIRPORT CONVENTION, TRADER HORN
Dyble, Mike; THE BARRY LEE SHOW
Dyble, Tony; THE BARRY LEE SHOW
Dymond, John "Beaky"; DAVE DEE, DOZY, BEAKY, MICK AND TICH

Eader, Gus; LOVE AFFAIR
Earl, Roger; SAVOY BROWN
East, Chris; LEGEND
Eaton, John; JOHN L. WATSON AND THE WEB
Edge, Graeme; GERRY LEVENE AND THE AVENGERS, THE MOODY BLUES
Edmunds, Dave; THE HUMAN BEANS, LOVE SCULPTURE
Edwards, Tony; JOHN L. WATSON AND THE WEB
Van Eijck, Hans; AFTER TEA
Elliott, Bern; BERN ELLIOTT AND THE FENMEN
Elliot, Bobby; SHANE FENTON AND THE FENTONES, THE HOLLIES
Elliott, Ray; THEM
Ellis, Glyn; (See Fontana, Wayne)
Ellis, Ian; CLOUDS
Ellis, Keith; VAN DER GRAAF GENERATOR
Ellis, Keith; JUICY LUCY, SPOOKY TOOTH
Ellis, Ralph; THE SWINGING BLUE JEANS
Ellis, Steve; LOVE AFFAIR
Ellison, Andy; JOHN'S CHILDREN
Emerson, Keith; GARY FARR AND THE T-BONES, THE V.I.P'S, THE NICE
Engel, Scott; THE WALKER BROTHERS
Ennis, Ray; THE SWINGING BLUE JEANS
Entwhistle, John; THE HIGH NUMBERS, THE WHO
Epstein, Brian; BRIAN EPSTEIN
Evans, Guy; VAN DER GRAAF GENERATOR, MISUNDERSTOOD
Evans, John; JETHRO TULL
Evans, Nick; THE ACTION, THE SOFT MACHINE
Evans, Rod; THE MAZE, ROUNDABOUT, DEEP PURPLE
Evans, Tom; THE IVEYS, BADFINGER
Eve, Mick; GEORGIE FAME AND THE BLUE FLAMES
Eyre, Tommy; THE GREASEBAND

Fairley, Pat; DEAN FORD AND THE GAYLORDS, MARMALADE
Fairweather-Low, Andy; AMEN CORNER
Faithfull, Marianne; MARIANNE FAITHFULL
Fame, Georgie; GEORGIE FAME AND THE BLUE FLAMES
Fantoni, Barry; BARRY FANTONI
Fardon, Don; DON FARDON AND THE SOUL MACHINE
Farlowe, Chris; CHRIS FARLOWE AND THE THUNDERBIRDS, COLOSSEUM, ATOMIC ROOSTER
Farndell, G.; THE BEAT MERCHANTS
Farr, Gary; GARY FARR AND THE T-BONES
Farren, Mick; THE DEVIANTS, THE PINK FAIRIES WITH TWINK
Feeney, Harry; THE ROCKIN' VICKERS
Feld, Mark; (See Bolan, Marc)
Felix, Mike; THE MIGIL FIVE
Fellana, Mike; THE CHICAGO LINE BLUES BAND
Fenton, Shane; SHANE FENTON AND THE FENTONES
Fenwick, Ray; AFTER TEA, THE SPENCER DAVIS GROUP
Fernandes, Manual; LOS BRAVOS
Ferry, Bryan; THE BANSHEES
Field, Tim; THE SPRINGFIELDS
Fields, Andy; THE NEWS
Fifield, Bill; THE ORIOLES, LEGEND, T. REX
Findlay, Bruce; THE SORROWS
Fingers, Freddie; SCREAMING LORD SUTCH AND THE SAVAGES
Finn, Mickey; HAPSHASH AND THE COLOURED COAT, TYRANNOSAURUS REX
Finn, Micky; MICKY FINN AND THE BLUE MEN
Fish, Alan; MR. TOAD, KISS, GROUNDHOGS
Fisher, Matthew; SCREAMING LORD SUTCH AND THE SAVAGES, PROCOL HARUM
Fisher, Morgan; LOVE AFFAIR, MOTT THE HOOPLE
Fleet, Snowy; THE EASYBEATS
Fleetwood, Mick; THE CHEYNES, THE PETER B'S, JOHN MAYALL, THE BO STREET RUNNERS, SHOTGUN EXPRESS, FLEETWOOD MAC
Flight, Graham; THE WILDE FLOWERS
Flint, Hughie; JOHN MAYALL
Flowers, Herbie; BLUE MINK
Fontana, Wayne; WAYNE FONTANA AND THE MINDBENDERS
Ford, Dean; DEAN FORD AND THE GAYLORDS, MARMALADE
Ford, John; ELMER GANTRY'S VELVET OPERA, THE STRAWBS
Ford, Perry; THE IVY LEAGUE, THE FLOWERPOT MEN
Foster, Colin; ELMER GANTRY'S VELVET OPERA
Foster, David; THE WARRIORS
Fowler, Mike; GRAPEFRUIT
Fox, Terry; COPS 'N' ROBBERS
Frampton, Peter; THE PREACHERS, THE HERD, HUMBLE PIE
Francis, Ritchie; EYES OF BLUE
Fraser, Andy; JOHN MAYALL, FREE
Freeman, Bob; THE OTHERS
Freeman, Gerry; THE APPLEJACKS
Fripp, Robert; KING CRIMSON
Froggatt, Raymond; RAYMOND FROGGATT
Fryer, Fritz; THE FOUR PENNIES
Fuller, Stewart; FEEL FOR SOUL

Gabriel, Peter; GENESIS
Gaffney, Joe; THE BEATSTALKERS
Gage, pete; THE ZEPHYRS
Gaines, Ron; EAST OF EDEN
Gale, Juliette; THE ABDABS
Gallacher, George; THE POETS
Gallagher, Rory; TASTE
Gallaher, Mick; THE CHOSEN FEW, SKIP BIFFERTY, HEAVY JELLY
Gantry, Elmer; HAIR, ELMER GANTRY'S VELVET OPERA
Gandy, John; THE FAIRIES
Gardner, Kim; THE BIRDS, CREATION
Gare, Lou; AMM
Garner, Bob; THE MERSEYBEATS, CREATION
Garrick, David; DAVID GARRICK
Garritty, Freddie; FREDDIE AND THE DREAMERS
Garwood, Rod; UNIT FOUR PLUS TWO
Gaydon, Christian (John); A BAND OF ANGELS
Gee, Rosko; TRAFFIC
Geere, Steve; LEGEND
George, Alan; THE GAMBLERS
Georgiou, Steven; (See Stevens)
Gerrad, Denver; WARM SOUNDS
Gibb, Barry; THE BEE GEES
Gibb, Maurice; THE BEE GEES
Gibb, Robin; THE BEE GEES
Gibbins, Mike; THE IVEYS, BADFINGER
Gibbons, Steve; THE UGLIES
Gibson, Colin; SKIP BIFFERTY, HAPPY MAGAZINE, GRYPHON
Gibson, Terry; THE DOWNLINERS SECT
Giles, Peter; KING CRIMSON
Gill, Geoff; THE SMOKE, CHORDS FIVE
Gillan, Ian; WAINWRIGHTS GENTLEMEN, EPISODE SIX, DEEP PURPLE
Gilmour, David; JOKERS WILD, PINK FLOYD
Gladwin, John; METHUSELAH
Glasgow, John; CHICKEN SHACK
Glover, Dave; THE SOUL AGENTS
Glover, Jeff; LOOT
Glover, Roger; EPISODE SIX, DEEP PURPLE
Godding, Brian; BLOSSOM TOES
Godley, Kevin; THE MOCKINGBIRDS
Goins, Herbie; ALEXIS KORNER, THE NIGHT TIMERS
Goodhand-Tait, Philip; THE STORMSVILLE SHAKERS
Gomesz, Tony; THE FOUNDATIONS
Goldberg, Terry; THE MARK LEEMAN FIVE
Goodritch, Sandra; (See Shaw, Sandie)
Gordon, Jim; TRAFFIC
Gorman, John; THE SCAFFOLD
Gosling, John; THE KINKS
Gould, Don; THE APPLEJACKS
Gouldman, Graham; THE WHIRLWINDS, THE MOCKINGBIRDS
Grabham, Mick; PLASTIC PENNY, PROCOL HARUM
Graham, Bryson; SPOOKY TOOTH
Graham, Ernie; EIRE APPARENT
Grant, Arthur; THE EDGAR BROUGHTON BAND
Grant, Eddie; THE EQUALS
Grant, Erkey; ERKEY GRANT AND THE FERWIGS
Grant, Keith; THE DOWNLINERS SECT
Gratton, Mick; SIREN
Gray, Dorian; DORIAN GRAY
Grech, Ric; FAMILY, BLIND FAITH, TRAFFIC
Green, Chris; FEEL FOR FREE
Green, Colin; GEORGIE FAME AND THE BLUE FLAMES
Green, Jack; TYRANNOSAURUS REX
Green, Jim; THE CHEROKEES
Green, Mick; JOHNNY KIDD AND THE PIRATES, CLIFF BENNETT
Green, Peter; THE PETER B'S, SHOTGUN EXPRESS, JOHN MAYALL, FLEETWOOD MAC
Greenaway, Roger; THE KESTRALS, DAVID AND JONATHON
Greenslade, Dave; CHRIS FARLOWE AND THE THUNDERBIRDS, COLOSSEUM
Gregg, Brian; THE TORNADOES, THE PACK
Gregory, Mike; THE ESCORTS
Gregory, Steve; THE ALAN PRICE SET
Griffiths, Brian; THE BIG THREE
Griffiths, Clive; TIMEBOX
Griffiths, Derek; THE ARTWOODS
Griffiths, Ian; THE OVERLANDERS
Griffiths, Ron; THE IVEYS, BADFINGER
Griffin, Dale "Buffin"; THE SHAKEDOWN SOUND, MOTT THE HOOPLE
Grimes, Carol; BABYLON, DELIVERY
Grodway, Rob; THE PACK
Grosvenor, Luther; THE V.I.P.'s, SPOOKY TOOTH, THE HELLIANS
Groves, Mick; THE SPINNERS
Grundy, Dave; (See Berry, Dave)
Grundy, Hugh; THE ZOMBIES
Guest, Lynton; LOVE AFFAIR, ENGLISH ROSE
Gurvitz, Adrian; GUN
Gurvitz, Paul; GUN
Gustafson, Johnny; THE BIG THREE, THE MERSEYBEATS, THE QUOTATIONS, JOHN AND JOHNNY
Guster, Keith; FLEURS DE LYS
Guy, Athol; THE SEEKERS

Hall, Cliff; THE SPINNERS
Halliday, Hugh; UNIT FOUR PLUS TWO
Halsall, Pete "Ollie"; TIMEBOX
Halsall, Ollie; TAKE FIVE, TIMEBOX
Halsey, John; TIMEBOX
Ham, Peter; THE IVEYS, BADFINGER
Hamilton, Alex; THE ROCKIN' VICKERS
Hamilton, Gary; HAMILTON AND THE MOVEMENT
Hammill, Pete; VAN DER GRAAF GENERATOR
Hammond, John; ATOMIC ROOSTER
Hancox, Paul; CHICKEN SHACK
Hardin, Eddie; THE SPENCER DAVIS GROUP
Hare, Colin; HONEYBUS
Harman, David "Dave Dee"; DAVE DEE, DOZY, BEAKY, MICK AND TICH
Harris, Terry "Jet"; THE SHADOWS, JEFF BECK
Harris, Tim; THE FOUNDATIONS
Harris, Tom; JOHN L. WATSON AND THE WEB
Harrison, Bobby; PROCUL HARUM, FREEDOM
Harrison, George; THE BEATLES
Harrison, Henry; COPS 'N' ROBBERS, THE NEW VAUDEVILLE BAND
Harrison, Mike; THE V.I.P.'S, SPOOKY TOOTH
Harrison, Phillip; THE TEMPERENCE SEVEN
Hart, Mike; THE CLAYTON SQUARES, THE LIVERPOOL SCENE
Hart, Tim; STEELEYE SPAN
Hartley, Keef; RORY STORM AND THE HURRICANES, PADDY, KLAUS AND GIBSON, THE ARTWOODS, JOHN MAYALL, THE KEEF HARTLEY BAND
Hartley, Roger; THE PACK
Harvey, Alex; THE ALEX HARVEY SOUL BAND, THE SENSATIONAL ALEX HARVEY BAND
Harvey, David; THEM
Harvey, Les; STONE THE CROWS
Harvey, Pip; THE DOWNLINERS SECT
Harvey, Tam; THE HUMBLEBUMS
Haslam, Annie; RENAISSANCE
Hastings, Pye; THE WILDE FLOWERS, CARAVAN
Hatton, Billy; THE FOURMOST
Hawken, John; THE NASHVILLE TEENS, RENAISSANCE, SPOOKY TOOTH
Hawkes, Chip; THE TREMELOES
Hawkings, Roger; TRAFFIC
Hawksworth, Mick; ANDROMEDA
Haworth, Bryn; FLEURS DE LYS
Haycok, Pete; THE CLIMAX CHICAGO BLUES BAND
Haydock, Eric; THE HOLLIES, HAYDOCK'S ROCKHOUSE
Hayes, Michael; (See Most, Mickie)
Hayward, Justin; THE MOODY BLUES
Heath, Fred; JOHNNY KIDD AND THE PIRATES
Heather, Roy; THE BLUE BEATS, THE NATURALS
Heckstall-Smith, Dick; ALEXIS KORNER, THE GRAHAM BOND ORGANISATION, JOHN MAYALL, COLOSSEUM, THE CYRIL DAVIES RHYTHM AND BLUES ALL STARS
Helliwell, John; THE ALAN BOWN SET
Henderson, Alan; THEM
Henderson, Dorris; ECLECTION
Hendrix, James Marshall; THE JIMI HENDRIX EXPERIENCE
Henrit, Bob; THE ROULETTES, ARGENT, UNIT FOUR PLUS TWO
Hensley, Ken; THE GODS, TOE FAT
Herbert, Ian; SPOOKY TOOTH
Heron, Mike; THE INCREDIBLE STRING BAND
Hewlett, John; JOHN'S CHILDREN
Hicks, Tony; THE HOLLIES
Hill, Dave; THE 'N' BETWEENS, AMBROSE SLADE
Hill, Rodney; THE WARRIORS
Hill, Tony; MISUNDERSTOOD, HIGH TIDE
Hinde, John; THE ZEPHYRS
Hine, Eric; SIMON DUPREE AND THE BIG SOUND
Hinkley, Tim; THE BO STREET RUNNERS, THE CHICAGO LINE BLUES BAND
Hiseman, Jon; THE GRAHAM BOND ORGANISATION, JOHN MAYALL, GEORGIE FAME AND HIS BLUE FLAMES, COLOSSEUM
Hoard, Steve; MISUNDERSTOOD
Hobday, Stuart; LEVIATHAN
Hodgkinson, Colin; ALEXIS KORNER
Hoffman, Red; THE MEASLES
Holder, Noddy; THE 'N' BETWEENS, AMBROSE SLADE
Holland, Bernie; FERRIS WHEEL
Holland, Dave; PINKERTONS ASSORTED COLOURS
Hollis, Peter; THE CHEYNES
Holmes, Chris; TIMEBOX
Holmes, Christine; FAMILY DOG
Holt, Derek; THE CLIMAX CHICAGO BLUES BAND
Honeyball, Ray; HEDGEHOPPERS ANONYMOUS
Hood, David; TRAFFIC
Hooper, Malcolm; THE VERSIONS
Hooper, Tony; THE STRAWBS
Hooper, Brian; THE WILDE FLOWERS
Hooper, Hugh; THE WILDE FLOWERS, THE SOFT MACHINE
Hopkins, Mike; THE IDLE RACE
Hopkins, Nicky; NICKY HOPKINS, THE CYRIL DAVIES RHYTHM AND BLUES ALL STARS, JEFF BECK, THE ROLLING STONES
House, Simon; HIGH TIDE, THE THIRD EAR BAND
Howard, Alan; BRIAN POOLE AND THE TREMELOES
Howard, Frank; DAVEY JONES AND THE KING BEES
Howe, Steve; THE SYNDICATS, THE IN CROWD, TOMORROW, YES, BODFAST
Howerd, Cephas; THE TEMPERENCE SEVEN
Hubbard, Neil; MISUNDERSTOOD, JUICY LUCY, THE GREASEBAND, WYNDER K. FROG
Hudson, Richard "Hud"; ELMER GANTRY'S VELVET OPERA, THE STRAWBS
Hughes, Glen; BRIAN AUGER TRINITY
Hughes, Harry; CLOUDS
Hull, Alan; THE CHOSEN FEW, LINDISFARNE
Hultgren, Georg; ECLECTION
Hunt, Alan; ELMER GANTRY'S VELVET OPERA, THE OUTCASTS, THE PIONEERS
Hunt, Marsha; MARSHA HUNT, HAIR, STEAM PACKET, ALEXIS KORNER, FERRIS WHEEL
Hunter, Ian; THE APEX RHYTHM AND BLUES ALL STARS, MOTT THE HOOPLE
Hunter, Russell; THE DEVIANTS
Hunter, Wes; SOUNDS INCORPORATED
Hunter-Morrison, Colin; THE PATHFINDERS, TRASH
Hurst, Mike; THE SPRINGFIELDS
Hutchings, Ashley; FAIRPORT CONVENTION, STEELEYE SPAN
Hutchinson, John; THE BIG THREE
Huxley, Rick; THE DAVE CLARK FIVE
Huxton, Chris; THE UNDERTAKERS
Hyde, Dave; THE MARK LEEMAN FIVE

Inkpen, Mick; BLUESOLOGY
Innes, Brian; THE TEMPERENCE SEVEN
Innes, Neil; THE BONZO DOG DOO DAH BAND
Iommi, Tony; EARTH, BLACK SABBATH, JETHRO TULL

Jacklin, Tommy; SKIP BIFFERTY, HEAVY JELLY
Jackson, Al; THE APPLEJACKS
Jackson, Dave; VAN DER GRAAF

GENERATOR
Jackson, Lee; ALEXIS KORNER, GARY FARR AND THE T-BONES, THE NICE
Jackson, Mick; LOVE AFFAIR
Jackson, Ray; LINDISFARNE
Jackson, Tony; THE SEARCHERS, TONY JACKSON AND THE VIBRATIONS
Jacobson, Steve; THE MOCKINGBIRDS
Jagger, Mick; ALEXIS KORNER, THE ROLLING STONES
James, Barney; LEGEND
James, Hugh; THE SPINNERS
James, Jimmy; JIMMY JAMES AND THE VAGABONDS
James, Joel; THE LEAGUE OF GENTLEMEN
James, Stu; THE MOJOS
Jameson, Steve; TRUTH
Jansch, Bert; PENTANGLE
Jarvis, Angus; THE BARRY LEE SHOW
Jay, Peter; PETER JAY AND THE JAYWALKERS
Jenkins, Barry; THE NASHVILLE TEENS, THE ANIMALS, HEAVY JELLY
Jewell, Jimmy; KISS
Jewry, Bernard; (See Fenton, Shane)
John, Clive; MAN
John, David; DAVID JOHN AND THE MOOD
Johnson, Bob; P.J. PROBY, STEELEYE SPAN
Jones, Allen; AMEN CORNER, JUDAS JUMP
Jones, Bob "Kongos"; THE HUMAN BEANS, LOVE SCULPTURE
Jones, Brian; THE UNDERTAKERS
Jones, Brian; THE ROLLING STONES, ALEXIS KORNER
Jones, David; THE CONRADS, DAVEY JONES AND THE KING BEES, DAVIE JONES AND THE LOWER THIRD (See Bowie, David)
Jones, Gloria; TYRANNOSAURUS REX
Jones, Jack; MARK FOUR, CREATION
Jones, Jeff; MAN
Jones, John Paul; LED ZEPPELIN
Jones, Kenny; THE OUTCASTS, THE PIONEERS, THE SMALL FACES, THE FACES, THE WHO
Jones, Les; FOUR PLUS ONE, THE IN CROWD
Jones, Mick; SPOOKY TOOTH
Jones, Micky; MAN
Jones, Neil; AMEN CORNER
Jones, Paul; MANFRED MANN
Jones, Paul; ALEXIS KORNER
Jones, Ray; THE DAKOTAS
Jones, Richard; THE CLIMAX CHICAGO BLUES BAND
Jones, Ronnie; THE NIGHT TIMERS
Judge, Alan; BERN ELLIOTT AND THE FENMEN
Jupp, Micky; THE ORIOLES, LEGEND

Kaye, Tony; YES
Keen, Speedy; THUNDERCLAP NEWMAN
Kefford, Chris "Ace"; THE MOVE, BIG BERTHA, ACE KEFFORD STAND
Kellie, Mike; THE V.I.P.'S, SPOOKY TOOTH
Kelly, Luke; THE DUBLINERS
Kemp, Gibson; RORY STORM AND THE HURRICANES, KING SIZE TAYLOR AND THE DOMINOES, PADDY, KLAUS AND GIBSON
Kemp, Rick; MIKE CHAPMAN, STEELEYE SPAN
Kemp, Samuel "Pinkerton"; PINKERTONS ASSORTED COLOURS
Ken, Hopping; SCREAMING LORD SUTCH AND THE SAVAGES
Kent, Jonathon; THE LEAGUE OF GENTLEMEN
Kerslake; THE GODS
Kilminster, Ian "Lemmy"; THE ROCKIN' VICKERS
King, Alan; THE ACTION
King, Danny; DANNY KING AND THE ROYALS
King, Jim; FAMILY
King, Jonathan; JONATHAN KING
King, Reggie; THE ACTION
Kinorra, Phil; BRIAN AUGER TRINITY
Kinrade, John; THE ESCORTS
Kinsley, Billy; THE MERSEYBEATS, THE MERSEYS
Kirby, Alex; ST. LOUIS UNION
Kirby, John; THE CHEROKEES
Kirchner, Peter; HONEYBUS
Kirke, Simon; BLACK CAT BONES FREE
Kirwan, Danny; BOILERHOUSE, FLEETWOOD MAC
Kittringham, Eric; TASTE
Knail, John; STACKWADDY
Knapp, John; LEGAY, GYPSY
Knight, Graham; DEAN FORD AND THE GAYLORDS, MARMALADE
Knight, Peter; STEELEYE SPAN
Knights, Dave; PROCOL HARUM
Knowles, Dave; KISS
Kogel, Mike; LOS BRAVOS
Koger, Marijke; THE FOOL
Konrad, Bob; THE MOJOS
Korner, Alexis; FREE AT LAST, ALEXIS KORNER
Kossoff, Paul; BLACK CAT BONES, FREE
Kramer, Billy J.; BILLY J. KRAMER AND THE DAKOTAS (See Ashton)
Kristina, Sonja; HAIR
Kuhlke, Norman; THE SWINGING BLUE JEANS

Laidlaw, Ray; LINDISFARNE
Laine, Denny; DENNY AND THE DIPLOMATS, THE MOODY BLUES, DENNY LAINE'S STRING BAND
Laird, Rick; BRIAN AUGER TRINITY
Lake, Greg; THE GODS, KING CRIMSON
Lamb, Keith; MR. TOAD
Lambert, Dave; THE STRAWBS
Lambert, Kit; THE WHO
Lambert, Red; THE MIGIL FIVE
Lamble, Martin; FAIRPORT CONVENTION
Lamd, Bob; LOCOMOTIVE
Lancaster, Alan; THE SPECTRES, TRAFFIC JAM, STATUS QUO
Lancaster, Phil; DAVID JONES AND THE LOWER THIRD, THE BUZZ
Land, Bob; THE MINDBENDERS
Land, Bob; WAYNE FONTANA AND THE MINDBENDERS, THE MINDBENDERS
Landerman, Barry; KIPPINGTON LODGE
Landon, Neil; THE IVY LEAGUE, THE FLOWERPOT MEN, FAT MATRESS
Lane, Ronnie; THE OUTCASTS, THE PIONEERS, THE SMALL FACES
Lantree, Honey; THE HONEYCOMBS
Lantree, John; THE HONEYCOMBS
Larke, Johnny; PETER JAY AND THE JAYWALKERS
Lavern, Roger; THE TORNADOES
Lawrence, Dave; THE WILDE FLOWERS
Lawrence, Ken; FOUR PLUS ONE, THE IN CROWD
Lawson, Dave; EPISODE SIX, THE ALAN BOWN SET
Lea, Chris; THE ROCKIN' BERRIES
Lea, Jim; THE 'N' BETWEENS, AMBROSE SLADE
Leahy, Ronald; THE PATHFINDERS, TRASH, STONE THE CROWS
Lease, Marc; THE ZEPHYRS
Lee, Albert; CHRIS FARLOWE AND THE THUNDERBIRDS
Lee, Alvin; TEN YEARS AFTER
Lee, Barry; THE BARRY LEE SHOW
Lee, Bernie; ORANGE BICYCLE
Lee, Dick; JOHN L. WATSON AND THE WEB
Lee, Ric; TEN YEARS AFTER
Leeds, Gary; THE WALKER BROTHERS
Leeman, Mark; THE MARK LEEMAN FIVE
Legend, Bill; TYRANNOSAURUS REX
Leigh, Andy; SPOOKY TOOTH
Leitch, Donovan; (See Donovan)
Lennon, John; THE BEATLES
Lennox, Davis; THE BEATSTALKERS
Leo The Flee; SCREAMING LORD SUTCH AND THE SAVAGES
Leonard, Roger "Deke"; MAN
Leverton, James; FAT MATTRESS
Lewis, Dave; ANDWELLA'S DREAM
Lewis,Ken; CARTER LEWIS AND THE SOUTHENERS, THE IVY LEAGUE
Lewis, Linda; FERRIS WHEEL
Linnell, Mike; THE MIGHTY AVENGERS
Litherland, James; COLOSSEUM
Little, Carlo; SCREAMING LORD SUTCH AND THE SAVAGES
Locking, Brian "Licquorice"; THE KREWCATS, THE SHADOWS
Lodge, John; THE MOODY BLUES
Lomax, Jackie; THE UNDERTAKERS, LOMAX ALLIANCE, HEAVY JELLY
Long, Tom; PINKERTONS ASSORTED COLOURS
Longford, Paul; THE BARRON KNIGHTS
Longhurst-Pickworth, Mike; (See Hurst, Mike)
Lord, Jon; ROUNDABOUT
Lord, Jon; THE ACTION, THE ARTWOODS, THE RIOT SQUAD, ROUNDABOUT, DEEP PURPLE
Lovelady, Dave; THE FOURMOST
Lowe, Nick; KIPPINGTON LODGE
Lowther, Henry; THE KEEF HARTLEY BAND, MANFRED MANN
Lubin, Howard; UNIT FOUR PLUS TWO
Lucas; THE MIKE COTTON SOUND
Lucas, Gil; THE MIGIL FIVE
Lucas, Trevor; ECLECTION
Luker, Mal; CHORDS FIVE
Luker, Mal; THE SMOKE
Lulu; LULU AND THE LUVVERS
Lund, John "Zeke"; THE SMOKE, CHORDS FIVE
Lynes, Rod; THE SPECTRES, TRAFFIC JAM, STATUS QUO
Lynne, Jeff; THE IDLE RACE, THE MOVE
Lynott, Phil; SKID ROW
Lynton, Rod; RUPERT'S PEOPLE
Lyons, Leo; TEN YEARS AFTER

Mac, Andy; THE GAMBLERS
MacBeth, Peter; THE FOUNDATIONS
McCarthy, David; LEGAY, GYPSY
McCartney, Paul; THE BEATLES
McCarty, Jim; THE YARDBIRDS, RENAISSANCE, TOGETHER
McCracken, Richard; TASTE
MacCrae-Brown, Douglas; THE YOUNG IDEA
McCullough, Henry; EIRE APPARENT, THE GREASEBAND
McCulloch, Jack; THUNDERCLAP NEWMAN
McCulloch, Jimmy; THUNDERCLAP NEWMAN, STONE THE CROWS
McDaniels, Pete; THE BIRDS
MacDonald, Ian; KING CRIMSON
McDonald, Robin; THE DAKOTAS
MacDonald McLaughlin, Marie; (See Lulu)
McDowell, Keith; THEM
McDowell, Paul; THE TEMPERENCE SEVEN
McGear, Mike; THE SCAFFOLD
McGinnis, John; STONE THE CROWS
McGough, Roger; THE SCAFFOLD
McGowan, Cathy; CATHY McGOWAN
McGuinness, Tom; CASEY JONES AND THE ENGINEERS, MANFRED MANN, McGUINNESS FLINT
McHugh, Paddy; THE EXCELLES, ARRIVAL
McIntyre, Mac; PETER JAY AND THE JAYWALKERS
McIntrye, Onnie; DREAM POLICE
McKechnie, Licorice; THE INCREDIBLE STRING BAND
McKenna, Barny; THE DUBLINERS
McKanna, Hugh; DREAM POLICE
McKenzie, Alistair; THE BIRDS
McAuley, Jackie; THEM, BELFAST GYPSIES, TRADER HORN
Mackintosh, Stuart; LUCAS AND THE EMPERORS
MacLagen, Ian; THE MULESKINNERS, THE TEA TIME FOUR, BOZ PEOPLE, THE SMALL FACES, THE FACES
MacLaine, Pete; PETE MACLAINE AND THE CLAN
McLane, Ian; ANDROMEDA
McLaughlin, John; GEORGIE FAME AND THE BLUE FLAMES, BRIAN AUGER TRINITY, PETE BROWN
McLelland, Geoff; JOHN'S CHILDREN
McLeod, Ken; BELFAST GYPSIES
McLintock, Ian; THE OTHERS
McNally, John; THE SEARCHERS
McPhee, Tony; HERBAL MIXTURE, THE JOHN DUMMER BLUES BAND, HAPSHASH AND THE COLOURED COAT, THE GROUNDHOGS
MacPherson, Bruce; LUCAS AND THE EMPERORS
Macrae, Shel; THE FORTUNES
McShee, Jacqui; PENTANGLE
McVie, John; JOHN MAYALL
Machon, Tony; THE MIGHTY AVENGERS
Mack, Freddie; THE FREDDIE MACK ROADSHOW
Mague, Ian; CHRIS FARLOWE AND THE THUNDERBIRDS
Maguire, Les; GERRY AND THE PACEMAKERS
Mair, Alan; THE BEATSTALKERS
le Maistre, Malcolm; THE INCREDIBLE STRING BAND
Makins, Tony; GEORGIE FAME AND THE BLUE FLAMES
Malcolm, Vic; INFLUENCE
Maldoon, Clive; BODFAST
Maldoon, Curtis; BODFAST
Male, Kerrilee; ECLECTION
Malone, Wilson; ORANGE BICYCLE
Mandala, Johnny; ATOMIC ROOSTER
Mann, Manfred; MANFRED MANN
Mansfield, Tony; THE DAKOTAS
Mark, Jon; JOHN MAYALL
Marriott, Steve; THE MOMENTS, THE SMALL FACES, HUMBLE PIE
Marsden, Beryl; BERYL MARSDEN, SHOTGUN EXPRESS, THE SHE TRINITY
Marsden, Freddie; GERRY AND THE PACEMAKERS
Marsden, Gerry; GERRY AND THE PACEMAKERS
Martin, Doug; THE POOR SOULS
Martin, Tab; THE TORNADOES, THE PEDDLERS
Martinez, Ray; GYPSY
Martinez, Tony; LOS BRAVOS
Marvin, Hank; THE SHADOWS
Mason, Dave; THE HELLIANS, DEEP FEELING, TRAFFIC
Mason, Laurie; THE OVERLANDERS
Mason, Nick; THE ABDADS, PINK FLOYD
Masters, Greg; MIKE SHERIDAN AND THE NIGHTRIDERS, THE IDLE RACE
Mattacks, Dave; FAIRPORT CONVENTION
Matthews, Ian; FAIRPORT CONVENTION
Matthews, Pauline; (See Dee, Kiki)
Maughn, Don; THE SORROWS, (See Fardon, Don)
Maus, John; THE WALKER BROTHERS
Maxfield, Mike; THE DAKOTAS
May, Brian; SMILE
May, Phil; THE PRETTY THINGS
Mayall, John; JOHN MAYALL
Mayhew, John; GENESIS
Meehan, Tony; THE SHADOWS
Meekham, Mick; HERBAL MIXTURE
Meikle, David; UNIT FOUR PLUS TWO
Mercer, Chris; JOHN MAYALL, MISUNDERSTOOD, JUICY LUCY, WYNDER K. FROGG
Middleton, Lester; LUCAS AND THE EMPERORS
Middleton, Max; JEFF BECK
Miles, John; INFLUENCE
Millar, Keith; ST. LOUIS UNION
Miller, David; LULU AND THE LUVVERS
Miller, Peter; PETER JAY AND THE JAYWALKERS, THE NEWS
Miller, Phil; DELIVERY
Miller, Steve; CARAVAN, DELIVERY
Millinck, Ronnie; THEM
Mills, Ray; THE ALAN PRICE SET
Millward, Mike; THE FOURMOST
Minns, Paul; THE THIRD EAR BAND
Mitchell, Mitch; THE PRETTY THINGS, THE RIOT SQUAD, GEORGIE FAME AND THE BLUE FLAMES, THE JIMI HENDRIX EXPERIENCE
Moe, Rick; MISUNDERSTOOD
Moeller, Billy; (See Smith, Whistling Jack)
Moeller, Tommy; UNIT FOUR PLUS TWO
Molland, Joey; BADFINGER
Money, Zoot; ZOOT MONEY'S BIG ROLL BAND, DANTALION'S CHARIOT, ERIC BURDON AND THE NEW ANIMALS
Monk, Jack; DELIVERY
Monroe, Tony; THE BIRDS
Moody, Mick; WILD FLOWERS
Moon, Keith; THE HIGH NUMBERS, THE BEACHCOMBERS, THE WHO
Moon, Roger; THE PLASTIC DREAMBOAT
Moore, Gary; SKID ROW
Moorhouse, Pete; THE ROCKIN' VICKERS
Morais, Trevor; RORY STORM AND THE HURRICANES, THE PEDDLERS, FARON'S FLAMINGOES
Moraz, Patrick; YES
Morrison, Van; THEM
Morton, Lionel; THE FOUR PENNIES
Moss, Geoff; PETER JAY AND THE JAYWALKERS
Moss, Paul; FEEL FOR SOUL
Moss, Tony; THE PURPLE GANG
Most, Mickie; MICKIE MOST
Moules, Pete; UNIT FOUR PLUS TWO
Muir, Lindsay; THE UNTAMED
Munden, Dave; BRIAN POOLE AND THE TREMELOES, THE TREMELOES
Murphy, Roscoe; LEVIATHAN
Murray, Chick; JETHRO TULL
Murray, Martin; THE HONEYCOMBS
Murray, Mitch; MITCH MURRAY'S MONKEYS
Murray, Tony; PLASTIC PENNY,

Nash, Graham; THE HOLLIES
Nelson, Ross; LULU AND THE LUVVERS
Newell, Vernon Dudley Bohay; THE BONZO DOG DOO DAH BAND
Newman, Andy; THUNDERCLAP NEWMAN
Newman, Sandy; MARMALADE
Newman, Terry; THE PIONEERS
Newman, Tony; SOUNDS INCORPORATED, JEFF BECK
Newman, Tony; PINKERTONS ASSORTED COLOURS
Newton, Paul; THE GODS
Nicholas, Paul; HAIR, SCREAMING LORD SUTCH AND THE SAVAGES, PAUL NICHOLAS
Nichols, John; ST. LOUIS UNION
Nicholson, Geoff; EAST OF EDEN
Nicks, Stevie; FLEETWOOD MAC
Nicol, Simon; FAIRPORT CONVENTION
Nolan, Larry; THE SOFT MACHINE
Noone, Peter "Herman"; HERMAN'S HERMITS
Norman, Chris; THE ELIZABETHANS
Nugent, George; THE UNDERTAKERS

Oakley, Vic; THE BYSTANDERS
O'Flaherty, Pete; SIMON DUPREE AND THE BIG SOUND
O'Hara, Brian; THE FOURMOST
Oldfield, Mike; THE SALLYANGLE
Oldfield, Sally; THE SALLYANGLE
Oldham, Andrew Loog; ANDREW LOOG OLDHAM
O'List, David; THE ATTACK, THE NICE, MISUNDERSTOOD, JOHN'S CHILDREN
Olsson, Nigel; PLASTIC PENNY, THE SPENCER DAVIS GROUP
O'Neale, Bob; THE BLUE BEATS, THE NATURALS
O'Neill, Jimmy; THE UGLIES, THE WALKER BROTHERS
Orde, Dougie; (See Stephens, Dave)
Osbourne, Ozzy; EARTH
O'Sullivan, Con; (See Carr, Johnny)
Other, A.N.; THE TEMPERENCE SEVEN

Packham, Phillip; THE SORROWS
Page, Jimmy; CARTER LEWIS AND THE SOUTHENERS, MICKY FINN AND THE BLUE MEN, NEIL CHRISTIAN AND THE CRUSADERS, THE YARDBIRDS, LED ZEPPELIN
Paice, Ian; THE MAZE, ROUNDABOUT, DEEP PURPLE
Pain, Pupert; SCREAMING LORD SUTCH AND THE SAVAGES
Palmer, Carl; CHRIS FARLOWE AND THE THUNDERBIRDS, ARTHUR BROWN, ATOMIC ROOSTER
Palmer, Clive; THE INCREDIBLE STRING BAND
Palmer, Poli; THE HELLIANS, ECLECTION, FAMILY
Palmer, Robert; THE ALAN BOWN SET
Parfitt, Rick; THE SPECTRES, TRAFFIC JAM, STATUS QUO
Paris, Jeff; THE BYSTANDERS
Parkes, Alan; BLUE MINK
Parkinson, Bill; THE FOURMOST
Parnell, Rick; ATOMIC ROOSTER
Paton, Hume; THE POETS
Patto, Mike; MIKE PATTO AND THE BREAKAWAYS, THE BO STREET RUNNERS, CHICAGO LINE BLUES BAND, TIMEBOX, SPOOKY TOOTH
Pauli, Peter; HIGH TIDE
Payton, Denny; THE DAVE CLARK FIVE
Peacock, Roger; THE CHEYNES
Peacock, Roger; THE MARK LEEMAN FIVE
Pearne, Nick; VAN DER GRAAF GENERATOR
Peeby, John; THE ZEPHYRS
Peel, John; JOHN PEEL
Pemberton, Bugs; THE UNDERTAKERS
Pender, Mike; THE SEARCHERS
Pendleton, Brian; THE PRETTY THINGS
Perfect, Christine; CHICKEN SHACK, FLEETWOOD MAC
Perks, Bill; (See Wyman, Bill)
Perry, John; TONY RIVERS AND THE CASTAWAYS, GRAPEFRUIT
Peterson, Colin; THE BEE GEES
Phillips, Anthony; GENESIS
Phillips, Arthur; THE STRAWBS
Phillips, Eddie; MARK FOUR, T.N.T., CREATION
Phillips, Ray; THE NASHVILLE TEENS
Phillips, Roy; THE TORNADOES, THE REDDLERS
Pickett, Kenny; MARK FOUR, CREATION
Pickett, Nick; THE JOHN DUMMER BLUES BAND
Pinder, Mike; THE MOODY BLUES
Pizer, Robin; LEGAY, GYPSY
Plant, Robert; BAND OF JOY, ALEXIS KORNER, LED ZEPPELIN
Platt, Harvey; THE NEWS
Pool, Malcolm; THE ARTWOODS
Poole, Brian; BRIAN POOLE AND THE TREMELOES
Poole, Terry; BAKERLOO
Pope, Roger; THE SOUL AGENTS
Pope, Roger; LOOT
Postuma, Simon; THE FOOL
Potger, Keith; THE SEEKERS
Potter, Brian; FLEURS DE LYS
Potter, Nic; MISUNDERSTOOD
Potter, Nick; VAN DER GRAAF GENERATOR
Potter, Ricki; THE BLUE BEATS, THE NATURALS
Povey, John; BERN ELLIOTT AND THE FENMEN, THE PRETTY THINGS
Powell, Clive; (See Fame, Georgie)
Powell, Cozy; JEFF BECK
Powell, Don; THE 'N' BETWEENS, AMBROSE SLADE
Powell, Jimmy; JIMMY POWELL AND THE FIVE DIMENSIONS
Powell, Keith; KEITH POWELL AND THE VALETS
Powell, Roger; THE ACTION
Presley, Reg; THE TROGGS
Preston, Earl; EARL PRESTON AND THE T.T.S.
Prevost, Eddie; AMM
Price, Alan; THE ANIMALS, THE ALAN PRICE SET
Price, Rick; THE MOVE
Price, Wez; THE SORROWS
Prince, Viv; CARTER-LEWIS AND THE SOUTHENERS, THE PRETTY THINGS, THE BUNCH OF FIVES, DENNY LAINE'S STRING BAND,

KATE, THE CHICAGO LINE BLUES BAND
Prior, Maddy; STEELEYE SPAN
Prior, Mike; THE TEA TIME FOUR
Pritchard, Barry; THE FORTUNES
Pritchard, Dave; MIKE SHERIDAN AND THE NIGHTRIDERS
Pritchard, Dave; THE IDLE RACE
Proby, P.J.; P.J. PROBY
Purslow, Dave; JOHNNY CARR AND THE CADILLACS
Pustelnik, Ken; THE GROUNDHOGS
Pye, Peter; THE HONEYCOMBS
Pyle, Andy; BLODWYN PIG
Pyle, Pip; DELIVERY
Pymer, Roger; THE VERSIONS, THE PRECIOUS FEW

Quaife, Pete; THE KINKS
Quickly, Tommy; TOMMY QUICKLY
Quinn, Derek; FREDDIE AND THE DREAMERS
Quinton, Dave; FEEL FOR FREE

Rafferty, Gerry; THE HUMBLEBUMS, JUICY LUCY
Ralphs, Mick; THE SHAKEDOWN SOUND, MOTT THE HOOPLE
Ramsden, Mike; THE SILKIE
Ransley, Tony; SIMON DUPREE AND THE BIG SOUND
Raskell, Gordon; FLEURS DE LYS
Rathbone, Don; THE HOLLIES
Ratledge, Mike; THE SOFT MACHINE
Ravell, Chris; CHRIS RAVELL AND THE RAVERS
Ravenscroft, John; (See, Peel, John)
Raymond, Paul; PLASTIC PENNY, CHICKEN SHACK, SAVOY BROWN
Read, Rod; LEGAY, GYPSY
Reading, Ron; ASHKAN
Rebop; TRAFFIC
Red; THE BASKERVILLES
Redding, Noel; THE JIMI HENDRIX EXPERIENCE, FAT MATTRESS
Reece, Red; GEORGIE FAME AND THE BLUE FLAMES
Reeves, Tony; JOHN MAYALL, COLOSSEUM
Reid, Terry; PETER JAY AND THE JAYWALKERS, TERRY REID
Relf, Jane; RENAISSANCE
Relf, Keith; THE YARDBIRDS, RENAISSANCE, TOGETHER
Renbourn, John; PENTANGLE
Renwick, Tim; JUNIORS EYES
Revell, Jeff; FEEL FOR FREE
Revell, Julian; FEEL FOR FREE
Revell, Steve; STACKWADDY
Reynolds, Peter; THE PRECIOUS FEW
Reynolds, Roger; THE BARRY LEE SHOW
Rice-Milton, Terry; CUPIDS INSPIRATION
Richard, Keith; THE ROLLING STONES
Richmond, Dave; MANFRED MANN
Rickell, Andy; THE PACK
Rickfors, Michael; THE HOLLIES
Ridley, Greg; THE V.I.P.'S, SPOOKY TOOTH, HUMBLE PIE
Riley, John; DAVE BERRY AND THE CRUISERS
Riley, Tommy; THE HUMAN BEANS
Ritchie, Billy; CLOUDS
Rivens, Graham; DAVIE JONES AND THE LOWER THIRD, THE BUZZ
Rivers, Tony; TONY RIVERS AND THE CASTAWAYS, HARMONY GRASS
Rix, Harry; THE RUBBER BAND
Roberts, Andy; THE CLAYTON SQUARES, THE LIVERPOOL SCENE
Robinson, Dee Jay; THE PURPLE GANG
Rocky; LUCAS AND THE EMPERORS
Roden, Jess; THE KEEF HARTLEY BAND, THE SHAKEDOWN SOUND, THE ALAN BOWN SET
Rodford, Jim; THE MIKE COTTON SOUND, ARGENT
Rodgers, John; THE ROULETTES
Rodgers, Paul; WILD FLOWERS FREE
Ronson, Mick; THE RATS, MIKE CHAPMAN, DAVID BOWIE, MOTT THE HOOPLE
Rose, Stephen; TWICE AS MUCH
Rosen, Mike; ECLECTION
Roskams, Alan; THE MARK LEEMAN FIVE
Rossi, Brian; WHEELS
Rossi, Frances; (See Rossi, Mike)
Rossi, Mike; THE SPECTRES, TRAFFIC JAM, STATUS QUO
Rostill, John; THE SHADOWS
Rothwell, Ric; WAYNE FONTANA AND THE MINDBENDERS, THE MINDBENDERS
Rowberry, Dave; THE MIKE COTTON SOUND, THE ANIMALS
Rowe, Keith; AMM
Rowe, Kenny; THE MOMENTS
Rowland, Steve; FAMILY DOGG
Rowlands, Bruce; THE GREASEBAND, WYNDER K. FROG, FAIRPORT CONVENTION
Rowley, Mick; THE SMOKE, CHORDS FIVE
Royal, Denny; THE NEWS
Royer, Ray; PROCOL HARUM
Rudolph, Paul; THE DEVIANTS
Rugge-Price, James; A BAND OF ANGELS
Russley, Bill "Faron"; FARON'S FLAMINGOES
Rutherford, Mike; GENESIS
Ryal, Michael; THE FIRST GEAR
Ryan, Barry; PAUL AND BARRY RYAN
Ryan, Paul; PAUL AND BARRY RYAN
Ryan, Phil; EYES OF BLUE
Rye, Steve; THE GROUNDHOGS

St. John, John; SOUNDS INCORPORATED
St. John, Mark; THE BYSTANDERS
St. Peters, Crispian; CRISPIAN ST. PETERS
Salt, Pete; THE ROULETTES
Samways, Norman; FEEL FOR SOUL
Samwell-Smith, Paul; THE YARDBIRDS
Sanden, Doug; THE HIGH NUMBERS, THE WHO
Sanden, Johnny; THE RENO FOUR
Sanderson, Alan; THE GAMBLERS
Sanderson, Duncan "Sandy"; THE DEVIANTS
Sanllehi, Pablo; LOS BRAVOS
Sawyer, Phil; THE CHEYNES, FLEURS DE LYS, SPENCER DAVIS GROUP
Sayer, Leo; PATCHES
Scales, R.J.; ORANGE BICYCLE
Scanling, Barry; THE ORIOLES
Schwarz, Brinsley; KIPPINGTON LODGE
Scott, M.; BELFAST GYPSIES
Scott, Simon; SIMON SCOTT
Sealey, Terry; KISS
Seamen, Phil; ALEXIS KORNER
Sears, Pete; FLEURS DE LYS
Selby, Rabin J.; THE BYSTANDERS
Sendall, V.; THE BEAT MERCHANTS
Seyton, Denny; DENNY SEYTON AND THE SABRES
Shannon, Pete; THE NASHVILLE TEENS
Sharp, Art; THE NASHVILLE TEENS
Shaw, Ciggy; THE ROCKIN' VICKERS
Shaw, Sandie; SANDIE SHAW
Sheaff, Lawrence; AMM
Sheahan, John; THE DUBLINERS
Sheldrake, Dougie; THE ORIOLES
Shepherd, Derek "Bugsy"; LUCAS AND THE EMPERORS
Sheridan, Mike; MIKE SHERIDAN AND THE NIGHTRIDERS
Shinn, Don; THE SOUL AGENTS
Shirley, Jerry; HUMBLE PIE
Shulman, Derek; THE ROADRUNNERS, SIMON DUPREE AND THE BIG SOUND
Shulman, Phil; THE ROADRUNNERS, SIMON DUPREE AND THE BIG SOUND
Shulman, Ray; THE ROADRUNNERS, SIMON DUPREE AND THE BIG SOUND
Silson, Alan; THE ELIZABETHANS
Silvester, Andy; SAVOY BROWN
Simmonds, Kim; SAVOY BROWN
Simper, Nick; JOHNNY KIDD AND THE PIRATES, SCREAMING LORD SUTCH, ROUNDABOUT
Simpson, Rosie; THE INCREDIBLE STRING BAND
Sims, Terry; ASHKAN
Sinclair, David; THE WILDE FLOWERS, CARAVAN
Sinclair, Richard; THE WILDE FLOWERS, CARAVAN
Sinfield, Pete; KING CRIMSON
Skinner, David; TWICE AS MUCH
Slade, Kenny; THE GREASEBAND
Slade, Ray; THE ALAN PRICE SET
Slater, Rodney; THE BONZO DOG DOO DAH BAND
Slater, Will; THE BASKERVILLES
Smart, Keith; THE UGLIES
Smith, Charlie; MARMALADE
Smith, Chris; VAN DER GRAAF GENERATOR
Smith, Whistling Jack; WHISTLING JACK SMITH
Smith, James Marcus; (See Proby, P.J.)
Smith, Jimmy; LULU AND THE LUVVERS
Smith, Legs Larry; THE BONZO DOG DOO DAH BAND
Smith, Mike; AMEN CORNER, JUDAS JUMP
Smith, Mike; THE DAVE CLARK FIVE
Smith, Moth; LEGAY, GYPSY
Smith, Nigel; ANDWELLA'S DREAM
Smith, Peter; (See St. Peters, Crispian)
Smith, Ronnie; THE BEATSTALKERS
Smith, "Smudger"; COPS 'N' ROBBERS
Smith, Steve; COPS 'N' ROBBERS
Smith, Ursula; THE THIRD EAR BAND
Smith-Howell, Dave; KISS
Sneddon, Andy; EAST OF EDEN
Somers, Andy; ZOOT MONEY'S BIG ROLL BAND
Somers, Andy; DANTALION'S CHARIOT, THE SOFT MACHINE
Spear, Roger Ruskin; THE BONZO DOG DOO DAH BAND
Spedding, Chris; PETE BROWN
Spence, Johnny; JOHNNY KIDD AND THE PIRATES
Spencer, Jeremy; FLEETWOOD MAC
Spencer, Roger; MIKE SHERIDAN AND THE NIGHTRIDERS, THE IDLE RACE
Spenner, Alan; THE GREASEBAND, WYNDER K. FROG
Spinett, Henry; THE HERD, JUDAS JUMP
Spoons, Sam; THE BONZO DOG DOO DAH BAND
Springfield, Dusty; THE SPRINGFIELDS, DUSTY SPRINGFIELD
Springfield, Tom; THE SPRINGFIELDS
Spyropoulos, Alex; NIRVANA
Squire, Chris; YES
Stainton, Chris; THE GREASEBAND
Stamp, Chris; THE WHO
Stanley, John; THE OTHERS
Stannard, Terry; THE ALAN BOWN SET
Stanshall, Vivien; THE BONZO DOG DOO DAH BAND
Staples, Pete; TEN FOOT FIVE, THE TROGGS
Starr, Freddie; FREDDIE STARR AND THE MIDNIGHTERS
Starr, Ringo; RORY STORM AND THE HURRICANES, THE BEATLES
Stax, John; THE PRETTY THINGS
Steadman, Raymond; THE LEAGUE OF GENTLEMEN
Steel, John; THE ANIMALS
Steel, Mike; THE BYSTANDERS
Steele, Andrew; THE HERD
Stephens, Dane; THE FAIRIES, COPS 'N' ROBBERS
Stevens, Cat; CAT STEVENS
Stevens, Tone; SAVOY BROWN
Stewart, Al; AL STEWART
Stewart, Chris; EIRE APPARENT, SPOOKY TOOTH
Stewart, Eric; WAYNE FONTANA AND THE MINDBENDERS, THE MINDBENDERS
Stewart, Ian; THE ROLLING STONES
Stewart, John; HEDGEHOPPERS ANONYMOUS
Stewart, Paul; THE OTHERS
Stewart, Rod; JIMMY POWELL AND THE FIVE DIMENSIONS, LONG JOHN BALDRY, THE HOOCHIE COOCHIE MEN, THE STEAM PACKET, SHOTGUN EXPRESS, JEFF BECK, THE FACES
Sticks, Johnny; THE ESCORTS
Stokes, John; THE BACHELORS
Stokes, Terry; THE CHEROKEES
Stone, Martin; THE ACTION, MIGHTY BABY
Stone, Ray; THE DOWNLINERS SECT
Storm, Danny; DANNY STORM AND THE STROLLERS
Storm, Rory; RORY STORM AND THE HURRICANES
Storme, Rob; ROB STORME AND THE WHISPERS
Stott, Mick; STACKWADDY
Strange, Kid; GREAT WHITE IDIOT, DOCTORS OF MADNESS
Stuart, Chad; CHAD AND JEREMY
Stuart, Hamish; DREAM POLICE
Stubbs, Mick; THE BLUE RONDOS, THE SYNDICATS
Sullivan, Terence; RENAISSANCE
Summerfield, Saffron; TRADER HORN
Sutch, David; SCREAMING LORD SUTCH AND THE SAVAGES
Sutcliffe, Stuart; THE BEATLES
Sutton, Johnny; THE DOWNLINERS SECT
Swarbrick, Dave; FAIRPORT CONVENTION
Sweeney, Glen; THE THIRD EAR BAND
Sweeney, Mike; THE CHEROKEES
Swettenham, Geoff; TONY RIVERS AND THE CASTAWAYS, GRAPEFRUIT
Swettenham, Pete; TONY RIVERS AND THE CASTAWAYS, GRAPEFRUIT
Sylvester, Andy; CHICKEN SHACK
Sylvester, Terry; THE ESCORTS, THE SWINGING BLUE JEANS, THE HOLLIES

Talmy, Shel; SHEL TALMY
Tandy, Richard; THE UGLIES
Tatler, Sylvia; THE SILKIE
Tatum, Brian; THE BASKERVILLES, FEEL FOR SOUL, MOOCHE
Taylor, Alan; DAVE BERRY AND THE CRUISERS
Taylor, Clive; AMEN CORNER
Taylor, Dennis "T-Cup"; DAVIE JONES AND THE LOWER THIRD, THE BUZZ
Taylor, Dick; THE ROLLING STONES, THE PRETTY THINGS
Taylor, Gary; THE HERD
Taylor, King Size; KING SIZE TAYLOR AND THE DOMINOES
Taylor, Mick; THE GODS, JOHN MAYALL, THE ROLLING STONES
Taylor, Roger; SMILE
Tench, Bobby; JEFF BECK
Tetsu; FREE
Thacker, Clive; BRIAN AUGER TRINITY
Thain, Gary; THE KEEF HARTLEY BAND
Theaker, Drachen; ARTHUR BROWN
Thomas, Bruce; BODFAST, WILD FLOWERS, VILLAGE
Thomas, Ray; THE MOODY BLUES
Thomas, Ron; THE LEAGUE OF GNETLEMEN
Thompson, Danny; ALEXIS KORNER, PENTANGLE
Thompson, Paul; INFLUENCE
Thompson, Richard; FAIRPORT CONVENTION
Thompson, Steve; JOHN MAYALL, SPOOKY TOOTH, STONE THE CROWS
Thorup, Peter; ALEXIS KORNER
Tierney, Tony; LULU AND THE LUVVERS
Tinsley, Mick; HEDGEHOPPERS ANONYMOUS
Tinsley, Tito; WHEELS
Tobias, Oliver; WHY NOT, HAIR
Took, Steve Peregrine; TYRANNOSAURUS REX, TWINK
Townson, Chris; JOHN'S CHILDREN
Treadway, Greg; MISUNDERSTOOD
Trower, Robin; THE PARAMOUNTS, PROCOL HARUM
Truelove, S.; THE SYNDICATS
Truscott, Ray; JOHNNY CARR AND THE CADILLACS
Tucker, Cy; CY TUCKER
Tucker, Mick; WAINWRIGHTS GENTLEMEN
Turnbull, Jon; SKIP BIFFERTY, HEAVY JELLY
Turner, Bruce; LOOT
Turton, Geoff; THE ROCKIN' BERRIES
Tuttle, Bob; LUCAS AND THE EMPERORS
Tuttle, John; KISS
Twink; THE FAIRIES, TOMORROW, THE PRETTY THINGS

Underwood, Dick; DAVEY JONES AND THE KING BEES
Unitt, Victor; THE EDGAR BROUGHTON BAND
Uttley, Terry; THE ELIZABETHANS

Valentine, Hilton; THE ANIMAL
Vanda, Harry; THE EASYBEATS, GRAPEFRUIT
Vicens, Miguel; LOS BRAVOS
Vickers, Mike; MANFRED MANN
Voorman, Klaus; PADDY, KLAUS AND GIBSON, MANFRED MANN

Waddell, Bruce; CHRIS FARLOWE AND THE THUNDERBIRDS
Wafer, Raymond; THE FIRST GEAR
Wakelin, Mike; THE BLUE BEATS THE NATURALS
Wakeman, Rick; THE STRAWBS, YES
Walker, Dave; THE REDCAPS
Walker, David; THE IDLE RACE
Walker, Peter "Lucifer"; THE PURPLE GANG
Wallace, Ian; THE WARRIORS, KING CRIMSON, ALEXIS KORNER
Waller, Gordon; PETER AND GORDON
Waller, Mickey; THE MICKEY FINN
Waller, Mickey; BRIAN AUGER TRINITY, JEFF BECK
Walsh, David; THE OVERLANDERS
Walter, John; THE ALAN PRICE SET
Walton, Dave; THE FIRST GEAR
Ward, Alan; THE HONEYCOMBS
Ward, Bill; EARTH
Ware, Bobby; GRAPEFRUIT
Warner, Alan; THE FOUNDATIONS
Warwick, Clint; THE MOODY BLUES
Washington, Geno; GENO WASHINGTON AND THE RAM JAM BAND
Waters, Roger; THE ABDABS, PINK FLOYD
Watson, Alan; THE MIGIL FIVE
Watson, Fraser; THE PATH FINDERS, TRASH
Watson, John L.; JOHN L. WATSON AND THE WEB
Watson, Peter; THE ACTION
Watts, Charlie; ALEXIS KORNER, BRIAN KNIGHT'S BLUES BY SIX, THE ROLLING STONES
Watts, Peter "Overend"; THE SHAKEDOWN SOUND, MOTT THE HOOPLE
Wayne, Carl; CARL AND THE CHEETAHS, CARL WAYNE AND THE VIKINGS, THE MOVE
Wayne, Mick; JUNIORS EYES
Wayne, Pat; PAT WAYNE AND THE BEACHCOMBERS
Weathers, John "Pugwash"; EYES OF BLUE
Weaver, Blue; AMEN CORNER, THE STRAWBS
Weaver, Mick; THE FAIRIES, THE KEEF HARTLEY BAND, WYNDER K. FROG
Webb, Dave; ST. LOUIS UNION
Webb, Captain Joy; THE JOY STRINGS
Webb, Stan; CHICKEN SHACK, SAVOY BROWN
Webster, Tony; PETER JAY AND THE JAYWALKERS
Weider, John; THE MOMENTS, JOHNNY KIDD AND THE PIRATES, THE ANIMALS, FAMILY
Weir, Alan; THE POETS
Welch, Bob; FLEETWOOD MAC
Welch, Bruce; THE SHADOWS
Wenthropp, Davw; MOOCHE
West, Keith; THE IN CROWD, TOMORROW, FOUR PLUS ONE, KEITH WEST
West, Ricky; BRIAN POOLE AND THE TREMELOES, THE TREMELOES
Westlake, Kevin; BLOSSOM TOES
Weston, Bob; ASHKAN
Wetton, John; FAMILY, KING CRIMSON
Whale, Pete; KIPPINGTON LODGE
Whatsisname, Ken; THE ROCKIN' VICKERS
White, Alan; HAPPY MAGAZINE, GRYPHON, YES
White, Chris; THE ZOMBIES
White, Frank; DAVE BERRY AND THE CRUISERS
White, Priscilla; (See Black, Cilla)
Whitehead, Alan; DEAN FORD AND THE GAYLORDS, MARMALADE
Whiteman, Ian; THE ACTION
Whitham, Mo; THE ORIOLES, LEGEND
Whitney, John "Charlie"; FAMILY
Widlake, Terry; THE OVERLANDERS
Wight, Stevie; THE EASYBEATS
Wilkie, Derry; DERRY WILKIE AND THE SENIORS
Wilkinson, Dave; A BAND OF ANGELS
Williams, Aaron; THE MERSEYBEATS
Williams, Adrian; JUDAS JUMP
Williams, John; THE HUMAN BEANS, LOVE SCULPTURE
Williams, Paul; ZOOT MONEY'S BIG ROLL BAND, JUICY LUCY
Williams, Ray; MAN
Williams, Terry; MAN
Williamson, Robin; THE INCREDIBLE STRING BAND
Williamson, "Tudge"; THE BEATSTALKERS
Wills, Ricky; JOKERS WILD, THE SMALL FACES
Wilmer, Eric; BERN ELLIOTT AND THE FENMEN
Wilsh, Mike; THE FOUR PENNIES
Wilson, Barrie "B.J."; THE PARAMOUNTS, PROCOL HARUM
Wilson, Bob; TEA AND SYMPHONY
Wilson, John; TASTE
Wilson, Mick; DAVE DEE, DOZY, BEAKY, MICK AND TICH
Wilson, Willie; JOKERS WILD
Winberg, Bo; THE SPOTNIKS
Wincott, Terry; METHUSELAH
Wingfield, Pete; THE KEEF HARTLEY BAND
Winston, Jimmy; THE MOMENTS, THE SMALL FACES, WINSTONS FUMBS, HAIR
Winwood, Muff; THE SPENCER DAVIS GROUP
Winwood, Stevie; THE SPENCER DAVIS GROUP, TRAFFIC, BLIND FAITH, CREAM
Witcher, Philip; THE SORROWS
Wood, Arthur; THE ARTWOODS
Wood, Chris; LOCOMOTIVE, TRAFFIC
Wood, Heather; YOUNG TRADITION
Wood, John "Junior"; FOUR PLUS ONE, THE IN CROWD, TOMORROW
Wood, Ronnie; THE BIRDS, CREATION, JEFF BECK, THE FACES, THE ROLLING STONES
Wood, Roy; MIKE SHERIDAN AND THE NIGHTRIDERS, DENNY AND THE DIPLOMATS, THE MOVE
Wood, Royston; YOUNG TRADITION
Woodley, Bruce; THE SEEKERS
Woodmansey, Mick "Woody", THE RATS, DAVID BOWIE
Woods, Gay; STEELEYE SPAN
Woods, Junior; TOMORROW, JEFF BECK, THE FACES
Woods, Terry; STEELEYE SPAN
Worman, R.; THE BEAT MERCHANTS
Wright, Dave; THE TROGGS, LOOT
Wright, Gary; SPOOKY TOOTH
Wright, Lennie; JOHN L. WATSON AND THE WEB
Wright, Rick; THE ABDABS, PINK FLOYD
Wyatt, Robert; WILDE FLOWERS, THE SOFT MACHINE
Wyman, Bill; THE ROLLING STONES
Wymer, Nick; NIX NOMADS, THE FAIRIES

Yamauchi, Tetsu; THE FACES
York, Pete; THE SPENCER DAVIS GROUP
Youldon, Chris; SAVOY BROWN
Young, George; THE EASYBEATS, GRAPEFRUIT
Young, Colin; THE FOUNDATIONS
Young, Roy; CLIFF BENNETT AND THE REBEL ROUSERS
Younghusband, Barry; WARM SOUNDS

Zagni, Ivan; THE NEWS